Behavioral Anthropology

Behavioral Anthropology

Toward an Integrated Science of Human Behavior

THEODORE D. GRAVES

A Division of
ROWMAN & LITTLEFIELD PUBLISHERS, INC.
Walnut Creek • Lanham • New York • Toronto • Oxford

AltaMira Press
A division of Rowman & Littlefield Publishers, Inc.
1630 North Main Street, #367
Walnut Creek, CA 94596
www.altamirapress.com

Rowman & Littlefield Publishers, Inc.
A wholly owned subsidiary of The Rowman & Littlefield Publishing Group, Inc.
4501 Forbes Boulevard, Suite 200
Lanham, MD 20706

PO Box 317
Oxford
OX2 9RU, UK

First AltaMira Press edition published in 2004
Originally published in 2002 by Marion Street Publishing Co. Reprinted by permission.

British Library Cataloguing in Publication Information Available

Library of Congress Cataloging-in-Publication Data

Graves, Theodore D.
Behavioral anthropology : toward an integrated science of human behavior / Theodore D. Graves.
p. cm.
Includes bibliographical references and index.
ISBN 0-7591-0572-3 (cloth : alk. paper) -- ISBN 0-7591-0573-1 (pbk. : alk. paper)
1. Ethnopsychology. 2. Human behavior. 3. Personality and culture. 4. Cross-cultural orientation. I. Title.

GN502.G73 2004
155.8′2—dc22 2003024536

Printed in the United States of America

∞™ The paper used in this publication meets the minimum requirements of American National Standard for Information Sciences—Permanence of Paper for Printed Library Materials, ANSI/NISO Z39.48–1992.

For Nan—
and for our children—
Chris, David, Laurie, Lisa, Kitt, and Rick—
who shared so much of this adventure with me

Contents

Introduction

This is an intellectual autobiography, focusing on my career as a research anthropologist. Except for part of chapter 2 devoted to aspects of my childhood and formal education, which seem relevant for understanding the kind of behavioral scientist I became, this book covers the period from 1959 when I joined the Tri-Ethnic Community Research Project at the University of Colorado to 1983 when Dr. Nancy B. Graves and I sent off for publication our last piece of empirical research (Graves and Graves 1985) and began devoting our full attention to training teachers in Cooperative Learning methods. (This latter phase of my career is a book in itself, but for another time and place.) An exciting and productive twenty-five years.

From 1967 on, when Nan and I joined our families, it is also the story of an extraordinary intellectual partnership, for she became a vital part of my professional as well as my personal life. It was she whose training in ethology (the observation of animal behavior) expanded my interest in the direct observation of human behavior. It was her professional interest in mother–child interaction that added a developmental dimension to our work. And it was she who constantly reminded me that women should be viewed as potentially different from men in the way they respond to their circumstances. We taught all our courses together, made many joint public presentations, coauthored more than a dozen professional articles, and traveled around the world together conducting our fieldwork in Latin America, East Africa, and the South Pacific, always with several of our six children in tow. Even during our honeymoon—an extended research trip throughout the length and breadth of Mexico (Graves, Graves, and Kobrin 1969)—her two youngest accompanied us in the back of our Ford van. We took as role models other professional couples—Dick and Lee Jessor, our teachers and colleagues at the University of Colorado, Florence and Clyde Kluckhohn, who had served as consultants to the Tri-Ethnic project, Louise and George Spindler whom we got to know better when we moved to California, but above all, Beatrice and John Whiting at Harvard, whose cross-cultural research on personality and child development was closest to our own.

Finally, this book tells the story of what I like to think is an important theoretical and empirical development within anthropology which came to be known as "behavioral anthropology," as distinct from British "social anthropology" or American "cultural anthropology." The former emphasizes non-Western systems of social organization, the latter descriptions of non-Western cultures. By contrast, "behavioral anthropology" attempts to understand and account for the range and variety of *behavior* observable within even the most homogeneous non-Western groups, by relating this to variability in other experiential, cognitive, affective, and structural attributes. Our hope, common to most anthropological enterprises, is that cross-cultural research of this kind may help us better understand our own society as well.

I was an "interdisciplinary" scientist from early on, having started my college training in the physical sciences. But people seemed infinitely more interesting to me than molecules, and their behavior more complex. So sequentially I majored in economics, sociology, history, and political science. When I finally came to a blend of psychology and anthropology in graduate school I was determined that the latter become an integral part of the other behavioral sciences by adopting much of their theory and methodology, but expanded to include more qualitative approaches common among anthropologists and their holistic vision of society as a system of interlocking and co-evolving parts.

William B. ("Pete") Rodgers lured me to UCLA from the University of Colorado in 1969, and it was he who coined the term "behavioral anthropology." As an ambitious young full professor now in mid-career I embraced the term and used it in my attempt to define a distinctive role for myself and my colleagues, now launching a new "Graduate Research Training Program in Behavioral Anthropology" at UCLA funded by the National Institute of Mental Health (NIMH). In my vision of glory, we would become the champions of a more quantitative and replicable "science" of anthropology which colleagues in other disciplines would respect and want to include as a core part of an emerging interdisciplinary science of human behavior. Anthropology without apology. Chapter 1 of this book is based in part on the "position paper" I wrote soon after joining the UCLA faculty to articulate the distinctive features of our approach.

My work falls through the disciplinary cracks. Based on cross-cultural field research in natural settings, it is not rigorous enough to suit the tastes of experimental social psychologists, but too quantitative and statistical for the average anthropologist, many of whom are "number phobic." During the 1970s and 1980s, furthermore, "interpretive anthropology" held sway within our field and quantitative research of the type we were producing fell out of favor. So my published articles have not been cited as often as I would have liked, despite twice receiving the Stirling Award in Culture and Personality from the American Anthropological Association (1971 and 1975). This was my original motivation for wanting to reprint a representative collection of these articles (Volume II, *Studies in Behavioral Anthropology*) in the hope that with the passage of time the demon of reflexivity would be exorcised, the world would again be recognized as real and worth knowing however flawed our efforts, and the field might advance to the point where my work would have something of theoretical and methodological interest to offer a new crop of anthropology students and professionals. For I firmly believe that anthropology has an important contribution to make to an integrated science of human behavior.

This volume provides a commentary on the research reports republished in Volume II, a behind-the-scenes description of how these articles came into being, and at points an expansion to include additional material both published and unpublished, not contained in those articles. Each chapter focuses on one or another aspect of my work, arranged as best I could both topically and historically. And each ends with a summary of the methodological lessons I had learned at that point in my career that seem relevant for behavioral anthropology in general. I hope these may prove useful to others engaged in the rough and tumble of systematic field research, whether within exotic societies or our own. Although engaging in behavioral science in cross-cultural settings is challenging, often frustrating and exhausting, the main message I would like to convey is how rewarding it is—and how much fun.

Acknowledgments

Throughout the years of my formal training, research apprenticeship, and professional career, many teachers, colleagues, and especially my graduate students, have played a prominent role in this story, contributing to my developing skills as a behavioral scientist. Rather than repeating their names here, as these come up in the text, know that I have been thinking of each with respect, love, and gratitude, especially my students, to whom this book is dedicated. I'm sure I learned far more from them than they ever did from me.

Special mention, however, should be made of Dr. Robert D. McCracken, student, colleague, and friend, who for many years has been encouraging me to write this book. Having published over a dozen books himself during his own productive career, Bob has served as an ongoing inspiration. But more than that, he finally followed me around with a tape recorder for several days, and the transcript of those sessions served as the core of chapter 2. That got me started. Then he kept prodding and encouraging, and directed me to his own assistant, Sandra Rush, who has done a spendid job with the layout of both this book and its companion collection of articles, which comprises Volume II of this series. And she caught many an error I missed.

I also want to express my appreciation to my editor and friend Shoshana Alexander, who first encouraged me to make this more than a memoir for my children. If anyone else is reading this now they have her to thank.

I am also grateful to H. Russell Bernard, who recommended these two volumes in their earlier incarnation to his publisher, Mitch Allen at AltaMira Press, and to both Mitch and his senior editor Rosalie Robertson for following through and enabling these books to reach a wider professional audience.

Finally, I want to express special thanks to my wife, Laurinda, who did not share in the life recorded here. But she has encouraged me with the patience and understanding of an experienced therapist to delve deeply into this bit of unfinished personal and professional business, and to reclaim my voice as a behavioral scientist, even though this work has often taken my attention away from my life with her. I am deeply grateful.

—Theodore D. Graves

1

What Is Behavioral Anthropology?

Introduction

With the maturation of anthropology as a social science our research interests are inevitably broadening. To a traditional interest in describing the typical culture of various groups we are increasingly adding efforts to plot and explain the range and distribution of their internal variations (Pelto and Pelto 1975; Boster 1987).[1] For "shared meanings" are not totally shared, cultural knowledge is not uniformly acquired, practice frequently falls short of ideal, and even the "ideal" differs from individual to individual. This developing research interest acquires further importance as the pace of culture change increases and the pressures for modernization thrust new problems upon us, problems whose understanding rests in within-group variation.

Shifts in research objectives require concomitant shifts in research strategies. With increasing frequency anthropologists are finding it necessary to adapt and employ in their research the tools of their sister disciplines—sampling procedures, survey instruments, structured interviews, systematic observations, psychometric and sociometric tests—together with multivariate statistical techniques for analyzing and presenting large amounts of quantitative data (Bernard 2002).

By chance circumstances I became a pioneer in this process. In 1969, when I was only 37, the Department of Anthropology at UCLA made me an offer I could not refuse: a tenured full professorship to direct their NIMH-funded graduate research training program. I was young and ambitious, eager to stake out a distinctive professional identity for myself, for this training program, and for the anthropology department at UCLA. So, to distinguish our approach from the rest of the field, we called it "behavioral anthropology."[2]

For the previous decade I had been working in the Institute of Behavioral Science at the University of Colorado, first on the inter-disciplinary Tri-Ethnic Community Research Project, and then as director of a graduate Research Training Program in Culture Change and an affiliated study of Navajo Indian migrants to Denver.[3] From this experience I had developed a strong commitment to systematic, quantitative, interdisciplinary team research—not what most anthropologists do. But this is what I strongly believe we *should* be doing, at least some of us, if we want to participate as full members in an ongoing and cumulative "science of human behavior." And it is what I wanted us to be doing, and training students to be doing, in our Research Training Program in Behavioral Anthropology at UCLA.

What Is "Behavioral Anthropology"?

In simplest terms, cultural anthropology studies norms of appropriate behavior; behavioral anthropology studies what people actually do. Currently, there is a growing trend within anthropology toward this focus on "praxis" (Ortner 1984). But behavioral anthropology is much more than that. By "behavioral anthropology" I mean *the formulation and systematic testing within cross-cultural field settings of theoretically grounded hypotheses concerning the causes, correlates, and consequences of variability in human behavior.* Traditionally "cultural" anthropologists have focused attention on *within-group regularities* and *between-group differences* in beliefs and behavior; by contrast, our approach requires that we pay attention to *within-group variability* in these as well, that we seek explanatory models which can cope with and help us to understand this within-group variation, that these models be capable of systematic empirical test, and that they be examined within a variety of contrasting cultural groups. The growing body of empirically grounded research which results will then constitute the first steps toward an understanding of what is humanly universal and what may be culturally idiosyncratic.

This change of focus from descriptions of a group's "culture" to explanations of behavioral variability within even the most homogeneous cultural group does not make me a Skinnerian "behaviorist." All we have to work with as social scientists—our data—are observations of overt human behavior, even if these take the form of verbal responses by our subjects to interviews, questionnaires, psychometric tests, or experimental procedures. But human behavior (and that of many experimental animals as well) is determined not just by situational cues—a simple Pavlovian Stimulus → Response sequence—but also by how these situations are *perceived* and *evaluated* by the actor: Stimulus → Perception → Response (T. Graves 1973, reprinted as article 7 in Volume II of this series). Furthermore, actors bring to every situation their own habits and predispositions, beliefs and expectations, values, goals, objectives and plans, all of which serve as important determinants of their behavioral responses. The model I use in my work looks more like this:[4]

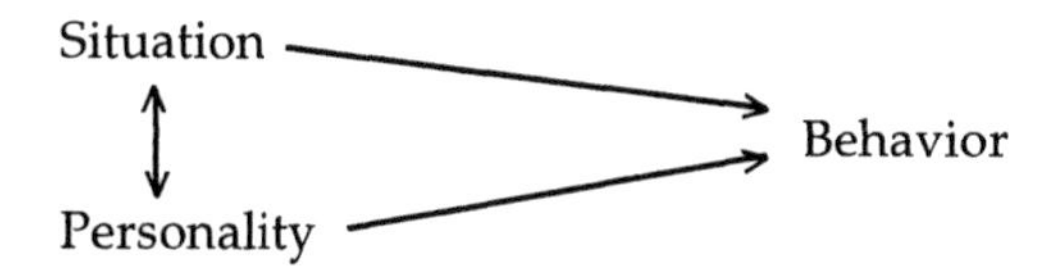

The "situation" includes the entire objective *context* within which a person operates, including other people, institutions, and artifacts. Measurable characteristics of complex situations obviously have some effect on how they will be perceived. But personal preferences also influence what arenas someone is likely to choose to enter. Thus the double-headed arrow between Situation and Personality. But both also have a direct (often complementary) effect on how a person will respond (Behavior). Finally, whenever possible I like to see the inclusion of a *historical* analysis of how a current situation came into being, and *developmental* research on determinants of a subject's personality predispositions at the time behavioral choices are made. This results in a *process* model which may look something like the following:

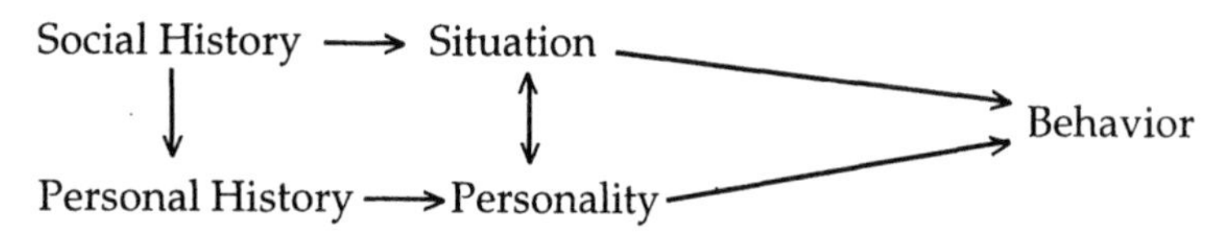

To pursue a model of behavior such as this requires that anthropologists add to their analyses of social history and cultural evolution the concepts and tools of sociology and psychology. Measuring relevant characteristics of the objective situation within which people operate is difficult—for example, the job opportunities available and level of unemployment when they arrive as migrants in some new urban setting—particularly if we recognize that actors may differ in their own situation as well: married or single, living alone or with a group of kin. Measuring their *subjective* personality characteristics is even more problematic. These determinants are *phenomenological*—they exist unseen within a person's head and must be *inferred* from what they say and do. This process is interpretive—*hermeneutic* if you will—and often subject to alternative interpretations. Our job as "psychological anthropologists" is to make this interpretive process overt and public, and our psychometric measures as appropriate to the cultural contest within which they will be used and as "reliable" and "valid" as possible. I will discuss these issues at greater length in chapter 6 on "Measuring Psychological Variables."

The Role of Culture in Human Behavior

What role does "culture" play in my model? The concept of culture grew out of the experience of Western explorers, missionaries, traders, and travelers confronting the many strange and wonderful customs of exotic tribes in "primitive" and "underdeveloped" areas of the world. Describing these novel customs before they were "lost" by contact, conquest, conversion, and co-option became the first priority of our profession. It served, and continues to serve, as a convenient basis for organizing museum displays and introductory courses in comparative society. Unfortunately, by emphasizing these between-group differences and within-group similarities it undoubtedly contributes to an all-too-common tendency among human beings to stereotype other groups and to ignore the many similarities among us in the ways humans respond to similar conditions.

Furthermore, a descriptive term used to refer to typical characteristics of some exotic group then became transformed into an "explanation" of their behavior. Anthropologists are wont to say that the Bula Bula behave as they do because of their "culture"—the traditional ways of thinking, feeling, and doing passed down to them by their ancestors. They speak Ki-Bula because they learned it at their mother's knee, and they worship Bulanese gods and goddesses because their people have always done so for as far back as anyone can remember.

This is still true to some degree of course, but it is becoming increasingly less true as the authority of tradition and of the elders is being undermined by Western contact. Furthermore, a group's "culture," when it is presumed to be shared by all its members, has difficulty accounting for within-group *variation* in belief and behavior which anthropologists have long recognized and reported within even the most isolated and homogeneous group. (For early references, see Dorsey in Sapir 1938; Hart 1954.) And since a group's culture is also conceived as basically self-perpetuating from one generation to the next, it cannot account for *change* in their behavior over time. When variation and change become the focus of our research we need new explanatory concepts. These are exactly the kinds of problems behavioral anthropologists typically want to address.

Even as an explanation of what between-group differences and within-group regularities we *do* observe, "culture" is a cop-out. It serves to conceal our ignorance of the underlying processes involved, not only from others, but from ourselves as well. By giving us a handy label to attach to our observations, it satisfies our curiosity before we are stimulated to seek more adequate explanations. Thus it can become a barrier to scientific progress.

In the last chapter of this book I will discuss these problems at greater length, and attempt to formulate and clarify roles the concept of "culture" may continue to play in an interdisciplinary science of human behavior. For now, I simply state that on purely pragmatic grounds I rarely found the concept useful in my work. During the first ten years of my professional life, for example, while participating in the Tri-Ethnic Community and Navajo Relocation Projects at the University of Colorado, we were able to explain most of the within- and between-group differences in drinking behavior among our subjects without recourse to the cultural heritage of the Native Americans, Hispanics, and Anglos we were studying. Instead, our explanations were lodged in the uneven distribution of economic opportunities and other structural variables among all the groups under investigation, which in turn had psychological parallels or consequences within the heads of our subjects. Regardless of their ethnicity, measures of these structural and psychological variables alone each successfully "predicted" their drinking behavior, and from a combination of the two types of variables, even higher levels of explanation could be achieved (Jessor, Graves, Hanson, and Jessor 1968; for examples, see chapter 4 below). From this decade of experience I concluded that a focus on psychological and structural variables such as these has far greater explanatory pay-off than attempts to describe the unique cultural traditions of the drinkers. And this noncultural orientation had substantial empirical success in our research among Navajo Indians. (See Volume II, part 2 and chapters 5 through 8 below.)

This focus on structural and psychological *variables* rather than on a non-differentiated and over-deterministic concept of "culture" has also enabled me to work closely with economists, sociologists, and psychologists who also may find "culture" a difficult concept to incorporate in their work (Bennett 1954).

Distinctive Features of Behavioral Anthropology

I would like to turn now to a more detailed examination of behavioral anthropology, its roots in more traditional anthropological method and theory, and the contribution I believe it can make to an emerging interdisciplinary science of human behavior.[5]

The distinctive features of behavioral anthropology are to be found at all stages in the research process: (1) in the selection of an appropriate problem for investigation; (2) in the type of explanatory theory invoked as a framework for research; (3) in the research design; (4) in the measurement of variables and data collection; and finally (5) in the analysis and interpretation of these data. Some of what follows is implicit in what has already been said; most will receive further elaboration in the rest of this book.

The Type of Problems Investigated

"Cultural" anthropologists typically select for investigation areas of belief and behavior in which there is *high concensus* among group members (D'Andrade 1987; 1995a). This is in line with, and helps reinforce, a concept of culture as a group's nonbiological, shared heritage, and "culture as concensus" continues as a focus of inquiry (Romney 1999). The group's *language* and other forms of *symbolic communication,* which are public expressions of group identity, require interpersonal agreement for their success, and provide constant opportunities for corrective feedback. These serve as prototypical "cultural" artifacts, and the rules of appropriate behavior which constitute a language's "grammar" provides a "model" for the concept of "culture" as a whole: the "grammar of interpersonal relations."

Among other typical topics chosen for investigation by ethnographers, *kinship terminology, marriage rules,* and related *kin-governed behavior* stand out as clear favorites. There is also a variety of similar *classificatory behavior* dealing with taxonomies of other things than people: like firewood, for example (Metzger and Williams 1966). *Social stratification* and associated *deference and demeanor* are other pet topics, and the more rigid the system (India's caste system and caste-like systems elsewhere) the better we like it. *Ceremonies, myths, and rituals* are also favored, usually being highly formal and tradition-bound. (They also make good cocktail conversation. And they generally occur too seldom during our fieldwork to challenge our assumptions of uniformity.) *Trading relationships* and other types of reciprocity also may assume near ritual form. These are the safe topics, the ones an ethnographer may choose when the rich diversity within a new setting overwhelms.

For this traditional interest of cultural anthropologists in the description of normative patterns and group regularities, behavioral anthropologists typically substitute an effort to explain within group *variation* in observable behavior. Behavioral diversity is to be found within even the most stable and isolated human groups, and its sources within these groups can certainly be usefully studied. But most examples of behavioral anthropology with which I am familiar are concerned with *culture change situations* and the diversity generated by contact with an alien way of life. (Historically, the roots of behavioral anthropology can probably be found in the emergence of *acculturation* as a problem, and the inadequacy of traditional anthropological approaches for dealing with that problem.) This does not involve simply the free adoption of alien patterns of behavior by some and not by others, though this is an important problem (Maher 1960;

Woods and Graves 1973). It may also entail explaining different *reactions* to the contact situation itself, including hostility and group conflict (Parker 1964), drinking and deviance (Graves 1967a; 1970), changes in childrearing practices (Boggs 1956; N. Graves 1971; Whiting 1996) and their effects on children's personality and values (Boggs 1958).

Despite the multiculturalism implicit in any acculturative situation, this emphasis on explaining within-group variation makes our work appear superficially like that of sociologists and social psychologists studying differences in beliefs and behavior within our own society. But closer examination reveals many distinctive anthropological features, which will emerge more clearly below.

The Type of Explanatory Theory Evoked

Many cultural anthropologists take as their model of all behavior the linguists' model of verbal behavior. The basic proposition underlying this model is that *all behavior is rule-governed;* the aim of anthropological inquiry therefore becomes the specification of the underlying "grammar" of "appropriate behavior" which serves as the guide for any observable act. Consequently, if you describe their culture—the norms and rules which they learned from their elders—you will understand their behavior. Some time ago Clifford Geertz provided an articulate example of this point of view: "Culture is best seen . . . as a set of control mechanisms—plans, recipes, rules, instructions (what computer engineers call 'programs')—for the governing of behavior," and mankind is "precisely the animal most desperately dependent upon such extragenetic, outside-the-skin control mechanisms, such cultural programs, for ordering his behavior" (Geertz 1965: 57). Many may rebel at this view of culture as a computer program, with human beings fed in like stacks of IBM punch cards and their behavior spewed forth on reams of printouts. And to be fair, Geertz soon backed off this definition and adopted what he refers to as "an interpretive theory of culture" in which "culture is not a power, something to which social events, behaviors, institutions, or processes can be causally attributed; it is a context, something within which they can be intelligibly—that is thickly—described" (Geertz 1973:14). Current theorists have recognized that there is no one-to-one relationship between "cultural models" and human behavior, and seek to investigate how action is "culturally informed" (D'Andrade and Strauss 1992). "In current anthropological theory there is no clear relation between *culture* and *action*. Of course, one can say 'people do what they do because their culture makes them do it'" D'Andrade observes. "The problem with this formulation is that it does not explain anything" (23). Nevertheless, these authors and many other anthropologists continue to expend inordinate time and effort in seeking ways to link shared "culture" to individual motivation (Jessor, Colby, and Shweder 1996).

Behavioral anthropologists have taken a different tack. Typically we focus on observed behavioral *diversity* and seek its explanation in the interaction between actors' personal attributes (both physical and psychological) and attributes of the environment (both material and social) within which they find themselves. These situational factors, in turn, have their roots in the history of the group, which also affects—through biological and social inheritance—many of the individual's personal characteristics as well, *but not uniformly or universally*. Finally, modification in any element within this system of concepts changes the context within which the other elements operate, producing waves of linked changes which can profoundly alter the environment of experience at both the individual and group level. This model is thereby capable of accounting for both continuity and change, both variation among actors at any point in time as well as individual and group variation through time.

This explanatory model is holistic and eclectic, in traditional anthropological fashion. Human beings are endowed with varying biological attributes, they are the product of differing historical circumstances and personal experiences, and they live out their lives within a multitude of changing physical and social settings. Most anthropologists, I believe, would find this explanatory model compatible with their traditional view of the world. The only element which is missing is the concept of "culture."

For interdisciplinary research on within-group variation in behavior and its correlates, an analytic approach which breaks the concept of culture into less global elements capable of being distributed unevenly within a population turns out pragmatically to be a more useful theoretical strategy, and one which other behavioral scientists can understand and work with. Thus we look at differences in the degree to which a community's members are mapped into certain social control structures, the degree to which they hold certain widely shared beliefs about the nature of the world, the degree to which they value certain commonly sought goals, and so forth. Not only does this strategy make possible within-group analyses such as we commonly pursue, it also permits more meaningful, because more differentiated, comparisons *between* groups, as in the Tri-Ethnic Research Project (T. Graves 1967a, Jessor, Graves, Hanson, and Jessor 1968), N. Graves' comparative study of parental feelings of personal control among Anglos, Hispanics, and East African Baganda (1971), and differences in consumption and violence between groups of Polynesian and Pakeha drinkers in New Zealand pubs (Graves, Graves, Semu, and Ah Sam 1981; 1982; reprinted in Volume II, articles 13 and 14).

Research Design

When I was a student the typical anthropological research design could be summarized as follows: Pick a spot, the remoter the better, and then go live there for a year. Since there are now more anthropologists than remote unstudied spots, we have been forced to reassess that approach. Behavioral anthropology is distinguished by far greater attention to research design. Usually the problem has emerged out of field investigation, as in traditional ethnographic inquiry, but strategies are then carefully specified for its systematic investigation. (See chapter 10.) Eventually, as more of the world becomes better known (and we shed our need to conduct our inquiries among the least-known groups available) we may frequently reverse this order, first specifying a problem, and then selecting a spot where this problem can fruitfully be investigated (N. Graves and T. Graves 1978; reprinted in Volume II, article 10). But even then preliminary exploratory work should precede the formulation of a research design, and then be followed by more systematic hypothesis-testing studies.

Anthropology as a whole is a *field* science, and behavioral anthropologists share this tradition. Our commitment is to studying behavior in its natural setting. This raises severe problems of "control" over the influences of mutually interacting forces that have operated over long periods of time. The effects of such forces can sometimes be "controlled" in the laboratory (Bruner and Rotter 1953). But since they are not controlled in nature, this procedure raises questions about the "external validity" of laboratory research findings: Would similar results actually occur in real-life settings? (See Campbell and Stanley 1966.) Because of our dedication to understanding how people behave in fact rather than in theory, we are generally willing to sacrifice laboratory controls for fieldwork reality. But we haven't yet devoted sufficient thought to methodological strategies for achieving alternative forms of control over the inferential ambiguity which natural settings introduce into our work (Jessor, Graves, Hanson and Jessor 1968:137-149). This is a challenge which confronts not only behavioral anthropologists but all of behavioral science, and I hope that our research strategies will help contribute to its solution. (See chapter 5 on "Research Design.")

As in traditional anthropology, the usual focus of attention of behavioral anthropologists is a single, non-Western group. Increasingly, however, I believe we will be adopting a *comparative* perspective. Because we are examining relationships between within-group variation in behavior and within-group variation in other attributes, and because the content of our measures (but not our analytic concepts) may be specific to a particular setting in which they are employed, direct comparisons between groups on the same operational procedures are often inappropriate. Such efforts by ethnologists have evoked justified criticism that the units of comparison are not truly comparable. Rather, I would hope that we can increasingly examine whether the same *pattern of relationship* between variables holds within two or more distinct ethnic groups (Jessor, Graves, Hanson and Jessor 1968; N. Graves 1971; T. Graves, N. Graves, Semu, and Ah Sam 1981; 1982; T. Graves and N. Graves 1985). This would provide us with cross-cultural validation of within-group processes, as well as making possible a *systematic* examination of the role group membership variables may play. (See T. Graves 1967a and the sociological literature on "structural effects.") This also turns out to be a useful enterprise for generating new theory or refining old ones, by specifying the conditions under which they apply (N. Graves 1971; T. Graves and N. Graves 1985).

Finally, behavioral anthropologists, like traditional ethnographers, are interested in creating explanations firmly grounded in the specifics of the situation we are studying. This is in line with a growing concern within social science to break free from the constricting influence of "inherited" grand theory, and to be actively engaged ourselves in the process of theory-building. Traditional anthropological methods of participant observation and key informant interviewing are useful "discovery techniques" for generating new explanatory theory, but we should be exploring others. (See chapter 11 on "The Interplay between Theory and Research.")

Behavioral anthropologists are concerned both with *generating* appropriate theory and systematically *testing* its explanatory worth. Thus we want to go "beyond ethnography," and our reports often begin just at the point where traditional ethnographic accounts conclude. (See chapter 10 for an example of "A Different Kind of Ethnography.") Fairly explicit hypotheses and their empirical examination are the typical result. But be warned: A theory to be of any value must be both testable and refutable. Thus behavioral anthropology is risky business, and our pet theories may crumble in the face of empirical reality (T. Graves 1974; reprinted in Volume II, article 6). But that, too, is part of the joy of the enterprise.

Measurement and Data Collection

An extended period of *participant observation* and interviews with a handful of *key informants* remain the major data collection procedures employed by cultural anthropologists. These methods may work reasonably well if our research problem involves the description of cultural knowledge and beliefs in which there is "high concensus" among informants. But when our focus of inquiry is on *within-group variation* in beliefs and behavior, these methods are totally inadequate. "What sort of scientists are they whose main technique is sociability and whose main instrument is themselves?" Geertz has recently asked (2000:94). Indeed.

Behavioral anthropologists are particularly distinguished from our colleagues by the field methods we employ. Hypothesis testing requires systematic quantitative data. Developing clear "operational definitions" of our key concepts has therefore become a focal concern of behavioral anthropologists (Pelto and Pelto 1978; Bernard 2002). And so we have been forced to look beyond the limited methods learned from our teachers. First, we have had to give up *inappropriate* uses of participant observation and key informant interviewing, and when testing our hypotheses, pay careful attention to sampling problems. (See chapter 8 on "Samples and Surveys.") Then we have become methodologically eclectic, borrowing field methods freely from sociology, social psychology, economics, etc. (See chapters 6 and 7 on "Measuring Psychological Variables" and "Social Channeling of Behavior.")

The easiest technique to borrow and apply cross-culturally is a survey interview of a random sample of the entire group we are studying (Graves 1966b). There are many anthropological purposes for which the survey interview is indispensable, and despite doubts of some colleagues, it clearly *can* be employed with success. But there are a host of other procedures which deserve attention: nonreactive techniques such as have been suggested by Webb, et al. (1966); the use of self-anchoring scales (Kilpatrick and Cantril 1960) and content analysis, which permit our subjects' own categories and dimensions to emerge (Graves and VanArsdale 1966); rating procedures (Chance 1965); projective tests designed for and tailored to the situation being studied (Goldschmidt and Edgerton 1961; Parker 1964; Michener 1971); and direct, but systematic observations of ongoing interpersonal behavior (Boggs 1956; Whiting 1963; N. Graves 1971; see chapter 9 on "Direct Observations of Behavior").

The use of quantitative procedures cross-culturally creates a new set of methodological problems peculiarly anthropological. But their solution, I believe, will make an important contribution to behavioral research within our own society as well. Sociologists and social psychologists, when they construct a measuring procedure, can draw on their own experience as members of the group they are studying to assess the appropriateness of their instruments. They are their own anthropologists. But when working cross-culturally, the "face validity" of a scale is far less dependable. Behavioral anthropologists need to devote more attention, and imagination, to the problem of *validating* the procedures we are using in the field. Here the traditional methods of participant observation and key informant interviewing can again be invoked, but for systematic ends. When conducting social science research cross-culturally, nothing substitutes for personal familiarity with the field (Woods and Graves 1973; reprinted in part in Volume II, article 9), or for involving a few key members of our subject population in the construction of our instruments (Graves, Graves, Semu, and Ah Sam 1982; reprinted in Volume II, article 15 and discussed in chapter 13 below.)

Analysis and Interpretation

One of the major limitations of conventional anthropological inquiry, particularly "interpretive anthropology" made popular by Clifford Geertz and his followers, is that it is highly dependent on the skills and insights of the ethnographer. These insights and interpretations must be taken "on faith" by others and are frequently not subject to verification. This problem was noted early in our history:

> It can be taken as a general rule that intensive research upon the same preliterate people by a variety of ethnologists gives rise to considerable controversy and disagreements over the nature of fundamental institutions and cultural expressions. Things which are accepted verbatim about groups reported on by single field workers are subject to considerable scrutiny and argument when the area is opened up to additional members of the profession. (Bennett 1946)

"Replicability" and "verifiability" stand at the very heart of science. A major critique of "interpretive anthropology" as practiced by Geertz and his followers has been its lack of replicability or verifiability (Spiro 1986). It is all too easy to project more uniformity and structure into our ethnographic observations, Homer Barnett warned us long ago, than may actually exist:

> All of us search for patterns in our information, and sometimes we find them when they are not there; or, if they exist, they are amorphous and protean. We are inclined to discern form and structure partly because our concept of culture leads us to believe they must be there despite the vagueness and vacillation of our informants on crucial questions, and partly because we need a basis for comparability between our findings and those of other ethnographers. (Barnett 1960)

Because at least some of the data collected by behavioral anthropologists will be quantitative in form, they are amenable to mathematical and statistical manipulation. (See chapter 4 on "Simple Data Analysis" and chapter 12 on "Multivariate Analysis and Causal Inferences.") This brings both advantages and risks. The obvious advantage is the grounding our interpretations then have in an objective and replicable body of empirical data. We may not agree on our conclusions, but we know with clarity wherein lies their basis. Furthermore, with a rich store of quantitative data to draw on, it is clear that we can discover relationships which are far too subtle to come to the attention of an ethnographic observer, no matter how sensitive (Woods and Graves 1973; reprinted in part as article 9 in Volume II). If these empirical relationships can then be interpreted through the aid of a rich store of personal experience within the setting being examined, representative case studies, and other more qualitative material, we would seem to be on pretty sound ground. Basing our reports on carefully collected quantitative data narrows considerably potential grounds for controversy. It also provides a basis for later observers to build on earlier work by others with greater confidence.

But the risks of employing quantitative data are also clear. First, you can be proven wrong and have to reformulate and retest your theories. This can be a slow and painful process (N. Graves 1971). Second, the more public your procedures and your data, the more susceptible your reports to challenge by your critics. But for those whose goal is understanding, these risks, too, will be cherished as priceless advantages.

Finally, there is a more subtle risk, and one to which it is easy to succumb. This is the danger that mathematical and statistical manipulations become ends in themselves rather than paths to valid understanding. Given the limitations inherent in anthropological field data, no matter how carefully collected, and the many resulting violations of the mathematical assumptions upon which most statistical inferences are based, wise researchers will not take their statistics too seriously. Here again traditional anthropological wisdom has something to offer, though in new form. Our claim to the validity of our interpretations should rest not on the level of statistical significance achieved, but on the consistency and interpretability of the *pattern* of interrelationships obtained. (Many examples from my own work are provided in Volume II of this series.) The more variables which are mapped into the analysis, the less likely that this pattern of relationships is the product of chance factors. The more operationally distinct the procedures and different the samples of people which yield similar results, the more confidence we can have in our conclusions.

Traditional ethnographers analyzing "cultural patterns" or "themes" also looked for the implications of their interpretations within a variety of distinct social contexts. And their analyses gained in compelling quality the more of these they could claim to have found. The same procedure is applicable here, but the firmer empirical grounding available should help us avoid charges of subjectivism, projection, and the systematic (if unconscious) omission of negative instances.

The Structure of This Book

This is an intellectual autobiography covering my thirty years of research experience as an anthropologist from 1954 when I began work among a group of hospitalized Navajo Indians until 1983 when our last research grant came to an end and Nancy Graves and I decided to leave the University of California at Santa Cruz and devote full-time to applied problems: training teachers in cooperative small group classroom methods. My goal in this book is to explicate as clearly as I can from a review of my own intellectual history what I see as the theoretical and philosophical foundations of Behavioral Anthropology, some of its research implications, and the contributions I believe anthropology and anthropologists can truly make to an integrated science of human behavior.

In the following chapters I will illustrate how my own approach to studying human behavior in cross-cultural perspective introduced in this chapter evolved over the years and how it differs from that of most anthropologists. The power of this approach to reveal subtle relationships which typically escape the attention of field anthropologists who concentrate on describing a group's "typical way of life"—no matter how "thick" that description—should thereby become apparent. Each chapter is devoted to a particular research issue that I was addressing at that time, from "Measuring Behavior" (chapter 3) to "Research and Application" (chapter 13). In the final chapter on "Anthropology in the Twenty-first Century" I will discuss the ways I believe behavioral anthropology can contribute both to a "new agenda" for our field, and to an integrated science of human behavior.

Notes

1. See also the entire issue of the *American Ethnologist* (Volume 2, Number 1, 1975) and the entire issue of the *American Behavioral Scientist* (Volume 31, Number 2) on intra-cultural variation, which these two essays introduce.

2. William B. ("Pete") Rodgers, who had been instrumental in luring me to UCLA, was the first to suggest the name, and I adopted it as providing a nice contast to "cultural anthropology."

3. For some representative publications emerging from this work, see parts 1 and 2 of Volume II of this series.

4. Physical anthropologists, sociobiologists, and evolutionary psychologists may want to add *biological* factors— genetic predispositions, for example—as a third direct determinant of behavior (and perhaps of certain personality predispositions as well). Ideally we would want to include such factors and deal with them; I am simply not competent to do so.

5. This section draws heavily on an essay written shortly after I moved to UCLA in 1969, which served as a "charter" for our new program in "Behavioral Anthropology." With its strong critique of the "poverty of culture," this essay (Graves 1972b) provides a good representation of the thinking of this brash young man at mid-career.

2

Becoming a Behavioral Anthropologist

Anthropologists, I am not the first to observe, are often "marginal people" wherever they reside, observers of their own and other's lives (Freilich 1970). I'm not only a marginal American, but a marginal anthropologist as well. How did I become such a maverick in the field? Looking back, I can see the seeds from my earliest memories.

I began my "anthropological" career in first grade, when I fell in love with a beautiful English refugee, Geraldine Shepherd. The year was 1938, war in Europe was imminent, and her parents had sent her to live with relatives in the United States. We were both new to our school and became inseparable playmates. "How many stones are you?" she asked as we balanced on a see-saw. My first awareness that there were other ways to measure weight than pounds and ounces. "There goes a lorry," she pointed. "What's a 'lorry'?" I asked. "Put it in the boot," she told me. "Where's the 'boot'?" My first awareness that there were people who used other words than those I had learned for the common things of everyday life.

I've felt like an "outsider" for as long as I can remember. I was raised in the gardener's cottage on a large estate in Llewellyn Park, a wealthy New Jersey "gated community." (Thomas A. Edison's youngest son, Ted, was a near neighbor and like a second father to me. Both he and his wife, Ann, were scientists, environmentalists, and deliberately childless.) Most of my friends had swimming pools or tennis courts; I envied them. I had a pony, chickens, ducks, and milked a cow. Perhaps they envied me. When I was invited to attend social events I felt awkward, like a "poor cousin." But in public school my classmates knew I lived among the rich, and therefore I often felt awkward with them as well. So I early learned to be an "observer" while I struggled to be an acceptable "participant."

My marginalization continued throughout my education. I was smart. I was also a slow maturer. So by junior high I was receiving far more social recognition from my teachers than from my peers. To win adult approval, I worked hard in school. Classes were "streamed" in those days, and I was always in the top, "college preparatory" stream. By tenth grade I had received a scholarship to attend a prestigious New England prep school. I hated boarding school. I considered my classmates snobs—not like my public school friends—and they in turn mostly ignored me as having come from "the sticks." Like me, my few friends there were the school's pariahs. And I missed girls. But I got a first-class education.

In my senior year I won a prize in chemistry, and since my father was an engineer it seemed natural to me to pursue a university degree in chemical engineering. My father was also a Harvard graduate. And so, along with most of my classmates, I was expected to go to Harvard. But I refused to consider another all-male institution (as Harvard was at the time) and won a scholarship to Cornell instead. After a heavy dose of the hard sciences—physics, math, and chemistry—I decided I did not want to spend the rest of my life sweating over a hot test tube, and switched to economics, the most "mathematical" of the social sciences. But I had obtained a solid foundation in the physical sciences and an appreciation of the scientific method.

In my sophomore year I fell in love again, with Carly Ayers, a warm and welcoming Quaker lass, and the next year I followed her to Earlham College in Richmond, Indiana. (Becoming a Quaker pacifist at the height of the Korean War further marginalized me from family and friends.) At Earlham undergraduates were treated like graduate students, leaving me convinced that small, liberal arts colleges of this type are the best possible preparation for an academic career. There I took courses in world religions, sociology, history, and political science, and learned how to argue with my professors and think for myself.

Acquiring the Tools of a Behavioral Scientist

When I graduated from Earlham in 1954 I had already been admitted to law school at the University of Pennsylvania. Gunther Solowjew, my

German roommate, discouraged me from pursuing this course, however, on the grounds that I didn't have enough respect for the law— which was true. At that time "The Law" served largely as a tool of "The Establishment." My intent, still novel at the time, was to use the law to empower the powerless. But for a chance meeting with a Quaker philanthropist, Marthana Cowgill, I might now be working with Ralph Nader.

Marthana and her sister Mary owned and operated a tuberculosis hospital for Navajo Indians in Boulder, Colorado. Shortly before my graduation she had returned to her alma mater for her fiftieth reunion. We met, and she invited me to join her hospital staff to fulfill my alternative service as a conscientious objector. So I decided to put off law school for a couple of years and work for Marthana. Tubercular Navajos from infancy to old age were sent to this off-reservation facility for treatment; I lived on the hospital grounds and worked as a teacher and recreational director. Marthana encouraged me to learn as much as I could about the Navajo. Several of us on the hospital staff studied the language with a tutor from the Wycliffe Bible Translators, and soon I was teaching the children to read in both English and Navajo. In my spare time I began taking graduate classes in sociology, psychology, and anthropology at the University of Colorado.

That first summer Marthana took me to the reservation as her driver, to sell handicraft produced by our patients at the annual tribal fair. By the second summer I had enough command of the Navajo language to travel around the reservation with a former patient, visiting the parents of children in the hospital, taking them photos and returning to the hospital with photos from home. Reservation life hadn't changed much yet: Most families still lived in scattered hogans and herded sheep, most roads were rutted and unpaved, more appropriate for wagons than for cars. I drove a 1936 Ford coupe; it was light and its high center and short wheel base made it an ideal back road vehicle. Still, we spent hours digging ourselves out of mud (when it rained) or sand (when it didn't), and several times had to ask for help from nearby Navajo "outfits." On this trip I learned a great deal about traditional Navajo life, and on my return to Boulder switched my graduate major from psychology to anthropology. I was hooked.

The Public Health Service had recently taken over responsibility for Indian Health. A more enlightened group than the Bureau of Indian

Affairs, they sponsored a conference in Gallup, New Mexico, in 1955 to encourage dialogue and cooperation between traditional Navajo healers ("hand tremblers" and "singers") and Western doctors. Each agreed to refer patients to the other when their symptoms suggested that they would benefit from doing so. Once a patient was "non-virulent" our own staff doctors frequently sent them back to the reservation on a leave of absence to participate in a traditional Navajo "sing." Attending this conference with several staff members from our hospital initiated for me a continuing interest in traditional healing methods and psychosomatic medicine. (See Volume II, articles 9, 11, and 15.)

It was fortuitous that my first psychology course at Colorado was taught by Richard Jessor. He was a student of Julian Rotter, who in turn traced his intellectual lineage to Edward Tolman. I had never been drawn to "behaviorism" with its roots in the rat lab. Too mechanistic for my tastes, too far from my own experience as a human being. Besides, I was severely allergic to rodents. But Tolman's and Rotter's theoretical models for understanding the behavior of both rats and humans immediately appealed to me. It was said that whereas Skinner treated human beings like rats, Tolman treated rats like human beings. He was interested in the phenomenology of rats: what was going on in their heads as they tried to make sense of the experimental world psychologists put them in. Tolman would have appreciated the memorable cartoon of two rats in a Skinner box: One says to the other, "Boy have I got that psychologist trained. Every time I pull this lever he drops another pellet of food into my box!"

Rotter's theoretical approach was based on decision theory: Just as rats running a maze choose one path over another because they believe it is more likely to lead to something they value, i.e., a pellet of food, so humans choose one course of action over the alternatives they see available to them, either consciously or unconsciously, because they think it is most likely to have a positive outcome or at least avoid a negative one. I'm sure I found this model of rational choice attractive because Jessor presented it so well, but it also fit my own subjective view of the way people usually behave. Rotter's recently published book on his theory, *Social Learning and Clinical Psychology* (1954), became my bible, and I began applying its principles in my research.

Through my work among the Navajo patients at the hospital, I became interested in "acculturation" as a topic for systematic investigation. As my first empirical research project I collected data from Navajo patients on their changing food preferences with exposure to a more Western diet. Even though most preferred a traditional diet of mutton and fried bread, variations among them in food preferences were evident from their requests and complaints. Rotter's decision theory seemed to me to provide an appropriate model for understanding these changes in behavior that take place with exposure to new ways of life. "Individual choice and culture change" would continue as an important research and teaching topic throughout my professional career. (See chapter 5.)

These choices are based on a person's values—what they like and want to achieve—and their expectations about the best way to do so. Values and expectations are key variables in Rotter's theory. As a young graduate student I became intrigued by the practical problems of measuring psychological variables such as these. The physical sciences, where my college education had begun, deal with the material world—something hard, tangible, against which you can place a ruler. Not until you get into the ethereal realms of quantum physics are you forced to measure by inference. But the situation in psychology is far more difficult: You are trying to measure what's going on within someone else's head, and even your subject may not be clear what that is. (See chapter 6.)

When you depend on subjects themselves to report on their internal states, for example, their values, expectations, hopes and fears, you have no way of knowing how accurate ("valid") or consistent and repeatable ("reliable") those reports may be. Even if subjects were able to report their internal states accurately, often they are motivated to deceive. For example, the use of psychological tests to select candidates for a job is highly suspect. Job candidates want the job very badly, and so naturally they're going to be saying to themselves, "Now, what are these guys wanting to find out about me, and how can I make myself look good?"

Kenneth Hammond addressed issues of this kind, and his course in psychometrics became one of my favorites at the master's level. I learned a tremendous amount from him. Jessor taught me theory, Hammond provided the practical nuts and bolts of how you go about doing behavioral research. He introduced us to the philosophic and practical problems of how to measure "subjectivity" objectively. I learned about forced choice procedures where the alternatives have equal "social desirability," and "projective techniques" such as the Rorschach inkblot test and the Thematic Apperception Test (TAT) where respondents are unlikely to be able to figure out what is a "good" or "bad" response. I was particularly attracted to "nonreactive measures" where subjects are unaware of the fact that they are being measured at all—ratings by other people, the use of work, school, and court records, unobtrusive observations. These would become a staple in my work. (See chapters 3, 5, and 9.) But perhaps what impressed me most was the wide variety of ways one could go about measuring psychological attributes in addition to self-reports. In the scientific study of personality I recognized a challenge worthy of all the energy and creativity I could muster. (See chapter 6.)

Because I was living and working among Navajo Indians, how to measure personality variables within culture groups other than our own became a scientific issue that I attempted to address as a young graduate student. What got me started on this was taking a course in Rorschach psychology during my second year from Victor Raimy, then Chair of the Psychology Department, in which I was introduced to the work of two psychological anthropologists, A. Irving Hallowell and Anthony F. C. Wallace, then teaching at the University of Pennsylvania. Right after the Second World War, Hallowell had started using the Rorschach test among the Ojibwa. Wallace was his student and he continued that work with other Native American groups. The thinking at that time was that the Rorschach test, which had been widely used as a diagnostic instrument during the war, was "culture free," and that anyone responding to these ambiguous inkblots, regardless of their background, would be revealing their personality traits in similar ways. What made this assumption exciting was the idea that you could then make valid cross-cultural comparisons between different groups responding to the same stimuli.

Now acting as a self-proclaimed "psychological anthropologist" like Hallowell and Wallace, I began collecting Rorschach protocols among the Navajo patients where I worked. I soon recognized (and this was a bit disillusioning so early in my career) that this instrument probably lacked cross-cultural validity. I was immediately struck by how different were the responses of patients when I administered the instrument in English and in Navajo, for example, and how different were their responses from those collected within my own culture. Not surprisingly, working in English as a second language, subjects provided much sparser material. But even in Navajo, the cultural meanings appeared to be so different from those that we in the West match to inkblot images that it seemed unlikely that comparisons across cultures were appropriate. A high incidence of "animal images," for example, probably wouldn't indicate psychological immaturity among a herding people living close to nature, as such images are thought to be within our own culture (Klopfer, et al. 1954).

I continued to believe, however, that this instrument might be a useful tool when working *within* another culture, because it wasn't language specific, and that within-group *variation* in response would still be valid. The Rorschach images were so ambiguous that people from any cultural background could respond to them, and I thought that alone would be exciting. So I kept playing around with this instrument, collecting quite a few Navajo protocols, looking at them and trying to evaluate how they differed from the norms of Westerners. This was the topic of one of my graduate student papers, which stimulated my further interest in psychological anthropology.

As I entered the field, my mission as an anthropologist, already formulated at this early point, was to help turn psychological anthropology into a "science": the behavioral science branch of our discipline, where we would be doing systematic, quantitative research on personality variables and their relationship to behavior. I was already thinking of *variation in behavior* as the thing to be explained, as most sociologists and psychologists would. It seemed natural and obvious to me; it just wasn't what *anthropologists* normally did. From my point of view, however, it seemed like that's what anthropologists *should* be doing, at least some of us.

When it came time to choose where to go for my Ph.D., I applied to Harvard and the University of Pennsylvania, and was accepted at both, including offers of financial assistance. A major attraction of Harvard, in addition to the leading-edge anthropological work being done there among the Navajo by E. Z. Vogt and his mentors, Clyde and Florence Kluckhohn, was the interdisciplinary approach being promoted within the Department of Social Relations, where sociologists, psychologists, and anthropologists were exploring ways to work more closely together. The major attraction of the University of Pennsylvania, besides a full scholarship, was that my intellectual heroes in psychological anthropology, Hallowell and Wallace, were both on the faculty. Another reason for choosing Penn, and ultimately the deciding factor, was that Dick Jessor's mentor, Julian Rotter, was also going to be a visiting professor there, and I could get firsthand exposure to him and his theoretical model.

With my master's degree at the University of Colorado completed in June 1957, my wife, Mollie, and I headed for Philadelphia. Though formally in anthropology, my degree was really interdisciplinary, including a lot of sociology and psychology and just enough anthropology to squeeze by. The fact that I was under-socialized as a cultural anthropologist at this early stage, I believe, was another important factor in my subsequent role as a maverick, enabling me to move easily beyond the limits of traditional ethnography.

Becoming a "Well-Rounded" Anthropologist at the University of Pennsylvania—1957-1959

I spent my first summer in Philadelphia taking an intensive course in Spanish to offer as a second language, along with the French I had studied in boarding school and college. Loren Eiseley was Chair of the Anthropology Department at the time and he took me under his wing as my faculty advisor. He was a physical anthropologist, an expert on evolutionary biology who had just published *The Immense Journey* (1957). When I first met him in his office I explained that I was there to become a psychological anthropologist. He looked at my transcript and said, "Well, you've already done a lot of psychology and psychological anthropology. We have a well-rounded program here. To fill in your deficiencies, what you really need now is a lot more physical anthropology and archaeology. So you had better sign up for my course, a course with Carlton Coon" (another physical anthropologist), "and a couple of archaeology courses. And when are you beginning work on your German?" "Why German?" I asked in dismay, "I'm offering French and Spanish." "We don't permit students to submit two Romance languages for their degree." So, since I had little interest in German anthropology, I spent the next two summers at Columbia struggling through intensive courses in Russian instead. Someday, I thought, I might have an opportunity to study the way indigenous peoples in the Soviet Union and the United States were treated by and responded to very different political systems. (That "someday" has never come.)

With most of my formal course work at Pennsylvania devoted to filling in these gaps in my background, my hopes for getting much specialized training in psychological anthropology at Pennsylvania were dashed; I ended up taking only one course each with Tony Wallace, Pete Hallowell, and Ward Goodenough, and they never became true mentors. Many years later Ward and I had lunch together and he told me that when the faculty met to discuss my candidacy they concluded that they really couldn't teach me anything. Since I wanted to be treated by them as a peer rather than a student, this was probably as much my fault as theirs. But it added to my professional marginality.

During my second year at Pennsylvania I was Eiseley's teaching assistant. This was the year of the Darwin Centennial, and Eiseley spent a lot of that year away from campus on the lecture circuit. So students who signed up for Loren Eiseley often got Ted Graves instead! From having to teach his evolutionary perspective this became an integral part of my own thinking as well, and I still view it as a fundamental aspect of an anthropological approach.

Studying archeology (including radiocarbon dating, etc.) and physical anthropology (including human genetics) reinforced my commitment to quantification, statistics, and other aspects of the "hard sciences." It also helped shape my holistic view of human behavior: You can't ignore history and geography, you can't ignore the social, psychological, or biological aspects of the human condition. I was already interested in human biology and its relationship to psychology and behavior. Seeing the benefits Navajo tuberculosis patients received from traditional healers, for example, I had taken a course in psychosomatic medicine at Colorado, back in the days when this subject was still considered controversial.

During the spring of 1957, while preparing for my master's comprehensive and oral exams, I experienced my own practical lesson in this topic. Although I felt confident about my academic work, I began experiencing serious stomach distress. Secretary of State John Foster Dulles had recently died of stomach cancer, and I began worrying that I might be suffering from this, too. But my doctor could find nothing physically wrong with me, other than the valve between my stomach and my small intestines seemed to be closed, preventing food from passing through and placing pressure on my diaphragm. Wisely, he asked when my MA exams would take place and recommended that I come see him again soon afterwards if my symptoms persisted. I never needed to do so. Stress and health subsequently became a special research interest of mine. (See chapters 5 and 13, and Volume II, articles 11 and 15.)

My work in physical anthropology at Penn reinforced and extended this interest. I avidly read Roger Williams' new book on *Biochemical Individuality* (1956), which argued that even the human body exhibited a wide range of variability. And I was intrigued by his theory that vitamin B therapy could help alcoholics recover from their addiction. I also read experimental studies of alcohol addiction in pigs and rats. It was during this period that I began thinking about Native American drinking problems as a potential interdisciplinary dissertation topic, and this led directly to my work on the Tri-Ethnic project.

Learning Interdisciplinary Research Skills, The Tri-Ethnic Community Project—1959-1962

While my efforts to obtain specialized training in psychological anthropology from Tony Wallace and Pete Hallowell were frustrated, I did manage to further my interdisciplinary goals by taking a couple of courses with Julian Rotter in the Psychology Department. And it was he who most directly influenced my choice of dissertation topic. Rotter was interested in cross-cultural applications of his theory, and had worked with some anthropology students at Ohio State, including Edward Bruner (Bruner and Rotter 1953). While taking a seminar with him during my second year at Penn, Rotter mentioned that he had a former student who was about to launch an interdisciplinary research project on Indian drinking behavior. Perhaps I might want to work with this student for my dissertation research, he suggested. "Who is he?" I asked. "Where is he located?"

"Dick Jessor at the University of Colorado."

I guess I had never told Rotter that I had gone to Colorado for my master's degree and knew Jessor well; all he knew was that I was an anthropologist taking his courses in psychology and was a good student. And coincidentally, I had already been thinking about Indian drinking as a possible focus for dissertation research, having worked enough around the Navajo reservation to have seen firsthand its devastating impact on their lives. It seemed like fate. I immediately began corresponding with Dick, and he in turn invited me to join the project as soon as I finished my course work in June, only six months after the project received its funding.

Omer Stewart, who had been one of my anthropology professors at Colorado,[1] had a long-standing interest in the Southern Utes, and it was he who first had the idea to apply for funds to study their drinking behavior within the context of the tri-ethnic community in southern Colorado where they lived. Why would three culture groups, Anglos, Hispanics, and Ute Indians, all living side by side in the same physical environment, exhibit such different behavior with regard to the use of alcohol? What role did differences in their cultures play, and what other factors were involved? At an early stage in the application process Stewart had enlisted Jessor as a coinvestigator, because he wanted to do an interdisciplinary project. Stewart was not a theorist and had no idea how you would go about doing something of this kind. He simply thought, "Well, we anthropologists will do our thing and Jessor and his crew will do their thing, and we'll get some sociologists to do their thing. We'll all be looking at the same problem through three different disciplinary eyes." This is a typical anthropological approach to interdisciplinary research, what John Bennett has called "Federation" rather than "Integration" (Bennett 1954:169).

Stewart's thinking was an important influence on me, however, because he was right that students from each discipline would be looking at different things, and looking at things differently. And he was right that the investigation would be enriched by having these multiple points of view. (This later became an important element in my own research design. See chapter 5.)

Jessor was intrigued, but he had his own vision. He wanted a more integrated approach, one where the basic theory itself would be interdisciplinary, one that would be equally applicable within all three ethnic groups. His goal was to explain ethnic differences in drinking rates without recourse to differences in their traditional "cultures," through the use of analytic variables which were differently distributed within each group, but operated in similar ways.

I moved back to Boulder in June and became an active part of Jessor's team, which now included Dick, his wife, Lee, a developmental psychologist, and the sociologist Robert Hanson. That first summer we sat around a table together generating theory to account for both between-group and within-group differences in drinking behavior. Then we set about designing a research project to test our theory.

What emerged from this effort was a nicely integrated, social-psychological theory of drinking behavior, which represented a substantial intellectual achievement at the time. Our empirical analysis of drinking behavior within these three ethnic groups then served as three replications of this guiding theory, thereby contributing to our confidence in its general applicability among human beings. But it did not address unique factors confronted by Native Americans or Hispanics by virtue of their history or their distinctive ways of life. The anthropological part seemed short-changed: I, the one anthropologist on this team, could not see how to integrate a holistic concept of "culture" in any systematic way within our conceptual scheme. We ran right up against problems Bennett had discussed in his paper on "Interdisciplinary research and the concept of culture" (Bennett 1954): Within each ethnic group "culture" is not normally treated as a variable.

It wasn't until well along in the analysis of our data that I was able to contribute something I considered interesting from an anthropological perspective. (See Volume II, articles 1 and 2.) But because of my background in sociology and psychology, I *was* able to contribute to the social-psychological theory. I had already been thinking about Indian drinking behavior from an interdisciplinary perspective, and that spring before joining the project I drafted a paper for Jessor suggesting that Robert Merton's sociological theory of "anomie" (1957) might serve as a testable explanation of high rates of Indian drinking within the community we would be studying. Merton saw drinking behavior as a "retreatist" response to a "disjunction" between a person's goals and their ability to satisfy these through the legitimate means available to them. It seemed to me that many Hispanics and Utes, living in this community side by side with the dominant Anglo residents, would be identifying with an Anglo way of life and wanting Anglo material goods. But because of their economic marginality, they would also be apt to experience Merton's "means-goals disjunction." Melvin Seeman (1959), another Rotter student, interpreted Merton's structural "anomie" as "alienation" at the individual level, providing just the type of link between the sociological and the psychological we were looking for. Subsequently, I applied "disjunction" theory to my secondary analysis of the Tri-Ethnic data, and then in several parts of my own research among Navajo migrants. (For a review see T. Graves and N. Graves 1978.)

Jessor's approach to the research was a typical one within social psychology: You start with theory, you derive hypotheses, you develop measures, and you test your hypotheses. This was familiar to me, having already been trained as a social psychologist. I didn't know any better at that point. Anthropology works the other way around: It's inductive rather than deductive. You go out there, you immerse yourself in the "culture," you let the "data speak for themselves" (which of course they cannot), and you come out with a theory about the nature of these people, which you call an "ethnography," a description of their "culture." But this is really your theory about what makes them tick. You've generated that theory from your observations.

I wasn't well-socialized in this ethnographic tradition, and I wasn't convinced that it was useful. My degrees were heavily diluted by sociology and psychology, which have the opposite epistemology, and I was an integral part of Jessor's team which ascribed to the standard social-psychological research model. Omer Stewart and his staff were doing the ethnography, collecting immense masses of data, talking with informants, keeping field notes on their observations, and duplicating historical documents. Stewart placed great value on collecting any type of public records bearing on the group he was studying. Those of us on Jessor's team thought of ourselves as the *real* behavioral scientists. I was scornful of the anthropological data that were being collected because I could see no way in which those data could be used systematically to enrich our analysis. We believed that data-collection should be guided by theory, and would jokingly say: "Omer has rooms full of data untouched by human minds."

As it happened, the police records Stewart collected later became an important part of our "global deviance" ratings, and these ratings proved to be our most powerful dependent variable: the behavioral outcome we ended up predicting most successfully within all three ethnic groups. I'll discuss this in the next chapter on "Measuring Behavior." This work, in turn, served as a model for my use of arrest records in the Navajo Urban Relocation Research Project. (See chapters 5, 6, and 7.) We also used employer records and records from the Bureau of Indian Affairs relocation office in Denver to study migrant adaptation. So I learned something from Omer about the value of public records. But in each case we had a clear theoretical purpose in mind, and this theory guided our systematic collection and use of these records.

At this point in my career, the one use for more "qualitative" data I could envision was to collect case studies of people who represented extremely deviant drinking behavior within the tri-ethnic community, to contrast with others who were quite acculturated, Westernized, but not deviant. I thought these illustrative individuals and families would "put flesh on the bones" of our statistical analysis. But even these data were not seen to be useful by Jessor—case material wasn't "hard" enough for him—and they were not included in our final report. In his opinion the statistics were enough and could speak for themselves. I also wrote an ethnographic introduction to the tri-ethnic community (Graves 1966a) which also did not get included in our final report. (Jessor would eventually come to see the value of ethnography, which he still equates with "qualitative data," as a complement to his more quantitative approach to social inquiry. See Jessor, Colby, and Shweder, 1996. And I would continue to seek ways in my own research to use case material in a systematic way, by carefully selecting subjects for intensive study who occupied strategic positions within the web of theoretical relationships. See chapters 5, 6, and 7, and Volume II, article 5.)

Working on the Tri-Ethnic project was superb training for a behavioral anthropologist. I learned a lot about conducting social-psychological research cross-culturally and a lot about interdisciplinary team research. And in the process I became a very different kind of anthropologist.[2]

In many respects, Jessor took a very conventional approach within social psychology. What made our project *unconventional* was that we were working within three ethnic groups, which is something psychologists don't normally do. So we had the opportunity for both *within-* and *between*-group comparisons, which is still quite unusual. If we could see the same theory play itself out within three different culture groups we would have much more confidence in its universal applicability. That goal is one I can trace throughout my research career, right up to the last article reprinted in Volume II (article 15), which also has three different ethnic groups and presents a theoretical model to explain within- and between-group differences in migrant health, a model which works equally well within each group. This ongoing theme in my work seems to me an important contribution of anthropology to an integrated science of human behavior.

Learning Strategies for Cross-Cultural Measurement—Dissertation Research—1959-1961

My own dissertation was developed and conducted among students within the tri-ethnic community's high school, to complement the adult project. In addition to Anglos, Hispanics, and Ute Indians, the high school student body included a large number of Navajo Indians residing in an off-reservation boarding facility. So we actually had *four* ethnic groups represented, though for most purposes we found empirically that we could treat the two tribal groups as a single Native American sample. Although Tony Wallace continued to be my formal dissertation advisor, my real advisor on a day-to-day basis was Dick Jessor, which probably further contributed to my marginality within anthropology. What we wanted was to design a small, independent, "hypothesis-testing" study that I could conduct among students, which at the same time would parallel and extend the adult survey study we were designing for the entire research team.

For my dissertation research I chose to study social-psychological correlates of "delay of gratification" among the Anglo, Spanish, and Native American high school students. Delay of Gratification is a category of behavior at the very core of the American middle-class value system (Schneider and Lysgaard 1953). We often refer approvingly to children's "ability to delay gratification"—for example, waiting until Christmas morning to open presents placed enticingly under the tree, or holding off on sweets until after dinner—as an indicator of their future success in school and in life. But many, of course, do not develop this ability until much later in life, and some never do. What leads some high school students to give up the pleasures and rewards of immediate gratification—

cutting classes, getting drunk—for potentially greater rewards—graduating from high school, getting a good job—later in life? Is this something he or she does rarely, or over and over again? In other words, is it a "behavioral predisposition" that we can count on and predict is likely to occur in future circumstances? And what are its social-psychological correlates?

One of Rotter's psychology graduate students, Walter Mischel, had just published a study of "preference for delayed reinforcement" in Trinidad (1958; see also 1961a and b), and this influenced my choice of "delay of gratification" as a dependent variable—the behavior I would try to explain. As "independent," or "predictor" variables, I wanted to choose personality attributes with anthropological significance. In discussion with Jessor, I took "time perspective" as a major focus of inquiry. "Temporal Orientation" was one of Florence Kluckhohn's five universal problems of mankind or "value orientations" (Kluckhohn 1953).[3] "Value orientations" she defined as "principles which 'guide,' 'channel,' or 'direct' behavior" (Kluckhohn and Strodtbeck 1961:5). With respect to a group's orientation toward time, she saw but three logical solutions: an emphasis on the past, on the present, or on the future. What she meant by a past, present, or future orientation is not explicitly spelled out but appears to rest in where a group finds its *main standard of authority* for engaging in a particular act: in past tradition, future consequences, or present desires. Although all people in all societies must have some concern with all three orientations, the *main* period governing their behavior will vary from group to group, she hypothesized. For example, Kluckhohn presumed that the dominant time orientation of Anglo-Americans would be toward the future, whereas that of Hispanics would be oriented toward the present. Native Americans would be more oriented toward the past, toward cultural tradition.[4] A group's *secondary* preference was also important in her scheme, as potentially indicative of the direction of *culture change*.

To test ethnographic hypotheses of this kind within five Southwestern culture groups—Texans, Mormons, Spanish-Americans, Navajos, and Zuni Peublós—Kluckhohn and her colleagues proceeded to develop five hypothetical situations bearing on time orientation, meaningful within all of these groups. She then offered her subjects these situations and three alternative reactions to each, representing a past, a present, or a future orientation.[5] Based on how subjects ranked these, group profiles were constructed. The great strength of this approach was that it provided an empirical basis for testing casual ethnographic observations, using responses from small, representative samples of subjects from each culture group.

My problem with her work, however, was that she adopted the typical anthropological approach of treating a group's time perspective as a *culture trait*, distinguishing that group from its neighbors, rather than as a *dimension* along which individuals within quite homogeneous culture groups would doubtless range.[6] I suspected that the distribution of this range might even overlap markedly with that of neighboring ethnic groups. The anthropological approach tends to reinforce group stereotypes; a psychological approach, by contrast, would help to break them down.

Furthermore, Kluckhohn's study lacked any *behavioral outcome* to which her variations in value orientation could be related. This set her work off quite clearly from what I was trying to do. For example, I anticipated that I would find clear ethnic differences in *both* time perspective and related behavior, with Anglo students generally displaying a more extended future time perspective *and* more ability to delay gratification than Hispanic and Native American students. Yet it was also clear than many Anglo students engaged in various forms of "immediate gratification" (often considered "delinquent" by the community). And although Hispanic and Native American students were stereotyped as more likely to "live in the moment," clearly many of them were as hard-working and conscientious in school and as controlled in their extra-curricular activities as their typical Anglo schoolmates.

Empirically, I hypothesized, these within-group variations in time perspective and delay of gratification would be correlated. My simple-minded theory was that an "extended" future time perspective, a tendency to look well into the future when making choices in the present, would be associated with planning behavior, feelings of personal efficacy, and a propensity to delay gratification. This in turn would be associated with lower levels of "deviant behavior": being tardy or cutting school, being disruptive in class, smoking, drinking, fighting, disobedience, using profanity, oscenity, lying, cheating, or stealing, as well as being seen by teachers and peers as not "likely to amount to something" in life.

My major focus at this stage in my career was not so much on the theory, which was a derivative of the wider Tri-Ethnic Project, but on measurement. A lot of my attention was devoted to developing reliable and valid measures of student *behavior* to serve as criterion measures—what we wanted to be able to predict and explain—something which anthropologists rarely do. I will discuss what I learned about doing this in the next chapter on "Measuring Behavior." Many of the strategies I explored at this early level of professional development are applicable to any behavioral scientist, whether working cross-culturally or not.

But my primary interest was *psychometric*—how to measure personality variables associated with this behavior. A second problem with Kluckhohn's work, for my purposes, was that her measure of time perspective did not seem "clean" to me in content and meaning: Subjects might be responding to her questions in terms of general optimism about the future, beliefs about the degree of predictability of the universe, of the inevitability of change, how much they could contribute to it through their own efforts, and whether change is desirable or undesirable.[7] More problematic for my purposes, it did not produce scores along a "variable" which in turn could be related to variation in behavior.

To develop my own measures of time perspective that could be applied cross-culturally, I combed the literature, selected, modified, and invented a number of alternative ways to measure various aspects of "time perspective," and then moved to the field. There in the small southwestern town of Ignacio my growing family and I lived and worked over the next two years. There I pretested and refined these measures among high school students in the neighboring tri-ethnic community of Bayfield, and then applied them and further refined them in the local Ignacio high school. This was my first major application of what I had been learning about psychological measurement cross-culturally.

My measures of time perspective included a story completion technique and a series of hypothetical situations to elicit possible outcomes and consequences. But my most effective technique, adapted from earlier work by Melvin Wallace among schizophrenics (1956), was simply to ask each student during an individual interview "to think ahead for a minute, and then tell me ten things you expect you'll do or expect will happen to you." In an exploratory effort to test the adequacy of Kluckhohn's theory (and as a modification of Wallace's technique) this process was then repeated to obtain a sample of ten *past* events as well. When I finished collecting this "Life Space Sample," I then asked my subjects, "How long from now do you expect [each future event] to happen?" and "How long ago did [each past event] happen?" To calculate their past and future "extension" scores I rank-ordered these responses from the shortest to the longest past and future events mentioned, and, after experimenting with a number of alternatives, used the length of time from the present to the *median* past or future event listed as my operational definitions.[8]

Since I was working with a variety of ethnic groups, I immediately saw cross-cultural differences in the responses to these measures, not only in the length of time they encompassed, but in content as well. In contrast to other groups, Native American responses often included the expectation of trauma—accidents, illness, and death. It was in the formal measure of past and future *extension*, however, that ethnic differences emerged most clearly. For example, when asked to look ahead and tell me a number of things they expected to do or have happen to them, my Anglo subjects typically mentioned events well into the future, followed by the Hispanics, and then the Native Americans. These Anglo–non-Anglo differences would have occurred by chance less than one time in a hundred, and Spanish-Indian differences less than five times in a hundred. See table 2.1:

Table 2.1. Ethnic Differences in Time Perspective: The Life Space Sample

	Anglos N = 46	Spanish N = 41	Utes N = 12	Navajos N = 24	Significance: A vs non-A	Significance: S vs I
Median future extension	3+ years	2+ years	5+ months	4+ months	p<.01	p<.05
Median past extension	2+ years	1 year	10 months	3+ months	p<.001	p<.05

Contrary to Kluckhohn's hypothesis, it was the Anglos, not the Native Americans, who displayed the most extended *past* time perspective as well, with our measures of past and future extension co-varying substantially: Spearman rho = .62. (Correlation coefficients are explained in chapter 4.) As a result, within each ethnic group, between 75% and 85% of the subjects had scores either above or below the median on *both* past and future extension. This suggested an empirical refinement of Kluckhohn's theoretical formulation: Our theory would better fit the data if we were to view "time perspective" as "extended" versus "restricted" rather than as past, present, or future in orientation. Among Anglo students, for example, 65% had an "extended" time perspective (above the median in *both* future and past extension); 39% of the Spanish students' responses were extended, but this was true of only 6% of the combined group of Native American students.

These empirical results fit well more casual ethnographic observations and Kluckhohn and Strodtbeck's empirical research. In their report Angloes had the strongest "future" orientation, Navajos (and Zuni) were clearly "present," and the Spanish-American subjects were intermediate.[9] But my data also demonstrated a wide range of within-group variability, with some Utes and Navajos responding to my measure in typical "Anglo" ways and some Anglo and Hispanic subjects responding like Native Americans. By employing carefully constructed *measures* of time perspective I could relate both these *between-group* and *within-group* differences to group and individual differences in conforming and "deviant" behavior. A variety of these behavioral measures will be discussed in the next chapter.

Other than these clear and anticipated ethnic differences, the results of my work at the end of the first year of testing in the high school were not dramatic. Nevertheless, almost all relationships between my psychological measures and student behavior were in the direction predicted, even when these correlations did not attain "statistical significance." This served as my dissertation, and also provided the basis for further refinement of my measures for a second year of testing in which our results were somewhat stronger. This may seem like a lot of work for a modest empirical pay-off. A major lesson learned, however, which I have carried with me throughout my career, and which has helped maintain my motivation to devote so much attention to cross-cultural measurement, was that *"the more reliable our measures of the psychological trait and the more valid our criterion measure, the higher the statistical association generally found"* (Graves 1961:256): Clean up your act and your results will improve. If they don't, the empirical associations you found were probably the result of chance influences, rather than the operation of underlying lawfulness.

The contributions my thesis made to anthropology also shaped my professional career as a behavioral scientist. First, I had taken some aspects of "worldview"—Kluckhohn's "value orientations"—reduced them to psychological constructs, developed replicable measures of these constructs, and then empirically demonstrated statistically significant ethnic group differences which previously had only been described ethnographically. This addresses an ongoing problem with ethnographic research: Where two or more anthropological observers might disagree on their more casual interpretations of a group's typical personality traits, those who challenged my results were free to replicate them. Other than Kluckhohn's work, I could find only one empirical demonstration of ethnic differences in worldview in the literature (Thompson 1948). "When research similar to our own is such a common enterprise within our sister disciplines," I noted, "it is somewhat surprising that it is so rare in anthropology" (Graves, 1961:273). And it is still rare. "However useful and suggestive anthropology may remain as an art-form," I concluded way back then, "if we do not begin employing methods which meet the scientific standards of our colleagues in related fields, they will be forced to do the job for us" (274).

But I was not satisfied just to demonstrate these ethnic differences, I also wanted to *explain* them. In my view, stating that they were the result of "cultural" differences, as anthropologists might be satisfied to do, would simply mask our ignorance. Instead, I treated "ethnicity" as a *residual explanation*, to fall back on only when we had explored obvious alternatives such as socioeconomic status, family stability, and IQ. In my dissertation I devoted considerable attention to this problem, and although I found significant associations with measures of a number of these variables, when I "controlled" for these associations statistically, I was unable to "empty out" all differences between the ethnic groups in time perspective and related personality attributes that I had demonstrated. (I will discuss some of these statistical issues further in later chapters on data analysis.) This was a problem to which we would return with greater success in the Tri-Ethnic project as a whole.

To me this was very important and addressed a major limitation in typical ethnographic research. By developing instruments which enabled us to examine within-group *variation* in "worldview" such as time perspective, anthropologists would also be better able to address problems of *psychological acculturation* (Graves 1967b; reprinted in Volume II, article 2), and related issues of *culture change,* such as psychological preadaptations for assimilation and mobility. These are topics that would continue to interest me in my subsequent research among Navajo and Pacific Island migrants. (See Volume II, articles 6 and 10.)

Finally, this study was the first within anthropology to demonstrate that within-group differences in worldview *made a difference,* that is, had a measurable effect on individual behavior. Previously, anthropologists had speculated about these linkages at the level of group orientations and modal group behavior, but rarely had even these speculations been put to a test.[10] My research went a long way beyond that: It demonstrated that both modal and variant patterns are important, and that persons from the same culture group who have come to differ in their worldview will also differ in predictable ways in their behavior. I concluded my thesis by noting, "If anthropologists will continue to subject their speculations to such tests, work which now serves only as a stimulus to scientific research by *others* can itself contribute directly to a science of human behavior."

Lessons Learned for Behavioral Anthropology

It is ironic that research in the *social* sciences tends to be so individualistic: Rarely do we work as part of a team. This is particularly true of anthropologists. Husband–wife teams are not uncommon, but because ethnographic reports are typically so dependent on the subjective impressions and intuitive interpretations of field workers, even husbands and wives may come to see their research subjects in quite different terms, as Margaret Mead and Reo Fortune did during their fieldwork among the Arapesh (Mead 1935; Fortune 1939). The result, in their case, contributed to the breakdown of their marriage (Mead 1972). For the public at large it contributes to a breakdown in our confidence in the reliability and validity of ethnographic reports. (Derek Freeman has made a veritable profession of trashing Mead's research among adolescents in Samoa. See Freeman 1983 and 1999.) Becoming part of an interdisciplinary team and following the cannons of behavioral science research helps innoculate anthropologists from criticism of this sort.

In order to be an effective member of an interdisciplinary team, however, an anthropologist must become familiar and comfortable not only with these canons, but also with the entire language and epistemology that guides the work of our sister disciplines. To contribute to an interdisciplinary team you have to become an *interdisciplinary person*. I was fortunate in having had so much training and professional mentoring within economics, sociology, and social psychology, and to conduct my dissertation research within the context of Jessor's team. But I did so at some cost to my training as an anthropologist. It was only in retrospect many years later that I began to see ways to integrate the contributions of anthropology into a truly interdisciplinary science of human behavior, an issue which I will address more fully in the last chapter of this book.

Notes

1. Stewart was a member of the Native American Church of the United States and an expert on its use of peyote as a sacrament. In 1954 or 1955 I invited him up to the tuberculosis hospital where I worked, and the Navajo patients loved hearing him sing peyote songs. He also introduced a number of the UC faculty and graduate students to the use of peyote as a spiritual path, long before Timothy Leary's work with LSD at Harvard. I suspect this may be one reason Boulder became such a high place so early in the psychedelic revolution, and remains so today.

2. John Bennett, speaking for himself and other anthropologists who successfully worked on interdisciplinary teams, reports a similar outcome. See Bennett 1954.

3. The Kluckhohns were consultants to the Tri-Ethnic project, but I was also familiar with their work because of my earlier interest in and experience with Navajo people.

4. Interestingly, LeShan (1952) theorized that these same "cultural" differences in time perspective would be found *within* Western society as *social class* differences, with the lower-lower class being predominantly *present* oriented, the upper-upper class predominantly *past* oriented, and the intermediate class predominantly *future* oriented. These differences, he theorized, were the result of class differences in typical childrearing methods, which he outlined. As a partial test of his thesis he collected responses to the stimulus "Tell me a story" from 117 eight- to ten-year-old children. As hypothesized, the action in the stories elicted from middle-class children were substantially more extended in time ($p < .01$) than those told by lower-class children. But he collected no evidence for a "past" time perspective among upper-class children.

5. As an example, which also illustrated many of the problems with her method,

here is her Philosophy of Life item (T3):

People often have very different ideas about what has gone before and what we can expect in life. Here are three ways of thinking about these things.

B (pres) Some people believe it is best to give most attention to what is happening now in the present. They say that the past has gone and the future is too uncertain to count on. Things do change, but it is sometimes for the better and sometimes for the worse, so in the long run it is about the same. These people believe the best way to live is to keep those of the old ways that one can—or that one likes—but to be ready to accept the new ways which will help to make life easier and better as we live from year to year.

A (past) Some people think that the ways of the past (ways of the old people or traditional ways) were the most right and the best, and as change comes things get worse. These people think the best way to live is to work hard to keep up the old ways and to try to bring them back when they are lost.

C (fut) Some people believe that it is almost always the ways of the future—the ways which are still to come—which will be best, and they say that even though there are sometimes small setbacks, change brings improvements in the long run. These people think the best way to live is to look a long time ahead, work hard, and give up many things now so that the future will be better.

Which of these ways of looking at life do you think is best?
Which of the other two ways do you think is better?
Which of the three ways of looking at life do you think most other persons in _____ would think is best?

6. Kluckhohn was aware of within-group variation, but her samples—roughly 20+ from each group—were too small to demonstrate this variation systematically.

7. Kluckhohn herself recognized this problem: "The value orientation which created the most difficulties [with respect to the purity of the orientation measured] was the *time* orientation. In general, we consider the items developed for it to have been the least successful in producing responses which can be considered as fairly clear-cut and accurate indications of the ordering of preferences on a single orientation." (Kluckhohn and Strodtbeck 1961:91.)

8. After collecting my dissertation data I discovered through careful item analysis that collecting five future events was quite enough to provide a reliable extension score. In the adult survey the procedure was modified further, and the five past events were collected first, followed by the future ones. Jessor, Graves, Hanson, and Jessor (1968) provides further details of administration, probes, etc. in appendix 2.

9. As reported by Clyde Kluckhohn and Kim Romney in Kluckhohn and Strodtbeck (1961:325): "At present the dominant *time* orientation among the Rimrock Navaho is clearly the Present one. This is born out by both the results of the value-orientation schedule and extensive field data on file in the Values Project."

10. I knew of only one example: Differences in modal beliefs about the nature of the divinity were shown to bear a statistically significant relationship to modal child training practices (Spiro and D'Andrade 1958).

3

Measuring Behavior

"Your first task," Dick Jessor instructed as I began planning my dissertation research, "will be to develop a series of reliable measures of your dependent variable, 'delay of gratification.' No test of a theoretical scheme can be any better than the adequacy of the measures of the behavior it is intended to explain."

The "adequacy" of a measure depends on two attributes: its "reliability" (internal consistency and stability or repeatability over time) and "validity" (how well it measures the theoretical concept it is designed to measure). A lack of reliability introduces random variation, which decreases correlations and increases the difficulty of demonstrating "statistically significant" differences between groups. So it is in a researcher's own professional self-interest, as well as in the interest of science, to devote attention to developing reliable measures. And since we have no pure, independent measure of a personality attribute or behavioral predisposition, the validity of our measures can only be judged *indirectly* by a variety of strategies such as the following: Seeing how well a series of alternative measures agree ("convergent validity"), differentiate between groups believed on an *a priori* basis to differ on the trait being measured ("discriminant validity"), and create a consistent pattern of correlations with theoretically related variables ("construct" and "predictive validity"). Furthermore, by using several alternative measures, the inadequacies of any one will not seriously jeopardize tests of your theory.

For a behavioral anthropologist our core interest is in understanding and accounting for *variation* in behavior within a particular ethnic group: Why are some Native Americans teetotalers or moderate drinkers, while others conform to the stereotype of the "drunken Indian"? Why are some Anglos "problem drinkers" despite "cultural norms" of moderation? And what accounts for variation in the drinking behavior of Hispanics, who have no clear cultural norms or stereotypes with regard to the use of alcohol? This was the confronting problem for our Tri-Ethnic staff, and together we constructed an interdisciplinary theoretical model to account for these within-group differences which involved a set of social pressures and constraints and a parallel set of psychological predispositions and inhibitors.

At this point in my career I did not yet call myself a "behavioral anthropologist." That would not happen until I moved to UCLA in 1969. But in my training as an interdisciplinary "behavioral scientist" and my experience on the Tri-Ethnic project, where I had my office in the Institute of Behavioral Science, along with economists, sociologists, and psychologists, I learned almost by osmosis the critical role played by measures of behavior in any research undertaking.

So during my years on the Tri-Ethnic staff I devoted a great deal of attention to developing reliable and valid measures of a person's typical *behavior*, including five nonobservational strategies: self-reports; ratings by friends who know the subject well; ratings by objective observers, usually in authority positions, like parents, teachers, and supervisors at work; the use of formal records over which a subject has no control ("nonreactive" measures); and a subject's choices in experimental situations which simulated the behavior under investigation. (Later in my career I developed measures based on *direct observations* of behavior. See chapters 9, 10, and 11.)

Self-Reports

The most straightforward method of measuring a person's typical behavior would seem to be to ask them. They usually know better than anyone else what they tend to do under a wide range of circumstances, if they are willing and able to tell you truthfully. Aye, but there's the rub! Most behavior that we as social scientists are interested in studying carries a heavy burden of "social desirability" or censure: generosity, honesty, empathy, sexual activity, delinquency, or drunkenness. Who wants to devote their professional lives to studying a neutral topic such as why some men part their hair on the left or on the right?

Most kids recognize that "delay of gratification" behavior is valued by adults because of the many exhortations by parents and teachers to "stop fooling around and make something of yourself." And much "immediate gratification" behavior is seen as no more than a form of "social deviance"—cutting up in the classroom, playing hooky, getting drunk, using illegal drugs, premarital sex. In fact, though the Tri-Ethnic project was undertaken to study and explain excessive drinking and drunkenness, especially among the Native Americans in our research community, Jessor insisted that the theory we develop and test be not just of alcohol abuse, but of "deviant behavior" in general. So my interest in "delay of gratification" and its psychological correlates became part of a larger research interest in the social and psychological determinants of deviation or conformity to middle-class standards of behavior among high school students (my particular focus) and in the community at large.[1]

So if we are to use our subjects themselves as "informants" or raters of their *own* behavior, we are usually asking them to report on behavior which they know we probably approve or disapprove of. Understandably, they will probably distort their answers to make themselves look good, even if only in their own eyes. How do we go about enlisting their honesty and their cooperation? Overcoming this type of "reactivity" in measurement is part of the challenge—and fun—of studying human behavior.

There are many strategies for doing this. One is to live in the community you are studying, build up rapport with the people, and become known for your nonjudgmental attitudes. This is the typical anthropological approach, and has much to recommend it. My family and I spent two years in the small tri-ethnic community where I was conducting my research, and I made a point to get to know and be known by as many people as possible, both adolescents and adults. To all who asked I explained my role as an anthropologist: I was trying to be an objective and nonjudgmental observer of the local scene whose goal was to understand their "way of life." I avoided attending the local churches, but was regularly seen in the local bars. I promised not to betray their confidence and took the risk of joining students on their drive-around evening outings, explaining that I wanted to see firsthand what teenage life in this community "was really like." They were delighted to show me. Finally, to get to know and interact with more Hispanic and Native American students in particular, since I was an "Anglo," I sponsored a "Teen Club" open to all adolescents in the community, but which particularly filled the recreational needs of these minority students. The club sponsored periodic record hops in town and weekly roller-skating outings to nearby Durango. And we held many discussions in my home about what it meant to be an adolescent or minority group member in this community and in the wider society.

Another strategy is simply to address the issue directly with your subjects. At the beginning of formal testing in the high school, and of each formal interview our team conducted in the community, we asked the subjects for their cooperation and honesty, citing the importance of the research we were conducting. We also reassured them that their individual responses would be kept private and anonymous, and only summary statements would ever be shared with school officials or the public.[2]

Another strategy involves wording questions in as nonjudgmental a fashion as possible. As one indicator of a tendency to "delay gratification," for example, I wanted a measure of students' tendency to plan ahead. So in individual interviews I asked them a series of questions about their *planning behavior* under different circumstances, prefaced by the statement, "Some people spend quite a bit of time planning their lives in advance; others prefer to take life as it comes. How about you?" This introduction was intended to convey the impression that whatever they said was okay, in the hope of diminishing their tendency to answer in what they might consider an "appropriate" or "socially desirable" manner. Six of the ten questions I asked formed a nice "Guttman Scale" with high "reproducibility," thereby at least demonstrating internal consistency ("reliability") in these student responses. (In a Guttman scale of high reproducibility, the responses to each item will accurately "predict" a subject's responses to most of the other items in the scale. The four questions which did not do so were discarded.)[3] And ethnic differences were in the direction expected ethnographically (an indicator of "discriminant validity"), with 61% of the Anglo students emerging as "high planners" on this scale, as compared with only 44% of the Hispanic students and 28% of the Native American students.

We also made a list of twenty typical types of adolescent misbehavior to tap a variety of immediately gratifying behaviors with potentially negative consequences later on, such as "gone on beer parties," "ditched school," or "gone to a movie the night before a test." This list was presented to students on the third day of our formal testing in the school, after they had become used to our asking intimate questions about their beliefs, hopes, and expectations. For each behavior in our list, students were asked to check whether they had never engaged in that behavior, had done so once or twice, several times, or very often. Their score was simply the sum of the scores on these items.

In addition to total score, these items divided into three sub-scores of roughly equal length: school-related behavior, drinking-related behavior, and other immediately gratifying behavior. These sub-scores correlated with each other positively from .44 to .69, suggesting a reasonable degree of consistency in such behavior within different domains. (I will discuss the meaning of a correlation coefficient in detail in the next chapter.) Although sex differences were large and highly significant, as we expected, no ethnic differences were found.

A "Projective Test" of Behavior

Measures of "behavioral tendencies" or "predispositions" can only be inferred from observations of behavior under as controlled conditions as possible. But if someone exhibits "delay of gratification" under many circumstances, we often say they have the "ability" to delay gratification. Is this a "personality trait"? How does it differ from a "behavioral tendency"? These are philosophic, theoretical, and practical issues which I will address again in chapter 6 on "Measuring Psychological Variables." Often you can end up with an empirical muddle: You must be careful to avoid circular reasoning of the sort, "They behaved the way they did because they had a personal predisposition to behave that way," based on observations of the very behavior you are trying to explain![4]

In the second year of testing, another graduate student, John Shybut, and I experimented with the use of a "projective test" for measuring a student's tendency to delay gratification, in the hope that they might reveal their own behavioral predispositions in a context where they might be less aware that they were doing so.[5] (I will discuss projective tests for measuring personality variables at greater length in chapter 6.) It is an indicator of the fine line between measures of general behavioral tendencies and measures of "personality traits," however, that we could use this simple projective test as one of our alternative measures of "delay of gratification" *behavior,* while Jessor would choose to report these measures in chapter 10 of our final report on the Tri-Ethnic project devoted to "The Measurement of the Personality System," along with my measures of "time perspective." (See Jessor, Graves, Hanson, and Jessor 1968.) Beware that circularity!

The procedure Shybut and I developed was novel, but can be applied under other circumstances and for other purposes. As part of a regular composition assignment in their English classes, and without their knowledge that this was actually part of our research, all students were asked to write a story about a hypothetical event in which the key figure was someone like themselves:

> Write a complete story suggested by the following theme: It was a weekday afternoon in a small southwestern town. A teenage boy (or girl) returned home from school to find a letter waiting for him (or her). Quickly he (or she) opened it and read the letter inside. "Dear Sir:" it read, "You will remember entering your name in our nationwide contest. The drawing has just been held and your name was the one selected. You will find a check for $1000 enclosed with this letter."
>
> Now begin your story and be sure to tell a complete story about what the boy (or girl) did with the money. A complete story would have a beginning, a middle, and an ending. In your story tell about any important things which you think would have happened. You will probably want to include answers to these questions in your story:
>
> 1. What did the boy (or girl) think about after getting the money?
> 2. What did he decide to do with the money?
> 3. Why did he decide to do this?
> 4. How did things work out?

The content of these stories was easily classified into delay *versus* immediate gratification responses, with interscorer agreement of better than 90%. (The normal procedure in content analysis, which we followed, is then to discuss disagreements between scorers and arrive at consensus, thereby further increasing the reliability of the measure.) This activity was fun and interesting from a methodological point of view, but empirically did not prove to relate well to the other measures of delay of gratification behavior or to its various predictors in our theoretical scheme. I mention it here because it serves as one more example of the variety of ways one can go about measuring behavior.

Behavioral Choice Procedures

John Shybut and I also experimented with two "behavioral choice" procedures to measure a student's "delay of gratification" behavior. Previous research on this topic had generally been undertaken with relatively young children, and usually involved giving the subject a choice between a small reward at the time of the experiment—a piece of candy, a nickel, a small toy—or a larger reward a few days later. Our procedures were modeled on this same paradigm. The choices were made to appear as "natural events," and students did not know that they were really part of our testing program.

The Dance Vote. In our second year of work in the high school, and at the beginning of the first day of testing we told students, "Because of your help with our research last year and this year, we want to do something in return." We then gave them an opportunity to vote, by secret ballot, either for a record hop "this Saturday" with all kinds of records, door prizes, refreshments, and decorations, or a band dance "a month from now" with a popular band ("the Zuni Midnighters") when we had had time to make the arrangements.

The Thank-You Ticket. On the final day of testing each student also received a thank-you ticket worth from 25 cents to 50 cents at a local drug store, depending on how long they waited to cash it over the following ten days. "Because there are so many kids in the school, you probably couldn't all fit into the store at one time," we explained. Like a traveler's check, they signed it at the time of testing at school, and then again in the store when they cashed it in. I collected these from the store at the end of each day.

It is perhaps less a measure of their ability to delay gratification than of their trust in me as a friend that 82% of the students voted for the dance band and 86% waited to cash their thank-you ticket until it was maximally valuable. And contrary to expectations, Hispanic and Native American students were even more "delayed" in their choices than Anglo students. (If you were a Hispanic or Native American teenager in this community it would have been very likely that you had attended one or more events sponsored by our teen club. But we had relatively few Anglo members.) Although these measures did not prove empirically useful in the Tri-Ethnic study, they alerted me to the possibility of using direct behavioral measures of this kind, which some years later Nancy Graves and I used very successfully on the island of Aitutaki. (See chapter 10 below and Volume II, article 10.)

Peer Ratings

If other people have an opportunity to observe your subject's behavior under a wide range of circumstances, they can often serve to provide behavior ratings which will be more objective than you can obtain from your subjects themselves. For example, fellow students are a convenient group from whom to obtain peer ratings of their classmates' general behavior (as are teachers, parents, and community members at large, see below). The local high school within which I was conducting my research was small: 128 students and 10 teachers. And the community, though tri-ethnic in composition, was also small and tight-knit. So everyone knew everyone else.

We included a "sociometric" questionnaire as part of our battery of procedures, in which students were asked to nominate other students in response to a variety of questions. For example, the first question asked, "Who are the four kids in this school you would choose to mess around with?" And at a later point in the questionnaire, "Which kids from around here do you *actually* mess around with the most?" Besides yielding information on cliques and cleavages, cross-ethnic friendship patterns, and other aspects of the student social structure, this sociometric test included several questions which could be combined into a general measure of "deviance-conformity." Students were asked to nominate "Which kids from around here act the way most adults approve of?" and "Which kids from around here get into trouble most?" Students were rank-ordered by the number of nominations they received, and the ranks (in opposite directions, of course) combined into a single score. (Adding ranks and reranking the sums is a good, simple way of combining the responses to questions of this type.)

One limitation of peer ratings is that they may be influenced by how well subjects are *liked or disliked* by their classmates ("halo effects"). Another limitation is that adolescents find it uncomfortable to "rat" on each other, even in situations of test anonymity. But these limitations are offset by the large number of raters involved. Even though some students may hold back, enough will be willing to make nominations that you will probably end up with a good measure.

Ratings by Authority Figures

Although they may not know their students as intimately as peers, teachers and others in authority may provide more objective measures of a research subject's behavior, at least within work or school settings, and for those behavioral domains of importance to the rater. In the tri-ethnic high school where I worked, for example, I asked all the teachers as well as the principal to rate the students in two complementary ways, which illustrate two different but contrasting strategies. For the first, more global rating, I defined two ends of a behavioral continuum as follows:

> This student is always on time, neatly dressed, courteous in language, quiet and cooperative in class, always has assignments completed on time, and in every way by his behavior, makes his teachers' jobs easier and more satisfying.
>
> This student disrupts orderly classroom routine, and displays such behavior as whispering, talking, giggling, gum-chewing, attention-getting, etc., and in other ways makes his teachers' jobs more difficult and less rewarding.

Names of all students had been typed on 3 by 5 cards, and I asked each teacher to sort them roughly into two equal piles, those whose classroom behavior *during this school year* had been closest to the first description, and those whose behavior had been closest to the second. Then I asked them to take these two piles and divide each roughly in half in the same way. Thus four roughly equal groupings were obtained from each rater, and the piles and the students within them were numbered from 1 to 4. Since teachers rated only students they had in class (only the principal felt able to rate all students), our subjects had different numbers of raters. So, each student's ratings were averaged, and the distribution of scores again broken into quartiles. This is another simple procedure for combining the behavioral ratings by different authority figures into a more stable and valid measure.

As an alternative measure, we used a series of eight specific behaviors considered by the principal to comprise the major forms which nonconformity to school norms might take. These included smoking, drinking, fighting, disobedience, profanity with students or teacher, lying, cheating, and stealing. Each was carefully defined. Then for each student and each behavior, teacher raters were asked to say whether *during the last school year* the student had to their knowledge (0) never exhibited that behavior, (1) exhibited it once or twice, or (3) exhibited it several times. Again, these ratings were summed and averaged across raters and the distribution of mean scores divided into quartiles. And again, this rating strategy can easily be applied to other behaviors in other settings.

These alternative procedures and alternative raters allowed us to explore some interesting methodological issues:

1. To what extent will multiple observers agree in their ratings of student behavior?
2. What are the relative advantages, if any, of global ratings as opposed to ratings based on a checklist of more specific behaviors?
3. To what extent may halo effects influence teacher evaluations?
4. Do different classes and different teachers have sufficient varying stimulus value for students that their behavior changes radically from one setting to another?

Correlations between teachers on the global measure averaged only in the high 40s, and 15% of the students were rated as highly conforming (top quartile) in their classroom behavior by one teacher and highly deviant (bottom quartile) by another. Another 38% were rated as highly conforming by one teacher and moderately deviant by another, or moderately conforming by one and highly deviant by another. Thus for *over half* the students we obtained evidence for fairly large shifts in behavior from one classroom to another. This suggests a high degree of situational specificity in classroom behavior. But what we wanted to predict was *a general tendency* to conform to middle-class standards of behavior, *regardless of the situation*. (See Ross and Nisbett 1991 for discussion of this general issue within social psychology.)

Correlations between teachers' ratings of the same student increased somewhat when they used the list of more specific behaviors, and now averaged in the high 50s. This suggests a general principle: that the reliability of behavioral rating can be improved by making the task more specific. Note, however, that then the *full range of behavior under investigation* must be clearly defined and sampled.

Correlations between a teacher's rating of each student on the global procedure and on the list of more specific behaviors were also in the high 50s, no higher than the correlations *between* teachers. This suggests that probably any "halo effect" was minimal.

Finally, we compared these ratings of specific behaviors with the global ratings. These quite different procedures correlated with each other .78. This suggests a second general principle: that the reliability of rating procedures can be vastly improved by combining the scores of several observers. For even if a student's behavior varies somewhat from one classroom to another, these variations will tend to average out. Furthermore, we are now closer to our goal of evaluating a *general behavioral tendency* across many varying (teacher/classroom) situations.

Teacher and peer ratings correlated .75, suggesting that these alternative procedures were converging on the same underlying behavioral predisposition. But since teachers and students knew our subjects under complementary conditions, we felt that combining their judgments would prove empirically fruitful. And indeed, the resulting "global deviance" measure (falling into the top quartile on *either* the teacher or peer rating scale) proved to be our most valid measure of adolescent "deviance," that is, the one having the highest correlations with quite different, but theoretically linked psychological and sociological measures. In fact, using only four "predictors"—two sociological and two psychological—we were able to specify groups of students who varied from only 9% "deviant" (the "optimal" pattern) to 100% "deviant" (the pattern departing most from optimal), with those groups falling in between increasing in the proportion "deviant" as the number of departures from an "optimal" pattern also increased. (See Jessor, Graves, Hanson, and Jessor 1968, table 11.13, reprinted here on page 82. I will discuss "pattern analysis" more fully in this next chapter on "Simple Data Analysis.") For a behavioral scientist, I learned, ratings by peers and authority figures can provide excellent measures of variation in the behavior you want to explain.

School Records

Because of the potential distortions inherent in any rating procedures, we also examined the possibility of using school records—in our case excessive absenteeism and tardiness—as objective and "nonreactive" measures of immediate gratification, that is, measures not under a subject's control or ability to distort. Over two-thirds of the students had no more than one "tardy" over a two-year period. The remaining third had a median of five tardies. Similarly, the distribution of absenteeism also appeared to be highly skewed. "Ninety percent of our absenteeism is caused by ten percent of our students," the principle noted. Of course, some absence is legitimate, due to sickness. By counting only the *occasions absent* (any period of absence bounded by a day of attendance) the contribution of several days of sickness was minimized and an emerging pattern of truancy highlighted. Excessive absenteeism and tardiness correlated fairly well with teacher ratings during our first year of analysis, and better than with student self-ratings. But they did not correlate well with other measures of "deviant behavior" or with our theoretical predictors of "delay of gratification." So in our final report we scrapped both of these measures based on school records (and also self-ratings of behavior) in favor of the combined teacher-peer rating of "global deviance" presented above. Nevertheless, finding ways to use public records as nonreactive measures of behavior was a challenge to our creativity as behavioral scientists, which in subsequent research among Navajos and Pacific Islanders turned out to be extremely useful.[6] (See especially chapters 5 and 10 below.)

Measures of Drinking Behavior

Besides my own dissertation research in the high school, I was also given major responsibility for developing and refining our measures of drinking behavior for the project as a whole. (See Jessor, Graves, Hanson, and Jessor 1968, chapters 7 and 8.) With Jessor's mantra clearly in mind—"The test of a theoretical scheme can be no better than the adequacy of the measurement of the behavior it is intended to explain"—we set to work. But the task was daunting: The "deviant" use of alcohol was not likely to be something subjects would be readily willing to honestly report.

Since the core of our data collection in the community would be drawn from formal interviews among a random sample of adults, we would need to use all the interview strategies known to maximize our subjects' veracity. We would first build rapport with nonthreatening questions, assure our subjects of anonymity, display a nonjudgmental attitude when asking about other intimate behavior, embed the drinking questions in as broad and unthreatening a context as possible, and word the questions with care, for example, "How many times have you . . ." (engaged in some behavior) rather than "Have you ever . . . ?" We were helped in this process by looking at a number of recent survey studies of drinking behavior conducted elsewhere in the United States, such as Maxwell's in the state of Washington (1952), Mulford and Miller's in Iowa (1959; 1960a, b, and c, 1963), and most particularly the work of Genevieve Knupfer and her colleagues in California (1963), whom we visited and conferred with at length.

The result in the adult survey was a complex and time-consuming procedure which took place near the end of the interview, when subjects were already tired, but we hoped ready to be honest and open with us. "Well, we've been going over a lot of different things, but now I'd like to concentrate on just one thing in more detail. The thing I'd like to talk about now is drinking; what I mean is alcoholic drinks like liquor, wine, or beer. Of course, whatever you say will be kept private." Subjects were then handed a card which read:

_____Three or more times a day
_____Two times a day
_____About once a day
_____Three or four times a week
_____Once or twice a week
_____Two or three times a month
_____About once a month
_____Less than once a month, but at least once a year
_____Less than once a year
_____Never

"Here's a card which says how often people drink. Let's take wine first. Which one says how often you usually have wine? Let's look at it." The interviewer then read these frequencies aloud, from "Three or more times a day" to "Never." This order of presentation, suggested by the California researchers, was intended to make it easier for fairly regular daily drinkers to admit to their high frequency by suggesting that we anticipated even higher frequencies among some subjects. (Actually, 8 of our 221 adult subjects did acknowledge drinking three or more times a day.) Subjects who reported drinking wine at least once a month were then asked how often they consumed various *quantities* of wine:

"When you drink wine, how often do you have five or more glasses?"

_____Nearly every time
_____More than half the time
_____Less than half the time
_____Once in a while
_____Never

"When you drink wine, how often do you have three or four glasses?" (Same categories.)

"When you drink wine, how often do you have one or two glasses?" (Same categories.)

This whole procedure was then repeated for beer and hard liquor, including mixed drinks.

Tedious as it was for both subjects and interviewers, we thought this procedure would have several advantages: By breaking down this complex behavior into its component parts we hoped to improve the accuracy of our subjects' recall. It also made possible a beverage-by-beverage analysis of their drinking habits. Finally, it would enable us to differentiate subjects who were moderate drinkers on a daily basis (like many of us on the research staff) from those who were pretty regular weekend binge drinkers (like many of our Native American research subjects).

As it turned out, we never used these data in the ways originally intended. Too complex. Instead, we converted each subject's intake of each beverage into ounces of absolute alcohol, multiplied by their frequency and added across beverages to produce a *single score*—average ounces of absolute alcohol ingested per day—which would permit correlational analyses and tests of group differences. Because of the way we had collected our data, however, reducing these responses to this single "Quantity-Frequency Index" created an extremely complicated scoring nightmare. It was also sobering to discover that many of us on the research staff, with our daily cocktail hour after work, had a "Q-F" score as high as the tri-ethnic community's "drunken Indians!"

Our survey also asked subjects how often they had been drunk in the last month or year, about various negative consequences of their drinking, such as problems with their family, friends, fights, accidents, their job, or their health, and questions about what made them feel like having a drink, with twenty-five response categories offered from "just to be sociable" to "helps you forget your problems." Fourteen similar to the latter, which indicated that alcohol was being used to cope with personal psychological problems, particularly those involving a negative self-image, clung together statistically, forming an index of what we called "Personal-Effects" drinking. Although all of these measures were based on "self-reports," each could serve as an alternative indicator of "problem drinking."

The procedures we used in the high school study were fairly similar. The third day of testing was devoted to a "Drinking Questionnaire." The day was introduced by explaining that "Many scientists have been interested in teenage drinking all over the country," and in a direct appeal for their cooperation, "It's important for this study that your answers be accurate and honest." As always they were assured anonymity. For this group-administered questionnaire, the "Quantity-Frequency" section was substantially simplified. Students were simply asked, "How often do you usually drink wine?" and then, "When you drink wine, how much do you usually drink at one time?" Scoring categories were provided from "One or two times a day" to "never," and from "A bottle or more" to "Never drink wine" and students were simply asked to circle the appropriate answer. Similar questions were then repeated for beer and liquor. This format is quite similar to that used by Mulford and Miller (1960a, b, and c) in their Iowa survey.

Following this students were asked, "When do you usually drink?", "Where do you usually do most of your drinking?", and "Who do you usually drink with most often?" followed by a list of various response categories to circle or space to write in their own answers. Then they were asked, "What kinds of things make you feel like having a drink?" followed by a series of twenty-eight items ranging from "just to be friendly" to "helps you forget your problems." As in the adult survey, fourteen responses of the latter type tapped "personal effects" reasons for drinking and empirically formed a single scale. Students were also asked, "How many times have you gotten drunk or pretty high in the last year?" with response categories from ten or more times to never, and responded to a series of questions about their attitudes toward drinking and its various negative consequences in their life. (Copies of all our student and adult questionnaires are available in Jessor, Graves, Hanson, and Jessor 1968).[7]

All this attention devoted to assessing drinking behavior proved worthwhile. Sex and ethnic differences in reported drinking behavior were substantial, and always in the direction anticipated from more casual ethnographic observations (*discriminant validity*). Correlations among these various measures were also reasonably high, ranging from .45 to .63 among adults and .47 to .86 in the high school (*convergent validity*). Since all these drinking measures were based on self-reports, however, some of the correlation among them could be a result of a generalized "willingness to be honest about my behavior" factor. (A possible artifactual correlation of this kind is always an issue when two or more of your measures in some theoretical scheme are based on self-reports.) Interestingly, the highest correlations in both settings were with the simple question "How many times have you gotten drunk (or pretty high) in the last year?" And among all these self-report measures this also proved to have the highest correlations with our theoretical network of predictor variables (*predictive validity*). In fact a "pattern analysis" of those who reported being drunk more than once during the previous year ranged from 0 in the optimal pattern to 53% in the four departure patterns among those in our adult community sample, and from 14% to 80% among the high school students. (This simple statistical procedure will be described more fully in the following chapter.) Accounting for more than 50% of the variation in reported drunkenness is a pretty impressive result in the behavioral sciences.[8]

Using Court Records

Because of the difficulties in obtaining accurate self-reports of socially disapproved behavior such as heavy drinking, we also made a major effort to obtain objective external evidence of problem drinking and other forms of (mostly drinking-related) deviant behavior by any of the 221 subjects in our adult survey sample by means of a thorough search of all court records in the area over the previous ten years: the U.S. federal courts in Colorado and New Mexico, two district courts, seven municipal courts in the surrounding area, magistrate and justice of the peace courts, the tribal court, and records from the law and order branch of the Bureau of Indian Affairs. Omer Stewart was responsible for suggesting we use these formal records as an alternative measure of social deviance, and it was he and his team who undertook the tedious task of scouring them for us. Like school records of absenteeism and tardiness among high school students, these court records provided another valuable "nonreactive" measure not under a subject's control, and my experience using them in the Tri-Ethnic study led directly to the use of court records in my first independent research project among Navajo migrants to Denver. (See chapter 5.)

Forty-five of the 221 subjects in our adult sample had court records of convictions for crimes other than civil suits, minor traffic violations, and game law violations, all of which were excluded. These 45 subjects had a total of 247 convictions, ranging up to 15 for one of them. From the records it was clear that 87% of these offenses were alcohol related; an independent investigation of the others might well have found alcohol implicated in many more. These records also supplemented our self-report data in significant ways. Of the forty-five subjects who had convictions, only twenty-six acknowledged this fact in our interview, when we asked specifically, "What (else) have you gotten into trouble with the law about?" So 42% of those who had convictions failed to acknowledge this fact, and sixteen of these nineteen (including ten women) had clearly *denied* it. Self-protection, when reporting on your own socially disapproved behavior, is clearly a problem for researchers trying to establish valid measures of behavior. The use of formal records is one strategy for helping to overcome this, and one which I would find particularly valuable in my research among Navajo migrants.

A problem specific to court records, however, is the possible skewing effect of ethnicity. Being a member of a conspicuous minority group, we have good reason to suspect, will lead to a higher rate of arrest by police and conviction by the courts. And public drinking norms may make some minority group members more visible when drunk and therefore more subject to arrest than majority group members who are more likely to drink at home. Finally, public records normally pick up only a small portion of the behavior under investigation. Two strategies address such issues. The first is to compare the record data with alternative measures of the same general behavioral domain: in our case, alternative self-report measures of drinking behavior. If they are reasonably well correlated, then composite measures can be constructed which provide a broader range of coverage. The second is to "control" for ethnicity by analyzing the correlates of these measures *within* each ethnic group separately. In the Tri-Ethnic study we employed both strategies.

Within all three ethnic groups, a record of having had a court conviction during the previous ten years was positively associated with each of our four different self-reports of alcohol use and attendant problems. See table 3.1 (based on table 8.4 in Jessor, Graves, Hanson, and Jessor 1968:199):

Table 3.1. Correlations between Court Records and Four Self-Report Measures of Drinking Behavior, Adult Community Survey

	Anglos (N = 93)	Spanish (N = 60)	Indians (N= 68)
Quantity frequency of alcohol use	.34	.07	.27
Drinking for its personal effects	.44	.18	.31
Drinking-related problems	.88	.69	.38
Times drunk during previous year	.85	.78	.46

Looking at this table it appears that *times drunk* last year can serve as the best single self-report measure of socially punishable ("deviant") drinking behavior—the one with the highest convergent validity.

Finally, as we had done in the high school study, for the adult community study we constructed a "global deviance" measure using all the information we had. Subject were classified as "deviant" (i.e., had repeatedly engaged in socially unacceptable, largely drinking-related behavior of some kind) if they reported having been drunk fifteen or more times during the previous year, *or* if they reported two or more instances of drinking-related problems or any other serious offense, *or* if they had a record of a court conviction during the previous ten years. Ninety-one of the 221 subjects in the adult sample were thereby classified as "deviant." As we will see in the next chapter, this proved to be our most "valid" measure of problem behavior, the one which we were best able to predict from our network of sociological and psychological variables (predictive validity).

Lessons for Behavioral Anthropology

Here are some of the lessons I learned from these exercises in behavioral measurement, which have been important to me in my career as a behavioral anthropologist:

1. Self-reports are a difficult way to get reliable information about a person's behavior, particularly when that behavior carries a strong valence of social approval or disapproval. Our natural tendency for self-protection and desire to make ourselves look good in others' eyes inevita-

bly introduce distortions which undermine the validity of these self-report data, and therefore our ability as behavioral scientists to test our theories about the determinants of that behavior.

2. Behavioral choice procedures and behavioral experiments are promising alternatives, particularly if they can be constructed in ways which conceal the behavioral tendency of interest. (Some social psychologists have been very creative in designing experiments of this type, for example in studies of honesty and empathy.) But since these experiments normally provide a *very limited sample* of your subject's behavior, many such choices would have to be provided under a wide variety of circumstances to yield a stable measure of an individual's "behavioral predisposition" across situations. Normally the cost of doing this precludes it being a realistic research option. An alternative is to pool these measures across *subjects*, rather than across situations. In this way you obtain more stable measures of the behavioral tendency for a *group* of subjects who have some potential determinant in common: background experience, personality attributes, social position, or ethnicity. Then the limitations of these measures on an *individual* basis tend to be canceled out, and theoretically interesting relationships can be examined. O. Michael Watson and I used this strategy when looking at Arab and American "proxemic behavior" (Watson and Graves 1966) and some years later Nancy Graves and I used this strategy effectively in our research in Polynesia. (See chapter 10 and Volume II, article 10.)

3. Behavioral ratings by others, particularly persons without strong emotional ties to your subjects, proved to be much more valid than self-reports. (We tried collecting behavioral ratings from our student subjects' mothers in the Tri-Ethnic study, but they proved not to be very objective raters of their children's behavior, and I haven't bothered to discuss them in this chapter.) And by using a number and variety of persons with differing opportunities to observe your subjects (in our case, peers and teachers) these ratings can be substantially improved, both in reliability and validity.

4. The more specific the behaviors being rated, the more reliable and valid the ratings. But then you need to be sure that the range of specific behaviors effectively samples the behavioral domain you want judged. A behavioral domain like "delay of gratification" at a relatively high level of

abstraction will require a larger sample of specific behaviors than a domain like "excessive alcohol consumption" at a much lower level of abstraction.

5. Finally, a general principle which emerged from this work is that although it may be possible to obtain reasonably reliable and valid self-report measures of a person's behavior, "nonreactive" measures over which a subject has no direct control, whether ratings by others or constructed from formal records or other sources, are likely to prove more "valid" than self-reports, and are much to be preferred. In my experience, these are the behavioral measures which we seem best able to predict and explain. Furthermore, measures of personality variables are almost always (but not inevitably) dependent on self-reports of a subject's internal state. (See chapter 6.) So, if these measures are to serve as "predictors" in some theoretical scheme, it is highly desirable that your behavioral criterion measures not *also* be based on self-reports. For then there will always be the suspicion that the correlations you obtain are the result, at least in part, of your subjects' own willingness or unwillingness to say negative things about themselves.

Formal records have their own limitations as a basis for a behavioral measure, however. Normally they are not specifically collected for research purposes, and inferences must be made from the records to some underlying behavior of interest. Then the "validity" of that inference will need to be demonstrated. We will run into this issue again in chapters 5, 6, and 7, where I will present our use of arrest records as a measure of excessive drinking among Navajo migrants to Denver.

Notes

1. The term "deviant behavior" created a lot of problems for my anthropological colleagues, who generally attempt to take a stance of "moral relativism," accepting whatever behavior they observe within other cultures without judgment. Much of what middle-class observers judge as "deviant behavior" is clearly "normative" in other times and places. Jessor devoted the whole second chapter of our book to defining the concept of "deviance." It would perhaps have made our work much easier, and I would have taken less flack from my dissertation committee at Penn, if we had simply focused our research attention on drinking and drunkenness.

2. In his research on sexual behavior Kinsey went one step further, asking that if his subjects were unwilling to answer his questions honestly, that they not participate in his study.

3. For a good discussion of the use of Guttman scales in anthropology, see appendix B in Pelto and Pelto (1978). Bernard (2002) also provides good coverage of Guttman scaling for anthropologists in chapter 12. For an example from my own work, see T. Graves, N. Graves, and Kobrin (1969).

4. The concept of culture, when defined as typical ways of thinking, feeling, and doing, can create the same problem of circularity for anthropologists as the parallel concept of personality, as an individual's typical ways of thinking, feeling, and doing, does for psychology. The way people have behaved in the past, whether as individuals or in groups, is still usually the best predictor of their future behavior, but doesn't provide much of an "explanation."

5. In retrospect, I doubt that this was true. In fact, students may have been more inclined to attempt to look good for their English teacher than they would for us.

6. Most anthropologists don't appreciate the value of looking for countable indices of theoretical variables. I remember when defending my thesis at Penn one member of the committee remarking that he hoped I would not spend my entire professional career as an anthropologist counting student tardies!

7. Ethnographers may feel that collecting open-ended interviews with a small sample of subjects from this community on, for example, their drinking habits and reasons they felt like having a drink might have been important and useful initially, or as a supplement to our more structured procedures. I would agree.

8. The pattern using alternative self-report measures of quantity/frequency, "personal effects" drinking, and drinking-related problems were similar, but less dramatic. See Jessor, Graves, Hanson, and Jessor 1968, tables 11.11 and 11.13, pages 360-361.

4

Simple Data Analysis

One of the things which most clearly distinguishes behavioral anthropologists from others in the field is our commitment to quantification wherever possible and appropriate, to counting, to the use of statistical analysis to examine empirically relationships between within-group variations in the *behavior* of our subjects and possible determinants or correlates of that behavior among background experiences (including socialization experiences), personality predispositions, and situational pressures and constraints. To do this requires at least a minimal understanding of simple statistics.

In sociology and psychology a command of statistics is assumed as a necessary requirement for a research career. With my strong math background from engineering I did well in my statistics courses. Ken Hammond therefore invited me to work as one of his research assistants on a project in the medical school. So I began applying my statistics from an early stage in a research context which made them more meaningful to me. I worked for months in a room full of graduate students pounding out chi square tests on desk calculators, something which only a few years later would take the university's new mainframe computer but an instant to produce. But this work gave me an intuitive "feel" for relationships among variables and a hands-on appreciation of "correlation coefficients" as the way we test our hypotheses about the possible causes of some behavior we are attempting to explain.

When I became an anthropology major, however, I soon realized that while students in physical anthropology and archaeology usually felt quite comfortable with numerical and statistical analysis, most of my fellow "cultural" anthropologists did not. So my interest in and command of statistics set me apart from them—and from most of their teachers as well. I'll admit to feelings of superiority in this regard: Quantitative research is what "real scientists" do, I believed. And I wanted my chosen field to hold its own among the other behavioral sciences. I vowed that when I became a professor myself, all my students would be required to take statistics, and to collect at least some quantitative data as part of their dissertation research.

But to have any influence in the field, I realized, I would also have to learn how to communicate with anthropologists who did *not* have my background, and who were frequently "number phobic." So during my apprenticeship I was constantly on the lookout for ways to simplify the presentation of quantitative data. This was the motivation behind my development of "pattern analysis," the major form in which the Tri-Ethnic data were presented. Because in addition to my other research duties, I was given the task of conducting most of the statistical analysis for the project as a whole on the university's new computer system and presenting the results in our final report (Jessor, Graves, Hanson, and Jessor 1968).

What Is a Correlation Coefficient?

When I start to present *numbers* to an audience of cultural anthropologists, whether students or colleagues, many eyes glaze over and minds turn off. So my challenge has been to develop ways to present fairly complex and sophisticated statistical analyses in a manner that *any* intelligent layperson can follow. Let's start with the simplest tests of co-variation, the basic tools of behavioral science.

A familiar example of co-variation is the relationship between height and weight. As we grow taller, we grow heavier. More bone mass, more tissue, more muscle. Height and weight co-vary. In fact, it is tempting to say that an increase in height "causes" an increase in weight. The converse, however, would not feel true: that an increase in weight "causes" an increase in height. "Causal inferences" from correlational data are common but tricky. We'll return to this issue later in this chapter and at greater length in chapter 12.

Now suppose a group of researchers from Mars wanted to study human development on Earth. They might scoop up some babies into a spaceship and observe them for twenty years. This would be a "longitudinal" or "developmental" research design. But suppose these Martian researchers only had grant funds to support their work for two or three years. Then they might choose as an alternative a "cross-sectional" design in which they scooped up a sample of humans and examined their physical characteristics to see which "co-varied" in theoretically predictable ways.

So suppose these Martian researchers came down and scooped up me. (I've always wanted to be picked up by aliens.) I'm a pretty average man in height and weight: 5' 10" and 155 pounds. Then suppose they scooped up the German super-model Claudia Schiffer. (What a great scenario!) She's a bit taller than me—5' 11"—but substantially lighter: 127 pounds. Then suppose they scooped up the San Francisco 49ers' star running back in their 1999 season, Charlie Garner. He's only 5' 9" but 187 pounds. With only this sample of three human beings in hand they might conclude that there is *no* relationship (co-variation) between height and weight among humans, or perhaps a slight "negative" one, because the tallest subject in their sample was the lightest, and the shortest was the heaviest. Perhaps as humans are being manufactured, these Martians might hypothesize, their original bulk of clay gets stretched, and perhaps a bit gets lost or used up in the process. Or perhaps they might conclude that they were dealing with three different "species" of human beings, each with their own distinctive developmental pattern.

To study this problem more thoroughly, our Martian scientists might decide they needed a larger sample. So they descend on the 49ers' practice field and scoop up the entire 1999 team (or at least 30 of the best-known players). The team roster with their jersey numbers, positions, heights, and weights is presented in table 4.1. (Note: this is not a "random sample" of humans, but like many researchers, our Martian scientists got what they could within the time and resources at their disposal.)

Now, despite their advanced technology, our Martian scientists are wise enough to begin their analysis by plotting their raw data by hand on a "scattergram" (figure 4.1). Height is shown along the horizontal (X) axis and weight along the vertical (Y) axis. So each point on the scattergram represents a real human being. There's Charlie Garner near the lower left-

Table 4.1. 1999 49ers Team Roster

No.	Name	Position	Ht.	Wt.	Ht. rank	Wt. rank	Rank diff.	(Rank diff.)^2
4	Chad Stanley	P	6' 3"	205	18	12	6	36
5	Jeff Garcia	QB	6' 1"	195	8	5.5	2.5	6.25
7	Wade Ritchey	K	6' 4"	200	24	9	15	225
8	Steve Young	QB	6' 2"	215	12.5	14	1.5	2.25
18	Steve Stenstrom	QB	6' 2"	202	12.5	11	1.5	2.25
21	R W McQuarters	DB	5' 9"	198	2.5	8	5.5	30.25
23	Pierson Prioleau	DB	5"10"	191	4	4	0	0
25	Charlie Garner	RB	5' 9"	187	2.5	2	.5	.25
27	Craig Newsome	DB	6' 0"	188	5.5	3	2.5	6.25
30	Lance Schultes	DB	6' 2"	195	12.5	5.5	7	49
38	Darnell Walker	DB	5' 8"	167	1	1	0	0
40	Fred Beasley	RB	6' 0"	235	5.5	18	12.5	156.25
44	Tommy Vardell	RB	6' 1"	238	8	19	11	121
46	Tim McDonald	DB	6' 2"	219	12.5	16	3.5	12.25
51	Ken Norton	LB	6' 2"	254	12.5	21.5	9	81
54	Lee Woodall	LB	6' 1"	224	8	17	9	81
55	Winfred Tubbs	LB	6' 4"	254	24	21.5	2.5	6.25
62	Jeremy Newberry	C	6' 5"	315	29	29	0	0
63	Derrek Deese	T	6' 3"	289	18	24	6	36
65	Ray Brown	T	6' 5"	318	29	30	1	1
67	Chris Dolman	G	6' 3"	297	18	27	9	81
74	Dave Fiore	T	6' 4"	290	24	25	1	1
80	Jerry Rice	WR	6' 2"	196	12.5	7	5.5	30.25
81	Terrell Owens	WR	6' 3"	217	18	15.5	3.5	12.25
83	J J Stokes	WR	6' 4"	217	24	14.5	5.5	30.25
85	Greg Clark	TE	6' 4"	251	24	20	4	16
88	Mark Harris	WR	6' 4"	201	24	10	14	196
90	Junior Bryant	DE	6' 5"	305	29	28	1	1
97	Bryant Young	DT	6' 3"	291	18	26	8	64
98	Gabe Wilkins	DE	6' 5"	305	29	28	1	1

Rank Diff. = (Ht. Rank – Wt. Rank); (Rank Diff.)^2 = Rank Difference squared

hand corner at 5'9" and 187 pounds. Just below him is the lightest member of the squad, the hapless defensive back Darnell Walker, at 5'8" and 167 pounds. And there in the upper right-hand corner of the distribution is the heaviest member of the squad, tackle Ray Brown (No. 65), at 6'5" and 318. Despite the fact that other players are scattered all over the graph, the general tendency for shorter players to be lighter and taller players to be heavier is obvious. Height and weight co-vary.

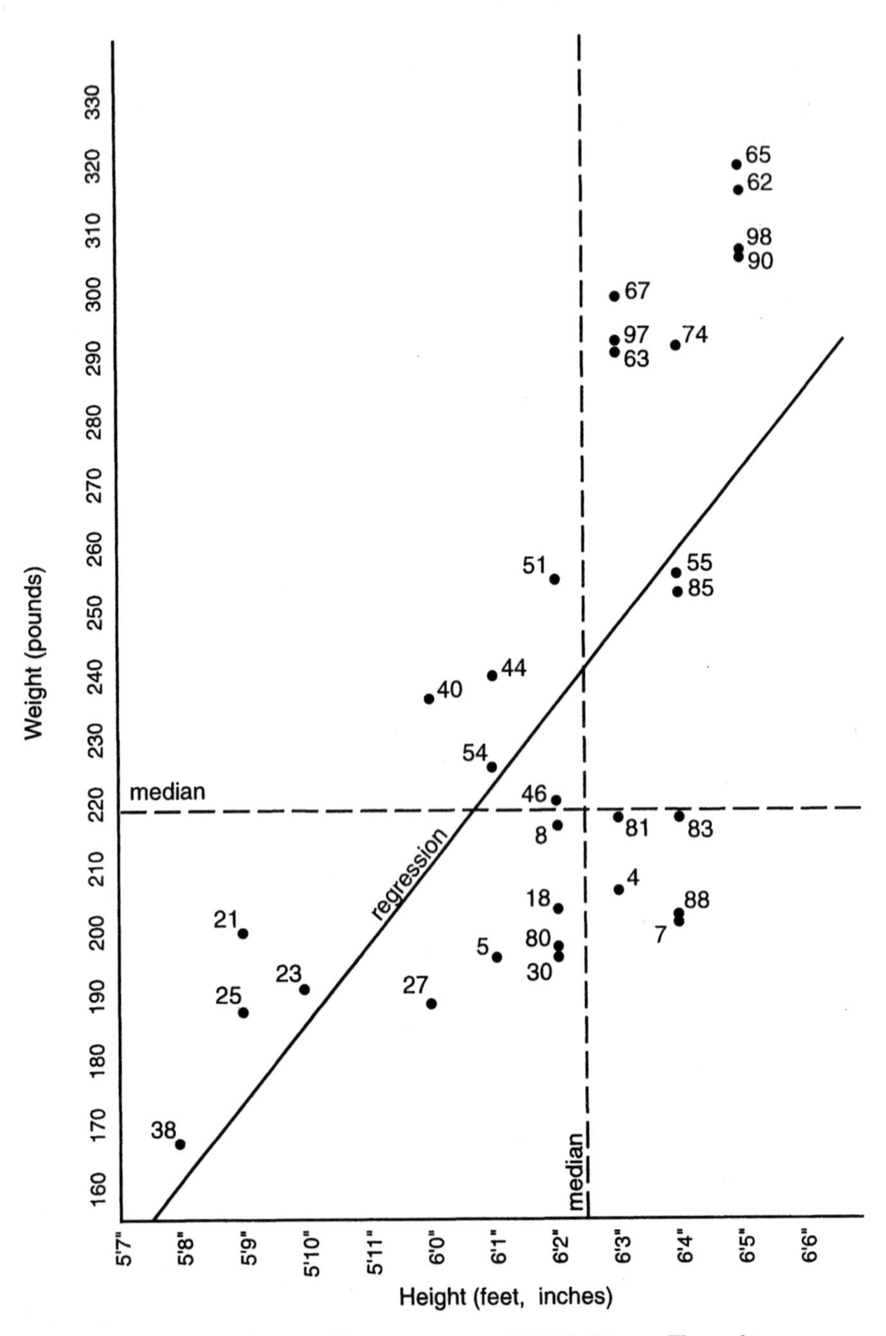

Figure 4.1. Raw Score Scattergram (1999 49ers Team)

But how strong is this relationship? If it were perfect all the dots in this scattergram would fall along the single solid ("regression") line I have drawn through the distribution, every inch of increase in height would lead to an increase of a little over 12 pounds in weight, and the correlation coefficient would be one (r = 1.0). If we had a "negative" correlation (the taller the subjects the lighter their weight, as in my first fantasy sample of three), the regression line would point upwards in the opposite direction, and if all the dots fell along it we would have a correlation coefficient of –1.0. The more scattered the dots, the weaker the correlation, until we have a situation where any height in the distribution is associated with any weight: r = 0.

One way to measure the strength of the co-variation in our data is by calculating the magnitude of this correlation coefficient, from –1 to +1. There are several different mathematical formulas for doing this, depending on your purpose and what kind of data you have.[1] Because it is intuitively easy to understand, I have calculated a "Spearman rho," a standard "nonparametric" correlation coefficient. In the fourth column from the right of table 4.1 I have ranked the players from shortest to tallest and in the next column from lightest to heaviest. For each player I then subtracted the lower rank from the higher rank ("difference") and entered this in the next-to-last column. Obviously, the smaller this difference, the stronger the association between height and weight (the closer they co-vary.) Three players had exactly the same rank on both "variables" and seven others were only 1.5 ranks or less apart. That's a third of the squad. I then squared each of these differences and put that figure in the last column. (Squaring gets rid of the positive or negative signs, which I ignored when subtracting one rank from the other. It also gives greater "weight" to players who deviate the most from our expected height–weight relationship. If you want to know "why" we do this, ask Dr. Spearman.)

Finally, I inserted these figures into the formula for calculating a Spearman rho:

$$\rho = 1 - \frac{6\Sigma D_i^2}{N^3 - N}$$

where D is the difference in weight rank and height rank for each player, and N is the number of subjects in the sample.

The coefficient turned out to be .71, which is very respectable in science: In a sample of 30 people, it would occur by chance less than once in a thousand times. So our Martian scientists will conclude that among human beings height and weight probably co-vary, and based on their (clearly biased) sample, a person's height probably accounts for roughly half the variation in their weight. (This estimate is arrived at by squaring the correlation coefficient and converting this to a percentage: i.e., .71 x .71 = 50%.)

Contingency Tables

Another, even simpler way to present these data is by means of a "two-by-two contingency table" (figure 4.2). In figure 4.1 I drew a dotted horizontal line at the "median" height of these players: between 6'2" and 6'3". Half the players are 6' 2" or shorter, and half are 6'3" or taller. I also drew a dotted vertical line at the midpoint in weight: 218 pounds. Half the squad is lighter, half is heavier. Then I simply counted the number of players in each quadrant and placed that number in the corresponding quadrants of the two-by-two table below. Ten players fall into the upper right-hand Quadrant B: They are both taller and heavier than average. And ten players fall into the lower left-hand Quadrant C: They are both shorter and lighter than average.

	6'2" or shorter	6'3" or taller	Totals
Over 218 pounds	A 5 (7.5)	B 10 (7.5)	15
Under 218 pounds	10 (7.5) C	5 (7.5) D	15
Totals	15	15	30

Figure 4.2. The Distribution of the 49ers Squad by Height and Weight

Again, the association (co-variation) between height and weight is obvious: two-thirds (10 of 15) of the tallest members of the squad are also the heaviest, and only a third of the shortest are among the heaviest. If there were no association between these two variables, height and weight, then "by chance" we would expect seven-and-a-half people to fall into each quadrant. (Thirty divided by four. I have placed these "expected cell frequencies" in parentheses.)

One of the nice things about a two-by-two contingency table is that you are dealing with groups of real people in each quadrant, rather than an impersonal (and less easily comprehensible) correlation coefficient. So just as when we looked at the scattergram, if you have other information about these people (as we do for the 49ers), you can look at those who do *not* fit your hypothetical expectations and see if there are good reasons why. This will enrich your understanding. (And this is why I had our Martian scientists select a known squad of football players.) For example, *all* the offensive and defensive linemen and defensive line backers on the team are above average in weight. These are the "Sherman tanks" of the squad whose main job is simply to push open a hole for one of their running backs to slip through or keep the opposing line from pushing open a hole for one of theirs. So three of the five men in Quadrant A who are below average in height (in this case 6' 1" or 6' 2") are nevertheless above average in weight. Otherwise they would not be able to do their job. The other two in this quadrant, Fred Beasley and Tommy Vardell, are running backs who have to slip through those holes, and often meet those Sherman tanks on the other team head on. (Charlie Garner is also a running back, but makes up for his lack of bulk by his agility.) Similarly, in Quadrant D are three of the team's outstanding wide receivers, Terrell Owens, J. J. Stokes, and Mark Harris, who have to be tall, but light and agile to catch passes while evading the defenders. The other two, interestingly, are the "special team" kickers. Height—long legs—without too much weight must be of advantage in their job.

(Note that if you are stuck in the field with only a hand calculator and decide to calculate a Spearman rho by hand, you will also be able to quickly spot the subjects who deviate most from your hypothetical expectations, because they will be the ones with the largest "differences" between their two ranks. You can then use other information to see if you can understand why. They are the ones in table 4.1 like Wade Ritchey—one of the two "special teams" kickers—and the wide receiver Mark Harris, both of whom fell in Quadrant D of our contingency table, plus Fred Beasley and Tommy Vardell, the two running backs who are heavier than you would expect from their height, and who fell into Quadrant A. These two approaches to looking at our data yielded similar information.)

Presenting your data in the form of two-by-two contingency tables makes your results immediately clear to a reader. If the percentage of subjects falling into each quadrant is quite different, as in this case, the *social significance* of your results can easily be judged by any reader. For example, if you knew that a player on the 49ers' squad was taller than half his teammates, then it would be a good bet that he was heavier as well. Two-to-one odds: You'd be right two-thirds of the time and wrong only one-third of the time. If there were *no* association between these two variables, if height was *not* a good "predictor" of weight, then you'd be right only half the time and wrong half the time—no better than chance. But because height *is* a good predictor of weight, by using this information you substantially improve your betting odds.

"Tests" of a "hypothesis" about "why" people vary in their behavior are really just "bets" of this type. We are gambling our reputation as behavioral scientists on some interpretation about co-variation. If we don't collect or present any data to support our interpretation, then readers are forced to accept our conclusions "on faith." And there will always be some skeptic out there who will challenge us. The time and trouble it takes to collect quantitative data often protects us from fooling *ourselves*, as well as our readers. It also offers us the possibility of discovering something we overlooked in our more casual observations, or had never anticipated.

Statistical Significance and Social Significance

Skeptics and hard-nosed statisticians will wonder if the relationship we just presented is "statistically significant": Might it have occurred by chance? By shifting the position of only a few players from Quadrant B to Quadrant A and from C to D you'd have no association at all. A test of "statistical significance" is simply a way to evaluate your "betting odds."

How much faith should you have in these results? How likely are they to occur again if you drew another sample of football players, or of people in general?

One way to calculate the "statistical significance" of our findings is to use a "chi square" test, one of my favorite simple statistics. This statistic is based on the difference between the "expected cell frequencies" (7.5 in our case) and the *actual* cell frequencies. In each cell this difference comes to two-and-a-half people. The bigger this difference, obviously, the stronger the association between the two variables. Using the formula for calculating chi square, you square this difference ($2.5 \times 2.5 = 6.25$), divide it by the *actual* number of subjects in each cell (5, 10, 10, and 5) and add across all four cells (1.25 plus .625 plus .625 plus 1.25). In this case, chi square equals 3.75. Looking up this value in a table of critical values of chi square in any standard statistics book you find that it is not quite large enough to be "statistically significant" at the .05 level; that would require a chi square value of 3.84. So a little more than five times in a hundred you might have obtained a distribution like this by chance alone. Is this a good bet?

Now suppose we *doubled* our sample size from thirty to sixty players, but still found the same relative distribution in the four cells. The *proportion* of players in each cell would be the same, but the chi square value would also double, to 7.5. (Try it and see.) So now your results are "highly significant" statistically, and would have occurred by chance less than once in a hundred times. The odds that your conclusions are based on "chance" are now very small.

This effect of sample size on "statistical significance" is why I like to collect samples of between 60 and 120 in each group I study. (This sample size also makes for pretty dependable estimates of other characteristics of your population, and permits cross-cutting your variables a couple of times while still maintaining a reasonable number of cases in each cell.) Then if I obtain results that are clearly socially significant, they will be statistically significant as well. The converse is also true, however. If your sample size is large enough, even a weak association in terms of the percentage of difference in each cell may still be "statistically significant" even though it is not large enough to matter in the real world. So don't be fooled by the magical phrase "statistically significant." As behavioral scientists we should probably be interested only in relationships between "predictor" and "outcome" variables that are large enough to be of social and practical importance (Morrison and Henkel 1970).[2]

One last thing: Notice that by cutting our predictor variable—height—and our outcome ("dependent") variable—weight—at their medians and grouping our subjects simply into "high" and "low" on each we lost a lot of information. When we used the full range of values to calculate a Spearman rho correlation coefficient the result was .71 and highly significant statistically. (A correlation coefficient calculated from our two-by-two table—the "contingency coefficient"—came to less than half that: .33.) But grouping data in contingency tables allows us to use much "cruder" data. It's much easier to rate people as "high" or "low" on some variable than to give them an "exact" score. Given the measurement problems in behavioral science, it is often wiser to use a crude but reliable (easily repeatable) measure than to pretend that your instruments are better than they really are. And if you get good results with crude measures, of course, it is likely that you would get even better results as your measurement instruments improve.

Finally, the use of crude contingency tables is a "conservative" approach: Generally speaking, my research goal has simply been to demonstrate *co-variation* among predictor and outcome variables, rather than trying to estimate the "true strength" of that relationship. Too often the strength of a relationship will vary tremendously, depending on the samples you have (the particular groups you are studying) and the measures you are using. But if I get the same *pattern* of associations among samples of Anglos, Hispanics, and Native Americans, for example, and if these associations are consistently in the same *direction* (even if they differ in magnitude) regardless of the measures I use, I can feel some confidence in the repeatability of my results within *other* groups at other times and places. This is what I call "sloppy replication," and it gives me greater confidence in the generalizability (universality) of my results than if the same results were obtained using the same instruments on very similar groups of people (classic replication), where perhaps your "findings" are the result of "artifacts" that may occur again when the study is carefully replicated.

So, despite this loss of information, two-by-two contingency tables are among my favorite ways to present data. Furthermore, often the only information I have is in the form of unique categories ("male" vs. "female") or the presence or absence of some feature (owns, does not own a radio). Finally, two-by-two tables are simple for most people to understand, and I like knowing that each quadrant constitutes a group of real people who share two characteristics (in this case high or low height and weight) and may therefore share other characteristics as well.

Analyzing the Tri-Ethnic Data

When I was analyzing my dissertation data in the field all I had was a desk calculator. So all my analyses took the form of the simple tests of association discussed above. But when I returned to Boulder, the University had installed its first mainframe computer, and I was given the task of preparing and analyzing the Tri-Ethnic project's data.

The Community Survey study was conducted during a two-week period in October 1962, which memorably coincided with the Cuban missile crisis. Twelve of us were in the field at the time conducting the interviews, and we all wondered if the world would go up in smoke while we were busy collecting our data! Despite these circumstances, 221 interviews were completed (plus only 10 refusals, a 4% rate which was gratifyingly low), representing a one-sixth sample of all adult Anglos and Hispanics and a one-third sample of adult Ute Indians. This was my first example of the feasibility of conducting a survey study cross-culturally using a carefully selected random sample from a total population census. (Four years later my students and I would conduct interviews with a stratified random sample of adult male Navajo Indians, the first to use the tribal census for such a purpose. See chapter 8.) The idea of interviewing a *representative sample* of persons from within different ethnic groups to substantiate our conclusions rather than simply a few "key informants" or a haphazard sample of anyone willing and available is still relatively rare within anthropology.[3] But it is such standard practice within our sister disciplines that if we want to contribute to an integrated science of human behavior we should give it a try. It is a lot easier than it may seem.

After the adult survey was completed we had the tedious job of checking and scoring all the interviews and punching all the data onto IBM cards to be fed into the computer. (There are much easier and faster ways of doing this today. See Bernard 2002.) While analyzing these survey data I had my first experience working with massive tables of correlation coefficients. I was doing the computer work, the statistical analysis, and the first time we got all the variables scored, punched, and correlations run, Dick Jessor and I set aside a day to analyze the printout. The new computer could give us an N-by-N matrix of correlations: each variable's statistical association with every other variable we had measured. We could then look at these correlations and test theory after theory, and every subtheory we could come up with, against the data.

Dick and I were eager to look at this matrix. It was exciting to have this powerful statistical output that the new computer made possible. It would have taken dozens of research assistants months and months to do this by hand, as I had been doing for Ken Hammond only a few years earlier. But it took the computer a single run. And we weren't dealing with chi squares, which are relatively simple to calculate, we were dealing with Pearson correlation coefficients, which are more mathematically complex.[4]

So we started looking at the matrix, and theory after theory that we had expected to be supported washed out. It was very discouraging. None of our theoretical expectations panned out that first day. But the mind is not capable, nor willing, to accept this meaninglessness outcome of data that we had worked for years to generate, to collect, to score, and then to correlate. So we started asking ourselves, "What correlations are there in the data that are significant and substantial enough to be meaningful?"

First, we circled all the big correlations, looked at them, and then began creating new theories to explain them. This is the old anthropological "inductive" method: You collect masses of data and then see if you can make sense out of it all. The deductive method hadn't worked. So we said, "We'll shift gears; we'll generate theory." And by the end of the day we had a new body of theory to explain all the outcomes. Great stuff, thrilling. We were feeling pretty good about the day's work.

That evening I was working over the data and I discovered that in the stack of IBM punch cards that we had fed into the computer, one card had been misplaced, which meant that the entire stack of cards was off by one card. Because each subject had several cards to record all their data, this meant that the machine was reading half of one variable and half of another in the placement of the cards into the computer. So in fact what was fed into the computer for analysis was essentially a random numbers table. That's why we got what looked like random numbers from the correlations coming out. Garbage in, garbage out. Of course, we laughed, and God laughed, sitting up there watching us toil away. We laughed because we were able to deal so easily with this random set of outcomes and make sense out of them. An important lesson for me, and one which I always share with students in my methodology classes. This is also one reason I am suspicious of "letting the data speak for themselves," and why I still value the deductive method, beginning with theory and testing it against your data, even though this approach has its limitations, too. The ideal way to proceed is to *generate* theory inductively, *test* it deductively, and then go back and *refine* it inductively, moving back and forth between the inductive and deductive methods. (See chapter 11.)

Pattern Analysis

The simple statistical tests we have discussed so far are all measures of association between an outcome and *one* predictor. But usually our theories are far more complex than this, particularly if they are interdisciplinary and involve testing the *joint* effects of several variables simultaneously, for example, psychological pressures and situational constraints. (See chapter 7.) We can test our theory one variable at a time, as I did in my dissertation, but it would be nicer to test these joint effects simultaneously. This involves "multivariate analysis," which can be quite sophisticated mathematically and hard for a nonstatistician to follow (or accept on faith). "Pattern analysis" was my simple alternative to more conventional "multivariate analysis" such as multiple regression and path analysis, both of which I will discuss in chapter 12.

Access to a powerful university computer was very useful in refining our measures, checking their internal consistency (reliability), and their relationship to other measures of the same theoretical variable or other theory-linked variables (validity). We then knew which of our measures were most effective in doing their job. But this computer power is also seductive. It would enable us to "regress" (run correlations) for all the sociological and psychological variables we had painstakingly measured against our outcome variables: drinking behavior and other forms of "social deviance." Then we could see which variables and which measures "worked" best (showed the highest co-variation with our outcome behavior) and how much of that variation in drinking and deviant behavior they jointly accounted for.

This is a tempting statistical strategy (to which Dick and I briefly succumbed), but would be "bootstrapping": maximizing our results on the basis of correlation coefficients unique to the measures and the particular community within which we were working. In the Tri-Ethnic project we had a more conservative goal: simply to demonstrate a meaningful *relationship* between our analytic variables and behavior, recognizing that the strength of these relationships would be highly dependent on our particular sample of people and the effectiveness of our measures. Our goal was to *test a theory* rather than to discover a statistical formula that would maximize prediction within our study population. The latter might look good in an article, but would be unlikely to stand up if attempts were made to replicate it elsewhere. Our goal was not simply publication but understanding. This statistical cautiousness has guided all my subsequent work.

Another goal was simplicity of presentation. We wanted intelligent readers without advanced training in statistics to understand rather complex theoretical and empirical outcomes. And I, in particular, wanted to be able to communicate our results to anthropological colleagues most of whom have limited statistical sophistication. This, too, has continued as a goal throughout my career, and modifications of pattern analysis have served me well in this regard. (See Volume II, articles 5, 7, 8, 10, and 11.) A side benefit is that this approach makes both the discovery and presentation of complex "interaction effects" much easier and clearer, a topic which I will discuss later in this chapter.

Pattern analysis grew directly out of my experience as a graduate student calculating hundreds of chi square tests for Ken Hammond's research project. As we have just seen, chi square is perhaps the simplest test of association between an "independent" or "predictor" variable and some outcome (the "dependent" variable). Subjects are divided into those who are high or low on the predictor variable, and then this division is crosscut by those who are high or low on the outcome variable. This is the way I analyzed my dissertation data.

From the time IBM punch cards were introduced as a way to record data, I had begun using a mechanical counter-sorter. Set the machine to read any one of the eighty columns on the punch cards and it will spew these out into different piles. I loved watching this machine at work. There were virtues in this hands-on process: I *saw* relationships emerging visually as cards piled up in certain cells. Furthermore, I immediately spotted *scoring errors* when a card would fly into some unintended slot. These would be lost within the black box of a computer and simply introduce random error that reduces the strength of empirical relationships. Finally, because this process is slow and tedious, I took more time to think through what relationships I wanted to examine and why.

For ease of understanding by readers, I would often collapse these two-by-two tables and simply present the *proportions* of subjects in the high and low half of the predictor who had some outcome. For example, two-thirds of the 49ers above the median in height were also above the median in weight, and among those below the median in height, only one-third were above the median in weight.

Combining more than one "predictor variable" into a multivariate pattern analysis was my own extension of this approach. Others had used some variant when presenting their findings, however. For example, I had long been interested in the work of the rural sociologist Everett Rogers (1962) on predicting those who would be most receptive to the adoption of technological innovations, a key issue in the literature on "culture change" and "acculturation." The article by Rogers and Havens (1962) is probably the closest thing to pattern analysis with which I was already familiar, and may have served as an unconscious model.

To construct a multivariate pattern analysis I would construct a two-by-two table from the "predictor" variables. Then I could simply crosscut each cell by a *third* predictor, and sometimes even by a *fourth.* I would then look at the proportion of subjects in each cell who display some outcome we were interested in, such as reporting being frequently drunk, or falling into our "global deviance" category. For clarity of presentation, I found that I could usually combine without distortion subjects who departed from an "optimal" pattern of predictors on only one of several "predictors" into a "one departure" group, and repeat this process for the two-departure or three-departure groups down to those who departed from an optimal score on *all* predictors (never more than four in my work). This yielded very clear and easily interpretable results.

Here are some examples. The analyses presented in our final report on the Tri-Ethnic Research Project (Jessor, Graves, Hanson, and Jessor 1968) are all derived from and test the original interdisciplinary theory we developed around the table together in 1969. This theory carefully relates three types of sociological variables (what we referred to as "the opportunity structure, the normative structure, and the social control structure") and parallel psychological variables ("the perceived opportunity structure, the personal belief structure, and the personal control structure") to various measures of drinking and other forms of deviant behavior.

Four of my favorite tables from this report (on pages 351, 353, 360, and 361) illustrate in a more graphic way than words both what pattern analysis looks like and a core lesson from our work: that sociologists and psychologists can usually find a set of "predictors" from within their own discipline which will relate to some behavioral outcome in a theoretically meaningful way at about an equal level of success. For example, looking at table 4.2 a sociologist might be tempted to crow about the power of three structural variables—"socioeconomic status" (one measure of the opportunity structure), "exposure to deviant role models" (a measure of the normative structure), and "absence of sanctioning networks" (a measure of the social control structure)—to predict rates of "deviant behavior" within the adult community. (I won't describe these measures in further detail; that is readily available in Jessor, Graves, Hanson, and Jessor 1968.)

But looking at table 4.3, a psychologist might be equally enthusiastic about the power of three psychological variables—"personal disjunctions" (a measure of the perceived opportunity structure), "attitudes toward deviance" (a measure of the personal belief structure), and "alienation" (a measure of the personal control structure)—to predict the *same* behavioral outcome. Each discipline has succeeded in accounting for well over half the variability in deviant behavior.

Table 4.2. Three Sociological Variables and Deviant Behavior Adult Community Study

		Percent deviant
Optimal pattern	(N = 43)	14%
1 Departure	(N = 81)	33%
2 Departures	(N = 75)	59%
3 Departures	(N = 20)	75%

Table 4.3. Three Personality Variables and Deviant Behavior Adult Community Study

		Percent deviant
Optimal pattern	(N = 43)	16%
1 Departure	(N = 56)	27%
2 Departures	(N = 63)	51%
3 Departures	(N = 42)	69%

Each disciplinary spokesperson is justified in proclaiming that they have uncovered a good piece of the truth. But this *does not preclude* the possibility that the other discipline (or even some third, fourth, or fifth discipline) *also* may have an equal claim to a part of the truth. In the search for understanding, interdisciplinary rivalry is rarely justified. Usually work within one discipline proves to be *complementary* to work within another. And when these efforts are combined, our understanding is enhanced even further, as table 4.4 (using two sociological and two psychological variables in a "field theoretical" analysis—Lewin 1951, Yinger 1965) illustrates.

Now we have defined a group with an optimal pattern of structural and psychological attributes, only 7% of whom have fallen into our "global deviant" category, and at the other extreme, a group without any positive scores on these attributes, 84% of whom fell into our deviant category. So we have accounted for over 75% of the variability in this behavior.

Within the high school study the four variable "field theoretical" pattern analysis did even better: From optimal to four departures the percent of students classified as "deviant" (in the top quartile of *either* the peer ratings *or* teacher ratings of their "deviant behavior"—discussed in the last chapter) ranged from 9% to 100%. This is a powerful replication of the adult study in a different setting, with different subjects and measures—a good example of "sloppy replication." In both settings, furthermore, a similar pattern appeared consistently (though sometimes less dramatically) regardless of the behavioral criterion measure used, including various self-reports of drinking behavior.

Table 4.4. Field Theoretical Pattern and Deviant Behavior Adult Community Study

		Percent deviant
Optimal pattern	(N = 28)	7%
1 Departure	(N = 54)	19%
2 Departures	(N = 54)	54%
3 Departures	(N = 40)	55%
4 Departures	(N = 19)	84%

Table 4.5. Field Theoretical Pattern and Deviant Behavior High School Study

		Percent deviant
Optimal pattern	(N = 11)	9%
1 Departure	(N = 19)	27%
2 Departures	(N = 28)	36%
3 Departures	(N = 22)	50%
4 Departures	(N = 5)	100%

Finally, within the adult study, where our number of subjects was large enough to permit more refined breakdowns, the same pattern was found within both sex groups and all three ethnic groups analyzed separately. In fact, among Anglos in this community, *none* with an optimal pattern of predictors had been classified as "deviants," and *all* in the four-departure group were "deviants." Four social-psychological variables accounted for *all* the variation in this behavior! We could not have done better.

These figures were still consistent in direction but less dramatic within the two minority groups (weakest among Native Americans), suggesting that there is something about being a member of a minority group in our society which was not being captured by our theory. For example, even those few Native Americans with an optimal pattern on our four predictors had higher rates of drunkenness and deviance than Anglos in a similar position. And a few Hispanic and Native American women, despite departing from optimal scores on *all* our predictors, managed to control their drinking and deviant behavior. (No Anglo women fell in the four-departure pattern.) So there is something about being a woman which inhibits her from getting drunk or displaying other forms of social deviance even when the social and psychological pressures on her to do so are great. For our minority group subjects and for women our theory was good but incomplete. (Ah, yes, the Tri-Ethnic theory was mainly developed by Anglo males!) Nevertheless, the *pattern* of relationships repeated consistently within these quite divergent groups and measures provides compelling evidence for the validity and cross-cultural, cross-gender generality of our findings and of the underlying theory on which they were based. Even though our theory was "etic" not "emic" it worked quite well.[5]

Interaction Effects

Although this empirical consistency is impressive, I found it tedious and not very interesting. (Perhaps I had been working with the theory and data too long, and had become bored.) Far more interesting to me as an anthropologist was a secondary analysis I conducted among our two non-Western groups. This analysis examined the very different responses of Hispanics and Ute Indians to the pressures of "acculturation." (See Volume II, article 1.) Since the beginning of the project I had been interested in the behavioral consequences of what Merton and others referred to as a "means/goals disjunction": in the sociological case, when lower-class people aspire to the material rewards of our society but are blocked from achieving them. I felt that within our tri-ethnic community, many Hispanics and Utes who were "acculturated"—who identified most strongly with an Anglo way of life and aspired to its material rewards—would be likely to experience just this type of disjunction and respond with excessive drinking behavior.

Briefly, what I discovered was a paradox: Using both a seven-item scale of "acculturation" and the amount of formal education subjects reported as alternative measures, among acculturated Hispanics deviance and drinking behavior consistently *increased* regardless of the measures I used, whereas among acculturated Ute Indians it consistently *decreased.* In other words, "acculturation" appeared to have an *opposite* behavioral consequence within these two groups.

This paradox was resolved when, guided by a theoretical hunch, I conducted a two-variable pattern analysis which crosscut my measures of acculturation by a measure of *access* (their job type): Within both ethnic groups, those who were high in acculturation but limited in access consistently had substantially higher rates of drinking and deviance than acculturated subjects who were high in access and thereby able to achieve their new goals, just as Merton's theory would lead us to expect. Again, consistently within both groups and across alternative measures, among those low in acculturation this measure of access made no difference in their drinking and deviant behavior, presumably because they were *not* aspiring to material goals which they could not expect to achieve.

What *was* different within these two groups, and here's where "culture" played a role, was that among the more traditional (unacculturated) Hispanics rates of drinking and deviance were relatively *low*, but among the traditional Ute Indians rates of drinking and deviance were quite *high*. The ethnic differences I had found among acculturated subjects could then be explained by the differential effect of acculturation on two types of traditional *social controls*: marital stability and church attendance. Among the more acculturated Hispanics, marital stability and church attendance *decreased*. By contrast, among the more accuturated Ute Indians these forms of social control both *increased*. With this the final piece of my empirical puzzle fell into place. (For further details, see Volume II, article 1.)

As both an anthropologist and a behavioral scientist this analysis fascinated me because it wasn't obvious and expected, as were essentially all the other analyses presented in our final report on the Tri-Ethnic study. And since these relationships were nonlinear they were not easily observable within our correlation matrices. Only by following through on a *theory-guided pattern analysis* was I able to discover them. I published this study independently a year before publication of our formal, book-length report on the rest of the Tri-Ethnic study, but it received only a paragraph of discussion in this final report (Jessor, Graves, Hanson, and Jessor 1968:416-417). Yet from my perspective as an anthropologist this analysis represented the most interesting one to emerge from the project.

Psychological Acculturation

I also published a study of "psychological acculturation" among Hispanics and Utes within this tri-ethnic community. (See Volume II, article 2.) In this article I attempted to demonstrate the way in which members of these two minority groups "took on" the value orientations of the dominant Anglo society—their norms of interpersonal behavior, feelings of personal efficacy and control, and extended future time perspective—as they were exposed to this society (through formal education), came to identify with it (as indicated by my seven-item "acculturation index"), and were given access to its resources and rewards (through achieving a semi-skilled or skilled job).

All the correlations among our carefully constructed and refined measures of these value orientations and their presumed determinants were positive and statistically significant, ranging from .18 to .5—respectable levels within social science. A multivariate "pattern analysis" combining the three measures of *exposure, identification,* and *access* yielded even clearer relationships. For example, among those with an "optimal pattern" (above the median on all three measures) 87% were also high in feelings of personal control, whereas among those in the opposite pattern (below the median on all three measures), only 11% fell above the median in feelings of personal control. (See table 4 in Volume II, article 2.)

But then I introduced an interesting *caveat*: What happens if we *reverse* the presumed direction of causality? "One could quite properly argue that those who, for reasons of personal history and temperament, have come to exhibit Anglo value orientations with respect to their relations to man, time, and the world will in turn remain longer in school, be more acceptable to Anglos as friends, acquire and hold better jobs, and so forth," I observed. Another pattern analysis using high scores on our three measures of value orientations (Volume II, article 2, table 5) illustrated how our data could equally support such a position. For example, of those Hispanics and Native Americans falling into the "optimal" (Anglo) pattern of value orientation, "95% succeed in remaining in school into high school (i.e., above the median on this variable). By contrast, without these Anglo value orientations, less than a third of the community's non-Anglos remained in school that long."

I concluded this paper with a speculation about this process of coevolution between personal beliefs and behavior and the wider social environment which I think probably represents the way the world really works:

> The objective contact situation exists external to the minority group members, who must operate within it, and limits the amount of exposure to the dominant group and the opportunities open to them. These, in turn, may have a significant impact on the psychological beliefs and values which the minority group members

> develop. In turn, the particular personality traits which each individual brings to the contact situation will affect their response to these objective opportunities and limitations. Thus a feed-back system is produced in which minority group members may help create further opportunities or help erect further barriers to their assimilation.

This was an issue that would occupy my attention in future research as well. (See chapter 11 in this book and articles 6 and 10 in Volume II.) Although not as interesting to me as the analysis reported in article 1, this study also made an important anthropological contribution. But it did not fit within Jessor's vision for the Tri-Ethnic project as a whole, and "acculturation" is not even listed in the subject index of our book. Jessor's sole interest in working with three distinct ethnic groups was to treat them as three replications of a single, uniform theoretical formulation.

Stepping Out on My Own

My research apprenticeship on the Tri-Ethnic project was superb preparation for a career in behavioral anthropology. Besides providing an opportunity to master simple statistics, a number of themes emerged at this early stage which would keep coming up throughout my career:

1. Cross-Cultural Measurement

During my research apprenticeship I devoted a great deal of time and attention to problems of cross-cultural measurement, and this would continue as a major topic of interest. I have also wanted my measures of key theoretical concepts to be as comparable as possible when used within different ethnic groups. This was a the source of my early interest in the Rorschach test. This goal may be a will-of-the-wisp. It may not be possible to develop measures that are totally comparable cross-culturally, but it's a goal I pursued right up until the last project that we conducted in New Zealand. (See Volume II, article 15, discussed in chapter 13 below.)

2. Psychological Acculturation

My interest in psychological acculturation had its early expression in my secondary analysis of the Tri-Ethnic data (Volume II, article 2). It was exciting to discover that measures of "exposure, identification, and access," the theoretical keys to successful social assimilation into another society, could be shown empirically to be associated with taking on that society's typical psychological attributes as well. Later I would discover some of the complexities and limitations of this process for minority group members attempting to assimilate into our dominant Western society. (See Volume II, article 6 on the "Culture of Poverty.")

3. Means-Goals Disjunctions

The stress created by a disjunction between the new goals non-Western peoples might acquire when trying to enter modern Western society and the limited opportunities they often had for achieving these goals, the "acculturation and stress" theory I had derived from the sociologist Robert Merton, received its first empirical support during my apprenticeship, and would be repeatedly supported in my future research. (See T. Graves and N. Graves 1978 for an early review, and articles 5, 7, and 8 in Volume II.)

4. Interaction Effects

During my apprenticeship I had my first experience with the thrill of discovering "interaction effects" among variables, where personality attributes are significant determinants of behavior only under certain structural conditions, but not under others. This sensitized me to look for such effects in my data throughout my career. (See Volume II, articles 5, 6, 7, 8, 11, and 15.)

5. Interdisciplinary Team Research

Above all else, however, I developed at this early stage a strong appreciation for and commitment to interdisciplinary team research. When you look at the world through different disciplinary eyes, you get a more well-rounded picture of reality. Each gives you a somewhat distinct and complementary view. No academic discipline has the whole truth, but each has a part of the truth. No discipline knows everything, but each knows something. Put them together and you get a richer, fuller, more complete picture of reality which exceeds the limitations of each discipline alone.

6. Multivariate Analysis

A related lesson is that multivariate analysis is a necessary adjunct to interdisciplinary research. Since different models of reality involve different variables, and each variable may account for a different portion of the outcome, by combining variables from several disciplinary points of view simultaneously your analysis will be enriched.

7. From Theory to Measurement

Moving from the theoretical level to the measurement of these variables is like looking at a set of Chinese boxes, each similar and each embedded in the next. Each theory is capturing a portion of reality. Each variable within a theory is capturing a portion of that theory. Each variable can be measured in a variety of ways. Each measure may include a variety of items. It's a similar structure at each level: what I call "methodological fractals."

8. The Method of Multiple Models

This interdisciplinary approach led directly to a major design feature of my first independent research project, presented in the next chapter: the use of multiple theoretical models. Each discipline has its own model of reality. Each model is a lens through which you see the world. And each focuses on certain parts of reality but tends to ignore or distort others. Sociologists, for example, look at the structure of interpersonal relationships and situational variables external to the person that mold their behavior in one way or another. So sociologists tend to look at the person as a victim of circumstances. "Don't blame the poor victims," a social worker may say, "look at the circumstances in which they grew up." That's a mind-set of sociology. Psychologists have an opposite mind-set. The psychologist will say, "It doesn't matter what a miserable situation you're in, because some people overcome their circumstances and some do not. Some Blacks turn out well despite their minority group status and miserable childhood circumstances. What's important is the way you *interpret* your circumstances." Both disciplines have their hands on a part of the truth.

If you are really interested in understanding something holistically, however, you need to approach it from several disciplinary angles, to "triangulate" on it, to use a physical metaphor. Each model, each discipline, is able to account for a portion of the variance, but certainly falls far short of accounting for *all* of the variance. Most empiricists in social science are very happy if they get .3-type correlations; .5-type correlations are just over the top. Yet a .3 correlation accounts for less than ten percent of the outcome. Ninety percent is still left for others to account for. Social scientists often pride themselves in statistically "significant" correlations of small magnitude, and then have the temerity to say, "I know why the so-and-sos do such-and-such. They do it because of *social class*," or whatever may be their variable of choice.

This is the height of professional arrogance. The job of the interdisciplinary theorist and researcher is to examine how these different ways of looking at the world complement each other and articulate.

9. Drinking Behavior as a Dependent Variable

Finally, a lesson about choice of subject. There is a sign on a country road in upstate Vermont which reads: "Choose your rut carefully, you'll be in it for the next ten miles." Your initial research topic is like this, and may well persist as a focus of inquiry for many years. In my case it was drinking behavior. This was not by preference: After spending many evenings in bars during my two years of fieldwork in Ignacio observing the drinking behavior of residents from all three ethnic groups and nearly getting my teeth knocked out in a barroom brawl, I wanted to switch my focus.

My research apprenticeship now completed, I was ready to step out on my own. In the next chapter I will describe the development of our research design for studying the personal adjustment of Navajo migrants to Denver, Colorado, where my students and I expected to be looking at things like their wages, their health, and how long they remained in the city. We did all this, but here again, problem drinking emerged as a necessary and central focus. Then several years later while working in New Zealand a Samoan graduate student in psychology, Vineta Semu, came to me for help with her plan for a systematic observational study of Polynesian drinking behavior because of my previous experience with this topic. And because of this experience I could apply for and get her substantial research funds to extend this study in several interesting ways. (See chapter 10 and Volume II, articles 13 and 14.) So choose your rut carefully!

Notes

1. For calculating the solid "regression line," running diagonally through the "scattergram" (figure 4.1), I have used a Pearson product moment correlation coefficient, explained in any standard statistical text, and in Bernard (2002: 589–594). This is the most common "parametric" correlation coefficient used in behavioral science because it lends itself easily to computer calculation. But it is a little more difficult to explain than a Spearman rho correlation. For an intuitive sense of it, turn figure 4.1 diagonally so that the regression line points straight up. Then think of it as representing an average of all the dots plotted on the scattergram—they are about equally distributed on either side. (If you summed the squared distances from this line to each of these dots on one side, it would exactly equal the sum of the squared distances to the dots on the other side.) See also footnote 4 below.

2. There is one sense in which there is some justification for taking an interest in small but "statistically significant" relationships when found. Most social science measurement falls so far short of the theoretical variable that it purports to measure that if you find the measurement, with all its flaws, to have *any* statistical relationship to some behavioral measure, you can probably assume that the underlying theoretical variable it's attempting to measure has a stronger relationship to that outcome, if you could only develop a better measure. You can determine that by seeing if when you clean up your measure, or add multiple measures of the variable, do you get stronger relationships? If you do, then you feel confident and you can say, "And probably the true relationship is even a little bit stronger than that."

3. Russ Bernard (2002, chapter 6) provides strong arguments for careful sampling for many research purposes, clear instructions on how to do it, plus a number of anthropological examples.

4. As explained in footnote 1, Pearson product moment (parametric) correlation coefficients are similar to the Spearman rank order (nonparametric) correlations I have explained in some detail in the text, but tend to be slightly more powerful, and lend themselves better to computer analysis. They were designed for data that fall into a "normal" (bell-shaped) distribution. But in my experience data can deviate quite widely from this ideal without causing you to draw false conclusions. When in doubt, calculate both types of "parametric" and "nonparametric" correlations and see how they compare. In our case, the Pearson correlation between height and weight was .67, essentially the same as we obtained using a nonparametric procedure.

5. Many anthropologists assert that when working within other ethnic communities and cultures only "emic" theory derived from the group's own categories of meaning is appropriate. If that were true, it would preclude all efforts to develop *cross-cultural* theories and conclusions, and "ethnology" would become impossible.

5

Research Design

When my dissertation was completed I was offered a position in the Anthropology Department at the University of Colorado to teach courses in culture and personality, culture change, and research methods. The year was 1962. I would be continuing my work analyzing the data we had collected on the Tri-Ethnic project for another four years. I would also continue to have my office in the interdisciplinary Institute of Behavioral Science at the University, which both physically and intellectually set me apart from the rest of my colleagues in anthropology. But the big change was that now I would be in a position to design my *own* research project and work with my *own* graduate students.

This was an exciting prospect. Despite the generous support I had been given for the last three years within the Tri-Ethnic project and the superb training I had received from Dick Jessor and other senior staff, I felt stifled by what I considered our rather rigid research design. What I wanted was a research laboratory within which my students and I could investigate a significant social phenomenon, while at the same time exploring *how* we as behavioral scientists might best go about studying such problems. I wanted a learning experience for all of us and an opportunity to be surprised and to discover things we didn't already know. This rarely happens in strict and carefully designed "theory testing" research such as the Tri-Ethnic project.

So, armed with a small grant from the University's Council on Creative Work I began exploring possibilities.

Designing the Navajo Urban Relocation Research Project

In 1952 the nearby city of Denver had been selected by the Bureau of Indian Affairs (BIA) as one of seven urban "relocation sites," and reservation Indians from all over the country were being encouraged to move there to find employment. Because of its proximity to their reservation, the largest tribal group of migrants in Denver were Navajo. Given my background experience with Navajo Indians in the Boulder TB hospital, their urban adjustment seemed like a natural choice for a research topic, and during the following year I applied for and received a three-year grant from the National Institute of Mental Health (NIMH) to do so.[1] This was supplemented by an NIMH Research Training Grant which provided additional funds to pay part of my salary and enable me to offer a number of prospective graduate students generous fellowships.

Initial planning and exploratory fieldwork in Denver to begin to understand the situation we would be studying more systematically was undertaken in the fall of 1963. As we had done in the Tri-Ethnic project, a small group of graduate students and I sat around a table at weekly staff meetings speculating about the process of migrant Indian adaptation to city life that we had begun observing informally. Our goal was different, however: not to come up with testable theory to explain some casually observed phenomenon like excessive Indian drinking, but *to discuss the range and variety of ways we might go about studying the migration process,*[2] both in Denver and on the Navajo reservation. Each graduate student involved was encouraged to come up with a different theoretical *model* of the migration process, insofar as possible from a different disciplinary perspective.

Six models of migrant adaptation were ultimately developed and investigated by our team. (See Volume II, article 3.) The first was a simple decision model, aimed at exploring factors which led to a potential migrant's decision to move to the city, and once there, to decide whether or not to return home to the reservation. A second examined the migrant's economic adjustment to urban life: the determinants of his job type and wage level, amount of unemployment, and employer satisfaction. A third looked at his social adjustment, friendship network, and assimilation into the wider Denver community. A fourth attempted to understand his psychological adjustment to urban life and the retreat into drunkenness common among so many. A fifth examined his psychological acculturation, his adoption of middle-class value orientations, and whether personality traits associated with the "culture of poverty" inhibited his economic achievement. And a sixth looked at the potential effects of urban stress on his health.

Note that each model directed our attention to a different set of explanatory variables: economic, social, psychological, and biological. And each had its own distinctive "dependent variable": the outcome we were attempting to account for and explain. This approach permitted the flexibility I wanted in an exploratory study without the theoretical anarchy typical of so much anthropological fieldwork. Although students each had a stake in their own particular model, their attachment to it would be diluted by having to consider several alternatives. This would free them psychologically, we hoped, to observe and accept disconfirming evidence and to make empirical discoveries. And the risk for the project as a whole was also thereby diminished, because if one model failed to account for a significant portion of the variance in migrant adaptation, others would probably do better. Finally, as likely as not these models would prove to be both theoretically and empirically *complementary*. This in itself would be an important issue to investigate.

The core of our project would consist of a survey interview which all of us would help design and administer, supplemented by records from the BIA, employers, and the police. This way students each would have their own theoretical model and body of empirical data to analyze and present for their dissertation.[3] My job, ultimately, would be to look for cross-model linkages and complementarities, and to integrate these models within a unified final report.[4]

Working on the Tri-Ethnic project, where our survey instrument typically took over two hours to administer and often seemed boring and repetitive for both subject and interviewer, I was determined that we design a survey instrument which would maintain both our own and the migrant's interest through variety and change of pace. Our questionnaire began with factual material which would be simple for the subject to answer and put him at ease. (At this point in the project we were only interviewing men.) We probed the migrant's background training, obtained a complete job history both in Denver and prior to relocation, and inquired about his health, social relationships, and spare-time activities. A sociometric test, based on our list of all known Navajo migrants in the city, yielded detailed information about social ties within his ethnic community.

Structured and semi-structured questions were alternated with open-ended ones. A battery of psychometric procedures ranging from forced choice scales to projective techniques provided measures of key psychological variables: attitudes, values, beliefs, and expectations. The projective tests used pictures drawn by Navajo artists, which immediately caught the migrant's attention and provided characters with which he could identify. (See chapter 6 and appendix B.)

About midway through the interview we provided our subject with an opportunity to stretch and relax before we took his blood pressure. Only toward the end of the interview were sensitive topics probed: his job insecurities and drinking behavior. Finally, the interview ended with an easy English language test, again employing pictures, and a chance for the subject to add anything he felt had been left out, or to ask further questions about the research and its aims (appendix A). Subjects were each paid five dollars for their time and attention, good pay where the average migrant's wage was only $1.25 per hour. Before we began systematic interviewing among Navajo migrants, the interview was pretested and refined using an urban Sioux Indian sample.[5]

In addition to providing a superb training laboratory for us all, Denver offered an ideal context for studying migrant adaptation. Practical logistic problems in an urban setting normally inhibits the longitudinal study of the *process* of migrant adjustment to their new environment. BIA sponsorship of the Navajo migrants whom we wanted to study meant that we could know *in advance* when potential subjects were going to arrive in the city and where they would be located, making it possible to interview them and follow their adjustment process from the day of their arrival through their first crucial months in the city. Besides our formal interviews, each student was encouraged to collect a case study from one or more of these new migrants. In addition, the BIA kept records on each Indian sponsored until they were either well-integrated into city life or had returned to the reservation. This supplemental information proved invaluable, and was carefully abstracted.[6] Finally, these records also provided us with a list of migrants already living in the city whom we could interview, as well as "returnees," many of whom we would later track down and interview on the Navajo reservation.

Ultimately, we interviewed 259 of the 518 known male Navajo Indians who had come to Denver since 1952. This included essentially the entire group living in Denver during 1963–1966 (N = 135) as well as about one-third of all former Denver migrants who had returned to the Navajo Reservation (N = 124). These "returnees" were interviewed during three summers of fieldwork on the reservation (1964–1966). Finally, in the summer of 1966 we also interviewed a comparison group of young men on the reservation (N = 113) who were not participating in the BIA relocation program. I will discuss this comparison group survey in chapter 8.

This idyllic research setting plus our team of eager student researchers made it possible for us to collect a wide range of information about migrant adaptation, and to employ a variety of different and complementary research strategies and techniques. The result was what I like to refer to as a *convergent* design, in which evidence from a number of sources is brought to bear on the same topic simultaneously.

The Decision Model

Soon after I joined the Anthropology Department in the fall of 1962 Minor VanArsdale and I became buddies. Van was an older graduate student, well-read, broad-ranging in his interest, with a keen mind, and we quickly established the kind of intellectual partnership I would like to have had with any of my own professors. A segue, but a Van story too good to skip: In November 1963 Van and I traveled to San Francisco to attend the annual meeting of the American Anthropological Association, where he was scheduled to deliver his first scholarly paper at a professional meeting. His session was chaired by Kimball Romney. Just as Van stepped up to the podium, Kim had to interrupt the proceedings to inform us that President Kennedy had been shot. Of course few in the audience paid much attention to Van's paper.

That evening Van and I walked the streets of San Francisco together, mixing with the quiet pedestrians sharing their grief. Shops were closed, many with informal memorials to the martyred president in their windows. The powerful emotions of that moment bonded us all, to each other, and to that time and place. I'm sure this is one reason why I still find San Francisco the friendliest and most beautiful city in the world. Now living in the Bay area, every time I cross the Golden Gate bridge I thrill to the sight.

Back in Boulder, fall 1963. "Decision theory" was in the air. Van and I had both read von Neuman and Morgenstern's *Theory of Games and Economic Behavior* (1944) and saw the way Rotter's social learning theory enriched this analysis. I was teaching a course in Cultural Dynamics, and in addition to covering topics like acculturation, modernization, urbanization, migration, and adaptation, I devoted a lot of attention to "cultural evolution." I was playing with the idea that "cultures" were to society as "species" were to biology and that a mechanism of cultural evolution similar to "natural selection" could be found in "social selection." Differential mate selection, a social choice, was a recognized part of natural selection, a part of the "environment" within which naturally occurring variations in physical attributes might survive and prosper. And Darwin was fascinated by the ability of breeders, through choice, to change quite radically and quickly the characteristics of domestic animals and birds. But these ideas hadn't been applied to nonbiological attributes of a group. So I set my graduate students the task of compiling propositions from the social sciences, particularly decision theory, under the general heading "Individual Choice and Culture Change." This, I hoped, might eventually form a general theory of cultural evolution.[7]

Our idea was that novel ways of doing things, styles of dress, formal and informal inventions, and so forth, are continuously springing up like mutations. Those that catch the eye of others and are adopted will survive and spread; others will be ignored and die. I had just read a book by Everett Rogers, a rural sociologist, on the *Diffusion of Innovations* (1962) and was presenting his ideas on the way innovations are selected and spread throughout a group, and what sorts of people are most likely to adopt them. These individual choices do not require a genetic underpinning to be perpetuated, and so novelties can spread quickly—like hula hoops and skate boards—leading to rapid culture change such as we are experiencing today. But for most of human history people have been very conservative in their choices, preferring the familiar to the unfamiliar. Nevertheless, over large numbers of "choice opportunities" certain principles obtain which make for highly predictable outcomes, such as "Zipf's Law" or "The Law of Least Effort" (Zipf 1949). This predicts that when two or more ways of doing the same thing are available, the one requiring the least effort will eventually prevail. This principle accounts for a great deal of cultural evolution, including why all over the world people are getting fatter: Everything we do now requires less effort than it used to.

This was the intellectual climate within which Van and I formulated the first of our "alternative models" of the migration process, which is fully explicated in article 3, Volume II. It is the simplest and most straightforward of our alternative models. Van had embraced Rotter's social learning theory, not because I had been raised on it, I hope, but because he recognized its value in enriching our understanding of human decision-making, a topic he had been deeply interested in himself. (One of the things I think I did right as a university professor is that I never attempted to create intellectual clones. Instead, I encouraged each of my students to find and pursue a topic which uniquely interested *them.* Although this has meant that I do not now have a following of former students carrying forward my own theoretical interests, they kept exposing me to new ideas and strategies which I might otherwise never have pursued on my own. Each different model of the migrant process illustrates the riches this approach has provided me.)

Most behavior is clearly goal-directed, aimed at accomplishing something of importance to the actor. If we can understand a person's goals and their expectations of being able to accomplish these by various alternative means available to them, we will go a long way toward understanding their behavioral choices. Any decision by a Navajo to migrate to the city and remain there, for example, seems likely to be a difficult one, beset with conflicts, since the familiar rewards of reservation life and supportive community of family and friends would have to be left behind. Strong incentives would be needed to induce such a move. And once in the city the migrant would daily face the question of whether or not he wanted to stay. "Harrison Joe" (a pseudonym), whose story introduces a major report on this research (Graves 1970; reprinted in Volume II, article 5), began contemplating a return home soon after his initial disappointments in Denver, and discussed it at length with a fellow migrant who was experiencing similar problems. In fact, he might have left the city a week earlier (and therefore avoided a drunken run-in with the police) if his packing had not been interrupted by a member of our research staff, Bryan Michener, who persuaded him to talk about his experiences in the city instead.

For testing this model, the primary behavior we wanted to understand was a decision to return home or to stay in the city. Our first task, therefore, was to obtain hard data on which migrants were still living in Denver, who had left, and how long they had stayed. This would not prove to be easy. From the beginning of the relocation program in 1952 until our research ended in 1966 at least 518 Navajo male heads of household had migrated to the city, 95% under BIA auspices. But most were no longer there. In fact, we soon discovered that almost half had left Denver within the first six months!

Although the BIA kept pretty good records on every migrant they sponsored during their period of initial job placement, and attempted a six-month follow-up to see how they were doing, their time and staff were limited, and their major focus, quite properly, was on getting new migrants settled in. They were well aware that the rate of return of government-sponsored migrants was high, and among insiders the program was jokingly referred to as the "Indian Fulbright Act," because it provided a means for young Indians to leave their reservations and visit the white man's world for a short time at government expense. But the BIA lacked reliable information. That task fell to us.

First, we abstracted all the official records available. If the migrant returned home fairly quickly after arrival, the whole history of his stay might be contained in the daily BIA record. If an Indian employee failed to report to work, his employer frequently called the BIA to find out where he was, and this would lead to an investigation. Landlords also called the BIA to report that a migrant had left town, often because he hadn't paid his rent. The official six-month follow-up also frequently revealed a return home. A letter to the BIA office nearest the migrant's reservation community would then result in a confirmation investigation and a date of return, which would be duly entered into the migrant's file. Finally, if a returnee subsequently requested the BIA for assistance in moving elsewhere (as about half did within two years of their reservation return, we discovered), this would bring his case to official attention and result in a date of return from Denver being recorded.

But this monitoring process was not systematic, and many migrants escaped official notice. For those Navajos whose current status in Denver was not officially known, all were assumed to be still living in the city. Our staff then attempted to locate each for an interview, using standard anthropological field techniques plus a good deal of less traditional detective work. Those who could not be located, or were said by their landlords, employers, friends, or relatives to have returned home, were followed up during our three summers of fieldwork on the Navajo reservation. In this manner we were able to establish either their continued presence in Denver or a definite date of departure (plus or minus about two weeks) for 504 of the 518 men in our migrant population (97%). See figure 5.1.

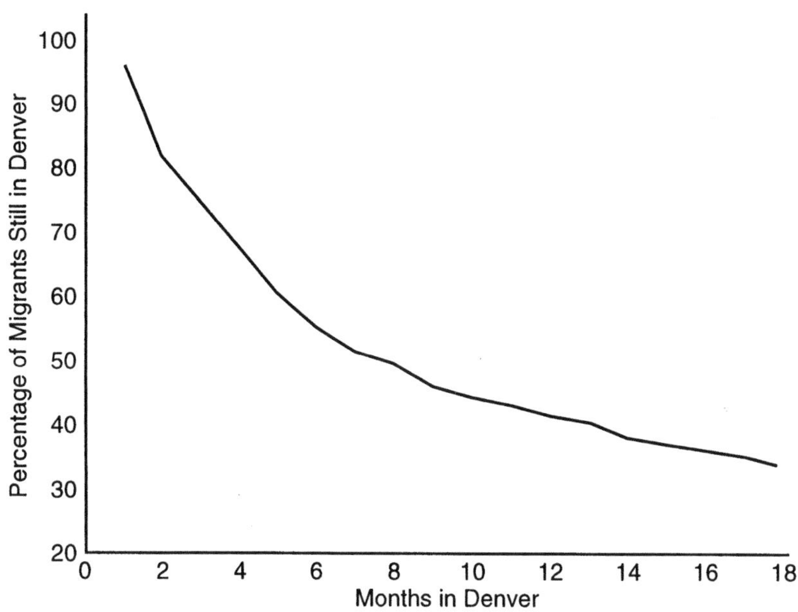

Based on data from 504 of 518 male Navajos who migrated to Denver for direct employment between 1954 and July 1965.

Figure 5.1. Rate of Return to Reservation by Navajo Migrants to Denver

These data can be summarized in the decay curve shown in figure 5.1, which plots the proportion of all migrants who were still in Denver after a certain length of time. Note that a quarter had left the city within three months; half had returned home within seven or eight. By eighteen months only 35% remained in the city. This analysis provided us with a solid criterion measure for investigating factors associated with this form of migration success or failure. On the basis of simple decision theory the following hypothesis could be derived and tested: *Those migrants who remain in the city have a personal goal structure more compatible with urban opportunities, and higher expectations for achieving their goals within the urban setting, than those migrants who leave the city and return to the reservation.*

Van took particular responsibility for developing and testing this model. He helped design, pretest, and initiate survey interviewing in Denver during the 1963–1964 academic year. And he was the first member of our staff to spend a summer (1964) on the reservation tracking down and interviewing "returnees" from Denver. At this early stage we didn't have the slightest idea how difficult a task it might be to find specific people scattered over 24,000 square miles of reservation. That first summer he only managed to find 20 from our preliminary list of over 200. Obviously this work was going to be extremely labor-intensive. (See chapter 8.)

In the fall of 1964, with our first 100 interviews in hand, including the 20 "returnees" Van had interviewed on the reservation, he and I conducted a preliminary analysis and test of the decision model which was published to illustrate our "multiple models" approach (Graves and Van Arsdale 1966; reprinted in Volume II, article 4). "Leavers" were defined as migrants who returned to the reservation within six months following our interview, or were interviewed on the reservation, and our exploratory strategy was to compare their responses with those of the "Stayers" and look for group differences.

This report did a good job of presenting migrants' views on the urban versus reservation "opportunity structure," based on a content analysis of four open-ended questions:

1. What are the things you like best about living in Denver?
2. What do you *not* like about living in Denver?
3. What do you like best about living on the reservation?
4. What do you *not* like about living on the reservation?[8]

Clearly, Denver was seen as a better place to get a good job than the reservation. But the reservation was overwhelmingly valued for access to kin and friends, and various traditional recreational and religious activities. So the conflict between the pursuit of economic goals which brought them to the city and traditional social and emotional goals which pulled them back home was starkly apparent. To achieve one set of goals another set had to be abandoned.

The use of these questions as an indirect measure of a migrant's *values*, as well as a measure of their *expectations* for achieving these valued goals, will be discussed in the next chapter.[9]

The Economic Adjustment Model

From the start we recognized that the quality of a migrant's economic adjustment would prove to be a critical factor in whether or not he remained in the city. A Navajo could not survive indefinitely in Denver, as he could on the reservation, through the charity of friends or relatives, and the extent of federal aid for which he was eligible under the BIA relocation program was limited by law. Of practical and theoretical importance, therefore, were factors in a migrant's background, such as education, vocational training, previous work experience, and even parental role models, which could be presumed to prepare him for a successful economic adjustment in Denver.

This model was straightforward and linear, but involved a quite different set of criterion measures: migrant wages and job level in the city, both on arrival and subsequently, the amount of unemployment he experienced, and ratings of his job performance by his employer.[10] Note that these *outcome variables* in this model would also serve as *predictor variables* in other models. Because the ultimate test of whether or not a migrant had made a successful adjustment to city life was whether or not he *remained* there.

With a background in economics, Robert Weppner took responsibility for developing and testing this model. His particular contribution was in recognizing and studying the role of employers as "gatekeepers" in the migrant's adjustment process. He obtained objective information on a migrant's wages from both BIA records and employers, to supplement the data given us in our survey interviews by the migrants themselves. He also interviewed all the Denver employers of Navajo migrants to tap their experience and learn how they perceived a potential employee's salable skills. He not only asked them how good a worker the migrant was in general, but more specifically, how well he carried out instructions, got along with his supervisor and coworkers, offered suggestions, and was dependable, ambitious, flexible, considerate, and able to plan ahead.

Bob needed a clear criterion measure for economic success. For this he also turned to our data on staying versus leaving. Recall that for our early paper Van and I defined as Stayers any migrant we had interviewed in Denver who was still there six months later, and Leavers anyone interviewed in the city who subsequently returned home, plus the small sample of returnees Van had interviewed on the reservation that first summer. (These two groups of leavers and returnees turned out to be very similar in their values and expectations, warranting combining them for comparison purposes. See Volume II, article 4.) But Bob wanted a criterion measure which would more clearly indicate that the migrant had made a *successful economic adjustment* to urban life.

By the end of the project we had collected enough interviews both in Denver and on the reservation that Bob was able to define "economically adjusted" Stayers as any migrant who remained in the city *at least eighteen months*, and "unadjusted" Leavers as those who returned home sooner than that, whether or not we had interviewed them in the city or on the reservation. (The Stayer group also included a few migrants interviewed on the reservation who had remained in Denver at least eighteen months before they returned home.) Since the BIA might help a migrant in various ways, including financial, during his first year in the city, Bob reasoned that if a migrant remained on his own at least six months beyond his first year, this should indicate that he had made a reasonable economic (as well as social) adjustment. Qualitatively, the typical reasons for a migrant's departure after eighteen months also appeared to differ from those who returned sooner, involving family crises on the reservation, sickness, retirement, new opportunities coming up, and so forth, rather than economic or social adjustment problems in Denver. For example, one migrant had returned to the reservation to die because he had been diagnosed with an incurable disease.

Bob's analytic approach was to compare our group of 108 Stayers with the 144 Leavers on a variety of economic and experiential predictors, including their preparation for urban life. (For published reports, see Weppner 1971 and 1972.) Table 5.1 presents the data on background variables.

Table 5.1. Stayer/Leaver Differences in Premigration Preparation for Urban Life

Variables:		Stayers (N = 108)	Leavers (N = 144)	Significance of difference
Father's occupation (% wage labor)		55%	49%	n.s.*
Family wealth (% "richer")		78%	57%	p<.001
Years of education	mean	8.0	7.4	n.s.
	(sd)	(2.9)	(2.8)	
Vocational training level	mean	1.2	1.0	n.s.
	(sd)	(0.9)	(1.0)	
Months of premigration work experience	mean	29.0	15.5	p<.001
	(sd)	(36.6)	(22.0)	
Highest premigration wage	mean	$1.63	$1.69	n.s.
	(sd)	(.56)	(.72)	
% having prior urban experience		40%	34%	n.s.

* Not statistically significant at the .05 level, two-tailed test.

We anticipated that migrants whose fathers had been involved in the wage economy would be better prepared for work in the city. We were wrong. Migrants were fairly evenly split between those from a traditional farmer/herder family and those whose father was a wage laborer, and this was true for both Stayers and Leavers. What *did* seem to make a difference, however, was *how successful* a migrant's family were perceived to have been economically. Those who reported that their families were "richer" than their neighbors were far more likely to make a successful economic adjustment in the city.

We were surprised to discover that formal education did not appear to be associated with economic success: Both Stayers and Leavers reported approximately the same amount of formal education, and roughly the same level of vocational training (scored 0 for none, 1 for semiskilled, and 2 for skilled). Prior *work experience* seemed far more important. Successful migrants reported almost *twice* as much work experience as unsuccessful migrants. Their wage level, however, and whether or not they had prior *urban* experience seemed unrelated to success.

A migrant's *initial economic experience* in Denver proved to be critical to their ultimate success. Table 5.2 summarizes these findings.

Table 5.2. Stayer/Leaver Differences in Initial Economic Experience

Variables:		Stayers (N = 108)	Leavers (N = 144)	Significance of difference
Initial % unemployed		12%	23%	p<.001
Initial job level	mean	1.8	1.4	p<.001
	(sd)	(.7)	(.6)	
Starting wage	mean	$1.48	$1.30	p<.001
	(sd)	(.38)	(.31)	

Here we found three powerful predictors of whether or not a migrant chose to remain in the city. Those who experienced relatively little unemployment during their first six months (or first half of their stay if they remained less than a year), those who obtained the best jobs (scored 0 for manual labor, 1 for semiskilled, and 2 for skilled work) and the highest starting wages were the most likely to stay in Denver at least eighteen months. (For a contrasting way to present these same data, and a *pattern analysis* which combines them, see tables 12.1 and 12.2 in chapter 12, below.)

Bob also looked at the subset of migrants who had received vocational training in school. Most never obtained a job in the field for which they were trained. Among Stayers, however, 45% received their first job in the type of work for which they had received training. This was true for only 27% of those who were soon to leave the city. This lack of relationship between what they had been trained for and what they actually did was a source of disappointment for migrants and complaint among their employers, who felt that most of the vocational training these Navajos had received in school was inappropriate or irrelevant to the work opportunities available to them in the city. Seeking to achieve a better fit between the training being offered these Indians (predominantly in boarding school) and the work environment for which they were presumably being trained is an obvious practical implication of Weppner's research.

An interesting but somewhat disturbing finding from Weppner's study came from his employer ratings of a group of fifty-nine Navajos who were making a good, long-term adjustment to city life (remaining over eighteen months), a small sample of nineteen Leavers whose employers could still remember them, and a comparison group of forty-one Anglo men holding similar jobs. Although their number was small and employers were probably influenced by their current absence, the Leavers had lower ratings on every scale. Of far more interest, on most seemingly relevant questions, the fifty-nine well-adjusted Navajos and their Anglo coworkers were rated as very much alike: how good a worker they were, how well they carried out instructions, got along with their supervisor and coworkers, were considerate, dependable, and low in absenteeism. But these "successful" Navajo workers were rated significantly *lower* than their Anglo coworkers in ambition, flexibility, offering suggestions, and being able to plan ahead. And they received significantly lower pay: an average of $1.91 per hour versus $2.17 for the Anglo. Yet we would find *no* wage advantage among Navajos who had adopted these very Anglo personality traits in which employers generally found them lacking. (See Graves 1974; reprinted in Volume II, article 8.) And considerable psychic cost (Graves, Volume II, article 7). Although we had no way to prove this, it appeared that wage discrimination might have been taking place. Given the crucial role which low wages played in their decision to return home, any discrimination in this area would prove critical in contributing to their urban "failure."

The Social Assimilation Model

One tacit goal of the government's Indian relocation program was to promote their assimilation into the mainstream of American life. Whether or not we agree with this aim (and most anthropologists probably would not), the process by which individuals may or may not shift their identity and loyalty to a new, and often powerful social reference group is a fascinating one to study. We also anticipated that such a shift might facilitate their urban adjustment.

Peter Snyder took major responsibility for developing and testing this model (Snyder 1968, 1971, and 1973). Initially, his goal was to examine the migrant's process of integration into the wider community, and the attenuation of his home reservation ties, as measured by visits and letters home. Who would identify with Anglos, adopt Anglo ways, and assimilate into Anglo society? And would such assimilation be associated with urban "success" as measured in other ways?

It soon became apparent from his initial ethnographic observations, however, that very little "assimilation" was taking place. Only 7% of the migrants reported participating in any clubs or sports groups in the city, and only 12% had ever attended an event sponsored by the pan-Indian White Buffalo Council. Although about half claimed to have at least one non-Navajo friend, over 80% reported getting together with fellow Navajos at least once a week. This was clearly their major social and recreational activity.

Our preliminary fieldwork also suggested that much of this recreational activity took the form of group drinking. So we began observing these recreational drinking groups and attempted to assess their effect on a migrant's success or failure in the city. Their major impact seemed to be to increase his consumption of alcohol, and therefore his likelihood of being arrested for drunkenness. Not a good outcome, since this often triggered a decision to return home. So the focus of Pete's work shifted toward observing and understanding these drinking groups and the mechanisms by which they encouraged excessive consumption.

Pete wanted to discover whether different friendship cliques had different drinking norms, and therefore differed in their potentially negative effects. To identify these core Navajo friendship cliques sociometrically, in a follow-up interview with ninety-four relatively stable migrants, each was presented with a list of all known Navajos living there and asked which ones he knew, and if so, had recently seen. Statistically, each person on this list was then treated as an "item" on a "test" and scored from 0 (unknown) to 2 (known and seen within the last month). These items were then factor analyzed, yielding clusters of items (people) to whom our subjects were responding in similar ways. By inverting the matrix we were also able to define clusters of subjects who were responding to these items (people) in similar ways. This enabled us to identify six Navajo social cliques, which Pete then validated through direct observation in the field. (See Snyder 1968.) Although these groups differed in their size (from three to thirty-three) and the background characteristics of their members, all six proved to be similarly high in arrest rates. Clearly, participation in *any* peer drinking group put a migrant at risk. The effect of these peer group pressures in conjunction with both psychological pressures to drink heavily and social constraints against drinking from their wives will be fully discussed in chapter 7 on "Social Channeling of Behavior."

The Personal Adjustment Model

When I applied for funds to study the adaptation of Navajo migrants to life in Denver, I had hoped at last to move away from the study of Indian drunkenness, which had preoccupied me for the last five years. But I could not. Soon into the project we learned that about half the migrants had been arrested at least once while living in the city, and about 95% of these arrests were for public drunkenness and its various consequences. So once again a major focus of our inquiry would necessarily need to be on the determinants of migrant Indian drinking behavior.

My work on the Tri-Ethnic project had led me to view much heavy Indian drinking as a form of psychological escape from the realities of their marginal and unhappy role within the White man's society, perhaps even a form of slow (and probably unconscious) suicide. Of course, Indian drinking groups can be boisterous and fun for participants as well, "an Indian weekend after a white man's week," as one described it. But with an arrest rate *over twenty times as high* as among similar working-class white men in the city, and *over eight times as high* as among a comparable group of equally vulnerable Hispanic migrants, the problematic nature of this behavior could not be easily dismissed. (Interestingly, because of the small numbers involved, the Denver police were unaware of these high arrest rates among Indians until we brought them to their attention. They believed the real problem of excessive drunkenness occurred among Hispanics. See Graves 1970; reprinted in Volume II, article 5.)

The Personal Adjustment Model, with roots in theories of psychopathology, considers frequent drinking and drunkenness as a response to the *disjunctions* which result from unfulfilled economic aspirations in the city. We have already seen in the Economic Adjustment Model how many migrants suffered from poor jobs, low pay, and unfulfilled economic hopes. We reasoned that economic marginality would also be associated with feelings of frustration and hopelessness, and therefore with higher rates of drinking and drunkenness. Navajo migrants appeared to be participants in a "natural laboratory" in which many would experience conflicts and frustration, with alcohol a readily available antidote.

Again, our first task would be to develop reliable and valid measures of the behavior we wanted to understand: in this case, excessive alcohol consumption and drunkenness. Because drunkenness is socially disapproved, it is difficult to get your subjects to admit their drinking problems, particularly to white researchers. (I have already discussed these measurement issues in chapter 3.) We had included a simplified version of the Tri-Ethnic project's drinking questionnaire in our survey instrument. (See appendix A, questions 73–80.) Among married Navajos in our sample, however, it was disturbing to discover a small but *negative* correlation between a migrant's self-report of his frequency drunk and how often his *wife* reported him drunk. Each was probably distorting their reports, but in *opposite* ways: he minimizing his drinking, she overwhelmed by the problems of controlling it. So I developed serious misgivings about using self-reports of drinking behavior as a dependent variable.

Fortunately, we were able to find an alternative in which I developed greater confidence: the use of arrest records.

As we began collecting police records on our Navajo migrant sample, we were struck by two facts: first, that about half our subjects had been arrested at least once while they were in the city, and second, that almost all these arrests were for public drunkenness or drinking-related offenses. Although obviously many subjects might have escaped getting arrested despite their heavy drinking, it seemed reasonable to assume that getting drunk with some regularity, particularly given the characteristic public drinking of our subjects, would increase the probability of being arrested. And it was exactly this "escape into drunkenness" that we wanted to explain.

The virtue of using arrest records as an indirect index of their drinking behavior was that it was a "nonreactive" measure, outside of our subjects' ability to control in an interview situation. Its limitations, however, were equally obvious: the relationship between drunkenness and arrest was *probabilistic*, making it a highly *unreliable* measure of an *individual's* behavior. Lots of error variance, which would lower correlations substantially. But, we reasoned, if we *pooled* subjects and only looked at *group differences*, this problem might be overcome. (This is a good strategy for any behavioral scientist working with unreliable measures.)

A second problem, however, initially seemed even more serious. The longer a migrant stayed in the city, the higher his probability of getting arrested. So arrests were *negatively* related to our other "nonreactive" behavioral criterion measure—returning quickly to the reservation. If our theoretical model predicted "staying" at least eighteen months, i.e., making a *good* urban adjustment, it would then probably *also* predict getting arrested at least once for drunkenness! This was *not* what we wanted to do.

The solution emerged quite serendipidously. In a provocative paper on "Indian criminality," Omer Stewart (1964) had presented police statistics from the United States as a whole and from Denver, comparing the rates of arrest of various ethnic groups, and the percentage of these arrests officially recorded as "alcohol related" (reproduced in Volume II, article 5, table 1). Not only did Native Americans exhibit arrest rates three or four times higher than any other minority group, and over seventeen times higher than "Whites" in Denver (not including Hispanics), but 76% of these arrests were officially designated as "alcohol related" nationally, and 86% in Denver. (Even this figure is probably low; when we examined the data case by case among our Navajo subjects the figure was about 95%.) Other ethnic groups had alcohol-related arrests of about 50% or lower.

Gross statistics of this kind are no better than the census figures on which they are based. This is a particular problem for Native Americans in the city, who may remain only briefly, get arrested, and then leave town before they are counted in any census. We had an opportunity to calculate far more accurate figures, using our samples of Anglo, Hispanic, and Navajo men of about the same age, all occupying similar jobs. These names (plus any known aliases), birth dates and the dates of their time in Denver were submitted to the City and County of Denver Police Department, who obtained permission from the FBI to turn over to us their complete police records for research purposes.[11]

Many Navajo migrants only stayed in Denver a short time. Nevertheless, by adding up the total number of months the entire group had been in the city, and dividing this by twelve, we found that they had spent 639 man-years in the city and been arrested 665 times, for a rate of 104,000 arrests per 100,000 man-years in the city. Using this same procedure the Hispanic migrants had an arrest rate of only 12,500 per 100,000 man-years in the city, less than one-eighth the Navajo rate, and the Anglo men had only 5,000 arrests per 100,000 man-years in the city. The Navajo rate was more than twenty times higher!

Having collected all these data for comparing ethnic groups, it then occurred to me to compare subgroups *within* the Navajo migrant sample, using this *same* procedure. For example, we found huge differences between Stayers and Leavers in their *rates* of arrest, as our theory and common sense would suggest. Stayers had an arrest rate of 67,000 per 100,000 man-years in the city. This is still over five times higher than the rate among our comparable sample of Hispanic men. But it is much lower than the rate among Leavers: 157,000 per 100,000 man-years in the city.

These results seemed promising, and led me to examine arrest rates among various groups in my *pattern analyses.* (See Volume II, article 5, tables 3-6.) These provided dramatic evidence for the explanatory power of our theoretical models. For example, using only three initial economic experiences we found arrest rates varying from 34,000 among those having an optimal pattern of initial economic experiences in the city to 214,000 among those with the least favorable initial experiences. This is a true *prediction* of problem drinking, since these initial economic experiences (based on BIA and employer records rather than self-reports) occurred right at the beginning of a migrant's stay in the city.

"The Personal Adjustment of Navajo Indian Migrants to Denver, Colorado" was published in 1970 and is reprinted in Volume II as article 5. In it the Personal Adjustment Model is fully presented and tested. But the article goes well beyond this one model, and in many respects can be viewed as a short summary and synthesis of *several* models.

The "Culture of Poverty" Model

President Johnson's "war on poverty" raised to conscious attention and popularity an anthropological theory about the "culture of poverty." This theory postulates that the poor within our society suffer from a self-perpetuating poverty "way of life," which includes certain characteristic personality attributes such as a tendency to live in the moment rather than to plan ahead, to feel fatalistic about life, and to lack ambition. (See the introduction to Oscar Lewis' 1966 book *La Vida,* on "a Puerto Rican family in the culture of poverty.") Some theorists argued that these lower-class personality attributes could be changed, primarily through education, and that those who adopted more "middle-class" beliefs and attitudes, would then behave in ways which raised them out of their poverty.

This theory has also been invoked to explain why so many Native Americans live in "multi-problem" families, with alcohol at the center of a cluster of related difficulties: intrafamilial conflict and marital instability, child neglect, poor health, delinquency, poor school attendance and early drop out. My dissertation research—discussed in chapter 2—was designed to test certain parts of this theory with respect to *immediate versus delay of gratification* behavior, but the full-blown "Culture of Poverty" Model came to public prominence several years later.

When we began the Denver project it seemed reasonable to assume that Navajo migrants would also vary on these personality traits, since many had a thorough exposure to middle-class beliefs and values through the work of Western missionaries, school teachers, and government officials. The Navajo Urban Relocation Research Project would therefore provide an opportunity to build on and extend my dissertation research, to see if these middle-class personality traits were related to better economic achievement in the city, to less problem drinking, and to a more satisfactory urban adjustment. Originally this work had been formulated within the Decision Model. But by the end of the project, with all our data now available, I recast these analyses within the framework of the by-then-popular "Culture of Poverty" formulation. The results were published in 1974 (Volume II, article 6), and will be discussed further in the next chapter.

The Migration Stress and Health Model

Braxton Alfred was an advanced graduate student ready to undertake his dissertation research at the time we began planning the Navajo project. As a result of his interest in the interplay between biology and behavior we included a Stress and Health Model which hypothesized that the migration process would be differentially stressful on migrants, depending, for example, on their economic success, and that this stress in turn would have a differential impact on their health, as measured by their blood pressure and a health symptom questionnaire.

When Braxton began checking the literature, he found a number of observers suggesting that the stress of "acculturation" might give rise to disease among a variety of quite distinct ethnic groups. (See the review in Volume II, article 3.) Most reports of this type were only concerned with migration as a generalized source of stress, which we felt sure many Navajo migrants to Denver would also be experiencing. In line with the general strategy of behavioral anthropology, however, Alfred's goal was more ambitious. He hypothesized that Navajo migrants might suffer *differentially* from urban stress, that this might manifest itself in elevated blood pressure or other psychosomatic symptoms, and that symptom formation might be related to differences among them in stress-buffering personal attributes or stress-inducing urban experiences.

Migrant stress and health seemed a promising topic for investigation, and we were also eager to include physiological attributes—blood pressure and psychosomatic symptoms—in our array of interdisciplinary measures. To test Alfred's model we bought every member of our research staff a stethoscope and sphygmomanometer and spent hours taking each other's blood pressure until we achieved a high level of consistency (reliability).[12]

Before coming to Denver all potential migrants under BIA sponsorship received a medical examination, and their blood pressures were available in their BIA records. When we subsequently interviewed them in the city they had significantly higher blood pressures than before migration. We liked these results, because the subjects involved in both rural and urban locations were the same people. (See Alfred 1970 for a published report.) But those *taking* the blood pressure measurement (the reservation doctors and us) were different. And when we also found elevated blood pressures among former migrants we interviewed on the reservation I lost faith in our results. Of course even back home these "returnees" may well have been experiencing the stress of failure and continued economic marginality. (See chapter 8.) But we were also unable to relate individual differences in blood pressure in the city to variations in stress-buffering personal attributes or stress-inducing experiences. Probably the process is far more complicated than the linear correlations we examined, and would have required the type of extensive "play" with the data that revealed these complexities and interaction effects elsewhere. Furthermore, blood pressure appears to be a relatively unreliable measure, varying considerably depending on circumstances, and so is poor at the level of *individual* correlations. Grouping our subjects in *pattern analysis* would perhaps have worked better.

The stress of urban migration and its impact on migrants' blood pressure has remained an important topic of research among a small group of anthropologists to this day. And they have experienced problems very similar to our own. (See Dressler 1999 for a recent review.)[13] Braxton graduated, however, and moved on to other things.

As a second measure of health status, Braxton suggested that we include in our survey interview our own version of the Cornell Medical Index (CMI). The original 195-item instrument was developed as an aid to taking medical histories. But shorter versions, with a focus on functional (psychosomatic) rather than organic symptoms, had been used cross-culturally by a number of researchers: Chance (1965) among Barter Island Eskimos, Langner (1965) in Mexico, Leighton et al. (1963) among the Yoruba, and Rotondo (1960) in Lima. Starting with Chance's version, we carefully selected, constructed, or reworded sixty items. After fifty-two interviews had been collected using this scale, item analysis led us to eliminate ten more items which had poor correlations with the total score.

Much of Braxton's dissertation was devoted to a careful evaluation of the reliability and validity of this instrument, and it's a model for how to go about doing this. With 144 interviews in hand, biserial correlations between each item and total score were run, which ranged from .22 to .94 and averaged about .6, quite respectable for an instrument of this type. (A biserial correlation measures the ability of each item to predict a person's response to the *other* items in a scale.)[14] A Kuder-Richardson test of its internal homogeneity was .9; this estimates the average correlation among all possible split-halves (for example, the correlation between the sum of the odd items and the sum of the even items). Forty-two subjects were interviewed again in Denver about six months after our first interview, as part of our effort to study the process of their urban adjustment over time. The test-retest reliability of this scale was .87, and 85% of their responses remained unchanged. This figure sets a lower limit on the instrument's true reliability (stability of measurement), since some actual change might be expected to have occurred over this period.

The validity of this scale (whether it actually measures the attribute it purports to measure) is harder to assess. Its *face validity* seemed clear, since we had carefully selected items which were ethnographically relevant to Navajos,[15] simple in language, and tapped functional rather than organic disorders. Another approach is *convergent validity*: how well this instrument correlates with other measures of presumably the same thing. Before administering our version of the CMI we asked subjects three general questions about their health:

1. How have you been feeling since you came to Denver? (on a scale from 0 to 3)
2. When was the last time you had to stay home from work because of sickness? How many days of work did you miss? (When was the time before that, etc. for the last six months.)
3. When was the last time you went to a doctor? (When was the time before that, etc. for the last six months.)

These three items all correlated with each other positively, ranging from .26 to .88, with frequency of going to a doctor having the highest values. And all three correlated positively with total score on the CMI, though these correlations were modest and only number of visits to a doctor was statistically significant (.23). But there was no correlation (actually, –.1) between the CMI and blood pressure. This was disconcerting, to say the least, and contributed further to my distrust of the blood pressure data.

Construct validity assesses how well an instrument fits within a network of theoretically related measures. We divided our subjects (at the median) between those who reported getting drunk three or more times last year, or less than 3 times. Similarly, we divided the sample into those who reported any of a series of drinking-related problems (such as fights with family or friends, trouble with the boss, etc.) and those who did not. Those who reported the highest drunkenness also reported a higher number of symptoms (almost significant at the .05 level), as did those mentioning any drinking-related problems ($p<.01$). This was encouraging, but these positive correlations with other self-report measures could result from a general tendency to be frank with us.

Finally, Braxton correlated CMI scores with all our measures of a migrant's background and urban experiences which might be expected to serve either as stress buffers or as stress enhancers. Unhappily, no correlations with any of these measures reached statistical significance, or were even higher than .12. You can imagine Braxton's disappointment, although he still received his degree.

Looking back I suspect that stress symptoms (including elevated blood pressure) have more complex, nonlinear determinants which we might have been able to discover with more subjects and more time. At the conclusion of data collection, however, I was focusing on other models and did not pursue this one. Nevertheless, Braxton's model of stress and health intrigued me, and his work strongly influenced me. Later in my career I looked at stress and health among Polynesians on one Pacific Island and Polynesian migrants in New Zealand, again using modified versions of the CMI. (See Volume II, articles 11 and 15.)

Lessons for Behavioral Anthropology

Several features of the Navajo Urban Relocation Research Project distinguish it from typical anthropological research. These distinctive design features characterize most of my later research, and may serve as a model for behavioral anthropology in general.

1. Team Research

Ethnographic research is typically an individual (and lonely) endeavor. Behavioral anthropology requires a radical departure from this model. The careful collection of a large quantity of systematic data bearing on relationships between some observable behavior in all its variations within a community and several potential, hopefully theory-based determinants of that behavior, is too large and complex a task for any one person to accomplish on their own, particularly if they are inexperienced behavioral scientists in training. They need the support and encouragement of others in the field with them, the ongoing feedback and guidance of experienced supervisors, opportunities to discuss and evaluate their field experience with others, and the diversity of viewpoints which only a team of researchers can provide.

2. Theory-Guided Research with Alternative Explanatory Models

Anthropologists have typically undertaken their research without explicit theoretical guidance, arguing that the data should be allowed to speak for themselves. But among the vast range of possible "data" spread before them, what they see and note is inevitably determined by their own implicit, unstated folk theories about what may be important. Far better to make these often unconscious theories conscious and explicit, so that the bias these may create can be known and taken into account.

A potential problem with "theory-guided research" is the stake a researcher has in a pet theory's explanatory power. We "test" our hypotheses, but are usually disappointed if the data fail to support them. This leaves us psychologically vulnerable to seeing what we want to see and overlooking negative data. This is one reason why "replication" of empirical findings by independent researchers—repeating the study within another group of subjects, often by a scientist somewhat skeptical of the initial results—is so important in science. And why it so often fails. We attempted to avoid this potential for self-deception by employing alternative explanatory models in our search for ways to understand and explain differences in migrant adaptation. From a methodological perspective, this was probably the most innovative aspect of the Navajo Urban Relocation Research Project.[16]

3. A Survey Interview of a Representative Sample

Typical ethnographic fieldwork depends in large part on interviews with a few "key informants" to gather a wealth of information about the group's "culture" which is not directly observable, or to interpret for the ethnographer what he or she may see. Normally it is assumed that these informants are representative carriers of their culture, and can therefore teach the ethnographer other aspects of their society's culture as they can teach its language. This has been a matter of considerable debate within the field, however, ever since Dorsey's classic observation reported by Edward Sapir, "Two Crows denies this." (Sapir 1938.)

Behavioral anthropologists typically avoid this problem by including as a core part of their research data collection from a representative sample drawn from the entire group under investigation. See chapter 8 on "Samples and Surveys."

4. Building In Discovery Techniques

The traditional ethnographic undertaking is inductive and theory generating, rather than deductive and theory testing. The great advantage of an inductive approach is the opportunity it provides for discovering something new that your guiding theory did not lead you to expect. My goal in research design has been to create an inductive-deductive mix. Our design therefore included at least three types of exploratory "discovery techniques":

a. Initial Ethnographic Fieldwork. Cross-cultural research in particular requires some initial opportunity for researchers to become acquainted with the field. This is essential if appropriate systematic measures are to be developed. A "behavioral anthropology" research project can often be built on the back of an earlier ethnographic study. In the Tri-Ethnic project, for example, Omer Stewart's long-standing ethnographic interest in Ute Indian culture served as its impetus. Alternatively, sophisticated members of the research community can be employed as team members in the design and implementation of the research. But nothing substitutes for an initial period of "fieldwork" by as many members of the project staff as possible to give them firsthand appreciation for the context within which the research is being conducted.

b. Case Studies. A closely related activity which also served as a way to become better acquainted with our field of research were the case studies undertaken by a number of students. Each core participant in our project was asked to follow one migrant with periodic reinterviews from the time of their arrival through their first few months of life in the city and/or their return home. Several of these case studies were summarized and included in our reports to add a human element missing from the Tri-Ethnic book, and Bob McCracken's subject became the focus of his dissertation and has remained a friend for thirty-five years (McCracken 1968).

c. Content Analysis of Open-Ended Questions. Some form of "survey interview" often serves as the core of a systematic field research project, as it did for our Navajo urban migration study. Ultimately we may develop enough experience working within our chosen research community to employ refined psychological tests and multiple choice opinion questionnaires which are easy to administer and score but still culturally appropriate. Initially, however, it is wise to use open-ended exploratory questions which permit subjects to share with you what is most relevant to *them*. But these are still amenable to systematic analysis and quantification, as we did with the four questions we asked migrants about what they liked and did not like about living on the reservation and in Denver. (See chapter 6.)

The most important "discovery technique" a scientist can bring to bear, however, is a general openness to the possibility of disconfirming evidence that does not fit your own theories or the received wisdom from others, a psychological skepticism, an eye for incongruities, and a delight in the unexpected outcome.

Finally, I once asked my graduate psychology Professor Ken Hammond, "What's the key to a good research design?" His answer: "You do your damnedest."

Notes

1. Grant No. 1-R 11 MH 1942-01, 02, and 03. I would like to acknowledge my debt to Thomas Gladwin, anthropologist cum Washington bureaucrat, Tri-Ethnic Research Project liaison person and consultant, who early adopted me as a protégé, encouraged me to seek my own research grant funds, taught me how to do so, and facilitated that process in many ways. I owe my success in obtaining research funds at both this point and throughout my career in large part to his support and guidance.

2. Initially we had intended a longitudinal study, reinterviewing migrants every six months from the time of their arrival to see if their urban experience, particularly their economic experiences, would have an impact on their personal be-

liefs, values, and expectations, which might influence their decisions about staying or leaving the city. But we soon discovered that relatively few new migrants were staying in Denver even this long, making a systematic study with samples larger than our case material impossible.

3. An M.A. thesis and four Ph.D. dissertations came directly out of this effort, and a fifth dissertation began here and was completed later in a Navajo high school. See:

Braxton M. Alfred, *Acculturative Stress among Navajo Migrants to Denver, Colorado* (1965)

Romola McSwain, *The Role of Wives in the Urban Adjustment of Navajo Migrant Families to Denver, Colorado* (1965)

Robert D. McCracken, *Urban Migration and the Changing Structure of Navajo Social Relations* (1968)

Peter Z. Snyder, *Social Assimilation and Adjustment of Navajo Migrants to Denver* (1968)

Robert S. Weppner, *The Economic Absorption of Navajo Indian Migrants to Denver, Colorado* (1968)

Bryan P. Michener, *The Development, Validation and Application of a Test for Need-Achievement Motivation among American Indian High School Students* (1971)

4. Whereas these students all fulfilled their tasks with flying colors, I flunked mine. Although I published six journal articles on the project, reprinted in Volume II, Part 2, the book-length manuscript which I completed early in 1972, *There But for Fortune: The Role of Alcohol in Urban Navajo Adaptation,* was never published, victim of a market slump for academic books coupled with my move to New Zealand. By the time I returned to the United States eight years later the research was old and my priorities had shifted. This was a great disappointment to the many students who worked on the project, as well as to me. This book is partial repayment of my debt to them.

5. The initial interview evolved a bit over our first six months of fieldwork, and was then modified for use among returnees to the reservation and our comparison sample living on the reservation. A synthesis of these various forms is contained in appendix A.

6. I am grateful to Dr. Phileo Nash, then Commissioner of Indian Affairs, and to the directors of the Denver Office of Employment Assistance, Dr. Solon G. Ayers and Mr. Maynard Gage and their staffs, for the many ways in which they facilitated our work.

7. This is one of those many "unfinished projects" in any academic career which never gets completed because of the more immediate demands of grant writing and research project administration, not to mention teaching and child rearing. Cultural evolution is still a hot topic. Susan Blackmore's popular book, *The Meme Machine* (1999), presents a synthesis of current thinking about cultural evolution which still lacks systematic consideration of what factors lead some memes to be selected and others to be ignored from the point of view of those minds doing the selection. Decision theory, I believe, could provide a mechanism for cultural evolution comparable to natural selection for biological evolution.

8. A methodological note: In modified form these four questions are an excellent source of information *from their point of view* about any contrasting situations your subjects may be experiencing. Note that subjects were first asked to provide

positive responses. This usually makes it easier for them subsequently to acknowledge and report their negative reactions.

9. The use of *decision theory* by anthropologists has come a long way since Van and I published our pioneering analysis in 1966 based on a conventional psychological model. The critique by Fjellman (1976) made explicit many concerns troubling anthropologists, who have quite properly been more interested in describing "natural" decision making under real-life conditions than "normative" decision making under experimental laboratory conditions (Quinn 1978). The development of "decision tree modeling" by Christina Gladwin (1989) and others has proved particularly fruitful, and I would consider her 1983 article on Guatemalan farmers' decisions concerning whether or not to plant maize or cash crops an excellent example of *behavioral anthropology*. I believe, however, that the types of analyses Van and I provided, as well as in the article on choice of medical treatment by Woods and Graves (1973; reprinted in part as article 9 in Volume II) would complement and extend some of the analyses being made within Gladwin's framework. See, for example, the clear limitations of the analysis of medical treatment decisions by Young (1980).

10. Our thanks to my friend Martin Hoffman, who owned an employment agency in Denver and provided invaluable insight into the workings of the Denver job market.

11. Given the increase in ethnic sensitivity and privacy concerns since then, I doubt researchers would be permitted to do this today. We are very grateful to Denver Police Chief Harold A. Dill for his cooperation and to Police Captain Doral E. Smith for the time he devoted to searching his records for us.

12. At that time taking a person's blood pressure involved some degree of judgment and skill; now there are digital instruments which make the process totally reliable in any interviewer's hands.

13. Interestingly, most studies have been able to demonstrate significantly higher blood pressure among migrants or urban samples at the *group* level, as we did, but have failed, as we did, to demonstrate consistent relationships between presumed urban stressors and elevated blood pressure at the *individual* level. The mechanisms by which hypertension is induced and manifested are obviously complex. Dressler (1999) has some promising theoretical leads which even now would be worth testing empirically in a reanalysis of our data.

14. Two graduate students, John Castellan and Steve Link, had written a computer program for the Tri-Ethnic project which carefully removed the contribution of each item to the total score before calculating these correlations.

15. During the two years I spent living and working with Navajo patients in a TB hospital in Boulder (1954–1956), I had heard many of their physical complaints.

16. Some years after publishing article 3 my father-in-law, Dr. R. Dana Russell, a prominent geologist, drew my attention to a precursor in two articles by Thomas Chamberlin (1890), another geologist, which describe "The method of multiple working hypotheses." But his goal was to evaluate which model served as the *best* explanation; ours was to explore their *complementarity*.

6

Measuring Psychological Variables

When I began my academic career, my first appointment was as a part-time instructor in the Psychology Department at the University of Colorado, teaching a course in "culture and personality." (They introduced me as "the anthropologist on our staff.") After my dissertation was completed I was invited to teach "culture and personality" in the Anthropology Department as well. (They introduced me as "the psychologist on our staff.")

With my strong interdisciplinary training and experience, my approach to "culture and personality" was quite different from that still popular in the field. Typically, an anthropologist would describe the "modal" personality of some exotic group, and then, based on a loose mix of Freudian theory, learning theory, and clinical insight, speculate about the ways that group's culture "molded" its children to display this "basic personality structure." Distinctive patterns of childrearing—nursing, swaddling, toilet training, and so on—received particular attention. Perhaps best known is Ruth Benedict's descriptions of the contrast between "Dionysian" Plains Indians and "Apollonian" Pueblos (1934).

Such ethnographic characterizations had to be accepted pretty much on faith. During World War II, studies of "National Character" attempted to make this process more systematic, but the results were still scientifically suspect. Critics pointed out that no anthropologist had ever demonstrated the presence of a "modal personality structure" empirically (Lindesmith and Strauss 1950) and that such stereotypic uniformity ran counter to the common experience of ethnographic fieldworkers (Hart 1954). More and more anthropologists came to acknowledge psychological *variability* even within the most homogeneous of simple societies. Using the Rorschach test, for example, Hallowell (1955) and Wallace (1952) had been unable to demonstrate empirically the existence of widely shared personality attributes ("modal personality") within the Native American groups they studied. In the face of such evidence, the idea that a culture "molds" the personality of its members into a relatively uniform pattern fell into disrepute.

The Role of Psychological Variables in Behavioral Anthropology

Instead of viewing this within-group variability in personality traits as a *problem* for us as anthropologists and a challenge to our concept of culture, it can be seen as an *asset*, enabling us to investigate both the sources of typical group traits and their behavioral consequences. For example, developmental psychologists are *also* concerned with the way in which personality attributes are acquired. They do so by examining how *variations* in childrearing and other background experiences may relate to *variations* in adult personality. When working cross-culturally they may then go on to demonstrate ethnic group differences in the *distribution* of certain personality attributes, as we did for time perspective and feeling of fatalism on the Tri-Ethnic project, and in the distribution of socialization experiences associated with these traits (Jessor, Graves, Hanson, and Jessor 1968). But this is a very different approach from that typically employed by anthropologists.

I wanted "psychological anthropology" to become a respectable social science using strategies of this type and measures of personality characteristics with demonstrable reliability and validity. In a highly negative review of Victor Barnouw's 1963 textbook on *Culture and Personality* (Graves 1964), for example, I concluded: "We can no longer afford to remain aloof from the main stream of social science, divorced from its theory and methodology, deaf to its demands for rigor and replicability. Anthropology has much to contribute to man's understanding of himself and his social milieu; it would be a shame if this contribution were lost by default." (Barnouw cried all the way to the bank; he was more in tune with the field than I, and his book became quite popular.)

Why Are Psychological Variables Difficult to Measure?

Psychological variables, both cognitive and affective, include beliefs, values, expectations, intentions, goals, plans, plus attractions, frustrations, angers, and fears—anything going on in the head of an actor. We have all experienced these thoughts and feelings, and we know they play a role in our behavior. So an integrated science of human behavior must take them into consideration.

But beliefs and feelings cannot be measured directly. We can ask our subjects about them, but they may or may not be willing or able to tell us about them accurately. So, they must normally be *inferred* from something we *can* observe, whether that is our subject's response to some structured task such as a behavioral choice, questionnaire, projective test, or reaction when placed in an experimental situation. Since these inferences are "interpretations" from observations of behavior, their validity is open to question and must be addressed.

As a self-proclaimed "psychological anthropologist," how to measure psychological variables successfully among non-Western people—cross-cultural "psychometrics"—had become a central concern of mine. And a fascinating challenge. The personality characteristics that we may consider typical of a culture group, I recognized, must be measured with all the care invested by psychologists working within our own society, but with the added issue of demonstrating the validity of these measures within an ethnic group other than our own. These are important skills for a behavioral anthropologist to develop.

Most psychological anthropologists take as their problem, "How do the typical experiences of a child growing up within this culture give rise to their typical personality attributes?" How does a "culture" mold "personality"? I'm interested in this too. (See chapter 8.) But my major focus has been, "How do personality attributes, whatever their origin, give rise to *behavior*?" The Navajo Urban Relocation Research Project, with its two clear, "nonreactive" behavioral criterion measures—returning home and arrest rates—provided many opportunities to pursue this goal. Three of our six theoretical models presented in the last chapter implicated psychological variables as important determinants of this migrant behavior.

In this chapter I will present a variety of strategies for measuring psychological variables cross-culturally, including inferences from objective, "nonreactive" indicators over which subjects have no control. Many of these measurement techniques can be generalized for use in other cross-cultural settings as well.

From Conceptual to Operational Definitions

The personality attributes we work with as behavioral scientists are *hypothetical constructs*, inventions of both folk and professional psychologists that have no objective reality.[1] Their value must be judged in purely pragmatic terms: How well do they explain and predict behavior? We observe someone at a party and say, "What a shy young man he is." "Shy" is a presumed "personality trait" which serves us as an (albeit circular) *explanation* of the behavior we just observed, which then becomes a basis for predicting his behavior in *new* situations. If our predictions pan out, we consider it a useful generalization. If not, we either refine our interpretation ("He seems to be shy in new situations, but not in familiar ones,") or invent a more satisfactory explanatory concept, such as "He seems to be *self-protective*."

When it comes to *measuring* concepts of this kind, the challenge is that since the concepts have no objective reality, the validity of these measures must be judged *indirectly* by a variety of strategies which serve to increase our confidence both in the usefulness of our concept and of our measuring instruments. This is a "bootstrapping" process that's dependent on weaving a convincing inferential web. This process is called "construct validation" (Cronbach and Meehl 1955), and was drilled into me by my mentors at Colorado, Dick Jessor and Ken Hammond, who had a strong professional interest in this approach. Critical to this process is the role of *theory* in both test construction and validation. (See Jessor and Hammond 1957.)

My effort to conceptualize and measure "future time perspective" at the dissertation level can serve as an example of the process. We start with a broad, verbal definition which attempts to capture not only the essence of the hypothetical construct, but also the network of theoretical relationships by which it is ultimately linked to observable behavior. Having no clear definition of future time perspective from Florence Kluckhohn's work, nor an agreed definition from the extensive psychological and sociological literature I reviewed (Graves 1961:8-40), I began by formulating a vague definition of my own, something like "how far into the future a person typically thinks when making day-to-day behavioral choices." The more long-term and extended their time perspective, I reasoned, the more future consequences, both positive and negative, they are apt to take into consideration, and "therefore" the more likely they are to chose behavior which has its major payoff in the future and the less likely to choose behavior which may be immediately gratifying but have long-term negative consequences. Thus the hypothesized link between an "extended" future time perspective and "delay of gratification" behavior already discussed in chapter 2.

Note that my definition of future time perspective did not exhaust its meaning, and that other theorists might have slightly different definitions.[2] The hypothetical construct is broader in its scope than any particular verbal definition of it. This is fruitful at the level of *theory generating*. But at the level of *theory testing*, which involves systematic data collection and analysis, clear *operational definitions* of all concepts in your theoretical scheme must be specified. Among anthropologists, even psychologically trained anthropologists, this process of operationalizing their concepts has often been poorly addressed (Pelto and Pelto 1978:43).[3]

That was my next task. I reviewed all the ways this concept had been measured by *other* researchers, and then selected, refined, and invented several approaches which I thought would be appropriate within the multicultural high school setting where I was working. For example, based on the most common method used by others (LeShan 1952), I asked students to complete four different stories that I started for them (two which introduced stories in an academic context, and two in a social context), to see how far into the future the action of their stories extended. (Most previous researchers had only used one story stem to measure future time perspective.) I also developed a series of life events (such as failing to get a high school degree) and conflicts between academic and social goals (such as whether or not to go roller skating with friends the night before an important exam) and asked them to tell me all the *consequences* they could think of for these events or choices. And finally, I asked them to "think ahead for a minute, and then tell me ten things you expect you'll do or expect will happen *to* you." This was followed by collecting a similar sample of ten *past* events, and how long from the present these events would or had occurred. This was the "Life Space Sample," which I had modified from work by Melvin Wallace (1956), and have already discussed briefly in chapter 2.

Each of these approaches provided a somewhat different "recipe" for assigning a numerical "future time perspective" *score* to each of my subjects: How far into the future the *action* of their stories extended (including *cognitive action* such as making plans); how many *consequences* they could imagine flowing from a variety of hypothetical situations; and finally, the median time from the present of the future (and past) events they named in their Life Space Sample.[4] Note again that these specific operational definitions do not exhaust the verbal meaning of the concept. No operational definition can. Each should be thought of as a more or less adequate *sample* of that meaning. Each gets at a slightly different aspect, but leaves a lot of "surplus meaning" to generate *other* approaches to the concept's measurement.

These methods were then pretested and refined in a neighboring multiethnic high school before use in my own research site. Pretesting measures with subjects *other than but similar to* those with whom you will ultimately be working is an important step in any research project, but particularly so when working cross-culturally. Instructions were improved, ambiguities corrected, and the best items selected for final use.

Pretesting also permitted me to estimate the *reliability* of these measures, both within the measure itself (*internal homogeneity*) and over time (*stability*). For example, the future events expected by each of the twenty-three pretest subjects were rank-ordered, and extension scores based on each item were compared, using Spearman rho correlation coefficients (discussed above in chapter 4). These correlations ranged from .56 to .78, quite respectable evidence for internal homogeneity. Except for the extreme scores, both short and long in temporal extension, correlations among the mid-range items (ranks 3 through 7) all fell in the mid to high seventies. This was an important consideration in ultimately choosing the time from the present to the *median* event mentioned as our operational definition of future extension. Finally, ten subjects were retested on the Life Space

Sample following Christmas vacation, five weeks after their initial testing. The Spearman rho correlation between their two future extension scores was .88.

After my data were collected in the Tri-Ethnic community's high school I was able to examine evidence for the *validity* of my time perspective measures. The *convergent validity* of the Life Space Sample—how well it correlated with our *alternative* measures of future time perspective— was disappointing: All were positive but nonsignificant (Graves 1961:177). But this could just as well have been because the story completions and consequences measures were not particularly good (as we later learned from other evidence). When correlations among alternative measures of the same concept are low, which is at fault? You have to decide on the basis of *other* evidence.

The *discriminant validity* of the Life Space Sample—the ability of a measure to distinguish between groups known to differ on the variable being measured—was strong, however. The ethnic differences in extension scores found were clear and consistent (and would later be replicated in the Navajo study). When rank-ordered from the least to the most remote from the present, every one of the ten future events collected from our subjects showed the same pattern: Anglos had the most extended future time perspective scores, both Native American groups had the least extended scores, and Hispanic subjects were intermediate. All Anglo–non-Anglo differences were statistically significant, most at better than the .01 level, and all but two of the Hispanic–Native American differences were also significant (Graves 1961:102). This same pattern of relationships among these three ethnic groups was found for our sample of *past* events, reinforcing our conviction that "extended versus restricted" was empirically a better way to conceptualize time perspective than a "past, present or future orientation."

I then carefully examined a variety of extraneous factors which might have been responsible for these ethnic differences: Socioeconomic status, family stability, Kuhlman–Finch IQ scores[5] (the test used in the local high school because it was considered to be fairly free from cultural bias), and verbal fluency, among other things. On balance, extension scores based on the Life Space Sample seemed to be more free from the effect of such factors (Graves 1961:125-173) than my alternative measures.

Evidence for the *predictive validity* of the time perspective measure at the dissertation level— its correlation with the various measures of behavior presented in chapter 3, was relatively weak, however. Although all correlations were in the direction predicted by my theory, they were small and nonsignificant. It can be taken as axiomatic that *all behavior has multiple determinants.* Drinking and other forms of deviant behavior among high school students is no exception. Empirically, an extended future time perspective appeared to play a very small role. As we saw in chapter 4, however, the wider theoretical net of social and psychological variables cast by the Tri-Ethnic Project as a whole was far more successful, and accounted for almost all the variation in deviant drinking behavior to be found within both the high school and the community at large.

Further evidence for the *construct validity* of this measure will emerge below and in Graves 1974 (Volume II, article 8). I turn now to the other measures we developed for testing our theoretical models of Navajo migrant adaptation to life in Denver.

Measuring Personal Goals and Expectations

In "Values, expectations and relocation," (Graves and VanArsdale 1966; Volume II, article 4) Van and I presented the Decision Model for staying or leaving the city, and how this decision was mediated by two psychological variables: The strength of a migrant's desire for economic success (his *goals)* and how sure he was of being able to achieve these goal either on the reservation or in the city (his *expectations).*

Content analysis of open-ended questions is a very flexible way to measure many psychological traits. The questions are treated as *projective tests* (to be discussed further below), where a person's responses are assumed to reflect their underlying psychological orientations. We employed this approach to measure a migrant's *goals,* using the four open-ended questions— discussed briefly in the last chapter—concerning what he liked and disliked about life in Denver and back home on the reservation. All responses to these four questions were placed on slips of paper, and Van and I independently sorted them into scoring categories. We agreed about 90% of the time, and then resolved our disagreements in conference. As anticipated in our hypothesis, we were pleased to discover that on three of these four questions migrants who remained in Denver were significantly more likely to mention economic-material features of life than those who returned home (Volume II, article 4, tables 1-4).

Approximately 40% of all migrant responses to these four questions referred to these material features of life, suggesting their high saliency for these migrants. As our project progressed and more migrants were interviewed both in Denver and on the reservation, we gave each subject an "economic value orientation" score based on the *proportion of all his responses* to these four questions which referred to economic-material goals.

As a measure of migrant *expectations* we used a *self-anchoring scale* (Kilpatrick and Cantril 1960). This is another flexible technique which can be used for many purposes.[6] We showed our subjects a ladder with ten rungs (numbered 0 to 9 for subsequent scoring). Then we asked them to think about the best and worst life they could imagine. Thinking about the worst life at the bottom and the best at the top, we asked them to indicate where they were *now* on this ladder with respect to achieving *their own goals* (whatever these might be), where they would be *five years from now if they stayed in the city* and again, *if they returned to the reservation.* Migrants who stayed in Denver were far more likely than Leavers to anticipate improvement in the city than back on the reservation ($p<.001$). Not a very exciting discovery. In fact, if the data had been otherwise our measure of personal expectations would certainly have been suspect.

Measuring Conflicts in Goals and Expectations

Far more interesting, however, was the potential *conflict between competing goals* which this early analysis suggested. This conflict analysis was reported in the next publication on the project (Graves 1970; reprinted in Volume II, article 5). The marginal resources of their reservation home condemn many Navajos to a peculiarly conflict-laden life. For those who come to value the material benefits of mainstream American society, the beautiful but barren reservation landscape and its limited opportunities for a cash income must present a discouraging vista. Much of the motivation to migrate, clearly, comes from this economic "push." At the same time, however, the reservation is a familiar and supportive environment, "home" in the most value-laden sense of the word, where an Indian is assured at least a minimum livelihood—and a warm welcome. Navajo society, of course, is not without its interpersonal conflicts and tensions, and life on the reservation is often physically strenuous. But particularly within traditional culture, where earth and its inhabitants constitute an integrated matrix, many of the rewards of life are intimately linked to familiar people and places. Thus when Navajos migrate to Denver they are forced to give up one set of potentially important goals in order to achieve another. For many migrants, we reasoned, this *conflict* between competing goals not only might serve as a motivation to return home (the Decision Model), but while still in Denver might be a factor leading them to get drunk (the Personal Adjustment Model).

Here our hypotheses were based on a "conflict-reduction theory" of drunkenness (Conger 1956). But this conflict between the rewards of urban and reservation life, we reasoned, would be *differentially distributed* among migrants, depending on the relative strength of their competing economic and traditional goals. The less important material success was to a migrant, or the more important a traditional reservation way of life, the more conflict the sacrifices of migration would produce, and therefore, we reasoned, the more drunkenness and arrest.

We could use our indirect measure of *economic value orientation* as one of our measures. To test this *goal conflict* theory of drunkenness, however, we needed a measure of the importance of a traditional Navajo way of life as well. Fortunately, the anthropologists Walter Goldschmidt and Robert Edgerton at UCLA had recently worked with William Nyddeger to produce a "picture interview" measure of Navajo traditionalism, modeled on one Goldschmidt and Edgerton (1961) had developed for another tribe, and they were gracious enough to lend it to us even before publication. The test consists of a series of pictures drawn by a Navajo artist, each of which presents a visual contrast or implied contrast between a traditional Navajo or a Western way of life. For example, one shows a doctor giving a Navajo a physical examination on the left side of the picture while a traditional medicine man ("singer") performs a ceremony over a sick patient on the right. Another shows a Navajo family in a pickup truck heading either to church or to a squaw dance. For each picture subjects were asked a standard set of questions and probes to elicit their personal value preferences.

Working together, two members of our research team, Braxton Alfred and Minor VanArsdale, wrote a scoring manual for this procedure, and all responses were scored independently by three researchers. A clear "traditional" orientation was scored zero, a mixed response (usually involving cultural "syncretism") received a score of one, and a clear repudiation of traditional ways or adoption of Western ways was scored two. To test for the internal homogeneity of this measure (reliability) we correlated the score on each of these six pictures with a total score based on the other five. As a result of this item analysis scores from three of the six pictures were discarded as unreliable. Scores on the remaining three were summed and subjects were divided into those above or below the overall median. (Each of these six pictures could *also* be viewed as alternative measures of Navajo traditionalism, and their intercorrelations as evidence of *convergent validity* or lack thereof. The distinction between internal consistency of a measure and its convergent validity is a slippery one. In general, the *more distinct* the measures, the more convincingly their correlation serves as evidence for their mutual validity.)

Then we looked at arrest rates among those in the high and low groups, along with arrest rates for those high or low in economic value orientation. The results are presented in Volume II, article 5, table 7. Looked at separately, each of these measures of personal goals had only a modest relationship to arrest rates. Nevertheless, in both cases, those whose personal goals were most *incompatible* with life in Denver had higher arrest rates. This was encouraging. When we combined these two measures into a pattern analysis, however, the results were far more striking, more than doubling from the most to the least conflictual pattern of values. (As an aside, it is worth noting that these value orientations had *no* correlation with a migrant's *actual* economic achievement in the city, or lack of it, which we will see below appears to account for a lot of their urban frustration and drunkenness. So these measures of *value conflict* are picking up an additional source of variation in arrest rates.)

Our measure of future expectations provides an alternative approach to this conflict-reduction theory of Navajo drunkenness. Regardless of his goals, our self-anchoring scale tapped his expectations of being able to achieve them either in Denver or on the reservation. (See Volume II, article 5, table 8.) As we anticipated, the lowest arrest rates were found among those who expected their lives to improve in Denver but not on the reservation. But the highest arrest rates were found among those who didn't expect their lives to get better in *either* location. Their pessimism may have been warranted, but their behavioral response—heavy drinking—undoubtedly contributed to a negative outcome as well.

Like all psychological measurement, these examples of conflicting values and expectations are *indirect* and *inferential*. But if we had asked migrants directly about feeling conflicted in the city, it seems doubtful that they would have been able to tell us, or perhaps even been aware of more than a generalized "dis-ease." By using measures of each element in the conflict and combining them we were able to create *new* measures of psychic conflict which proved to be strongly related to our measure of excessive drinking.

Using Economic Data as Indirect Measures of Psychological Distress

Another approach to measuring migrant feelings of conflict and frustration was even *more* inferential, and therefore even more in need of validation. These were "nonreactive" measures derived from the migrant's objective economic experiences based on BIA and employer records, and therefore out of the control of the migrants themselves. But each involved an inference about how migrants might be *feeling* about these experiences, which has to be supported by their relationship to other variables.

The main motivation for a Navajo to move to Denver was to get a *job*. Jobs were scarce on the reservation. If jobs also proved to be hard to get and poorly paid in Denver, we reasoned that a migrant could be expected to feel frustration and disappointment, and this in turn might serve as an important motivation to get drunk.

For many migrants such job frustration began on the day of their arrival. The job market in Denver has never been particularly good, especially for relatively untrained laborers like most of these Navajos. But their schoolteachers and the relocation officers had often given them exaggerated expectations concerning the splendid opportunities the city would provide. Some even came to the city with the mistaken belief, perhaps unwittingly fostered by BIA officials eager to promote relocation, that a good job would be waiting for them upon arrival.

The first indication they had that perhaps their dreams were unfounded was sitting around the BIA Office of Employment Assistance for seemingly endless days, and going out for fruitless and stressful job interviews that did not lead to jobs. Over half the Navajos who came to Denver were in the city for a week or more before they landed their first job. When we talked with these new migrants informally, while they sat around the BIA office of Employment Assistance waiting for possible job interviews, many shared their feelings of frustration and disappointment concerning their prospects in the city. During this initial period they faced no real economic hardship, for unlike migrants from other ethnic groups, they had the BIA, which gave them a weekly subsistence allowance until they got settled and began receiving a steady paycheck. So at this point their problems were purely *psychological*. But even if unfounded, we reasoned, anxieties felt and hopes unrealized might provide powerful motives for getting drunk.

Even a migrant for whom the BIA found a job fairly quickly was often disappointed by what he got. Frequently his first job would be a temporary affair, a stint washing dishes, janitorial work, or other menial tasks to tide him over until a more suitable job was found for him. Other initial jobs might not work out because neither the BIA staff nor the migrant himself yet knew where his talents and interests lay. So then he'd be back in the BIA office again, waiting around while they looked for something else.

A measure of his initial rate of unemployment over the first six months (or first half of his stay if he returned home in less than a year) provided an objective measure of early economic frustrations. As anticipated, an initial period of economic instability was associated with substantially higher arrest rates than among those in more stable jobs right from the start: 128,000 arrests per 100,000 man-years in the city for those with 15% or more initial unemployment versus 73,000 for those with less initial unemployment. See Volume II, article 5, table 3. Almost every other economic indicator we looked at told the same story: Those migrants who had the most negative initial experience in Denver, whether through temporary work, menial jobs, or low wages, had substantially higher arrest rates, and therefore were clearly drinking more, than those with more favorable economic experiences. With time, of course, their drinking behavior was probably itself *contributing* to their economic problems, and this is suggested by even stronger associations between *subsequent* economic experiences and arrest rates. Compare tables 3 and 4 in Volume II, article 5.

A validation of our *psychological* interpretation of these findings emerged when we looked at a migrant's wages relative to what he might legitimately be *expecting* to receive. When we compared a migrant's starting wage with the highest wage he had ever received *before* migration, the level of association with subsequent arrest rates *increased* substantially from that for low starting wages alone. Table 6.1 (abstracted from Volume II, article 5, table 3) makes this comparison clear:

Table 6.1. Initial Economic Experience Relative to Previous Experience *versus* Denver Arrest Rates

	Proportion of all migrants	Arrest rate per 100,000 pop.
Starting wage		
More than $1.25 per hour	38%	77,000
$1.25 per hour or less	62%	93,000
Starting wage relative to highest premigration wage		
Same or higher than premigration wage	48%	54,000
Lower than premigration wages	52%	116,000

From a psychometric point of view *Starting Wage Relative to Highest Premigration Wage* (referred to below as "Relative Starting Wage") is a particularly interesting measure. Technically, it is an objective and nonreactive *index* of a subjective psychological state which cannot be measured directly. It involves an inference, a leap of faith, however logical. Because of the problems with self-report data discussed in chapter 3, we looked for these objective indices wherever possible. Since we knew these Navajos were coming to Denver mainly in the hope of getting better jobs than were currently available to them on the reservation, *all* our economic measures, when low, served as indirect indices of potential disappointment. But looking at one economic fact relative to another economic fact proved in this case to yield an index of even greater empirical power. And one which seemed particularly convincing to us.

This index, Relative Starting Wage, led me to formulate what I came to refer to as "the paradox of experience." Sadly, the more successful a Navajo had been *before* migration to Denver, the more likely it was that he would be dissatisfied in Denver, even though in absolute terms he might be better off than his fellows. A corollary, which I will come back to later in this chapter, is that those migrants with the lowest aspirations for success in the city appear to tolerate its inevitable frustrations best.

Measuring Retrospective Distortion

Because of the many complaints we heard from migrants sitting around the BIA office while waiting for jobs, we decided to test the effect of this initial frustration on subsequent drinking behavior. So we carefully abstracted the BIA records and calculated the number of working days between a migrant's arrival in Denver and his first job. The length of this period of initial unemployment was empirically unrelated to any aspect of a migrant's own background, such as age, education, and prior work experience. But it was strongly related to the general level of unemployment in Denver at the time of his arrival ($p=.65$). So it is easy and accurate for a migrant to externalize the blame when this period of unemployment is protracted.

Despite these complaints, however, those who got jobs quickly had a subsequent arrest rate no different from those who were unemployed for a week or more before getting their first job. Were the complaints we were hearing of no psychological consequence? Had these events occurred too early to have lasting impact? Or were they overridden by subsequent experience?

These questions were not addressed again for several years, until I undertook a secondary analysis of *retrospective distortion* in their memory of this initial unemployment experience (Graves 1973; reprinted as article 7 in Volume II.) As part of his individual interview, each migrant had been asked how long he was in the city before getting his first job. Since for most migrants we had good BIA records, this question was included only to supplement incomplete or absent records, and to evaluate the validity of self-reports; initially no theoretical significance was attached to discrepancies. Then one day it occurred to me that *the amount and direction of distortion* in a migrant's memory of these events might have psychological significance. With this we hit empirical paydirt.

Table 4 in Volume II, article 7 presents the relevant data. Whether long (a week or more) or short, those who *underestimated* their initial period of unemployment—those for whom it was apparently not psychologically important—had an arrest rate only about *half* as high as those who were accurate in their recall or overestimated this period. (This article presents data demonstrating the value of looking at a variety of ways by which a migrant can influence the impact of his objective economic situation, for better or worse, through his perception of it: the Stimulus → Perception → Response model presented in chapter 1.)

Psychometric Measures for Testing the "Culture of Poverty" Model

The third psychological model of urban adjustment presented in chapter 5 was based on the popular notion that certain personality predispositions typical of members of the poverty class interfered with their economic goal attainment and therefore contributed to a perpetuation of their impoverished state. By contrast, many assumed that acquisition of American middle-class personality traits would facilitate their economic achievement and end their state of poverty. To test this model among our Denver migrants we chose to measure three of these psychological variables: a foreshortened time perspective, feelings of fatalism about their life, and low motivation to strive for achievement. These also correspond roughly to non-Anglo orientations on three of Florence Kluckhohn's universal "value orientations": Time Perspective, Man's Relationship to Nature (control over, harmony with, or subjection to) and Activity (doing versus being).

Because of the difficulty of psychological measurement cross-culturally, especially with respect to the appropriateness and validity of these measures for use among the group(s) being studied, I devoted more space to these issues than would normally be appropriate in a journal article (Graves 1974; reprinted in Volume II, article 8.) This is useful reading for any behavioral anthropologist interested in psychological measurement in cross-cultural settings.

1. Open-Ended Tasks—Measuring Time Perspective

For the Navajo urban migration project I turned again to the "Life Space Sample" I had used on the Tri-Ethnic project. After collecting my dissertation data I had discovered through careful item analysis that collecting five past and five future events was sufficient to provide reliable extension scores. So to save time in the adult community survey this was all we had requested. For the Navajo project the procedure was further simplified: Since it was really *future* time perspective we were interested in measuring, we decided not to bother to collect a sample of *past* events as well. (Also recall that past and future "extension" scores were strongly correlated.)

Even when we had reduced our request to five future events, however, this task proved difficult for more than half of our Navajo subjects. "We Navajo are not like you weather forecasters," one dourly remarked (quoted in Volume II, article 8). This created measurement problems, since the average number of future items we could collect was only about three. But the internal homogeneity of this measure—as reported above—is high, and scores based on different sample sizes appear empirically to be very comparable. In Denver, Anglo–Navajo differences in time perspective were again substantial, and similar to those we had obtained among high school students in the Tri-Ethnic project. Indeed, Navajos (and other Native Americans with whom I have worked) typically seem to be living more "in the moment" than Anglos. Nevertheless, there is wide within-group variation in their time perspective scores, with standard deviations substantially larger than the group mean.

The validity of this and the other two psychological measures presented in article 8 was derived from notions of *construct validity,* already discussed above, and is largely based on the consistent relationships these measures of the "culture of poverty" syndrome had with economic and behavioral variables. "Empirical correlations then serve a dual purpose: they validate the measures being used at the same time that they test theoretical hypotheses about relationships among the underlying concepts being measured. Of course, if no substantively significant and theoretically meaningful pattern of relationships emerges, the researcher is left in doubt as to whether the cause is poor measurement or poor theory. But that is always the case" (Volume II, article 6:113).

2. Forced Choice Tests—Measuring Locus of Control

Many psychological measures take the form of a series of "items"—statements which sample different aspects of the theoretical concept—to which your subjects are asked to respond in various ways, such as "true-false" or "agree-disagree." A serious problem with this format is how easily subjects may answer in a *socially desirable* manner they think will make them look good or please the interviewer, rather than expressing their true beliefs or feelings. One way to overcome this problem is illustrated by the scale we developed to measure migrant beliefs in "external" luck, fate, chance, versus personal ("internal") control over their destiny:

Our measure was a modification of the "Social Reaction Inventory," which had frequently been used by Rotter and his associates in their research on what they refer to as "locus of control" (Rotter 1966). A brief history of our efforts to develop and validate this measure for use cross-culturally is instructive. Those choosing to engage in behavioral science cross-culturally have their work cut out for them.

Before I joined the Tri-Ethnic staff, Jessor had created a forty-item "forced choice" measure of "locus of control," based on work by his friend Shepherd Liverant, a psychologist at Ohio State. For each "item," subjects were offered two statements—one expressing feelings of "internal" control over their lives, and the other expressing more "external" control, but "matched" for its degree of social desirability. Then they were asked which statement they agreed with more. During the spring of 1959 Jessor administered this inventory to a tri-ethnic population of youthful inmates at a nearby prison in Englewood, Colorado. Analysis of these data suggested the need to rebuild this inventory in several ways, simplifying the language and making a better match in *content* as well as in social desirability between the two halves of each forced choice item. This was one of the first tasks I was given when I joined the Tri-Ethnic staff that summer.

Constructing measures of this type is a lot of fun. Several of us would sit around a table and try to come up with statements which expressed in simple language feelings of personal control over one's destiny. For example, "A person can pretty well make whatever he wants out of his life." Then we would brainstorm a matching statement which expressed a fatalistic viewpoint: "No matter how much a person tries, it's hard to change the way things are going to turn out." Since a belief in personal control over our fate is considered "good" within middle-class culture, our goal was to come up with alternative statements which were equally reasonable and compelling, so that roughly half of our subjects would choose the "internal control" option and half the "external." If this proved to be empirically true, then we knew the sentence-pairs were roughly matched for "social desirability." If not, we would try rewording one or both halves of the pair to make them more equally attractive. For example, "If you've got ability, you can always get a good job," versus "Getting a good job depends partly on being in the right place at the right time." This item also illustrates how the use of words like "always" and "partly" can change the "social desirability" or "pull" of one side of the forced choice pair to produce a more equal distribution of choices.

My experience working in the tri-ethnic high school, and that of other social psychologists working elsewhere with this concept, had indicated that people may feel different degrees of personal control within different areas of their life. Their feelings may have *situational specificity.* For example, in the rural tri-ethnic community we were working in the Navajo boarding school students didn't feel much control over their academic achievement, but on the basketball court they dominated, in part because like World War II "code talkers" they could call out plays to each other in Navajo and their opponents wouldn't know what they were saying. Hispanic students felt more personal efficacy in the social realm, and Anglos in the academic realm. So to achieve a measure with *cross-situational generality* (our definition of a "personality trait") it was important to devise items which sampled a wide variety of life areas.

That fall I administered this revised forty-item inventory to all the juniors and seniors in the local tri-ethnic high school. A scaling analysis of these data suggested further revisions, which we undertook in the fall of

1960. This revised forty-item version was administered to all the high school students as part of my dissertation research in the spring of 1961 (Graves 1961). Further analysis of these data enabled us to modify and select the best thirty items for use in the high school study the following year. This is the version reported in our book (Jessor, Graves, Hanson, and Jessor 1968). Even then, during analysis we discarded seven items which failed to correlate well with total score, and constructed each student's *internal control* score from the remaining twenty-three. Biserial correlations (the ability of an item to predict a high or low score based on the remaining twenty-two items) averaged .4, which suggests a reasonable degree of internal homogeneity or generality of this belief across the domains sampled by these items. We also produce a seventeen-item adult version of the Social Reaction Inventory for use as part of our Tri-Ethnic community survey in 1962. Only twelve of these items survived this type of item analysis.

When we administered this questionnaire in either the high school (as a paper-and-pencil task) or among adults (as part of a formal interview) we assured our subjects that there were "no right or wrong answers" and that even though they might believe that both statements were true or neither was true, their task was to chose which statement in each pair they believed to be *more* true. We also included a few "buffer" items in each questionnaire to break any "response set" by our subjects. For example, "I don't spend much time thinking about the past" *versus* "I often think about the things I did as a child."[7]

The final versions of this scale took three years of development, and although Anglos consistently expressing the strongest feeling of "internal control" as anticipated ethnographically, the measures failed to produce a single significant correlation with any of our behavioral outcome measures. I did not know this at the time we began the Navajo project, or I might have been discouraged from trying to measure this personality trait once again. This is just as well, because although we again failed to find the *linear* relationship between a belief in internal control over one's destiny we anticipated and economic achievement in the city or arrest rates, we *did* find a fascinating *nonlinear* relationship in interaction with *actual* achievement, as we will see below.

In the interest of simplifying the language even further for use with Navajo migrants in Denver, and to make the task more concrete, we ultimately scrapped most of the items used on the Tri-Ethnic project and tried constructing new items within a different format. A situation was presented with two alternative explanations, and a subject was asked to choose which seemed to him "more true." For example:

> Suppose a man loses a lot of his livestock during the winter. Would this probably happen
>
> 1. because he didn't take proper care of them? *or*
> 2. because of bad luck?

After pretesting and item analysis we selected twenty items for our final questionnaire: eight from the original Tri-Ethnic work and twelve of these new, more concrete items. As we had come to expect from ethnographic reports and our Tri-Ethnic community experience, Navajo migrant scores on this measure were more than a full standard deviation *lower* (more fatalistic) than for our matched group of Anglos in similar jobs (*discriminant validity*). This also shows how "culture traits" can be measured and group differences demonstrated.

3. Projective Tests—Measuring Achievement Motivation

It stretches your creativity to attempt to measure concepts in a variety of ways: The more diverse your methodology, the better. The "tyranny of the method" was a principle that I learned to resist at an early stage. When I was a graduate student Jessor had been concerned about my fascination with the Rorschach test. What happens, he warned me, is that you develop expertise in the use of a method like the Rorschach test at great cost, and then you are tempted to use the Rorschach test for everything you do. This had been true to some extent for Pete Hallowell and Tony Wallace, for example, and Dick's warning probably helped save me from investing more than a single semester of study in that method. Instead, I incorporated the *principle* of projective testing in my work, and used this at various times in my career to help develop a number of alternative projective tests designed for specific purposes.

The basic principle of a projective test is that you provide your subjects with some *ambiguous* stimulus to which they can respond in a variety of ways. The type case, of course, is the now-familiar Rorschach inkblots, but you could just as well use cloud formations. (Most of us as children have lain on our backs looking up at the sky and seen various creatures passing by.) Since subjects must *project* meaning into your ambiguous task, that meaning is assumed to reflect their personality. In the case of the Rorschach test, psychologists have then developed an extensive literature on how to "score" a subjects' responses for various (typically psychopathological) attributes.

The only virtue of using a standard set of stimuli like the Rorschach test is that there is this large body of accumulated experience with the task to which you can compare the responses of your own subjects. But when working within cultures other than our own, this body of experience is usually of little value, as I had already learned when interviewing Navajo patients in the TB hospital where I first worked (chapter 2). So why not just construct *new* tasks which will elicit responses more relevant to your own theoretical purposes and then accumulate your *own* body of experience?

This is what we did on the Navajo project to measure migrants' "achievement motivation." Since measures of "need-achievement" have predicted "success" within modern Western society (McClelland 1953; McClelland et al. 1958; 1969), a measure suitable for use among Navajo subjects seemed like it might serve as a useful predictor of their successful economic integration in Denver as well.

We decided to model our measure on the Thematic Apperception Test (TAT) used by McClelland and his associates for their measure of achievement motivation, but modified specifically for use with Navajo subjects.[8] One member of our team, Bryan Michener, undertook this task, and his experience provides an object lesson for behavioral anthropologists in the development and use of projective tests in cross-cultural research (Michener 1965; 1971; see also Lindzey 1961).

Drawing on our experience living and working among the Navajo, we contrived a series of situations which would be familiar to our migrant subjects yet sufficiently ambiguous that they could be responded to in a number of ways, including, we hoped, "achievement" themes. I then hired my friend George Nez, one of the Navajo tuberculosis patients still living in Boulder, and an accomplished artist, to draw stimulus pictures representing these situations. We then selected what seemed to us the best six for our use. (See appendix B.) In order of presentation within our survey questionnaire, these included a picture of a young man speaking to an employer, a young man seated in a classroom, a young man watching a piece of Navajo jewelry receive a prize, a Navajo family boarding a bus, a young man speaking to an assembly of Indians, and a young man counting a handful of paper money. Note that in all these pictures there is a young man of about the age of our subjects with whom they could identify.

In the interview our subjects were asked to "tell a story" about each picture (including a series of standard probes—see appendix B) and their responses were tape recorded and transcribed. After we had collected about fifty interviews, Bryan began the arduous task of preparing a scoring manual. This effort is fully described in Graves 1974 (Volume II, article 8). Even today, to my knowledge, no cross-cultural projective test of this type and its scoring manual has ever been so carefully constructed, analyzed, and validated.

Testing the "Culture of Poverty" Hypothesis

This lengthy development effort outlined above and in Volume II, article 8 proved worthwhile when we were finally ready to relate migrant scores to their economic achievement and arrest rates in the city. Here fascinating, and hardly self-evident interaction effects were found which were identical in form for all three psychological measures. Our hypothesis was that more middle-class American personality traits—an extended future time perspective, feelings of personal control over one's life, and strong achievement motivation—should lead to a better economic adjustment in the city: more stable jobs and higher wages. Empirically, however, this was not true. When it came to acquiring and holding good jobs, these middle-class personality traits appeared to be totally *irrelevant*. See Volume II, article 8, table 2.

Negative findings of this type are discouraging, ambiguous, and hard to get published. You never know whether the reason for your failure is that your theory is wrong, or that your measures are poor. In the Navajo project, however, *I had confidence in the measures.* The economic outcome measures—wages, job type, unemployment rates—were all objective and outside our subject's control. And we had constructed the three personality measures with great care. So this led me to challenge the validity of the popular "culture of poverty" theory instead.

When we looked at these personality measures in relationship to arrest rates, several interesting empirical facts emerged. As we had anticipated, migrants having strong feelings of personal control over their lives had arrest rates only *half* as high as those acknowledging fatalistic feelings. But having an extended time perspective and high achievement motivation—middle-class personality traits which theoretically should have been associated with *lower* arrest rates, actually had *higher* arrest rates than those who were more present oriented and less ambitious. See Volume II, article 8, table 3.

Even more interesting, however, were the *interaction effects.* If a migrant was doing *well* in the city, with a stable job at good wages, his arrest rates were relatively low, and all three of these personality traits appeared to be pretty irrelevant, at least with respect to his drinking behavior. But if he was doing *poorly* economically, then fatalistic feelings, an extended future time perspective and a high need for achievement apparently *added* to his misery, and were associated with *more* drinking and drunkenness, as indicated by substantially *higher* arrest rates. See Volume II, article 8, tables 4, 5, and 6.

Our interpretation of these empirical findings was that migrants with poor jobs but a high need for achievement felt a *disjunction* between this need and their actual performance, and if they had an extended future time perspective, they anticipated that this negative situation would continue as did those holding a fatalistic view that there was nothing much they could do about this situation. Note that the first two associations are with middle-class personality attributes, the latter with one associated with the "culture of poverty." So the associations are not simple or straightforward, and only occur under adverse economic conditions.

Article 8 in Volume II presents my analyses in full, including a discussion of their practical implications. Although the "culture of poverty" idea had been criticized by a number of anthropologists on theoretical and ethnographic grounds (Leacock 1971; Valentine 1968), and others had demonstrated that these traits may serve to protect the mental health of those living in poverty (Parker and Kliner 1970), as far as I know this was the first time these psychological attributes had been demonstrated to have no relationship to economic performance. My paper on the culture of poverty won the 1971 Stirling Award in Culture and Personality from the American Anthropological Association, but the social and psychological issues it addressed remain unresolved.

Lessons for Behavioral Anthropology

Measuring psychological variables is hard work under the best of circumstances; it is doubly hard when working in a culture other than your own. So the task demands that you employ all the care and creativity you can muster, which is what makes it fun. Basically, you are trying to measure something which can be neither seen nor touched, a common problem in the physical sciences as well, and must therefore be inferred from measures of something else.

Since psychological variables are subjective phenomena, the usual strategy is to ask people to report what's going on in their heads. "How strongly do you believe . . . , Very strongly, strongly, not too strongly, not strongly at all," etc. But then you are faced with all the problems of self-report data: whether or not your subjects are willing—or able—to report these phenomena accurately.

The use of more indirect procedures, where the subject may not be as clear about what you are trying to get at, has its own problems. The reports are a *behavior*, whether or not they are your subjects' choices between carefully matched forced choice items on a scale like the Social Reaction Inventory or the stories they tell in response to TAT pictures. From these behavioral responses we *infer* some underlying psychological attribute giving rise to this behavior. The validity of this inference must somehow be demonstrated.

For example, as a measure of our migrants' "economic value orientation" we analyzed their responses to open-ended questions about what they liked or did not like about life in Denver and on the reservation. What we observed was a *behavioral tendency* among some to mention economic/material factors far more often than others. What we *inferred* from this was that underlying this behavior was a higher *psychological value orientation* toward economic/material goals. We validate this inferential leap by showing that under conditions of economic failure in the city this "value orientation" is associated with higher rates of drinking and drunkenness (as inferred from higher arrest rates). This also illustrates the issue, touched on in chapter 3, that the distinction between a "behavioral tendency" and a "personality predisposition" is a slippery one at best.

The Navajo project provided us with an opportunity to explore a wide range of psychometric strategies. The Social Reaction Inventory, with its large number of carefully constructed forced choice items, was the most conventional. Content analysis of open-ended questions, a self-anchoring scale in which subjects defined the ends of the continuum on which they then placed themselves both now and in the future, and projective techniques designed specifically for Navajos were more unusual. But most unusual of all were the large number of measures in which we *inferred* underlying psychological predispositions from the *interaction* between various measures.

These included, for example, conflict between competing goals (economic value orientation and Navajo traditionalism), conflict between competing expectations (success staying in Denver or returning to the reservation), and a large number of feelings which were presumed to emerge only when objective economic conditions were poor: *disjunctions* between high economic goals or need for achievement and a poor job, *frustration* in the form of distorted memories about how long it took to get even this poor job, *fatalistic feelings* about ever doing better, and for those with an extended future time perspective, a tendency to project this failure into the future. Perhaps most interesting of all, we inferred a dissatisfaction with their decision to migrate if their job did not earn them as much or more than they had previously earned before migration.

From a psychometric point of view this latter measure is particularly interesting because it is based on a comparison between two objective measures—wages before and after migration—rather than self-reports of migrants' internal states. Since all psychological measurement is inferential, drawing inferences about feelings of frustration and disappointment from objective measures such as wages is really no more problematic—perhaps less problematic—than responses to a direct question such as "How satisfied are you with your life here in Denver? Would you say, very satisfied, somewhat satisfied, not too satisfied, or not satisfied at all?"

This would be a typical "psychological" self-report question, but one which we never bothered to ask.

Since behavioral science is still in its infancy, I hope that my work contributes not simply to the body of empirical "facts" about human behavior, but also to the corpus of useful *techniques and strategies* for collecting these facts. For my own pleasure I try to use as wide a variety of procedures as possible. I approach research a bit like a non-Western farmer who resists the recommendations of well-meaning agricultural "experts" to plant his entire field with a single crop. If something goes wrong he'll starve. Instead, he prefers to intercrop with a variety of plants in a number of small plots with differing soils and microclimates. Not only does he learn from experience what "works" best, but also if one crop fails another may flourish and his family won't go hungry. No researcher wants to go hungry either.

Notes

1. Hypothetical constructs such as "gravity" are also common in the physical sciences, and can only be inferred and measured by their presumed effects.

2. For example, Lawrence LeShan (1952:589) defined time perspective as "the perceived relationship of the individual and his goals in time," and elaborated in the form of a series of questions: "How far ahead is the time span with which the individual is concerned? What is the crucial time limit during which he will frustrate himself in order to attain a goal? Does he relate his behavior primarily to the far future, the immediate future, the present, or the past?" Melvin Wallace (1956:240) limited his analysis to "future time perspective," defined simply as "the timing and ordering of personalized future events," including both their "extension" and "coherence."

3. Russ Bernard (2002:38-42) discusses operational definitions for anthropologists in chapter 2 as part of the foundation of social research.

4. Wallace used as his measure of temporal extension the difference between his subject's present age and their age when the most remote event mentioned was expected to occur. Not only does this waste 90% of the data, but we found that extension scores based on the most extreme items were less stable and less consistent (reliable) than an extension score based on the median.

5. Although this test had been consciously constructed to minimize cultural referents, we found highly significant Anglo–non-Anglo differences within our test population. These can probably be accounted for by differences in verbal skills, since for most Native American and Hispanic students English was their second language.

6. For a good discussion of this and other scaling techniques currently being used by anthropologists, including Guttman scales (Graves, Graves, and Kobrin

1969) and the Semantic Differential, which we used to measure Type A and Type B personality traits among an ethnically mixed group of subjects in New Zealand (Graves and Graves 1985), see chapter 12 in Bernard (2002).

7. For a full discussion of this procedure and a copy of both the high school and adult version, see Jessor, Graves, Hanson and Jessor, 1968:297-299 and appendices 2 and 3.

8. William Henry (1947) developed a modified version of the TAT, using a Native American artist, and collected protocols from about 1,000 children ages six through eighteen among five tribes: Papago, United Pueblos, Hopi, Navajo, and Pine Ridge Sioux. But his monograph only compares the general psychological characteristics of Hopi and Navajo based on these TAT protocols with ethnographic impressions of modal personality structure.

7

Social Channeling of Behavior

When we asked Navajo migrants themselves for the cause of their heavy drinking, they usually mentioned social pressure from their friends. "Whenever I see another Navajo," one migrant complained, "he wants me to have a drink with him." The previous chapter makes clear that this is by no means a complete explanation of migrant drunkenness. Psychological motivation to get drunk, grounded in economic marginality, proved to be extremely important. In an integrated science of human behavior, however, our goal is to tap a wide range of economic, social, psychological, and cultural determinants. Peer group influences cannot be dismissed as pure rationalization. Nor can cultural norms of what these peers will consider appropriate behavior. This chapter will deal with the complementary influences of social pressures and constraints, and the way these channel individual motivation within a framework of culturally prescribed patterns of drinking behavior. *All* of these influences contribute to our understanding of within-group variation in behavior, in what Abraham Kaplan has aptly referred to as a *concatenated* explanation (1964: 329ff).

Peer Group Influences on Migrant Behavior

As his task within our research team, Pete Snyder took major responsibility for looking at a migrant's *social* adjustment to life in Denver (Snyder 1968, 1971, and 1973). As we saw in chapter 5, his initial model involved studying the process of assimilation into the wider, non-Navajo community. But as our research team began to learn from our interviews and case studies, as soon as a new migrant arrived in the city, most began seeking out other Navajos, and would then spend much of their spare time in each other's company. For the vast majority of Navajo migrants, (over 80%), a get-together with other Navajos became at least a weekly event and constituted their most significant social activity.

The reasons seem self-evident: The city is a strange and lonely place where a young Navajo migrant cannot help but perceive himself as an outsider. Unfortunately, however, almost all recreational activity among their peers, we came to appreciate, included alcohol. Thus the search for companionship usually resulted in drinking and drunkenness, with a consequent increase in the probability of arrest.

Anthropologists who have studied problems of urban migration and adjustment throughout the world have almost universally emphasized the important role of ethnic group members in the city in facilitating a new arrival's adjustment to urban life. (See the review by N. Graves and T. Graves 1974.) Nowhere, to my knowledge, however, have these observers raised the possibility that this urban reference group might *also* serve to socialize the new migrant to various forms of *undesirable* behavior. One conclusion of our Denver research, which I want to explore in this chapter, was that *the Native American peer drinking group can be treated as a* "deviant subculture," *and that those migrants who are most integrated into this subculture will have the highest rates of arrest for drunkenness and drinking-related problems.*

Calling a migrant's drinking behavior the result of his participation in a "subculture," however, is just another "cultural" explanation, undifferentiated in content and monolithic in scope. Equally important is an examination of why individual migrants *differ* in their frequency of participation in that subculture and once there, differ in their degree of conformity to its norms. For this purpose we found it useful to examine the complex interplay of *social pressures* and *social constraints* bearing on each migrant, and their interaction with his *psychological predispositions*. Finally, I will argue that *the norms themselves* are grounded in objective circumstances and the psychological needs of the actors. Thus they, too, are subject to "explanation," and therefore cannot simply be deferred to as a final court of explanatory appeal.

Native American Drinking Group Norms

What a group considers appropriate behavior (such as their drinking group norms) can be determined in at least two ways: (1) by asking members what would be proper or improper to do under various circumstances, and (2) by observing what behavior actually receives social rewards and punishments from others in the group. Both approaches are useful and in many ways complementary. But the second is particularly strategic, because it reveals both the norms themselves and the mechanisms by which conformity to those norms is promoted.

As the anthropologist on Jessor's Tri-Ethnic team, I regularly spent time both observing and participating in the research community's many recreational drinking groups, particularly those of the local Ute Indians. Such "participant observation" is fun fieldwork, you may say. But returning home at 4 or 5 A.M. after spending the previous four to six hours passing around bottles of fortified Tokay wine, I wasn't always sure. My field notes were illegible and my head pounding.

So I was strongly motivated to moderate my intake in these situations. But my fellow drinkers made this impossible. No excuse of professional role or social vulnerability was acceptable. I was welcome to participate as long as I passed the bottle around with everyone else. I tried slipping my tongue into the mouth of the bottle to decrease the volume of my swig. Soon catching me at this deception, my drinking companions laughingly indicated with a finger on the side of the bottle just how much I was expected to swallow each round. The obvious goal was equal consumption and equal intoxication.

Drinking in the community's two local bars was no better, although I could at least go home at closing hour if I didn't feel up to extending the evening at one of the private parties which usually followed. At the bar drinkers sat around in clusters talking and laughing and buying rounds of beer for their entire group. This set up obligations for reciprocity among their friends, which inevitably led to more consumption than any one member might have bought on his own. As usual, I had difficulty keeping up with the pace of consumption, and my deviance became increasingly obvious as more and more unfinished bottles accumulated before me.

"Hey, what's wrong with you, man? Drink up!" my companions would admonish.

Public bars were the preferred setting when money was available, and beer the preferred beverage. In Ignacio, Ute Indians would be seen in the bars with greater frequency during the two weeks following monthly "per capita" payments from the tribal treasury; on Friday and Saturday nights when they had weekly paychecks in pocket; and early in the evenings. As their money decreased, business at the local liquor stores would pick up for a while ("more kick for a buck"), beer would be replaced by fortified wine, and consumption would shift from public to private settings. Thus the "periodicity" of "binge drinking" in this rural-reservation community, as well as the choice of beverage and setting, appeared to be grounded as much in available resources as in group norms.

Among the Navajo migrants we studied in Denver, recreational drinking fell neatly within this same general pattern. Since cash was far more available than on the reservation, and weekly paychecks were usually received on Friday afternoons, the vast majority of single males (like their working-class non-Indian neighbors) could be seen drinking beer with their friends in local bars on Friday and Saturday evenings. Several of my students and I observed these drinking groups in action and recorded the mechanisms by which participation was fostered and rewarded. These mechanisms were familiar to me and quite similar to those reported among various Indian drinking groups elsewhere (Curley 1967; Devereux 1948; Du Toit 1964; Ferguson 1968; Heath 1964; Honigmann and Honigmann 1945; Hurt and Brown 1965; Lemert 1958).

The large, predominantly male Navajo drinking groups we observed appeared to be relatively constant from weekend to weekend, though individual members might come and go. Both individuals and groups would circulate among the eight or ten preferred bars during the evening, with core members finally ending up at someone's apartment after closing hours. Arms around each other, participants displayed a great deal of companionship and conviviality. Those with money would periodically buy beers all around, the same pattern of "rounds" drinking I had observed in Ignacio. Sanctions for less than full participation included appeals to their ethnic identity ("Aren't you an Indian, man?") and ridicule ("Don't be a sour-faced white!") A few older Navajo couples might be seen sitting to one side of the bar, or a young couple more interested in each other than in their drinks. But solitary Indian drinkers were conspicuous by their rarity.

As reported in chapter 5, these friendship groups were subsequently identified in a more formal and systematic way through the use of a sociometric test. (See Snyder 1968, 1971, and 1973.) These observational data were also supplemented by quantitative material on drinking patterns obtained from interviewing the migrants themselves. Although some under-reporting of their quantity and frequency of alcohol consumption is to be expected (see chapter 3), there is no reason to believe that reports on beverage preference and the social context of their drinking would be biased. As we will see below, these interview data make it clear that descriptions based on field observations alone, however valuable and rich in content, present far too uniform a picture of Indian drinking behavior, and overemphasize the role of the conspicuous (and easily observed) peer drinking group.

Based on our interview data, the one ethnographic generalization that can be made with confidence concerning the drinking behavior of these Navajo young men is that the major beverage consumed *and desired* is beer. About 90% of the drinkers said they preferred beer, and 95% reported that this was their usual beverage, whether we interviewed them in the city or on the reservation. (This was true of 83% of our matched comparison group interviewed on the reservation as well.) So we are no longer dealing with the "winos" of more traditional ethnographic description, at least among younger Indians with money in their pockets. Only two subjects in our entire migrant sample (N = 259) expressed a preference for wine, and only seven reported that this was their "usual" beverage. Only four within the reservation comparison group (N = 113) said they preferred wine, and only five said it was their "usual" alcoholic beverage. So much for the validity of more casual ethnographic conclusions (Heath 1964).

But beyond beverage choice our generalizations break down. Among those interviewed in the city, 59% said they usually drank in public places with their friends. So the peer drinking group described above is clearly the *dominant* pattern. But 41% of drinkers said they usually drank in private homes, either alone or with their families. So this is a substantial *secondary* pattern, one rarely observed by anthropologists (including ourselves), and never reported in the literature. It is this *variation* in participation in the peer drinking group which provided us with an important opportunity to test its role in promoting problem drinking. Clearly, participating in a peer drinking group in a public bar, and therefore being subject to its norms of behavior, was a *choice*.

The relationship between the degree of participation in these public, recreational drinking groups, drunkenness, and arrest rates proved easy to demonstrate empirically. (See Volume II, article 5.) In an effort to tease out the differential impact of Navajo peers on a migrant's drinking habits (as well as other aspects of his social adjustment in the city) each was asked (*before* questions about their drinking behavior) whether or not they had any Navajo kin or friends in the city when they first arrived. Then they were asked at the time of the interview, "How often do you get together with other Navajos in Denver?" Similar questions were then posed concerning social contacts with Indians other than Navajos and with non-Indians. These questions enabled us to determine how readily a migrant could become mapped into a Navajo friendship group, the *frequency* with which he was currently interacting with his Navajo peers, and whether or not they constituted his *exclusive reference group*.

The relationship between three measures of social integration and urban arrest rates is presented in table 7.1. Regardless of the measure used, those migrants who were most thoroughly mapped into the Navajo ethnic community in Denver had the highest arrest rates.

Table 7.1. Social Relationships in Denver versus Arrest Rates

	Proportion of all migrants	Arrest rate per 100,000 pop.
Kin and friends at arrival:		
None	47%	71,000
Any	53%	108,000
Frequency of Navajo interaction:		
Less than once a week	18%	43,000
Every weekend	46%	98,000
More than once weekly	36%	114,000
Friendship pattern in the city:		
Some non-Navajo friends	52%	72,000
Exclusively Navajo friends	48%	118,000

These figures are impressive evidence that the recreational drinking groups we were observing put their members at risk by putting a lot of pressure on them to get drunk. To say that these Indians were conforming to a "cultural pattern" of heavy recreational drinking, however, is to say little of explanatory interest. Even to recognize that some migrants are more quickly and thoroughly mapped into these groups than others, and therefore more subject to their norms, only affirms that the situation is more complex than most ethnographic observers acknowledge. We still needed to understand what factors were responsible for these *differences* in frequency of participation.

Social Controls against Drunkenness: The Role of Wives

One factor that proved crucial was the role of *wives*. Whatever social controls there may be on the reservation, these are clearly attenuated when an Indian migrates to a city. More than most urban dwellers, he is apt to be relatively anonymous, and no longer under the eye of kinsmen or elders. Eighty percent of the Navajos coming to Denver, for example, were unmarried on arrival, and had left all family controls behind. And almost half (44%) were under twenty-one. Like most single young men away from home for the first time, a Navajo migrant is particularly subject to the temptations to engage in behavior he may have had less opportunity to try before. Heavy drinking is one of these.

Among married migrants, Navajo wives have powerful incentives to keep their husbands' drinking under control: not only does it use up family time and resources, but it increases the probability of sexual dalliance, spousal abuse, or a run-in with the police. Empirically, we found that among married migrants drinking problems were significantly reduced and their chances of remaining in the city were significantly increased.

Romola McSwain, a visiting graduate student from the University of Hawaii who joined our project to conduct her M.A. thesis, took particular responsibility for this part of our study. Since we were still in an exploratory phase when she arrived, Romola started her research by interviewing every Navajo migrant's wife we knew of in the city at that time (N = 28) using appropriate parts of the survey interview being administered to the men, plus a more open-ended interview guide that she developed herself. She then carefully selected eight women for in-depth case studies who represented differing degrees of contact with non-Navajos, variation in the balance of power with their husbands, and apparent success or failure in promoting their family's economic and social adjustment to urban life. A ninth case study of total failure was reconstructed from an interview with the husband while he was in jail, BIA records, and comments from other Navajos (McSwain 1965; this same case is subject to further systematic analysis in Ziegler and Graves 1972).

Almost every migrant wife Romola interviewed considered drunkenness, or the danger of drunkenness, as the foremost problem in her marriage. Keeping her husband away from his drinking companions, extracting promises of abstinence or at least moderation, and punishing his indiscretions, was a major activity—and preoccupation—of migrant wives. They spoke of it freely and at length. In one case, for example, most of the courtship consisted of a demonstration by the prospective bridegroom that he was capable of controlling his drinking (McSwain 1965).

Bryan Michener's case study of "Harrison Joe," which introduces my article on the personal adjustment of Navajo migrants (Volume II, article 5), illustrates how quickly the problem arises for a typical single migrant, and how likely it is to lead to arrest and a night in jail. This was quite enough for Harrison Joe. With only a lousy job from which he was soon fired, lonely and discouraged, he returned to the reservation only a couple of weeks after arrival.

Being married, however, doubles the probability that a new migrant will remain in the city at least eighteen months (from 23% to 46%) and more than halves his probability of arrest (from a rate of 128,000 per 100,000 man-years in the city for migrants who were single their entire time in Denver to 62,000 for those married at arrival, and only 32,000 for those who remain married throughout their stay).

Bob McCracken, another member of our Navajo research team, collected a remarkable hour-by-hour diary of his first two weeks in Denver from Andy Bodie, a married migrant, which illustrates how wives can intervene to keep their husbands sober (McCracken 1968).[1] On his fifth day in the city, Friday afternoon, Andy met by chance his unmarried "brother" (doubtless a cousin) on the street. Andy hadn't known he was in town, and they hadn't seen each other in years. His brother immediately invited Andy up to his apartment for a beer, Andy's first drink in the city. On returning home to his wife, Andy reports, "I told her I met my brother on my way coming back. Told her I drunk beer at his apartment. Then she said the next time don't drink any beer or don't fool around with him because if he gets you drunk he might let you alone and you might get hurt. So don't bother to fool around with him she said. I said okay." The subject arose again while they prepared dinner. "She must have thought I was just drinking around down town."

The following Wednesday, when Andy visited his brother again, his wife accompanied him, remaining discretely outside. Andy timed all his social interactions for us, and reported only staying in his brother's apartment for about five minutes: "Then I told him I have to see some one soon then I lift." When he returned to his wife, she asked, "What took so long? I told her we have been talking about something special. We start walking toward Safeway. I told her everything we talk about."

The following Sunday his wife again accompanied Andy to his brother's apartment, and when the brother left to purchase a six-pack of beer, she lectured Andy on the dangers of drink. "She said how like to drink with your brother? I said just to have a little fun. She said you shouldn't do that. Because he might get you in trouble. I said well I won't do that any more. She said be careful what you do."

From the other family case material Romola collected, far from being an unusually possessive and demanding wife, Mrs. Bodie appears quite typical. Navajo women have strong personal motives for keeping their husbands sober. As the arrest rates presented above indicate, most wives were successful in this campaign. But five gave up and returned to the reservation alone. Their husbands' arrest rate was an astonishing 226,000 per 100,000 man-years in the city!

A shift in the *context* of drinking with marriage can be documented from our interview data as well, but would probably have been overlooked if we had depended solely on the conventional ethnographic methods of participant observation and key informant interviewing. See table 7.2. Although almost as many married migrants reported drinking at least weekly as did single migrants, most of this drinking now took place at home. And usually they drank alone or with their family, where they would not be

Table 7.2. Effects of Marriage on Frequency and Context of Drinking*

	Married (N = 48)	Single (N = 50)
Frequency drink?		
At least weekly	58%	63%
Less than weekly	42%	37%
Usual location?		
Public	33%	64%
Private	50%	32%
Both	17%	4%
With whom?		
Friends	44%	74%
Family	15%	00%
Alone	42%	26%

* Based on those interviewed in Denver who admitted to being drinkers: N = 98.

subject to peer group pressure to get drunk, or be so readily exposed to potential arrest. So this shift in the *context* of drinking serves as an important explanation of their substantially lower arrest rates.

Psychological Motivation and Social Conformity

We have now shown that a few sociological variables—marital status and peer group membership—have gone a long way to explaining within-group variation in excessive drinking among Navajo migrants to Denver. But an integrated science of human behavior directs us to look at a migrant's psychological *motivation* to get drunk as well. It is in the interplay between external pressures and constraints and internal motivation and inhibition that our greatest understanding of human behavior will be found.

In the last chapter we saw that the understandable frustration associated with the economic marginality experienced by many migrants clearly leads to heavy drinking and high arrest rates. This doubtless leads to even further frustration and economic problems, thereby initiating a vicious cycle which typically results in a decision to return home. As in the case of Harrison Joe, staying in Denver just doesn't seem worth it.

So now we are able to formulate another testable hypothesis which takes us further beyond ethnographic description to an explanation of the variation among migrants in their drinking and arrest rates, even among married migrants: *Those migrants who receive the least economic rewards in the city will have the greatest motivation to get drunk, and will therefore be the most likely to seek out peer drinking groups, conform to their heavy drinking norms, and get themselves arrested, even if they are married.*

As we saw in the last chapter (and reported in more detail in Volume II, article 5) a variety of economic indicators all show the same results: Those with the greatest amount of unemployment, lowest wages, and especially those whose wages were no higher than they had received before migration, all had substantially higher arrest rates than those in a more favorable economic position. When we look at any of these economic indicators, crosscut by marital status, a very similar pattern emerges: When a migrant's economic position is reasonably *good* and his psychological motivation to get drunk is therefore *low*, his drinking behavior appears to be relatively controlled, and his marital status is of little importance with regard to drunkenness and arrest. But when his economic situation is *poor* and his motivation to get drunk is therefore *high*, his marital status becomes a crucial factor in whether or not he drinks enough to get himself arrested.

Table 7.3 offers a typical example, using the indicator that best seems to tap a major source of frustration: a low starting wage relative to what he had earned before moving to the city. In the upper half of the table, where our subjects wages are relatively good, arrest rates are similar and relatively low regardless of marital status. But in the lower half of the table where we infer that our subjects are feeling economic frustration arrest rates are substantially higher. But being married reduces these rates by half.

Table 7.3. Economic Pressures and Marital Controls

Starting Wage	Proportion of all migrants	Arrest rate per 100,000 pop.
Higher than highest premigration wage *and*		
Married	7%	43,000
Single	34%	42,000
Same or lower than highest premigration wage *and*		
Married	14%	72,000
Single	45%	154,000

We consistently found a similar pattern when we looked at the interaction between economic pressures and peer pressures. Economic pressures provided the *psychological motivation* to get drunk, peer pressures provided the *social context* to do so. Regardless of what measure we used of how fully a migrant was mapped into his Navajo peer group in the city, when crosscut by his economic status we obtained similar results. Here is a typical example:

When a migrant's wages are relatively good, getting together with his friends even quite frequently does not increase his risk of arrest. (Although 31,000, 59,000, and 17,000 arrests per man-year in the city do not form a linear trend, they are all low compared with the 76,000 arrests per man-year in the city among those experiencing economic disappointment who interact with peers the *least* often: less than once a week. And for those getting together with their friends the *most* often, more than once per week, the difference between subjects with relatively good wages—low psychological motivation to get drunk—and those with relatively poor wages is dramatic. See table 7.4.)

We conclude that if a migrant perceives his wages as *poor*, then he is apparently far more likely to get drunk—and therefore arrested—whenever he gets together with his friends. And the more often he does so, the higher his risk of arrest. Peer pressures and marital controls seem to be operating in a very similar manner: *Social pressures and constraints have their greatest effect on migrant drinking and arrest rates when their economic position is marginal and their motivation to get drunk is therefore high.*

Table 7.4. Economic Pressures and Peer Pressures

Frequency of Peer Interaction	Proportion of all migrants	Arrest rate per 100,000 pop.
Less than once per week *and*		
Present wage higher than premigration	8%	31,000
Same or lower than premigration	7%	76,000
Once per week *and*		
Present wage higher than premigration	27%	59,000
Same or lower than premigration	21%	157,000
More often than once per week *and*		
Present wage higher than premigration	16%	17,000
Same or lower than premigration	21%	231,00

The Indian Peer Drinking Group as a "Deviant Subculture"

One final question needs to be addressed: Why do Navajo migrants choose *drinking* as a preferred form of recreational activity rather than bowling or basketball? Is this a matter of historical accident or the absence of alternative recreational opportunities? Or is this choice itself and the peer drinking group norms which result, as I have come to believe, a logical response to the psychological needs of the participants?

A number of observers of Native American drinking on various reservations have echoed Lemert's suggestion that Northwest Coast Indian drinking groups arose in part "because there is nothing else to do" (1958:336; see also DuToit 1964 and Dozier 1966). But in Denver there were plenty of available alternatives, even recreational groups specifically oriented toward Indian participation. Several churches sponsored "Indian Centers," and for those turned off by church sponsorship, there was the Indian-run "White Buffalo Council" and numerous Indian dance groups and ball clubs. But few Navajo migrants chose to participate, and among those who did, the same names kept cropping up repeatedly on various membership roles. So again, participation in peer recreational drinking groups is a deliberate *choice* among a range of possible alternatives.

As we had learned, those migrants who got the poorest and least stable jobs on arrival in the city quickly sought out Navajo drinking groups. And as we have just seen, for any given level of social participation, those who were economically most marginal participated the most frequently and drank the heaviest within these groups, therefore getting arrested the most often. From this converging evidence I came to formulate the following interpretation: *Peer group drinking parties are being chosen by these Indians as a major recreational outlet because drunkenness is a particularly appropriate response to their economic, social, and historical circumstances, and to the psychological needs which these circumstances have generated.* These recreational drinking groups fit neatly within an explanatory model which handles a wide range of social phenomena within our own society, from delinquent gangs to groups of drug users: the emergence of a "deviant subculture."

Our focus on "deviant behavior" in the Tri-Ethnic project often drew criticism from my anthropological mentors and colleagues. In general, anthropologists consider "deviance" to be a Western middle-class prejudice, a lack of conformity to Calvinist dictates of "proper" behavior, rather than a judgment-free analysis of different patterns of social behavior on their own terms. The vast anthropological literature on drinking behavior in non-Western societies rarely mentions any negative consequences of this behavior, even when these would seem obvious to any casual observer, including the participants themselves (Heath 1987). You don't have to be a missionary to note the undesirable results of drunken stupor or drunken brawls. Within the context of a Western urban society, furthermore, drunkenness is clearly "deviant" in that it calls forth legal sanctions: arrest and incarceration. Even though he may be "conforming" to the norms of his peer group, a Navajo drinker *knows* the potential consequences of his drunkenness, and chooses to do so anyway.

The more I have studied and experienced Native American peer drinking groups the more I have been struck by their *similarity* among various tribes with quite different contact histories, cultural traditions, and physical circumstances. Consequently, an understanding of these peer drinking groups requires a set of explanatory principles which are applicable to Native Americans as a *social category*, regardless of tribal affiliation. As I noted in chapter 2, from my earliest work on the Tri-Ethnic project I was struck by how neatly Native American peer drinking groups fit Robert Merton's (1957) description of a "retreatist" adaptation to "disjunctions" between the goals this class of people were seeking, and their low expectations of being able to achieve these goals through the "legitimate means" available to them. These are exactly the conditions for the emergence of a "deviant subculture."

Cloward and Ohlin (1960:108), major spokespersons among deviant subculture theorists, describe the structural conditions under which such groups may arise:

> When a social system generates severe problems of adjustment for occupants of a particular social status, it is possible that a collective challenge to the legitimacy of the established rules of conduct will emerge.

These same structural conditions have also been seen at the root of individual psychopathology (Rotter 1954). Why, then, has a *collective* mode of adaptation arisen so commonly among Native Americans? (This does not mean that structural marginality may not *also* be at the heart of individual Indian psychopathology.) Such a collective response is common, Cloward and Ohlin believe, when members of a particular social status have grounds for challenging the legitimacy of the social order and feel unjustly deprived of access to opportunities to which they are entitled (1960:117).

Among Navajo migrants such feelings of injustice doubtless arise both because they have been led to expect a good deal more than the city is able to deliver, and because they are confronted by highly visible barriers to achievement in the form of economic and social discrimination. This "system blame" is reflected among our subjects by their significantly stronger feelings of *external control* than comparable whites, feelings which we saw in the last chapter are strongly associated with high arrest rates when they are in fact occupying poor and unstable jobs. By contrast, Cloward and Ohlin believe, solitary adaptations are more common when the blame for personal failure is placed on one's *own* inadequacies.

System blame—and resulting alienation—breeds tension toward the carriers of the dominant ideology, who are also recognized as the source of their oppression. Overt hostility toward Whites is rarely observed among Native American drinkers, who usually direct their alcohol-released aggression toward other Indians (particularly members of other tribes) or their wives. But it is my conviction, based on a good deal of personal experience with drunken Indians, that this represents displaced aggression, and that the true target of their hostility can and does emerge when social barriers to its expression are removed. My evidence is anecdotal, however, rather than being grounded in systematic data, and needs to be tested.

One example: Many years ago I picked up a hitchhiker on the Navajo reservation, and we shared his bottle and engaged in friendly banter for many miles. The drunker he became, however, the more he began ranting against the injustices of white society, injustices which I readily acknowledged. When we finally stopped at a campground and used the public toilets, I was shocked and surprised when with angry epithets toward "Whites" he suddenly pulled a knife and attacked me. This was sobering, and I managed to lock him in the latrine until I could find some Navajo police to subdue him. In retrospect, I believe that by giving him a ride and sharing his bottle I had reduced the social distance between us to the point where I lost the protection which my white skin normally provides.

Flaunting violations of the "White man's" mores in the form of public drunkenness serves as an indirect display of anti-White feelings and a challenge to the legitimacy of their laws. Collective support for such acts, in the form of group pressures to get drunk, the antithesis of middle-class white norms of moderation, provides social validation for this form of "deviant" behavior.

Finally, why has a "retreatist" mode of adaptation developed among Indians rather than a more active effort to overcome their structural marginality through personal betterment, illegal behavior, or rebellion? The answer, I believe, lies in the helplessness and hopelessness which so many Indians feel as a result of a long history of oppression, exploitation, and dependency since the European invasion. "Retreatism" through alcohol and drugs, Merton and many other theorists now believe, is a response to repeated failure to obtain the rewards of the dominant society through other routes. Certainly military pacification is an important historical factor for all Native Americans, as is racial discrimination. And despite occasional displays of "Red Power," most Native American young people appear to recognize the political limitations inherent in their small numbers (Steiner 1968). Native Americans, furthermore, have as little access to the *illegitimate* opportunity structure of big city crime as they do to the *legitimate* opportunity structure. For those whose lack of education and marketable skills condemns them to inevitable failure, drunkenness is a convenient, readily available, and relatively inexpensive avenue of temporary escape.

Thus the peer recreational drinking group, which provides so many positive interpersonal rewards as well, is a social invention which ideally serves the psychological needs of a large proportion of Native American young men in the United States today.

Obviously there are exceptions. The current president of the Navajo Nation, Kelsey Begaye, for example, hopes that his own life story may serve as an inspiration for Navajo youth.[2] After being discharged from a Navajo communications unit in Vietnam in 1971, he spent several years going from job to job, quitting or being fired, and ended up, he acknowledges, a drunken migrant bum on the streets of Los Angeles. After returning to the reservation in 1975 he met his future wife, Marie, who befriended him despite his alcohol problems, and helped guide him into a Christian revival conversion experience. He has been alcohol-free ever since, and became an alcohol and drug abuse counselor for many years. He now hopes as Tribal President to help other Navajos acquire the vision he lacked as a young man.

One last point. Over 80% of our Navajo migrant sample participated in these recreational drinking groups in Denver at least weekly. Not all of them were experiencing frustration and failure in the city. But once a pattern of group drunkenness becomes normative, it also serves as a standard of behavior for some participants who might not have the psychological needs which generated the pattern in the first place. The existence of the subculture itself, as mediated by the social pressures exerted by core participants, becomes one cause for the drinking behavior of others who come in contact with it. (Including myself!) This could well account for the fact that even among groups of migrants who otherwise appear to be relatively well-adjusted to urban life, at least with respect to their economic achievement, arrest rates (indicative of drunken excess) are substantially higher than for comparable working-class groups of Hispanics and Whites. This residual of unexplained drunkenness can perhaps best be explained by their participation in this pan-Indian deviant drinking "subculture." In conclusion, "cultural norms" do have a role to play in understanding group differences in human behavior, and in channeling that behavior in distinctive ways. But they are only *part* of the explanation.

Methodological Lessons for Behavioral Anthropology

All behavior is multi-determined. Social structural variables, as I first learned on the Tri-Ethnic project, are usually as good predictors of behavior as psychological variables, (see chapter 4, tables 4.2 and 4.3), and many social psychologists believe that these situational variables are the best predictors of all (Ross and Nisbett 1991). In our Navajo project, for example, *economic* variables proved to be our best predictors. But this was particularly true *when we looked at the way they were likely to be perceived by our subjects* (a psychological interpretation). Anthropologists, through their study of "norms of appropriate behavior" (an important aspect of a group's "culture") also have hit upon a part of the truth. People normally *do* conform to social expectations, *when they are motivated to do so.* Thus each discipline has a legitimate claim to part of the truth, and the explanatory importance of its own pet concepts. But no one discipline can claim *all* of the truth.

As a corollary, no one explanation of a phenomenon such as Indian drunkenness is ever complete, and given the present crudity of research strategy and measurement in the social sciences today, no one approach to explanation is alone very convincing. What we need is to *converge* on the problem, bringing evidence to bear on the same topic from a number of sources simultaneously with each piece of empirical data deriving its significance in part from the way it articulates with others.

This analysis of Navajo migrant drinking behavior in Denver is as thorough and "concatenated" an explanation as I have ever been able to mount. It is also the closest thing to a traditional "anthropological" analysis as I have presented, with its attempt to demonstrate the existence of a Native American "deviant subculture": weekend "binge drinking" by participants in recreational peer drinking group. But the limitations of this "normative" analysis have been recognized and three additional questions addressed:

1. Why do some members of a group *choose* to participate in some cultural pattern of behavior more often than others?
2. When they do choose to participate, why do some *conform* more fully (in our case, get drunk more often) than other participants? And finally,
3. How did these norms of appropriate behavior *come into being*? What functions do they serve the individual participant and the group?

When these issues are fully dealt with, through systematic economic, sociological, and psychological analyses, then the contribution of more qualitative ethnographic observations to a more complete understanding of some behavior of interest can be recognized and appreciated.

One other lesson for behavioral anthropology emerges from this work. Conventional ethnographic work has its place within a unified science of human behavior, as even Dick Jessor has come to recognize. (See his introduction to Jessor, Colby, and Shweder 1996.) But generally speaking more casual ethnographic observations should serve as the *beginning* of an investigation rather than its *end*. And they need to be treated as *hypotheses* in need of support and validation through the collection of more quantitative data. Frequently, "qualitative" observations and speculations, as I have drawn on here from my own field experience, can illuminate and help us to interpret more fully our quantitative data and their statistical relationships: a "qualitative/quantitative mix." But as we have seen in this chapter, ethnographic conclusions—without being supported by more systematic data from a representative sample of a large number of subjects—are suspect, and can be way off the mark. The quantitative data take time and energy to collect and analyze. But they can often lead to surprises, and to a far richer and more differentiated picture of a group's "culture" than most anthropologists present.

Notes

1. Andy Bodie is the only subject in our research reports who, at his request, is referred to by his real name. Bob continued to collect diary material from Andy periodically, even after he returned home to the reservation, and 35 years later they are still in regular contact. An autobiography is projected.

2. Based on a report in the San Francisco *Chronicle*, December 20, 1999, page D4.

8

Samples and Surveys

Whenever anthropologists talk with one or more "key informants" we are "sampling." Each serves as a "spokesperson" for some segment of their group who shares their characteristics. If we have been careful in their selection, most important segments of the population will be included: older women, older men, younger women, younger men, "traditional" or modernized, etc. A key issue is their *representativeness:* how adequate are they as spokespersons for their community? Because from what they tell us we will be tempted to draw inferences and make generalizations about the group as a whole. How convincing are these generalizations?

Most early anthropologists, right up through Margaret Mead, had the notion that each group's "culture" was so homogeneous and so widely internalized by all members of the group, that just about anyone could serve as a spokesperson for the group as a whole. We know better now. In the past, our choice of informants was often a matter of convenience: who was available, willing, and able to talk with an outsider, and reasonably knowledgeable about the topic under investigation. If our focus was on factual material—whether or not the community possessed various "culture traits" from Kroeber's list—or aspects of their way of life about which there was high consensus, such as language, kinship structure, the annual ceremonial round, "convenience sampling" of informants probably didn't matter much. If a handful of them essentially all agreed on some point, little further information would be obtained by more careful sampling of additional spokespersons. Romney and his associates have demonstrated mathematically that if informants have a reasonable level of "cultural competence" and the questions are a matter of "fact" (such as whether a disease is "contagious" or not) then interviewing six to ten of them is probably quite enough to establish these facts "accurately" at a high level of confidence (Romney, Weller, and Batchelder 1986). If the research questions are more interesting, however, such as when Weller asked her informants what diseases they believed to require "hot" or "cold" medicines for their treatment (Weller 1983), a lack of widespread agreement among respondents makes it impossible to specify the "correct" cultural belief, even using the mathematically sophisticated methods suggested by Romney et al. For questions of this kind there simply is no "cultural consensus."

But it is just these kinds of questions, where there is a *lack* of consensus and a wide range of within-group *variability* in our subjects' responses that behavioral anthropologists are most interested in asking. Because it is just these beliefs and expectations, attitudes and values, lodged inside their heads that we want to relate to variation in their behavior in order to predict and explain that behavior. Even if our goal is simply to demonstrate ethnic group ("cultural") differences in these beliefs and behavior, careful sampling of the population(s) under investigation is necessary to ensure that all segments are proportionately represented and the full range of variation documented. Then the reader will have greater faith in the validity of our generalizations, and future investigators can build on our results with confidence, to compare with other groups, for example, or to show changes over time.

So drawing a representative sample of subjects from the population being studied is a typical task confronting the behavioral anthropologist. Each subject who falls within our sample will be a "spokesperson" for all those with similar beliefs and values who did not happen to be selected. So we want to feel confident that no important segment of our research population fails to have a "spokesperson," and that the number of these spokespersons within our sample is proportional to the number of persons they represent in the larger group we are studying. Then, when we administer a questionnaire, psychometric procedures, or make other systematic observations of their behavior to infer what is going on in their heads (chapter 6) we will know that the full range of within-group variation is represented, and that we can reasonably and accurately infer the distribution of these attributes within the population as a whole. How to do this?[1]

The Tri-Ethnic Samples

Whenever you draw a sample, you need some way of defining the universe from which they will be drawn. In the Tri-Ethnic community research project Omer Stewart and his colleagues had conducted a careful house-to-house census of the school district, which served to define the geographic boundaries of our research community (Jessor, Graves, Hanson, and Jessor 1968:150-151). This gave us a full list of adults between the ages of twenty and sixty-five from whom to draw our survey sample. By dividing this list by sex and ethnic group and then taking every sixth name from among the Anglos and Hispanics, and every third name from among the Ute Indians we insured that our samples would be the size we wanted and representative of the community as a whole. (This is called "stratified random sampling.") The final samples actually interviewed consisted of 93 Anglos (45 men, 48 women); 60 Spanish (30 men, 30 women); and 68 Indians (35 men, 33 women).

The size of these samples is about right for most anthropological purposes. (See chapter 4.) Unless variability is very great, about sixty subjects is sufficient for making reasonable population estimates (Hansen, Hurrowitz, and Madow 1953). It is also large enough to insure expected cell frequencies of at least ten in a typical chi-square test. Doubling this number provides enough subjects for a three-variable pattern analysis (chapters 4 and 12). Collecting data from much more than this is probably a waste of your time; usually it is better to collect in-depth case material from a small group of representative subjects to flesh out the bones of your statistical analyses, as we did on the Navajo project. Furthermore, the larger the sample, the smaller the group difference or correlation which will be "statistically significant" (Morrison and Henkel 1970). As already discussed in chapter 4, our real interest is in *socially significant*, rather than statistically significant results. Samples of about this size normally yield both.

The Navajo Migrant Samples

For the Navajo project we had records from the Bureau of Indian Affairs on all Navajo men who had come to Denver under their relocation program, and we simply decided to interview every one of them who was currently living in Denver, or who arrived there during the life of the project. This yielded a group of 135 subjects. We also decided to interview a roughly equal size group of *former* migrants who had returned to the reservation. This was a far more formidable task, both because the reservation is much larger geographically than Denver, and because we did not have as clear and current addresses as we had for migrants living in Denver and in contact with the BIA Office of Employment Assistance on a regular basis. But during three summers of fieldwork we developed strategies for finding returnees, and ultimately interviewed one-third of them (N=124). About half of these were interviewed on a non-random basis employing geographic quote sampling methods. After we had gained experience, the second half of this sample was collected on a strictly random basis from what was now a full list of 373 names.

Knowing that "opportunistic samples" such as ethnographers typically rely on can yield quite different results from carefully selected random samples (Honigmann and Honigmann 1955), we decided to compared these two groups of returnees on all the variables we had measured. Since our field-workers had conscientiously attempted to find subjects from even remote areas of the reservation, we were pleased to discover that these two groups—those selected randomly and those selected on a more opportunistic basis—were essentially identical in their characteristics, permitting us to combine them and treat them as representative of *all* returnees from Denver.

The Reservation Comparison Sample

For our final summer of fieldwork (1966) we decided to interview a representative group of young men living on the reservation who had *not* migrated to a city. Our hope was that by examining how migrants differed from the average young man living on the reservation, we might better understand factors which led to their decision to leave the reservation. This work provided some interesting surprises.

The first thing Van and I had to do at the beginning of the summer was to draw a strictly random sample of young men from the Navajo tribal roles in the eighteen to thirty-six age range, carefully matched to our migrant sample. This would not have been possible even the previous summer, since the first systematic population register of 106,000 reservation residents had only just been completed and available on IBM cards a week earlier. So we were the first researchers to use this brand new database, which was exciting in itself (Graves 1966.)[2]

At this point the new population register was in a constant state of correction and revision, and we had no idea how accurate it would prove to be. Furthermore, young men in the eighteen to thirty-six age group could be expected to be particularly mobile, with many leaving the reservation in search of work. We therefore had no idea in advance how many predesignated names would be needed in order to obtain the number of completed interviews we wanted.

Our solution to this problem was simple, and could be useful to others faced with similar uncertainty. From the previous summer of fieldwork seeking out a random sample of "returnees" from Denver, we estimated that we might be able to find and interview about 50% of any predesignated group of young men. (This turned out to be a remarkably accurate guess!) Since we wanted roughly 120 completed interviews, this suggesting a predesignated sample of about 250.

But to be safe we drew 400 names. How then to ensure that those we actually found and interviewed would be a truly "random" sample of the age group from whom these names were selected? We accomplished this by assigning random numbers (hereafter called "priority numbers") from 1 to 400 to our random sample. Since there would be eight of us interviewing,[3] the sample was divided geographically into eight roughly equal groups, and within each of these groups the predesignated names were ordered by priority number. Each field-worker was then asked to obtain interviews from the fifteen available subjects on his list *who had the lowest priority numbers*. ("Unavailable" was defined as dead, working or living fairly permanently off-reservation more remote than the neighboring border towns, or completely unknown in his home area.) The priority numbers thus provided us with a set of randomly designated *replacements* for the unavailables, and assured that our interviewed sample would be random and representative, whatever the size of that sample might turn out to be. This is a form of "multi-stage" sampling, where we were sampling a sample.

After three weeks of field-work we all met in Flagstaff for a weekend of rest and relaxation, trading information, and horror stories. There we swapped names of persons on our lists who had moved to another researcher's area, and settled on a priority number cutoff. Since by this point we had already tracked down most of the people on our lists; even if we hadn't interviewed them as yet, we knew pretty well who was likely to be available. We could therefore estimate how high a priority number we would have to reach in order to obtain the desired number of completed interviews. (In our case we settled on a priority number of 250, the number we had previously estimated.) Such a system provides complete flexibility to meet any field contingency while still maintaining sampling rigor.

One hundred and thirteen comparison subjects were actually found and interviewed. A few of the 250 predesignated subjects were dead or unknown, but most of the others were living and working off-reservation, and were therefore similar to our migrant sample interviewed in Denver. Subjects were interviewed wherever we found them, using a modified version of the standard interview form we had used in the city. We had no refusals.

Finding Subjects in the Field

Our first step was to go to the headquarters of each school district within which our subjects lived, where we were told that current census information by families was maintained.[4] But these data proved to be of quite variable quality, often stored in old ledgers, new families added at the back, etc. And for common names like Begay and Yazzie, we were forced to thumb through endless lists. Finally, if the subject had assumed a last name which differed from that of his parents or guardians, it was almost impossible to find his family in these lists.

Local informants proved far more helpful. Sometimes there was a school census taker recruiting children for the fall who knew most of the families in the area. Also helpful were the public health nurses, chairmen of the local chapter houses, members of the local grazing committee (who had to see that all families in the area dipped their sheep each year), local traders (or more commonly, their Navajo assistants) and Navajo school employees who came from the area. Once pointed in the right direction, we asked anyone we saw.

The Navajo reservation is divided into "chapters," each of which elects a representative to the tribal council. Working through local chapter officials proved to be very helpful. Chapter houses have regular meetings, often weekly, to which many families from the area come. Chapter officials were happy to let our field-workers describe their job and its purpose at one of these meetings, and to read off names of those being sought from the area. One such meeting was worth 500 miles of driving.

Through the cooperation of the Navajo tribe our field-workers were able to obtain local high school students as field assistants, under the Navajo Youth Corps program. Their knowledge of local people and places made them well worth their modest pay. Furthermore, almost 20% of our random sample were unable to communicate adequately in English, a problem we had not run into among migrants in Denver. For factual questions, such as education and job history, these young Navajo assistants served quite adequately as interpreters as well.

Anyone who has worked on the Navajo reservation, or some third world site, will recognize how time-consuming and frustrating transportation problems can be. This is particularly true when tracking down predesignated subjects over long distances. Finding individual homes required a great deal of back-country driving. Most key access roads on the Navajo reservation were already paved, and the American Automobile Association had published a good map of the Navajo reservation. Other maps were available from the U.S. Geological Survey. But no maps showed the maze of local wagon tracks leading to individual homes and water supplies. These could only be learned from a knowledgeable assistant or by local inquiry.

Despite caution, cars do not last long when subjected to reservation roads. During our six weeks stay about half of us had car trouble serious enough to cost a day or more of field time. Small vehicles with a high center, short wheel base, and light weight, such as a VW car or bus, proved the most satisfactory. This last feature minimizes getting stuck in mud or sand, and makes getting unstuck relatively easy. Vans and SUVs, though more powerful, are also much heavier. And overhanging rear ends tend to bounce disconcertingly over rough roads. We always equipped our cars with a "Handyman" jack, tow chain, shovel, and extra gas and water.

Spring rains on the reservation generally end in May and don't begin again until August. But short storms can be dangerous at any time. And if the mud doesn't get you, the sand will.

The biggest problem in the field was not finding where a subject lived and how to get there, but catching him for an interview. Since our subjects were young males, many were working at least part-time during the summer: Only fifty-six, or about a quarter of the eligibles on our predesignated lists, were unemployed, and most of these were not sitting at home waiting to be interviewed. This meant returning to a subject's house periodically whenever his family thought he might show up, or tracking him down in the countryside or at work.

But even the closest kin were apt to be vague as to a subject's whereabouts. After a twenty-five-mile back-country drive we found the brother of one subject, who told us he was probably at his mother's place. Another five miles. There his mother said he was staying with his wife at her parents' sheep camp. Fifteen miles more. The wife hadn't seen him in days; come back next week. Next week we returned. The subject hadn't been home yet. The following week we returned. The wife had learned through a friend who knew one of the subject's friends that he had decided a couple of weeks before to go to California for work!

Another problem which was particularly acute for us, working among young males, was drunkenness and associated consequences among some of our subjects. Many young men on the reservation, particularly in the peripheral areas, spend a great deal of time hanging around the border town bars, and this sometimes proved to be a good place to look for them. After searching them all in Holbrook, one field-worker was led by a small boy into the bushes over the railroad tracks, where a subject was found sleeping it off with a group of friends. Several hours work thoroughly sobering him up yielded an interview. Another subject was interviewed in the Aztec jail, and a third while on the lam from the police. That the field-worker was able to obtain this interview at all is a credit to his ability to convince the subject that the research was not a tool of the white power structure, and that his confidence would be respected.

Perhaps the wildest chase occurred in the Tuba City area. A subject was reported to be living in Cameron, but no one seemed to know him there. Finally his home was found a few miles out of town. But there he was reported to be at his sheep camp near Flagstaff. One of the subject's brothers volunteered to serve as guide.

On arrival, after some thirty miles over back-country roads, we learned that our subject had left for the nearest bar, about twenty miles back the way we had come. There the bartender reported seeing him much earlier, and suggested we check the drunks stretched out in the sagebrush out back. Each was rolled over and identified, without success. Finally it was decided to return to the sheep camp and wait.

Later that afternoon, back at the camp, our subject's horse returned riderless, and his family decided he must have fallen off. So we back-tracked to the bar. There a new shift of bartenders suggested that he might have been arrested, so we went to Cameron, the nearest town, to check with the Navajo Tribal police. They were most cooperative, but didn't have him, and suggested maybe he had been picked up by the highway patrol, with headquarters in Tuba City. Since Tuba City, some twenty miles away, was home base and it was now late, we headed back there.

The highway patrol knew our subject well, but didn't have him. They suggested the Arizona State Patrol, with local headquarters in Flagstaff, and agreed to radio down there and check for us. And sure enough he was there, with a thirty-three-day sentence to serve.

We now thought we had him for sure. The Arizona State Police were very cooperative, and agreed to have our subject ready and waiting for us at 8 A.M. on the day he was due to be released. (He got out in eleven days on a two-for-one work program and good behavior.) And so we were at the Flagstaff jail promptly at 8, only to learn that he had been released 25 minutes earlier. The morning shift had overlooked the message on the blackboard to hold him.

So we went to the highway and checked five Indian hitchhikers without success. We then tried the bars. At the third he had been seen, and at the fourth he came to us, panhandling for the price of a beer. Our response was to recruit him for an interview and pay him for his time.[5]

Paying Subjects

When conducting survey interviews I have always believed it important to pay our subjects for their participation. This is an interesting practical and philosophical issue. Generally speaking, anthropologists prefer not to pay key informants for their help, feeling this might undermine their relationship and would rather reciprocate in other ways. But when conducting a survey among a large number of subjects whom you will perhaps never spend time with again, payment seems both warranted and useful. It shows respect for the value of their time and the seriousness of your research enterprise. (See Bernard 2002:200-202.) Perhaps our offer of payment also contributed to the fact that over my years of conducting cross-cultural surveys in a variety of cultural settings, refusals to participate have been rare. (Offering a token $20 payment for participation in a mailed survey which McCracken and I conducted recently among film directors, who obviously did not need the money, more than trippled their participation, and proved to be highly cost-effective. See McCracken 1999:14-15.)

Migrants versus Nonmigrants

Those of us interviewing our comparison sample on the reservation during the summer of 1966 were quick to notice that these young men seemed on the whole far better educated and acculturated than our migrant "returnees" interviewed during the previous summers. "Something must be wrong with our sampling," some of us feared. But the sample was good. What was "wrong" was that "migrants" are in no sense a "random sample" of Navajo young men. Overwhelmingly, we discovered to our complete surprise, migrants are drawn from those with a *middle* range of education, leaving behind them both the well-educated and the essentially illiterate. (See table 8.1.) The former are able to command the limited jobs that *are* available on or near the reservation, and thus have little motivation to migrate. The latter, by and large, have too few skills to enter the job market at all.

Table 8.1. Migrant/Nonmigrant Differences in Education

	Stayers (N = 108)	Returnees (N = 144)	Comparisons (N = 113)
Years of formal education			
11 or more	23%	10%	40%
8 to 10	37%	29%	20%
5 to 7	29%	50%	21%
4 or less	11%	11%	19%

The consequences of this phenomenon, particularly for migrants who return home, can be readily appreciated. They left the reservation in the first place because of hopeless competition for reservation jobs with better educated Navajos. Then in the city further selection takes place, when they find themselves in competition with better educated whites and other minority group members for even the poorest unskilled work. The best prepared Navajos can make it and stay. Consequently, *those who fail and quickly return home are now the residue of at least two selection processes: They first failed on the reservation, and then failed in the city.*

Back home again this unequal struggle continues. In economic terms it is vividly illustrated by comparing these Returnees with the Comparison group on their *reservation* employment. (See table 8.2). Three-quarters of the Returnees could command no more than unskilled manual jobs, significantly higher than the 62% among the comparison group. Their usual wage, $1.00 an hour, was significantly lower, and they spent significantly more time unemployed. The average Returnee found wage employment on or near the reservation only 10% of the time, whereas the Comparison group was employed on the average 25% of the time. The cumulative effect of these differences on annual income is even more striking. Whereas the median annual income for Returnees was only about $200 per year, for the Comparison group it was *well over three times higher.*

Table 8.2. Returnee vs. Comparison Group Differences in Economic Position on the Reservation

	Returnees (N = 144)	Comparisons (N = 113)
Reservation job type		
Semi-skilled or better	25%	38%
Unskilled manual labor	75%	62%
Normal wage		
Over $1.25 per hour	30%	52%
$1.25 or under	70%	48%
(Median wage)	($1.00/hr.)	($1.50/hr.)
Percent time employed		
75–100%	27%	33%
25–74%	15%	19%
Under 25%	58%	48%
(Median % employed)	(10%)	(25%)
Average yearly income		
(Median wage x 2000 hours x median % employed)	$200	$750

These figures further highlight the economic dilemma for former migrants. Their greatest problem back home was *underemployment*. Half were employed no more than 10% of the time and earned no more than $200 per year in wages. So the economic pressures to try migration once more were strong. And in fact, most did so: Within two years half of the Returnees had left the reservation to try to make it in some urban area once again. See figure 8.1. And the curve showed little sign of tapering off. But again the majority would fail. For them, the reservation becomes a final refuge for a group of human beings highly selected for failure wherever they may live. It is these men, I came to believe, trapped in a revolving door of economic failure, who would constitute the hard core of problem drinkers who are such a conspicuous and pathetic feature of Gallup, New Mexico, and of most reservation border communities throughout the United States.

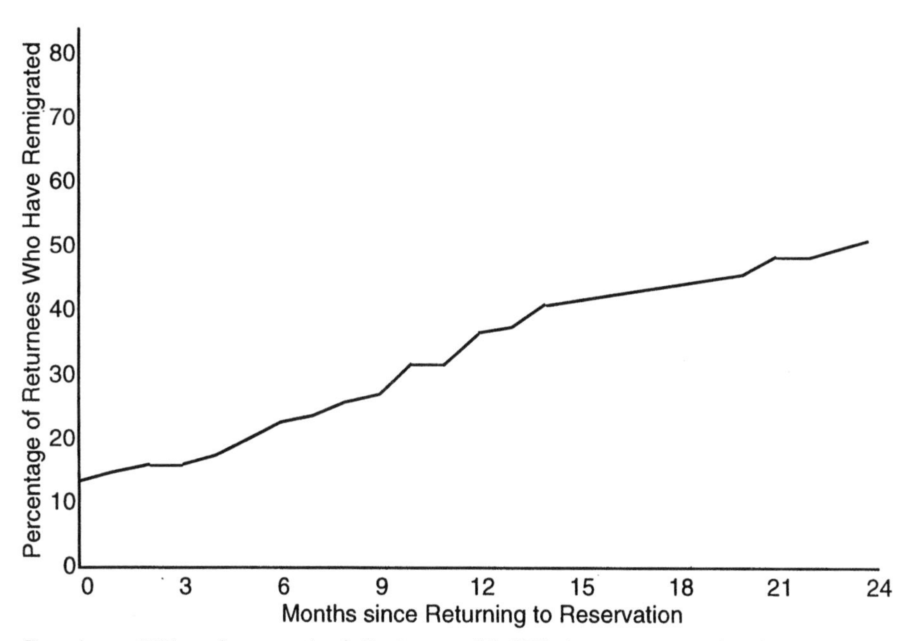

Based on a 25% random sample of all returnees (N=109) plus accurate remigration information on 112 cases.

Figure 8.1. Rate of Remigration by Reservation Returnees

Drinking on the Res

Because it was randomly selected form the reservation population as a whole, our Comparison sample provided an ideal opportunity to assess the typical drinking behavior of young reservation males in the late teens to mid-thirties age range. And because it was carefully matched to the age distribution of the Denver Returnee sample, it also provided an opportunity to test the hypothesis that former migrants caught up in a revolving door of failure contribute disproportionately to the problem drinking behavior so much in evidence on and around the reservation.

To address these two issues we turned to the section of our interview which asked subjects about their drinking behavior. The strategies used to maximize valid responses have already been discussed in chapter 3 on "Measuring Behavior." Self-reports concerning behavior which is socially disapproved are obviously subject to both conscious and unconscious distortion by subjects, and in evaluating our results this must be taken into consideration. But in describing the *context* of their drinking, including beverage preference, drinking location, and companions involved, such potential distortion seems less likely than when reporting the *quantity consumed and frequency drunk*. And from a pragmatic point of view, in the absence of arrest records such as we were able to use in Denver, these are the only data available to us concerning the reservation drinking behavior of our subjects.

Thirty percent of the Comparison sample reported currently being *abstainers*. For most of these (about 85%), however, this was not a lifelong pattern, but a more recent change in their lifestyle as a result of such factors as health, cost, problems on the job, accidents and fights, and pressure from religious teachers and family members, particularly their wives. So the drinking patterns described below are based on the reported typical drinking behavior of the 70% who said they were current drinkers.

Among young men on the reservation, the vast majority of drinkers (81%) both prefer and usually consume *beer*. Only five subjects said they preferred and drank only wine. (None of these fell in the eleven or more years of education category.) All the rest reported drinking beer, wine, and/or liquor in various combinations. This preference for beer may be an emerging new pattern among young Navajo males since the sixties, but it certainly calls in question the Navajo "wino" image reported in the ethnographic literature.

The *setting* and *social context* within which this drinking normally takes place are also of interest. These fall into six categories. In order of frequency: (1) the most common was an off-reservation town bar with friends and/or relatives—"brothers" and "uncles," Navajo kin terms for own and ascending generation males—42%; (2) next, similar companions, but in their own or someone else's home—20%; (3) then their own home, either alone or with nuclear family members (their wife, sister, or parents)—15%. (This is an emerging adoption of an "Angle" beer with dinner or TV pattern.) Next, (5) 8% reported usually drinking with their friends and/or relatives somewhere outside ("out of sight," as one candidly reported), behind a liquor store, in a car, or at a squaw dance; finally (6) another 6% in similar settings but alone. These categories and their ordering were essentially identical, regardless of educational level.

As among migrants in Denver, most Navajo drinking on the reservation was *social* (70%) and most of this took place *in public*. But unlike the situation in Denver, whether a young man was *married* or not seemed to have *no* impact on where he did his drinking and with whom: The proportion reporting most of their drinking within these six categories was essentially *identical* regardless of marital status.

More problematic are reports of *how much* these young Navajo men typically drank at a sitting, *how often* they drank, *how often they were drunk* during the last year, and whether or not they had ever been arrested for a drinking-related offense.

Estimates of how much subjects usually drank at a sitting (often reported as "a couple of beers" or "a six-pack") seemed so crude on examination that I won't bother to present them here. In the Tri-Ethnic study, which employed a far more refined set of repetitive questions to establish a "quantity-frequency index," expressed in average ounces of absolute alcohol consumed per day (a procedure which was unduly boring for both researchers and subjects), this measure consistently proved to be the poorest of our several measures of drinking behavior. (See chapter 3.) The simplified procedure developed for the Navajo project, however, appears on its face to have been even less reliable and valid.

How often our subjects reported having a drink seems a somewhat better measure. Thirty-seven percent of the sample reported drinking at least weekly, but those with eleven or more years of education were significantly less likely to do so (24%) than those with less education (47%). (Chi square = 4.15, $p<.05$.) There was no difference between these two groups in the proportion reporting that they got drunk ten or more times during the last year, however (36% and 38%, respectively), or had been arrested for a drinking-related offense (42% and 45%, respectively). Apparently, even better-educated young Navajo men were often drunk on the town and subject to arrest. And again, unlike the situation in Denver, whether or not the young man was married has *no* apparent effect on his reported drinking behavior.

The Denver Returnee sample, asked these same questions about their reservation drinking behavior, provide a basis for testing my "revolving door of failure" hypothesis. If a pattern of economic failure both on the reservation and in urban settings is a source of continuing psychological frustration assuaged by alcohol, as it was for migrants studied during their time in Denver itself, then we might expect that Returnees should be drinking more, and more frequently, than the Comparison samples who did not have this type of "revolving door" experience.

Given the logical basis of this hypothesis and the clear associations we had found between economic failure and high arrest rates in Denver, it was surprising to discover that overall, our Returnees reported essentially *identical* drinking behavior to our Comparison sample. Only thirteen subjects in our returnee sample had received eleven or more years of education, so differences between this group and those with less education were neither meaningful nor statistically significant. But like the Comparison group, the better-educated Returnees tended to report slightly less frequent

Table 8.3. Returnee vs. Comparison Group Differences in Reservation Drinking Behavior

	Returnees (N = 124)	Comparisons (N = 113)
Proportion of abstainers	31%	30%
Proportion drinking at least weekly (drinkers only)	40%	37%
Proportion frequently drunk (at least 10 times per year)	38%	37%
Proportion arrested for a drinking-related offense	44%	44%

drinking and drunkenness. Overall, nevertheless, Returnees and Comparison subjects appear amazingly similar. See table 8.3.

It is always sobering and healthy when your data fail to support your hypothesis, particularly if it is a favorite one, such as my "revolving door" hypothesis. Keeps you honest. But how to interpret the results? Is your hypothesis wrong? Or were your measures poor? Or your samples inappropriate? In our case the samples were appropriate and carefully drawn. As we have noted all along, self-report measures of drinking behavior are problematic. But I have no reason to believe that subjects in the Comparison sample would be any more or less likely to over or under report their drinking behavior than Returnees of comparable age and education. So if substantial behavioral differences between these two groups actually exist, as I had expected, these should have been reflected in differences in reported behavior, even though those reports were subject to bias. My tentative conclusion is that my "revolving door" hypothesis is wrong, that Returnees apparently sustained little or no "psychological residue" from their failure experiences in Denver, so that back home on the reservation they were no different in their drinking behavior from other young Navajo men of equivalent age and education. This negative conclusion is further supported by the survey research conducted on the Navajo reservation over the years by Stephen Kunitz and Jerrold Levy (1994 and 2000) who also failed to find any association between urban migration and reservation drinking problems.

One possible interpretation of these results, worthy of further investigation, is that whereas in the city Navajo drinking is the product of an interplay between psychological and social determinants, as we have shown in the last three chapters, on the reservation *situational* determinants (such as the absence of drinking establishments on reservation near their homes) may be over-determining, and psychological variables play little role. Since we carefully collected a lot of good data—background information, economic status, and a variety of psychological measures—from both the Returnees and Comparison group, this hypothesis could be tested, but would require the use of unreliable self-report data for our measure of drinking behavior. With so little evidence of group differences in these preliminary analyses, I chose to move on to other things.

Where Have All the Migrants Gone?

Thirty-five years after these data were collected, Bob McCracken finally persuaded me to consider undertaking a restudy of the Navajo young men we had interviewed in Denver and on the reservation. The availability of a Returnee sample and a matched Comparison sample, both interviewed under similar conditions on the reservation, would now provide the basis for a further test of my hypothesis about the vulnerability of former migrants to becoming trapped in a vicious cycle of repeated failure, with consequences for their drinking behavior and physical health. Specifically, I would anticipate that *former migrants will have a higher rate of premature mortality than members of the comparison group*, and that within both groups, *those with the least favorable psychological profile, background training, and economic experiences will also have higher rates of premature mortality.*

Premature death is the ultimate "nonreactive" measure of "failure." The death rate before the age of fifty is disturbingly high among Native American males, much of it the result of alcohol-related problems: auto accidents, cirrhosis of the liver, drunken exposure, fights, etc. Because of the lengths we went to in 1963 to 1966 to collect high-quality, systematic data over a wide range of background, education, economic, social, psychological, behavioral, and health issues, all of these hypotheses and others could now be put to a test thirty-five years later.

Whether the Navajo Tribe will ever permit non-Navajo researchers to undertake such a study today, however, even in partnership with tribal personnel, has proved to be problematic. When I was a young graduate student in the early fifties, you could drive down to the reservation, pick up a hitchhiker, and begin your research. Not today. The Tribe now firmly exercises its sovereignty; it has instituted research review procedures and privacy laws to prevent outside researchers from freely interviewing tribal members. I respect these laws, and because I was a part of it, understand the history which gave rise to them. (Those of us bothered by unwanted telephone surveys could wish for similar government protection.) Nevertheless, should permission ever be granted to proceed, the baseline data are available.

Lessons for Behavioral Anthropology

1. Behavioral anthropology requires us to collect our data from a carefully selected, representative *sample* of the group under investigation. At the time of my work on the Tri-Ethnic project and the Navajo research projects this was relatively rare within anthropology. It is much more common today. In the past, ethnographers usually based their conclusions on their own observations, supplemented by interviews with a handful of "key informants." This resulted in generalizations about the group which might be insightful and even fairly accurate in their description of "typical" or "modal" beliefs and behavior. But since "key informants" are not likely to be "typical" members of their community, and since anthropologists have limited opportunities even during a year of fieldwork to observe a wide range of behavior by the people they may be studying, particularly "private" behavior, we as readers have had no way to evaluate the validity of these accounts. Neither can the full range of within-group *variation* in beliefs and behavior be documented, nor can variation in one set of attributes be related to variation in others. Yet it is this *variation* which serves as the core material by which hypotheses can be tested and scientific conclusions drawn.

2. To gather such data usually requires some form of survey interviewing using a carefully constructed interview guide or questionnaire. Even systematic behavioral observations (chapters 9, 10, and 13) are often supplemented by survey questionnaires to obtain other information about your subjects, such as their schooling, family characteristics, job histories, beliefs and expectations, and self-reported behavior not easily amenable to direct observation.

3. Once a research population has been specified, usually by some form of census, it is relatively easy to draw a truly *random* sample of subjects to be interviewed, to insure that the full range of attitudes and beliefs present within the group at large will be tapped. Finding and interviewing these subjects in the field, however, may prove more difficult. The practical exigencies of a field situation, such as we faced on the Navajo reservation, often make it impossible to know how much time and energy it may take to collect a reasonable sample (between 60 and 120 subjects),

or how many of the predesignated sample may prove to be dead, absent, or ineligible for some reason. How do you insure that whatever size sample you end up with is still random? An easy way to do this is initially to select a random sample at least double the size you would finally like to interview. Then assign the names within this sample "priority numbers" on a random basis, and work down your list from number one to however far you need to go. This insures that replacements for absent or ineligible subjects are *also* random, and that if you run out of time or energy your final sample will also be random. I have not seen this flexible form or "multi-stage" sampling discussed elsewhere.

4. A well-chosen comparison group is a wonderful thing. At a very general level, anthropologists have often used the "method of controlled comparison" in their research. The differences between the way Hispanics and Ute Indians responded to acculturation (Graves 1967a; reprinted in Volume II, article 1), however, could be far more fine-grained and compelling than most such comparisons because it was based on systematic survey data collected from a representative sample of both groups. The Navajo comparison group described in this chapter was particularly enlightening as well, because it was drawn from the same culture group, with subjects matched by age to our earlier migrant sample. Differences between these two groups therefore highlighted important structural differences which possibly account for some of the economic difficulty Navajo migrants faced, both in Denver and back home on the reservation. It was not just a matter of their being ill-equipped for success in the city, they were also ill-equipped for success even on their home ground. This places their plight within a larger systemic context, and helps us to appreciate more fully some possible sources of problem drinking.

5. Survey interviews are a basic tool in the behavioral sciences, but are only now being used more frequently by anthropologists. My students and I were not the first to use these methods cross-culturally (Stykos 1966), or even the first to conduct survey research among the Navajo (Strieb 1952). If we want to join our sister disciplines as equal partners in the development of an interdisciplinary science of human behavior, however, behavioral anthropologists will need to use systematic surveys more often in our work. There is a rich literature on survey research methods, mainly by sociologists, which anthropologists can draw on

with profit. See, for example, Goode and Hatt (1952), which was my own major resource, both for myself and my students. Discussions of survey research methods by *anthropologists*, however, specifically aimed at promoting their use within non-Western settings, began appearing only *after* our Navajo fieldwork was completed (Bennett and Thaiss 1967; Pelto and Pelto 1978). More recent books on research methods for anthropologists by Russ Bernard (1988, 1998, 2002) now deal with this subject at some length.

Cross-cultural survey research serves both to document within-group behavioral diversity in non-Western settings and to relate this diversity to variation in other attributes. Even for the conventional concern of anthropologists to describe "typical" ways of thinking, feeling, and doing within non-Western cultures, generalizations based on empirical data collected from representative samples of subjects is far more convincing than generalizations based on the "insight" and "sensitivity" of even the most respected ethnographer. Often empirical data of this sort will serve to "validate" more casual ethnographic generalizations, as my dissertation research did for "time perspective" among Native Americans, Hispanics, and Anglos. But these data *also* serve to remind readers of the wide range of within-group variability on almost any so-called "cultural" attribute, and the substantial overlap *between* ethnic groups which is typically found. This helps prevent an unfortunate tendency for ethnographers to engage in stereotypic overgeneralizations about the "culture" of the groups they are describing, and to ascribe more within-group homogeneity than actually exists.

But these data permit much more: systematic tests of hypotheses about *why* these groups differ in the ways they do, as we attempted to do in the Tri-Ethnic research project (Jessor, Graves, Hanson, and Jessor 1968). We still have much to learn about how to measure important variables cross-culturally, particularly psychological variables. But when we gather our data from representative samples using instruments with reliability and validity that others can evaluate, the credibility of our conclusions is much enhanced.

Finally, *other* behavioral scientists can build on and use our data with a degree of confidence rarely accorded an ethnographic report. Even thirty-five years later we could now go back and use the data we collected among

Navajo men in their twenties and early thirties to test new hypotheses about how their lives turned out well into their fifties and sixties.

Notes

1. Chapter 7 of Pelto and Pelto (1978) provides excellent coverage of key sampling issues relevant for anthropologists. For recent coverage, see Bernard (2002), chapter 6.

2. Among other issues, this report discusses in detail potential sources of omission and duplication in census coverage, as we learned from conducting our survey of a random sample drawn from it. I want to thank the Census Office of the Navajo Tribe and particularly their director, Mr. Melvin Wise, for providing us with access to these census materials.

3. Kenneth L. Kuykendall, Robert D. McCracken, Bryan P. Michener, Minor Van Arsdale, O. Michael Watson, Robert S. Weppner, C. Roderick Wilson, and myself.

4. If we had it to do over again, our first step would be to check out the *family number* of each predesignated subject at the main census office, and record on our lists the parents and spouse of each subject. In the long run this would have saved time by making it easier for local informants to identify our subjects in the field.

5. My thanks to Ken Kuykendall for this detailed account and for his persistence in obtaining this interview!

9

Direct Observations of Behavior

The Graduate Research Training Program at Colorado needed a better mix of men and women than I had been able to recruit. And those women I did recruit were often uncomfortable in the intellectual give-and-take typical within academe. At least one good female student who dropped out of the program confessed to me that she felt intimidated by the rough and tumble of our weekly staff meetings, where each of us in turn presented our research ideas and progress for a collegial critique. "We're not criticizing people, only ideas," I explained to her. Students needed a strong and assertive ego to hold their own, however, and I didn't yet know how to facilitate this process in a way that would make it both more comfortable and more constructive, particularly for some women. Ideas, like babies, are fragile early in their development and easily destroyed if their obvious weaknesses receive too much critical attention. Far more fruitful is a general principle of creative group problem solving, which I would not learn for several more years, where the focus is directed to a fresh idea's potential for growth and its weaknesses are allowed to wither away from lack of attention, or can be addressed much later in the process.

Nancy Kitts could hold her own with the best of them. Nancy had chosen me as her advisor in 1964 because she heard we were doing exciting things over at the Institute of Behavioral Science, and she wanted to be a part of our team. Also, because she was married with three small children, her first departmental advisor had suggested she go for a terminal master's and a high school social science teaching certificate. This pissed her off—she wanted a Ph.D. Although I did not have a place for her within the Navajo migrant project and had used all my training fellowships to support students involved in that research, I recognized her potential and encouraged her to apply directly to the National Institute of Mental Health for a fellowship. She had training in ethology (the direct observation of animal behavior), spoke Spanish fluently, and proposed to use these skills in a study of migrant families from rural Colorado adjusting to life in Denver, with an emphasis on how migration changed patterns of mother–child interaction. The NIMH review board liked her proposal and her qualifications and awarded her a generous fellowship in national competition.

Nan's major contribution to behavioral anthropology has been to demonstrate the value of direct, systematic observations of behavior in cross-cultural settings. In her research among rural Hispanic families living in the San Luis Valley and among migrant families from the same area who had moved to Denver, quantifiable observations of mother–child interaction were her centerpiece, supplemented by parent interviews and in-depth case studies. This work provided a view of the urban migration and acculturation process very different from what we were learning among Navajo men. Nan and I came to value our complementarity in many other areas as well, and for the next twenty-five years we became partners in both our personal and professional lives.

Systematic Observations of Proxemic Behavior

Although there are many ways to measure individual variation in behavior, as I have discussed in chapters 4 and 5, certainly systematic observations are the most direct. Before I met Nan, my only experience with observational data was helping another graduate student in our program, O. Michael Watson, design and conduct an empirical study of "proxemic behavior": How people relate physically to each other when interacting. Edward T. Hall's book *The Silent Language* (1959) had stimulated Mike's interest. Although Hall had published a system of notation for recording observations of proxemic behavior (1963), he had presented no quantitative data based on that system. We felt it would be fruitful and fun to test Hall's theories about ethnic differences in proxemics through systematic observations of Arab and American students in a controlled laboratory situation (Watson and Graves 1966).

Whenever you plan to observe behavior systematically it is necessary to develop objective scoring procedures which you can use to record it. These serve as your "operational definitions" of the behavioral dimensions you will be reporting and relating to other variables. In Hall's 1963 paper, for example, he had divided proxemic behavior into eight different categories, five of which we selected for our study:[1] how close subjects sat to each other, the angle of their shoulders—from face to face to back to back—the frequency and intimacy of any touching during their conversation, the directness of their eye contact, and the loudness of their voices (measured by a decimeter attached to a microphone in the room). For each of these we assigned unambiguous scoring categories, and during initial trials two independent observers recorded identical scores.

Sixteen male Arab students at the University of Colorado, four friends from each of four different Arab countries, and sixteen American students, four friends from each of four regions of the United States, were recruited to participate in our study. Each subject was asked to sit with one of his other friends in an observation room containing a one-way mirror and engage in casual conversation for about seven minutes. This procedure was repeated with each of their three friends. After a couple of minutes of warming up time, observations were recorded for five minutes, one line of notation of the subject pair's proxemic behavior along each dimension per minute. Each group of four students therefore had a total of thirty lines of notation: five for each of the six pairs. Group means were then calculated and group differences tested.

As we had anticipated, Arab/American differences were substantial: On all five dimensions there was *no overlap* between the distribution of mean scores among the four Arab groups compared with the four American groups. For example, no touching occurred within *any* American group, but touching was observed within *all* Arab groups. By contrast, the proxemic behavior of subjects from the four Arab countries were quite similar, as was the behavior of subjects from the four U.S. regions, and differences were usually small and statistically nonsignificant. (For further details, see Watson and Graves 1966.) The only "explanation" for this within-group homogeneity and massive between-group differences available from our data was *culture*, making this a relatively poor example of "behavioral anthropology" as it would later be defined. But it is a good example of a limited but interesting domain—nonverbal communication behavior (Hall's "silent language")—which appears to be so highly patterned and homogeneous within any group that "culture" serves as an appropriate, though limited explanation.[2]

This was the first systematic empirical study of Hall's thesis, and was well received in the field, perhaps because it strongly *supported* anthropological theories about the nature of culture rather than challenging them. Mike went on to expand this research for his dissertation, to include 110 male foreign students from Latin America, Northern and Southern Europe, India and Pakistan, and Asia. (See his book, *Proxemic Behavior, A Cross-Cultural Study,* 1970.)[3]

For behavioral observations to take their rightful place within the repertoire of behavioral anthropologists, however, they need to be a part of a larger research effort where additional information about each subject is available through other procedures. Then measures of behavior based on systematic observations can become a powerful research tool, as Nan would teach me.

Systematic Observations of Child-rearing Behavior

Nan's research on the effects of urban migration on child-rearing practices among Hispanic families in the United States, which she subsequently replicated among the Baganda in East Africa, provides a case study in behavioral anthropology, and illustrates many of the strengths and difficulties when using systematic observations of behavior as a dependent variable, i.e., the thing we want to understand. (See N. Graves 1970; T. Graves and N. Graves 1978.)

Nan's research hypotheses were derived from acculturation theory and Rotter's social learning theory; her adaptation of Rotter's ideas concerning "internal versus external control" was both novel and fruitful. Within the domain of child rearing, she reasoned, high *mother efficacy*—feeling she had the ability to influence the kind of person her child would become, i.e., "internal control" in the realm of child rearing—and high *child potential*—a belief that her child had the capacity to learn how to contribute to the family—should both be associated with a substantial use of what Nan called "future-oriented" child-rearing behavior: explanation, teaching information, instruction, and suggestion. At the other end of this continuum would be mothers who felt they had little control over how their child turned out (low mother efficacy and low child potential), and therefore would devote much more of their attention simply to "keeping the lid on" through "power-assertive" and "immediate reactive" behavior such as commands, demands, and threats.

On the basis of the ethnographic literature Nan anticipated that Hispanic mothers would have more feelings of external control ("fatalism") than Anglo mothers with respect to their own efficacy as parents and the way their children turned out. She also anticipated that in an acculturation situation such as urban living provided, Hispanic mothers would have greater *exposure* to Anglo norms of family life, come to *identify* more with Anglos as a personal reference group, and therefore adopt more "Anglo" beliefs about their own efficacy as mothers and their children's potential for learning. This, in turn, would lead urban Hispanic mothers to display more Anglo-type, future-oriented child-rearing behavior, and less power-assertive, immediate reactive methods than their rural counterparts.

This is a complex web of hypothetical relationships. To test these hypotheses not only required Nan to construct and refine a reliable notation scheme for recording her observations of mother–child interaction, but also reliable measures of each of the other social-psychological variables in her scheme. For tapping the acculturation variables, she developed a formal interview and psychometric scales for measuring each mother's degree of exposure to and identification with Anglos and adoption of Anglo family and childrearing norms or retention of traditional Hispanic norms. She also included in her design an open-ended, tape-recorded interview of each mother in her sample, following an interview guide, which included questions such as "What sort of person do you want your child to be when he/she grows up" and "Do you feel there are any special ways you could treat him/her to make him/her that way?" These were designed to elicit a mother's child-rearing goals, her feelings of efficacy as a mother in producing such a child, a belief in her child's potential for acquiring these personality traits, and her reported child-rearing strategies (which could later be compared with what was actually observed). Nan developed a scoring manual for standardized coding of the interview content, and checked her reliability with a second researcher who was not privy to her research hypotheses.

From a larger pool of eligible subjects, matched samples of ten urban Anglo, ten urban Hispanic, and ten rural Hispanic families were selected for intensive interviewing and observation. To control for socio-economic status all families in her study qualified to enroll their preschool children in Project Head Start, and all had fathers present in the home. The urban Anglo and Hispanic subjects all lived in the same Denver neighborhoods, and the rural Hispanic families lived in the San Luis Valley in southwestern Colorado, an area typical of the rural environments from which most Denver Hispanic families had originally come.

The heart of her research involved systematic observations of mother–child interaction, which prior to her work in the mid-sixties was rare.[4] At the beginning of her investigation she and a coworker developed and pretested a series of twenty-one fairly concrete behavioral categories such as "explanation," "command," "comfort," and "help," at a level of abstraction somewhere between the very detailed level used by Barker and Wright (1954) and the much higher level of abstraction used by the Whitings and their students (1966). These categories could be observed and recorded at approximately 80–90% reliability. She also used three modifiers: simple symbols to indicate whether the behavior was verbal or nonverbal (v, –v), given or received by the target child (>, <), and positive, neutral, or negative in emotional tone (+, o, –). This resulted in over 300 logical possibilities, but still enabled her easily to record and prescore her observations sequentially in small, unobtrusive notebooks. Later these more specific categories were combined into more abstract, theoretically based categories of "future-oriented" or "power-assertive" and "immediate reactive" behaviors. Each mother was observed with her children in hour-long sessions for a minimum of three hours that included at least sixty interactions, to ensure relatively stable mean scores (Hansen, Hurowitz, and Madow 1953.)

Nan's project also included one year in Uganda (1967–1968) to replicate her study among Baganda families who were migrating to their capital, Kampala, but not simultaneously experiencing acculturation to a dominant ethnic group. They *were* the dominant group. This is a good example of a typical anthropological "controlled comparison" which proved to be both theoretically and methodologically instructive. While in Africa for my own purposes, I served as her support system, taking care of her youngest children (ages five and eight) while she conducted fieldwork in Kampala and a Baganda village to the south typical of those from which urban migrants were drawn. While the children were in school I analyzed data from the Navajo project and our honeymoon research in Mexico (T. Graves, N. Graves, and Kobrin 1969), and lectured at the university. When the children and I visited Nan in the village I did the cooking, and learned to peal green bananas with a huge bush knife almost as well as five-year-old girls. This was a matter of some local interest, since cooking was not a task normally undertaken by rural men. (In Kampala, however, single men were often seen preparing a meal.) During the summer months our three other children (ages eight, ten, and ten) joined us, and the seven of us travelled together in a VW square-back throughout the East African game parks, camping at night where the sounds of wild animal nearby might interupt our sleep. A wonderful bonding adventure for a newly blended family!

In both the United States and Uganda Nan's research involved preliminary fieldwork in each of the rural and urban settings; identifying eligible families and selecting her samples; constructing and translating her psychometric scales; conducting her formal and open-ended interviews; making her observations; preparing and refining her scoring manuals; coding and analyzing her data.[5] This was an ambitious research undertaking, and Nan devoted five years to the project. The results were well worth the effort, however.

As anticipated, among *both* the Spanish and Baganda mothers, a belief in their own efficacy as parents and their children's potential for learning were *positively* related to their observed use of future-oriented teaching behavior and *negatively* related to their use of power-assertive behavior. The Spanish sample yielded multiple correlation coefficients of +.46 and –.49, and among the Baganda the multiple Rs were +.44 and –.24 respectively. (I will discuss multiple correlation coefficients in chapter 12.) Even though the number of subjects was small, the care with which her measures were constructed and the consistency of her findings within quite different cultural settings gives us confidence in the validity and generality of her results. To this day I know of no other cross-cultural study of child rearing that has been able to demonstrate such compelling empirical relationships between a mother's beliefs and her observed behavior.

The results bearing on the acculturation hypotheses were more complex, however, and required a reconceptualization of the acculturation/urbanization/modernization process. Although there is considerable overlap among these three processes in practice, it is useful theoretically, and for purposes of developing appropriate measures, to distinguish them. Nan reserved the term "acculturation" for the results of *exposure* to a dominant group, possible *identification* with it and *access* to its rewards, as well as changes in the distribution of power and authority which this exposure produces. She used the term "urbanization" exclusively for changes in the environmental setting from rural to urban, and "modernization" for changes in characteristic technology and ideology, such as a shift toward an extended future time perspective and delay of gratification, feelings of internal control and achievement motivation such as I had documented among Hispanics and Ute Indians in southern Colorado and Navajos in Denver (T. Graves 1961 and 1974).

Contrary to her expectations, in both Denver and Kampala the many negative aspects of city living seemed to be responsible for *lower* feelings of mother efficacy than in the countryside, *less* confidence in their children's capacity to learn and contribute to the family welfare, and a *decrease* in warmth and *increase* in cold and angry reactions toward her child. For Spanish mothers, furthermore, these negative effects appeared to have been compounded by being a member of a disfavored minority group. (These interpretations of raw correlations were made possible by her extensive fieldwork and open-ended interviews with the mothers.)

Nan made an interesting distinction between voluntary and involuntary responses to a contact situation, crosscut by whether these responses were adoptive or reactive. "Voluntary adoption" constitutes assimilative responses, such as changes in dress, language, food, etc. in situations not required by the new situation. "Involuntary adoption" involves various accommodations in language, dress, food, etc. which may be forced upon an unwilling migrant by the new situation. "Voluntary reactions" are attempts to recreate or preserve the old way of life in the new setting. And "involuntary reactions" include a variety of (usually negative) responses such as irritation, tension, frustration, and strained family relations which may also result in or include psychosomatic symptoms, psychological maladjustment, drunkenness, or other forms of problem behavior. She considered the decrease in feelings of personal efficacy among her urban mothers and the increase in their power assertiveness and coldness toward their children to be "involuntary reactive" responses to their new urban environment.

Finally, recall that Nan's study included both the mother's reported and observed use of future-oriented "teaching" methods as part of her child-rearing behavior. Among the Hispanic mothers there was a respectable correlation of .55 between what they reported and what Nan observed. But among the Baganda this correlation dropped essentially to zero (.07). This means that there was *no* relationship between what these mothers *said* they did and what she actually *saw* them doing! Although Nan developed modest competence in Luganda during our year in East Africa, her mother interviews there were conducted with the aid of a trained interpreter/assistant. Whether or not translation might have contributed to this lack of congruence with what she saw, if Nan had not used observational procedures as her primary measure of these mothers' child-rearing behavior, she would not have obtained cross-cultural replication of her results.

The fact that theoretically expected relationships were supported by the observational data but not by the self-report data in the case of the Baganda suggests that the observations were a more *valid* measure of their child-rearing behavior than what mothers told her they did (or what she recorded them as saying). This conclusion is based on the principle of *construct validity*, already discussed in previous chapters. Furthermore, the observations also provided measures of the *affective* quality of child rearing—negatively impacted by urban living—which would have been difficult if not impossible to measure through interview procedures.

In general, direct observations usually provide more accurate and richer information on mothers' child-rearing behavior (as well as their children's responses to it) than they can recall or report. But the length of time required to obtain these observations meant that Nan had to keep her groups of mothers small, treating them in some ways like in-depth case studies.[6]

Inclusive versus Exclusive Interaction Styles

In 1970 Nan and I were teaching at UCLA, the campus was in turmoil as a result of President Nixon's Cambodia incursions, and Governor Reagan was making university life increasingly unpleasant. When Tony Hooper and Judy Huntsman, anthropologists at the University of Auckland, wrote us suggesting that we might be interested in their research among Polynesian migrants to New Zealand, we thought this would be a good time to take a couple of years off for some additional fieldwork of our own. So at the end of 1971 we packed up our blended family, (hers, mine, and ours), and became migrants ourselves, surprising everyone, including ourselves, by not returning permanently to the United States for another eight years.

Nan and I arrived at Auckland University in New Zealand's north island in January 1972 just a few weeks before the start of the academic year, which in the Southern Hemisphere coincides with the calendar year. I had been invited to assume the duties of the recently retired Professor and Chair of the Anthropology Department while the man they wanted as permanent department head, Ralf Bulmer, completed fieldwork in New Guinea. My duties included teaching an undergraduate course in "race relations." Since we were Americans, department members assumed we knew all about such things. In fact, neither of us had ever taught a course in interethnic relations, but I love the challenge of teaching a subject I know nothing about. We would simply turn the course into a "learning community," and take ethnic relations in New Zealand as the topic of a research project for *all of us*, students and professors alike, to investigate together. This material could then become the basis during the year for comparisons with other multiethnic societies, and perhaps for developing some general principles of our own. For us this was the epitome of "active learning"; for our colleagues socialized in a British academic tradition in which professors are assumed to be deeply knowledgeable "experts" in their field, it was scandalous.

After the first few weeks of classes at Auckland University class attendance is normally spotty, a large proportion of students drop out, and others simply read the professors' lecture notes, which have been circulating for years, and show up for the final exam. Our confession to over a hundred eager undergraduates on the opening day of classes that we knew almost nothing about the topic we were about to teach doubtless reinforced their stereotyping of us as brash and arrogant Americans. But when we explained what we planned to do they quickly entered into the spirit of our joint endeavor, attendance during the year was nearly perfect, and by the end of the year we had more students enrolled than we had started with.

As traditionally taught, this course had focused on "race relations" in Canada, Switzerland, and other safely distant societies. But we wanted to understand *New Zealand* ethnic relations. So we began the year by having students collect data from family, friends, and neighbors on their *attitudes* toward various ethnic groups within their society. (This research on inter-ethnic attitudes will be discussed in chapter 13.) Following this, we set them to work observing encounters between Polynesians and Pakehas in public places. ("Pakeha" is the relatively non-pejorative term commonly used for White New Zealanders of European ethnic heritage.) This active approach to learning was a novelty for New Zealand students, and was still remembered by many of them years later. Former students would stop us on the street to recall, "You taught me to *see* my society in a new way!"

We began by instructing our students in how to record simple narrative descriptions of cross-ethnic encounters. In the initial, exploratory stages of social research, naturalistic observations are among the most productive methods for generating theory (Glasser and Strauss 1967). After sensitizing our students to notice nonverbal (proxemic) behavior as well, such as eye contact, body orientation, closeness, touching, etc., we asked them to choose a public setting which appealed to them, and to record several observations within that setting. (Wherever possible, students were encouraged to observe three different interacting dyads in the same setting: Pakeha-Pakeha, Pakeha-Polynesian, and Polynesian-Polynesian.) Students then met within small teams of others working in similar settings to discuss their observations and attempt, under our guidance, to construct generalizations about their findings which could in turn be tested later through more systematic observations.

Nan took a particular interest in the group of students conducting their observations in elementary and preschool settings. (She herself had taught in preschools in Germany and the United States.) To maximize the possibility for discovering systematic variations in behavior inductively,

Nan encouraged her team to choose school settings with different ratios of Pakeha and Polynesian children, teachers, and mothers, and to observe participants in a variety of activities: indoors and outdoors, structured and unstructured. From this material it was possible to conduct "controlled comparisons" where some factors were matched between settings and others were left to vary. Over a two-year period twenty-two students under her direction recorded observations on sixty-six occasions in twenty-six different preschool classrooms or play areas, and one integrated preschool became the focus of intensive investigation for a master's thesis by Edite Denée (1973).

One of the rewarding aspects of teaching in New Zealand was that we had both Polynesian and Pakeha students in our classes, who could bring their own contrasting ethnic experience to bear on a subject. From content analysis of the observations in preschool and primary school settings we evolved a contrasting set of principles called "inclusive" versus "exclusive" behavior. These were observed in many different contexts, and seemed to have widespread implications for understanding differences between Polynesian and European-based cultures (N. Graves 1974).[7]

As we came to define it, "inclusion" is a principle for interaction which aims at fostering a sense of belonging or solidarity among persons, by incorporating them into a group. Acts of inclusion are composed of greetings, welcomes, invitations to join an activity, and organized or spontaneous group activities with a common goal. Group boundaries are flexible and loosely defined. By contrast, "exclusion" is a principle for interaction in which a person engages in solitary activities even in the presence of others (e.g.: "parallel play") or a one-to-one intensive relationship with a *single* other person. Frequently the qualifications of that other person must be ascertained and approved. In order to maintain such "exclusive" relationships, other persons must frequently be ignored or rejected. Three very quickly becomes a crowd. When this principle is operating, "groups" of children often prove to be conglomerates of two-somes, or several children vying for the exclusive attention of one popular member.

The adults in learning situations often set the tone for appropriate interpersonal relations in that setting. Contrasting examples from a Polynesian-run play center and a Pakeha-run kindergarten will illustrate this point:

Polynesian-run Play Center

A well-dressed Pakeha mother with her four-year-old boy arrives at the door, looks around, and takes a seat near the play-house, with her back to the group of other mothers. Looking up from where she is playing with the children, the casually dressed Polynesian supervisor notices the new mother and child. Walking up to where they sit she smiles and says "hello" brightly. The mother smiles briefly, then looks down to get a cigarette. The supervisor turns to the boy, saying "Hello, Michael. Come and play with the other children." She leads him by the hand toward the trolley, bending close to his head and talking all the while. She plays with the children on the trolley for about ten minutes.

Later, when seeing a new four-year-old boy working on a solitary task near his mother, she comes over, puts her arm around him and says, "Come on, Peter, shall we go build something?" She directs him toward the block corner. "Lets make a bridge, honey. Can you bring me some of those long blocks?" Soon a Polynesian girl comes to look, and the supervisor invites her to join in. "You want to build, too, Mary? Come on, now!" Seeing a Pakeha boy at the doorway with his mother, she again invites, "Come on, John, you want to build, too?" A group activity begins to form around the supervisor.

Pakeha-run Kindergarten

The Pakeha supervisor, fashionably dressed in a white skirt and blouse, stockings and heels, is standing near the painting easels, watching a child paint. A casually dressed Pakeha mother enters with her four-year-old son, goes up to the supervisor and greets her with a "hello" and a smile. The supervisor replies with a smile, saying "Hello, Tommy" to the child. The child looks away, embarrassed. The mother prompts, "Tommy, this is your teacher." "Carol," says the supervisor, smiling again. The mother and supervisor sort out the proper time for arrival at kindergarten in the future, while the child looks cautiously around the room. Then the supervisor says to Tommy, "If you need any help, just ask." The boy looks at the floor. The supervisor continues to smile, but does nothing further. Tommy looks up at his mother and suggests, "Lets look around the school, Mummy," pulling at her hand.

Tommy then chooses the one area where no other children are playing at the moment, the block rug. Later, when he goes to the toilet, he returns to find other children playing there. He complains to his mother, who encourages him to continue playing. He does so, but ignores the other children, and they ignore him.

The supervisor comes over to a Pakeha boy near Tommy and says, "Bobby, this is Tommy. Tommy, this is Bobby." Both boys look down. "Do you remember when you first came, Bobby?" she continues. "You didn't know anyone, did you? Remember how alone you felt? That's how Tommy feels." She continues explaining Tommy's situation, crouching beside Bobby, but touching neither child. Bobby and Tommy ignore each other. She leaves, without speaking to either of the two Polynesian boys also playing on the rug. Tommy, evidently feeling exposed and uncomfortable, goes outside.

In the first example, the Polynesian supervisor used an often-observed technique for integrating the new child: drawing him physically into a group and then interacting with all the children together. A second method, used later, was to involve a child in a fascinating activity in which the teacher participated wholeheartedly as well, making loud comments and enthusiastic remarks. She would then invite other children to join this obviously enjoyable game. She used everyone's name frequently, so no formal introductions were necessary. Peter was never confronted with his "new boy" status, and the other children came to know him in the context of a group activity with their teacher.

By contrast, in the second example the Pakeha supervisor was friendly and welcoming, but somewhat formal and distant. She did not touch the children, and not dressed for play, she mainly watched them at their various activities. She expected them to choose their own activities and to ask her for help if they wanted attention.

Left on his own, the new child, apparently feeling shy and out of place, did not choose a group activity, but wandered alone from area to area. The supervisor's technique for integrating him was a formal introduction and a request for empathy from another child, which only seemed to embarrass both boys. When this did not produce the desired result, she let the matter drop.

This Pakeha kindergarten was equipped with separate cubbyholes for personal possessions and separate washcloths and towels for each child. At snack time children were each expected to serve themselves from a little table, picking out their own glass from a tea tray whenever they chose.

By contrast, at the Polynesian-led play center all the children used a common basin and towel, and were fed their snack as a group during a communal gathering for singing and dancing. All the mothers and children were drawn together to participate.

These inclusive/exclusive principles obtain with respect to parental involvement in school governance as well. Observations at a number of parent–teacher meetings in different schools indicated that when Pakeha leaders were in charge the procedures tended to be formal and restrained, and usually focused on specific tasks or activities (a new reading program or other change in curriculum, a sporting event, a fund-raising activity) with little parental discussion and participation. After the meeting parents had to initiate contact with teachers or principals, who often stood as though at the head of a class. With so little initial attention devoted to greetings and inclusion, Polynesian parents often seemed to feel uncomfortable and unwelcome, even though no direct acts of exclusion occurred.

By contrast, at a Polynesian-run play center parents' meetings started with welcoming activities which encourage full participation. Formal procedures, such as reading minutes, were usually discarded. "You may not find it quite orderly," a Polynesian supervisor warned us. "People get quite involved and carried away." A Maori woman, given the opportunity to organize a parent meeting at her school, found that she was highly successful in encouraging parent participation by treating the situation as if they were on a Maori *marae*, the open space or courtyard in front of the communal meeting house.[8] The *marae* is the "stamping ground" (*tuuranga wae wae)* where matters of significance to the group are thrashed out in lengthy discussion. No one is excluded from this process, and decisions are arrived at gradually by group consensus.

Even among mothers participating in a Polynesian play center, cultural differences in patterns of interaction with the children were found. In one play center an equal number of Polynesian and Pakeha mothers were systematically observed for the extent to which they interacted exclusively with one child (whether or not their own) or inclusively with a group (of which their own child might or might not be a member). During twenty sessions over a six-month period 75% of the "inclusive" episodes involved a Polynesian mother, and 83% of the "exclusive" episodes involved a Pakeha mother (Denée 1973:27).

These values are reflected in Polynesian/Pakeha differences in conception of "the good child." Denée interviewed both Polynesian and Pakeha mothers from this play center, asking them to describe the three-year-old child they would like best for themselves. Polynesian mothers typically expressed a concern for getting along in the community or social group: two-thirds (67%) of their responses described a child that was well-behaved, obedient, nonaggressive, sociable, or sharing. The Pakeha mothers, on the other hand, more often gave individualistic, child-centered descriptions: 80% of their responses referred to a child who was happy, healthy, independent, or inquiring (Denée, 1973:30). These findings are strikingly similar to the differences Nan had found between Spanish and Anglo mothers' descriptions of the "ideal child" in Colorado.[9]

Polynesian and Pakeha children also displayed these contrasting modes of interaction. Although both Polynesian and Pakeha children expressed both styles from time to time, Polynesian children were far more likely to be observed in inclusive acts, particularly in settings where the student body was predominantly Polynesian. Pakeha children were more likely to be observed in exclusive interaction. And both groups were observed informally "teaching" their own preferred style to the other:

Inclusive Polynesian Children's Behavior

Two Polynesian girls, Sally and Venetta, both about six, are walking along holding hands, talking and giggling. Sally laughs and places her arm around Venetta's neck, giving her an affectionate hug. Suddenly they both stop. Sally has seen a Pakeha girl, Wendy, standing silently alone, looking very sad. Sally goes up to her and asks, "What's the matter?" She puts her arm around Wendy while maintaining her relationship with Venetta, her arm around her neck. The Pakeha child does not respond, turning her head away and avoiding eye contact.

Sally releases her hold on her Polynesian friend and places both arms around Wendy. She turns her head toward Venetta, however, and remarks, "I think she's lost that other girl." Wendy remains very rigid in Sally's arms, continuing to look at the ground.

Venetta then suggests, "She's over there. Come on!" At this Wendy looks up and appears to relax a bit, although still upset. Sally and Venetta arrange themselves on either side of her, putting their arms around her. They turn and walk together toward the jungle gym.

As the trio approaches, a Pakeha girl playing on the jungle gym looks up, jumps off, and moves quickly away. Wendy follows her departure with her eyes. Then, seeming to undergo a change of mood, she smiles and takes Sally's hand. Venetta moves closer to Sally, who gives her a playful push. All three girls laugh and begin to play together.

Here we saw two Polynesian girls engaged in what might be considered an intensive, exclusive relationship. Yet they are sensitive to the plight of another child abandoned by her playmate, and immediately include her in their group. They also try to solve her social problem by finding the girl who left her. When this girl rejects her once more, the Pakeha child turns to her Polynesian friends and accepts their warm inclusion wholeheartedly for the first time. If there is any jealousy on the part of Venetta, as might be indicated by her approach toward Sally after the Pakeha girl takes her hand, it is handled lightly with a playful push and quickly forgotten.

This solution to the threesome problem is in sharp contrast to that encountered by a Maori boy in an otherwise all-white kindergarten in an upper-middle-class Pakeha neighborhood:

Exclusive Pakeha Children's Behavior

A Pakeha girl, Susie, has been playing for some time with a Maori boy, James. Susie flits from activity to activity, seemingly using this device to keep James under her influence. After initiating play on the climbing frame, she runs off, calling him to follow. She sits down at the rear of a group listening to the supervisor reading a story.

When James approaches, Susie greets him with a loud "Hi, James!" The supervisor stops reading and looks up at James, as do all the children, turning around on their mat. The supervisor looks annoyed. James drops his eyes and moves away from the group. Susie then follows him, and the supervisor resumes her story.

James begins playing in a large box, and invites Susie to join him. "Wait for me, James," Susie responds as she runs up to him. James calls across to another girl, "Julie, come on! We'll let you in. Enough room." Susie asserts herself by also calling "Hurry up, Julie!" But when the girl arrives, Susie blocks her way, crying "There's no room!" Following her lead, James also says "There's no room for you." But Julie pushes her way into the box anyway, and the other two move over to make room for her.

As the three children leave the box, Julie says to James, "I'm going to be Susie's friend!" James ignores this remark and follows Susie to the swings. Susie retorts to Julie, "No, I'm James' friend," and James echoes, "She is." Thereupon Julie kicks James in the shin, but he ignores her.

This scene illustrates the way in which a Polynesian child, highly motivated by a need for inclusion, learns and comes to adopt his Pakeha friend's preferred interaction style: intense involvement with one person, to the exclusion of others. Although his natural tendency seems to be to invite others to join their activities, his friend prefers to keep him to herself.

Although our data are limited, these contrasting patterns of behavior were seen in the upper grades as well. In a South Auckland high school, for example, with a high concentration of Polynesians, the physical education teacher told Nan that she found Polynesian girls much more interested in team sport than Pakeha girls, more cooperative with her and other children, and less "catty" and "cliquey." During gym period, Nan observed that all but one of the girls who chose basketball, a team sport, were Polynesian. Friendly conversation, joking, and encouragement, both among team members and between teams, was the general pattern during the game. The rest of the girls, all white, chose to play patterball—a less energetic game between two persons—with little friendly interchange between pairs.

These ethnic differences in interaction style were not uniformly displayed either within or between settings, and both individuals and schools varied in the amount of inclusive and exclusive behavior observed. But in over 1500 acts recorded on this dimension at thirteen preschools and eleven primary schools, (excluding the intensive work by Denée and her team in one school) Pakehas were overwhelmingly exclusive in their behavior, while Polynesians were overwhelmingly inclusive. (See table 9.1.)

Table 9.1. Inclusive–Exclusive Behavior in 24 School Settings*
(Based on over 1500 acts)

	Polynesians		Pakehas	
School Level	Inclusive	Exclusive	Inclusive	Exclusive
Preschools	64%	36%	31%	69%
Primary schools	63%	37%	20%	80%

*From N. Graves (1974)

Polynesian behavior appears to be somewhat influenced by the proportion of Pakehas in the school. Where Polynesians were in the majority, 74% of their acts along this dimension were inclusive. In schools where they were a minority of at least 10%, this dropped to 65%. And in schools where they were a tiny minority (less than 10%) this dropped even further, to 41%. But even when severely outnumbered, Polynesians remain far more inclusive in their behavior than Pakehas, the vast majority of whose acts along this dimension were exclusive (varying from 64% to 82%) regardless of whether they were in the majority or the minority.

Social scientists with research experience in Polynesian or other traditional societies will readily recognize as typical what we call "inclusive" behavior. Placing a child within a peer group, for example, is a common socialization strategy in many Polynesian societies. (See, for example, Boggs 1973; Firth 1963; Gallimore, MacDonald and Boggs 1969; Hocart 1929; Howard 1970; Levy 1969; Mead 1928, Ritchie 1957.) Ritchie (1972) has labeled this form of child rearing a feature of the "co-relative" family, where the child is raised and trained by many other children and adults. Ritchie postulates that this should result in a "flexible accommodation to the needs of others, what Riesman once called 'other direction' (1950), low long-term personal aspiration levels, but great social responsiveness" (Ritchie 1972:91). This socialization style places great emphasis on sharing and cooperation, behaviors which are highly adaptive in small, closely knit societies with subsistence economies. By contrast, Western children raised within small nuclear families have far less opportunity to acquire the level of skill in interpersonal relations and group functioning which is commonly exhibited by Polynesian children. These ethnographic insights would become important background for our own fieldwork on a Polynesian island, discussed in the next chapter.

Methodological Lessons for Behavioral Anthropology

1. When using systematic behavioral observations in our research behavioral scientists need to formulate clear, theory-based operational guidelines. What are we observing and why? In our research on proxemic behavior these theoretical and operational guidelines had been provided by Edward Hall. All Mike Watson and I needed to do was to design a

setting and sampling procedure for collecting our systematic data. More typically, however, work of this kind requires a preliminary period of less structured, narrative observations from which theoretically meaningful categories can be derived and refined to serve as a basis for more systematic data collection. This was the sequence followed by Nan and her students in their work on inclusive versus exclusive behavior.

2. The categories used in behavioral observations can be constructed at different levels of abstraction. In the proxemic behavior research these categories were at an extremely low level of abstraction and required essentially no inference on the part of the observers. As a result, inter-observer reliability in observing and scoring this behavior was essentially 100%. Nan's dissertation research involved the development of categories at an intermediate level of abstraction, with an initial reliability level of between 80–90%. Later these relatively specific behavioral categories were combined into more abstract, theoretically based categories of "future-oriented" or "power-assertive" and "immediate reactive" behaviors. Since Nan did all the observations herself, the major "reliability" issue involved how consistently she used the specific categories over time. In her work in Polynesian preschools the raw observations were more open-ended and narrative in format, so that they could be made and recorded by a large number of students with little research experience. At a later stage she broke these narratives into behavioral units which she and her students, both Polynesian and Pakeha, had derived, and later scored them into theoretical categories of "inclusive" versus "exclusive" behavior.

3. The *setting* in which the observed behavior takes place is important to consider. In our research on proxemic behavior this setting was standardized, so that we could logically infer differences in behavior to be based on the ethnicity of the actors. Where the setting is allowed to vary, as in the proportion of Polynesian and Pakeha students in play centers, or deliberately contrasted, as in rural families versus urban migrants, the situation itself becomes a potential factor in the outcome behavior. In the next chapter, where observations were conducted in even more freely varying circumstances we will also see the effects of differences in the nature of the *personnel* present and their relationship to the target child.

4. Systematic observations of culture group differences in behavior, such as we recorded between Americans and Arabs and between Pakehas

and Polynesians, can be interesting and a big improvement over more casual ethnographic stereotypes. But behavioral observations are far more interesting when linked to other variables—the physical and social setting in which the behavior takes place, the beliefs, attitudes, and values of the actors, their amount of acculturative experience, etc. This requires complementary research among the actors being observed, using other data-collecting strategies, such as survey interviews, questionnaires, and psychometric procedures. In her dissertation research Nan collected a good deal of systematic data from the mothers she observed. In the next chapter the behavioral observations are complemented by even more information from both children and parents. And we will also look at systematic observations used as adjuncts to other behavioral experiments.

Notes

1. Since we would only be working with men and all would be seated, his first category, "postural-sex identifiers," was unnecessary. His "thermal" and "olfactory" codes could not be measured observationally, and we found our subjects unable or unwilling to talk about these in interviews: Could they feel the heat of their partner's body or smell its odor? So these too were dropped from our study.

2. "Culture" serves as a reasonable explanation for linguistic and other forms of communicative behavior, and children probably learn norms of "proxemic" behavior in the same way they learn their language, with peer influences perhaps more important than parents. Among immigrants, is there such a thing as a proxemic "accent"?

3. As we had found, as Hall postulated, and as Hediger had found among animal species in general, these subjects fell quite neatly into "contact" and "noncontact" groups, with Latin Americans and Southern Europeans joining Arabs within the contact grouping, and Northern Europeans, Asians, Indians, and Pakistanis joining North Americans in the noncontact grouping.

Systematic research on proxemic behavior continues to this day, and there is now a whole journal—the *Journal of Nonverbal Communication*—devoted to the topic. Video technology has facilitated systematic field research on proxemic behavior in natural settings and led to refinements. Hall's distinction between "contact" and "noncontact" cultures has stood up well, however, as have the Arab/American differences we first documented. Our pioneer work in this area continues to be cited. See, for example, the critique by Mazur (1977) and recent research by Remland et al. (1991 and 1995).

4. The Six Culture Study directed by the Whitings at Harvard used systematic coding of mother and child behavior as early as 1954, but these results had only recently been published when Nan designed her research (Whiting 1963). As far as we know, Stephen Boggs (1956) is the earliest *published* anthropological study using systematic observations of mother–child interaction.

5. In both rural and urban U.S. settings Nan worked with bilingual Hispanic research assistants who helped her with the development of her observational categories and the collection of her systematic observational data. This provided the basis for developing and testing the reliability of these data. She followed the same procedure with two bilingual Baganda research assistants in Africa.

6. Nan completed her dissertation in 1970 and produced a book-length manuscript, *City, Country and Child Rearing,* which was accepted for publication by Greenwood Press the following year. Unhappily it fell victim to the professional book publishing slump of the mid-seventies when that press was sold.

7. Unless specifically credited to Denée, all quotes and data in the following sections are taken from N. Graves (1974).

8. The *marae* also stands as the symbol of the home territory of the sub-tribal group (the *tangata whenua,* the "people of this place"). Rules of inclusion and exclusion are incorporated into Polynesian languages in personal pronouns. Only after the welcoming ceremonies for visitors are completed is the use of the exclusive "we" (*maatou*) by the home group ceremonially changed to an honorific *taatou* (an inclusive "we") when referring to everyone present. After this visitors can freely participate in the activities of the *marae,* including standing with the *tangata whenua* when welcoming the next group of visitors. See Salmond (1975).

9. In chapter 14 I will discuss another example of similar findings: Bea Whiting's research in Kenya (1996).

10

A Different Kind of Ethnography

Like most anthropology students, I was raised on a heavy diet of classic ethnography. Some of these books were fascinating, some were boring. All were based on a substantial period of "fieldwork" by sensitive observers, plus interviews with a handful of "key informants" who had become their friends. None were "science," at least as I had been taught to do science within the fields of economics, sociology, and psychology.

Science requires objectivity and repeatability. In theory, anyone else should be able to follow the same procedures as the original investigator and come up with similar data, from which similar conclusions can be drawn. But classic ethnography is dependent on the sensitivity and insightfulness of the ethnographer. And typically, when two or more ethnographers study the same group they come up with different conclusions.[1] The "culture" being studied and described often appears to be a Rorschach test that tells us as much about the ethnographer's personality and values as about the society under investigation (Bennett 1946).

Although I spent most of three years "in the field" during my dissertation research, I did not write a classic ethnography, an anthropological "rite of passage" I missed.[2] Instead, as described in chapters 2 and 3, I conducted a fairly straightforward social-psychological study of "deviant behavior" among high school students (Graves 1961). The one thing "anthropological" about this study was that I worked among three ethnic groups—Anglos, Hispanics, and Native Americans—and documented ethnic differences in certain "typical" personality traits—future time perspective and fatalism—which were in line with what we expected from previous anthropological reports. But unlike more casual ethnographic observations, mine were statistically significant differences in the *distribution* of scores on carefully constructed psychometric *measures* of time perspective and fatalism ("locus of control") of known *reliability* and *validity*. What my research also demonstrated was dramatic *variability* in these psychological traits within each of these ethnic groups and substantial *overlap* among them. This is exactly what other psychological anthropologists typically find whenever they systematically measure personality attributes cross-culturally, and raises questions about the validity of more stereotypic "cultural" descriptions found in conventional ethnographies.

How might a behavioral scientist go about conducting an ethnographic study? Nan and I were given an opportunity to try our hand at this task when I was awarded a two-year fellowship by the Royal Society of New Zealand in 1973. Our proposal included a year of fieldwork in the Cook Islands to explore the impact of Western industrial society and market economy on island life, on Islanders' personality and interpersonal relations, and on their motivation to migrate. We had chosen to focus on Cook Islanders, the second-largest group of Pacific Islanders living in New Zealand, because Samoans, the largest island group in New Zealand, were already being studied by our colleagues in the Sociology Department David Pitt and Cluny Macpherson (1974).[3]

The Cook Islands and New Zealand constitute a single "system" of relationships. As New Zealand citizens (with a status somewhat similar to Puerto Ricans in the United States), Cook Islanders are free to move back and forth between the two countries, and at the time of our research about half the Cook Islands population were living in New Zealand. (Samoans, by contrast, are not New Zealand citizens, and therefore not as free to migrate. This makes for interesting comparisons.) This continual flow of Islanders to New Zealand and back again, along with the "remittances" of wages from migrants to their families back home, meant that island life was already being radically affected by New Zealand influences.[4] Perhaps some Islanders were becoming "preadapted" to Western life, we reasoned. And perhaps these would be the most likely to migrate.

This comparison study of life on a "typical" island from which migrants to New Zealand were being drawn, was also intended as a "baseline" to compare with the lives of Cook Islanders living in New

Zealand, as Nan had done with her study of Hispanic migrants to Denver and Baganda migrants to Kampala. The Royal Society wanted us to conduct a quick social-psychological survey within one or more island communities. We resisted that idea. Instead, we wanted our study to be more in the manner of a traditional ethnography, by living and working on one of the Cook Islands for at least a year. We argued, I believe correctly, that behavioral scientists, when conducting research in non-Western settings, require an extended period of ethnographic fieldwork within those settings to formulate theory and hypotheses and construct measures which are relevant and appropriate to that setting.

Conventional ethnographies attempt to document essentially all aspects of a community's way of life. This of necessity spreads the researcher's energy very thin. But ours would be a different kind of ethnography: We would go with a clear problem focus, limit our investiation to changes in economic life, demography, personality, and behavior, and ultimately base our conclusions on systematic data collected from large and representative samples of subjects. Our goal would not be to describe Polynesian "culture" in stereotypic terms, their typical ways of thinking, feeling, and doing, but to account for the *range of within-group variation* we expected to find on this island in economic activity, family structure, personality, and behavior.

Selecting Our Research Site and Beginning Our Fieldwork

This focus on within-group variation and its correlates and change over time meant that our criteria for selecting our field site would be quite different from the ones typically used by anthropologists in the past. Instead of looking for the most isolated and exotic aboriginal community still available, we wanted one with substantial Western contact, with some people living quite traditional Polynesian lives and others more Westernized in education, occupation, and family structure.

During the August school holidays in 1973 we made an exploratory trip to the Cooks with our two teenage daughters and our youngest son, to choose a site for extensive fieldwork the following year. Aitutaki, situated about 125 miles north of the capital island of Rarotonga and the second largest of the fifteen islands in the Cook group, seemed a perfect choice. (See maps on facing page.) Not only did it exemplify the finest of traditional Polynesian life, but within its seven-mile perimeter and population of about 2,500, it contained a full range of variation from extended families cooperatively engaged in fishing and subsistence agriculture to highly Westernized professionals, government clerks, and business people. Thus it served as a stage on which the economic, social, and psychological changes of the last 300 years in the West were being reenacted within the space of a few decades.

Although the island had been missionized for more than a century, major Western influences date from the Second World War, when Aitutaki served as a military base in the South Pacific. The good airport built at that time provided scheduled flights to and from Rarotonga, and the island was regularly served by trading ships bringing in Western goods and taking cash crops—bananas, oranges, tomatoes, and copra—back to New Zealand. Since we intended to bring our four boys with us during the following year of fieldwork, another consideration was that Aitutaki had a small hospital and a Western-trained Cook Islands doctor in residence, Dr. Terepai Maoate. (He later became a leader of the Democratic Alliance Party, and in 2000 became his country's prime minister.) All these amenities contributed to Aitutaki's intermediate degree of Westernization. Nevertheless, at the time of our fieldwork tourists were still rare.

In May of 1974 we sailed to Aitutaki with our four boys,[5] fully equipped for at least a year of residence (including a water bed, which I highly recommend in a tropical climate). For the first six months of our fieldwork we were mainly "participant observers," getting settled, attending various churches and village meetings, participating in the weekly village work groups, and observing informally in homes and schools. During our earlier scouting visit we had arranged to rent a vacant house in Amuri Village from Tai Turia, principal of the nearby elementary school which our youngest son (age 5) would be attending. We enrolled our 12-year-old boy in the island's only middle school,[6] planted a garden, and began taking daily instruction in the language and culture from Tangaroa Elia, a retired schoolteacher and herbalist. Our two older boys, both 16, spent their mornings studying correspondence classes and their afternoons fishing. (They supplied us with most of our protein!)

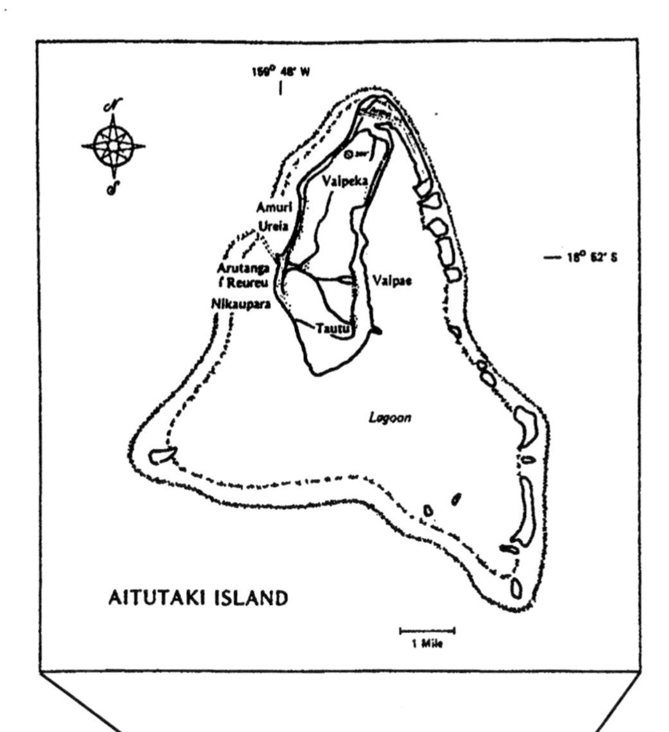
159° 48' W
Valpeka
Amuri
Ureia
Arutanga
Reureu
Nikaupara
Valpae
Tautu
18° 52' S
Lagoon
AITUTAKI ISLAND
1 Mile

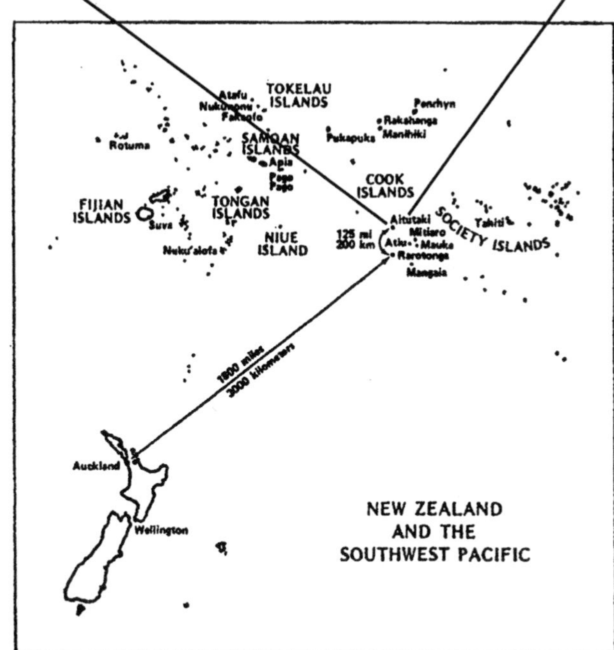
TOKELAU ISLANDS
Atafu
Fakaofo
Penrhyn
Rakahanga
Manihiki
Pukapuka
Rotuma
SAMOAN ISLANDS
Apia
Pago Pago
COOK ISLANDS
FIJIAN ISLANDS
Suva
TONGAN ISLANDS
Nuku'alofa
NIUE ISLAND
Aitutaki
Mitiaro
Mauke
Rarotonga
Mangaia
125 mi
200 km
SOCIETY ISLANDS
Tahiti
Auckland
Wellington
NEW ZEALAND AND THE SOUTHWEST PACIFIC

The American "Invasion" of Aitutaki

On the fourteenth of November, 1942, Colonel R. T. Garity landed on Aitutaki with a thousand American troops, half Black and half White. Aitutaki had been selected as a potential "fall-back" position in case the war in the western Pacific went badly. Since the local population at that time was only about two thousand, half of them children, American men outnumbered Aitutaki men by two to one. And even though the main troop contingent remained there only a year, two to three hundred troops were left behind to maintain the base until the end of the war.

This major "invasion" had been preceded in May by a small advanced contingent of American and New Zealand engineers, complete with bulldozers and other road-building equipment, who hired local men to clear land at the north end of the island for an airstrip. The airport was finished and the first planes began landing about two weeks after the arrival of the main troops in November. Aitutaki has never been the same since.

Everyone worked for the Americans. During the initial period of constructing the airport and base facilities probably two-thirds of the able-bodied men were regularly employed as laborers. They were paid forty cents for the first eight-hour shift and after a break, sixty cents for a second eight-hour shift, or about a dollar a day, seven days a week for the first six months or so. These wages had been deliberately set low by the New Zealand government "to prevent disrupting the local economy." But since there was almost no wage labor employment available to the average local at that time, cash was a novelty, and these wages were viewed as a tremendous boon.

Women and children were also employed. On Mondays about 500 adult women were washing clothes for the thousand troops, one bag per man per week, for which they were paid a dollar per bag. Each soldier made his own arrangements with a local woman, but almost every household had at least one member washing clothes. The local rate for other favors was also a dollar. "You could get anything for a dollar," we were told. In the evenings there were dances—one for the Black soldiers, one for the Whites—where local women, outnumbered more than two to one by American troops, were much in demand. (Two groups of offspring—one lighter than most Islanders and one darker—resulted from this period.) Illegal gambling and other activities provided more opportunities for American dollars to pass into local hands. (We found a 1943 American penny when digging up the floor for our cookhouse; it turned out to have been a popular gambling spot for the troops which our host remembered well from his childhood.)

The troops made their headquarters in the island's central school building, and school was closed for six months until four small, decentralized schools could be built closer to their students' homes in case of an invasion. So during this initial six-month period most children over twelve were also working for the Americans, cleaning rifles, polishing shoes, and running errands. It was an exciting and memorable period. In all, the average household on Aitutaki was probably earning upwards of $15 per week. This was the first regular paid employment most Aitutakians had experienced.

After six months the work tapered off. The troops built their own laundry and hired about forty local women to do the work full-time. After the airport and support facilities were completed many local men returned to their subsistence activities. But until the end of the war over a hundred men were regularly employed by the Americans, and forty or fifty were still working at the airport when New Zealand took it over at the end of the war. During this brief period a taste for "quick money" had been introduced to almost every household, which would never be lost.

Economic Changes since World War II

One of our early ethnographic tasks was to mine existing formal records to document major changes in economic and demographic conditions since World War II. A dramatic change was the increasing proportion of men engaged in nontraditional employment. The 1951 New Zealand census on Aitutaki listed only sixty-nine wage and salaried jobs, ten men worked in shops or bakeries, and six received some income from various churches as pastor or missionaries. The other 498 men age fifteen and over (85%) were full-time planters and fishermen. At the time of our fieldwork, however, 45% of the adult men on Aitutaki were on the government payroll: the Public Works Department, which constructs and maintains roads and public buildings; and the Agriculture Department, which was taking increased responsibility for cash crop activities, the airport, schools, hospital, electric power, post office, police, community development, and central administration.

With the increase in money provided by government jobs there had also been a concomitant expansion of private commercial activities: small retail shops and bakeries, a handful of self-employed men in the building trades, and the sale and servicing of motor mowers, motorcycles, trucks, and cars. Over 150 motorcycles were licensed on the island in 1974, though the actual number, estimated from our family survey, was probably closer to 250. There were also about fifty cars and trucks on the island, half owned by the Cook Islands government. Motor mowers were a recent import, but were already owned by 45% of the 109 households in our survey.

Employment opportunities for women, though far fewer, were also increasing. At the time of our fieldwork there were about sixty full-time jobs available for women on the island, mainly as teachers (twenty-two), but also as shopkeepers, office workers, nurses, and house girls. These represent only 12.5% of the available workforce, but their number had risen by a third since 1966. The rate of change is indicated by the fact that 80% of the employed women were under age forty, and almost 60% were under age thirty.

We obtained occupational data from the New Zealand censuses of 1951, 1956, and 1961, a census conducted by the Cook Islands government in 1966, the 1972 voter registration roll, and our own enumeration of all wage and salaried jobs available on the island, which we checked against self-reported occupations listed in the voter registration rolls in November 1974. Together, these showed a steady increase in nontraditional occupations among men. To fill in the blanks between these dates we classified the occupations of the male parent/guardians listed in the birth register each year, averaging these over three-year periods since World War II. The results are shown in figure 10.1. By 1972 a *majority* of the men on Aitutaki were involved in nontraditional occupations.

Effects of Wage Labor Employment on Work Patterns

Wages in all these occupations were extremely low, however, with those in typical laboring jobs earning only about forty cents an hour, or perhaps

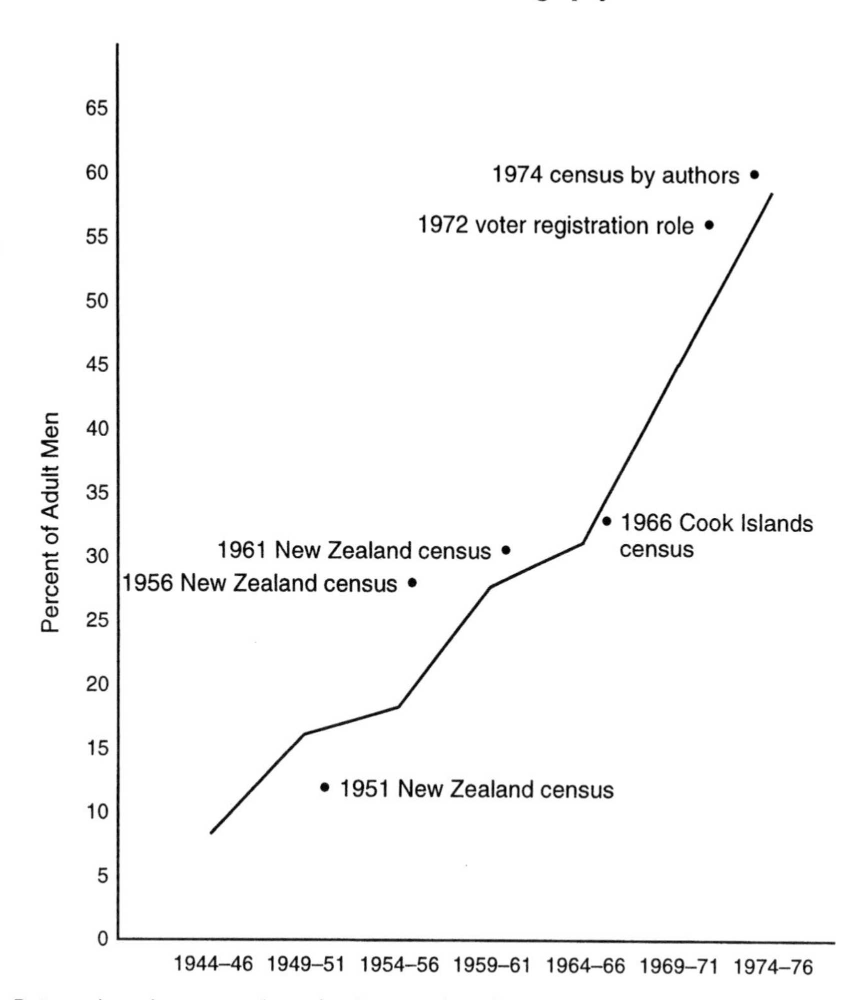

Data are based on occupations of male parent/guardian listed in birth register.

Figure 10.1. Nontraditional Employment on Aitutaki, 1945–1975

$15 a week in take-home pay. Even a top foreman or schoolteacher would earn only double that amount, and a senior public servant earned less than $3,000 a year. With prices in the local stores roughly double those in New Zealand, nearly all employed men also had to fish and maintain a garden for food crops, and many supplemented their income with cash crops: copra, bananas, and oranges. These activities now had to be fitted in around his formal employment.

Traditionally, the ideal pattern for a man on the island was to work in his plantation from six to ten in the morning, rest during the heat of the day from ten to three, then do some more work in the late afternoon from three to six. He would also spend one to three evenings a week fishing, depending on the catch. Once a man had an eight-hour wage labor job, however, this pattern was radically disrupted. He could squeeze in an hour or so before work in the morning, and perhaps another couple of hours or so after work until dusk. So where traditionally he could comfortably spend up to about thirty-five hours per week on his plantation while still leaving a couple of afternoons for sport and one day over the weekend for church,[7] now the maximum available time for planting during the week was cut in half. And this, of course, on top of a tiring forty-hour week of wage employment.

One result was a sharp diminution in subsistence and cash crops during the postwar years: At the time of our fieldwork informants estimated that the amount of land under cultivation was perhaps only a third of what it had been. A local village women's committee would periodically inspect each family's taro plot to be sure enough land was kept under cultivation to feed their family and prevent theft, but shortages of root crops were still sometimes felt. With the growing availability of "quick money" (wages) time devoted to earning "slow money" (cash crops) also declined. By the mid-1960s copra exports had declined by 22%, citrus fruit by 55%, and bananas by 90% (Johnston 1967; Bassett and Thomson 1968), and when we arrived tomatoes had ceased to be grown for export, replaced by hothouse tomatoes grown in New Zealand.

With increased pressure on a man's time and energy, there also had been a decline in voluntary communal labor. In the village where we lived every able-bodied man was supposed to contribute his labor to communal activities on Monday afternoons: cleaning the paths, roads, and vacant lots of weeds and overhanging branches, reroofing the palm-thatched homes of the sick and the elderly, repairing the village hall, etc. When we first settled into our village life, these were fun social occasions in which I was delighted to participate. (On one of these occasions my neighbor seriously asked me, "Do White men sweat?" He had never seen a White man working; even during the war years they were the supervisors and foremen, while local men provided the back-breaking labor.) But even during the year we were there participation noticeably declined.

Some of those working for wages full-time made voluntary cash contributions to the village to compensate for their absence. Others were fined, but these fines were rarely collected, because to do so would have required a confrontation and strained social relations. As the voluntary workforce decreased, of course, the amount of work remaining for those who *did* participate *increased*, serving as a negative reinforcement. Also, with fewer and fewer participants, the work projects were less fun as *social, community-wide* events, and with few formal sanctions being applied, more and more local villagers were tempted to skip out, producing further resentment among the faithful, annoyed at seeing their neighbors off fishing, resting, or working in their own gardens.

At the time of our last visit to the island in 1980 the voluntary community work parties on Monday afternoons had ceased all together. Our host, Tai Turia, the former village head man, explained that community leaders had attempted to set a good example, but even they became discouraged when the number of participants fell to no more than a handful. When he found himself working alone two weeks in a row, he confessed, he, too, stopped coming. And so ended the last of the regular weekly voluntary work parties on the island. "Who does the communal work now?" Nan asked. "Oh, we've made progress," he answered wryly, pointing down the road to where a group of men were hard at work, under the supervision of an island policeman. "We have prisoners now." Drunkenness, theft, and violence had become new problems.

Choosing a Research Focus

During our first six months in the field we kept asking ourselves, what should be the specific focus of our fieldwork? What variation in behavior do we want to document and understand? Our initial idea was to predict those young people most likely to leave the island for New Zealand. At the time of our fieldwork Cook Islanders going to New Zealand were required to obtain "Certificates of Identity" in lieu of passports. During 1973 and 1974 these certificates had been issued to 613 persons on Aitutaki, for an average rate of out-migration of 25.5 per month. Most of these (over 60%) were in the productive age range between fifteen and fifty-nine, and many young parents left their infant children behind in the care of grandparents or siblings. Some were on short trips for various purposes such as visiting New Zealand relatives. But uncounted were those migrating to Rarotonga each month (because they did not require these certificates), though many of these would not return.

To explore the rate of out-migration among young people in more detail, we systematically traced the whereabouts of everyone listed on the school records who was born between 1952 and 1958. Key informants from each of the seven villages were used, so that the present location of almost all the 575 young people in these seven age cohorts was obtained. (One had died, three were unknown to our informants and assumed to have left, and the present location of four was uncertain, though they were known to have left the island.) A decay curve displaying the proportion of young people in each age cohort remaining on the island as of September 1974 is presented in figure 10.2. By age twenty-two about 85% of these young people had left the island. Clearly, the best predictor of out-migration from Aitutaki was being born there! No amount of carefully constructed social-psychological measurement was likely to improve on this.

Given the dramatic impact of this out-migration stream—over 10% of the island's population each year and ultimately 85% of its youth — it is small wonder that local people *perceived* their society as changing rapidly and radically in its composition, a paradoxical misconception which became the focus of our first publication on our fieldwork (T. Graves and N. Graves 1976).

Systematic Data Collection: Learning Altruism on Aitutaki

We had not gone to Aitutaki specifically to study prosocial development in Island Polynesia, but we had a strong interest in this topic. So when predicting out-migration became uninteresting, prosocial development became the major focus of our work. Our observations of inclusive versus exclusive behavior in New Zealand, discussed in the last chapter, had sensitized us to the prosocial behavior typical of Polynesian children (and adults). Our

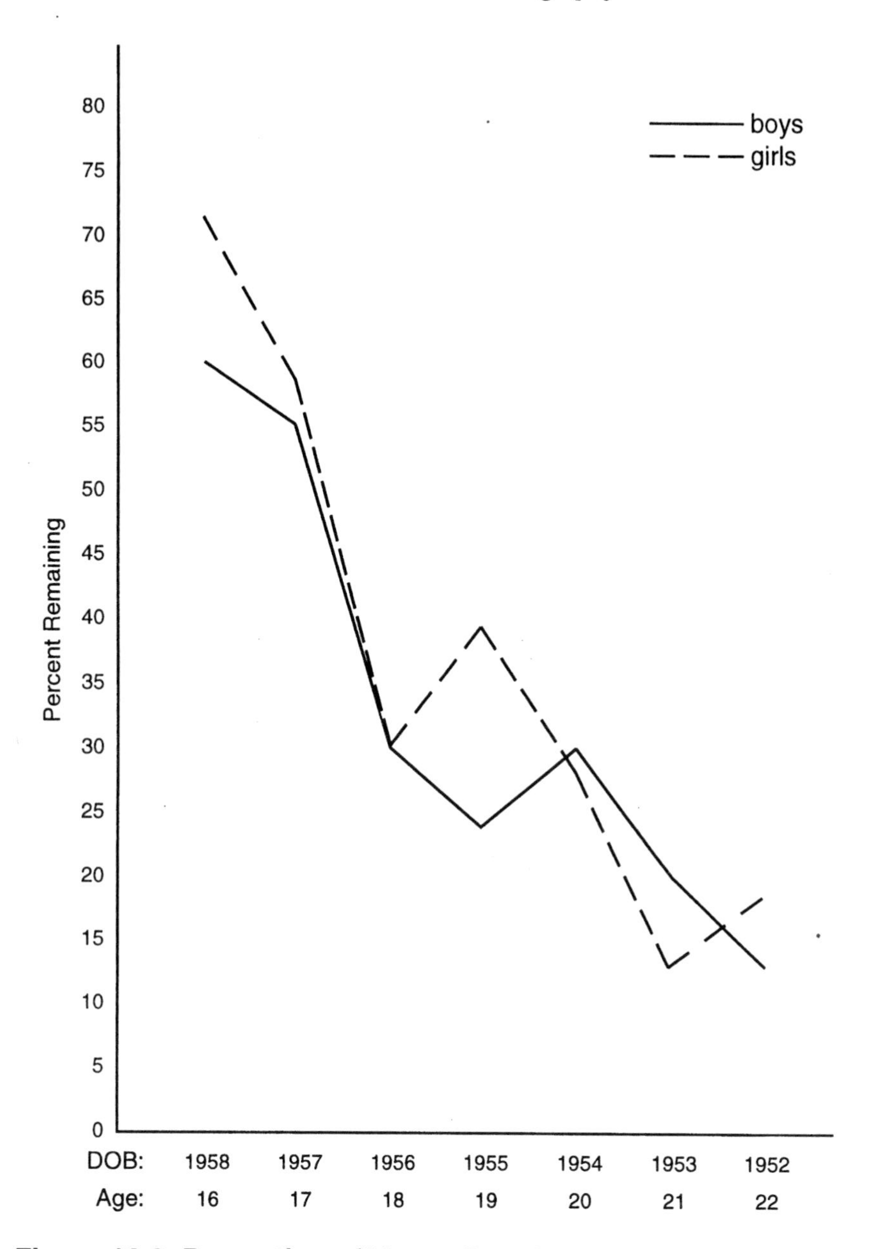

Figure 10.2. Proportion of Young People Remaining in Each Age Cohort as of September 1974, Aitutaki, Cook Islands

friend David Thomas, a social psychologist at the University of Waikato, had also introduced us to the work of Millard Madsen and Spencer Kagan on cooperation and competition among Mexican and Anglo-American children (Madsen 1967; Madsen and Shapira 1970; Kagan and Madsen 1971 and 1972) and shared with us the striking results he had recently obtained comparing the behavior of Polynesian and White ("Pakeha") children on the Madsen Cooperation Board (Thomas 1975a and 1975b). He urged us to conduct similar experiments among Cook Islands children in Aitutaki which we could compare directly with his. So we had taken with us the simple equipment required and arrived prepared to do so. In addition, we developed a coin distribution task in the field, building on earlier work by Kagan and Madsen (1972). Both simpler in format and more complex in content than their technique, our task, we found in pretesting, was suitable for use with subjects as young as five, yet retained the interest of sophisticated adults. It would therefore be appropriate for developmental studies, and for comparisons between parents and their children. Finally, Nan would work with several local schoolteachers to develop systematic procedures for observing preschool children in their natural settings. These experimental tasks and direct observations would provide our measures of behavioral variation. Differences in objective circumstances, economic activities, family structure, plus a survey interview among the parents and a variety of questionnaires and tests administered to their children in school would provide measures of our explanatory variables.

By September we had decided to make five-year-old preschoolers and form I children (roughly equivalent to U.S. sixth graders), plus their parents, the focus of our systematic research. Our goal was threefold: To examine psychological, structural, and experiential variables which might predict cooperative and altruistic behavior among young people; to observe how these behavioral tendencies were learned in early childhood; and finally, to measure the impact Western contact and other acculturation experiences among adults on island personalities and island life.[8]

Experiment One: The Coin Distribution Task

The most successful and productive of our systematic data collection procedures was the Coin Distribution Task we developed in the field.[9] Like many behavioral experiments and psychometric measures, it occupies an intermediate position between a pure measure of "generous" or "rivalrous" behavior and an indirect measure of underlying psychological tendencies or personality predispositions to engage in that behavior in interpersonal situations. (See chapters 3 and 6.) And in fact we used this task in both ways: as a measure of one "dependent" variable—behavior which we could explain or predict through its relationship to *other* measures—and as a measure of one "independent" variable—a personality or behavioral "predisposition" which helped to predict cooperative behavior in small groups on a very different task. (See Experiment Two below.)[10]

Our procedure involved each subject choosing one card from each of nine pairs of cards on which different numbers of pennies are placed for both the chooser and an observing child of the same age and sex. (For details of format and administration, see N. Graves and T. Graves 1978; reprinted as article 10 in Volume II.) Metaphorically, these choices were designed to represent behavioral choices confronting Islanders in everyday life. By inference they can also be seen as measuring the relative strength of four psychological motives: *rivalry* ("beating" the other, either by maximizing one's own gain relative to other or by minimizing the other's gain); *generosity* (maximizing the other's gain in absolute or relative terms); *equalization* (attempting to equate both one's own and the other's gain either on a particular trial or over the nine trials); and *self-maximization* (attempting to get the most for oneself without regard for the other).

Although Kagan and Madsen treated their own procedure as if each choice were an independent event, we found that subjects usually appeared to develop a general strategy across all nine choices. Because of the way the task is designed, however, the pursuit of any strategy involves trade-offs, and most subjects compromised somewhat. Subjects who made rivalrous choices on at least six of the nine opportunities were classified as *rivalrous* in both behavior and predisposition; those who made such choices three or less times were classified as *generous*; and those with intermediate scores of four or five were classified as *equalizers*. Each subject also received a *self-maximization* score, which is independent of the other three strategies.

We tested 261 boys and 212 girls on this procedure, virtually all the children in the first three grades (equivalent to K–2 in the United States), grade 5 (U.S. grade 4), and forms I and II (U.S. grades 6 and 7). The distribution of scores by age and sex can be seen graphically in Volume II, article 10, figure 1. Although at the start of their school experience less than 20% of these children displayed what we termed rivalrous behavior, by forms I and II about 40% of the girls and over half the boys were rivalrous. We concluded that the greater their exposure to Western schooling, the more rivalrous these basically generous children became. This is not just a matter of maturation; we validated our conclusions about the effects of exposure to the individualistic and competitive norms of Western schooling through a complex net of correlations, reported in article 10, as well as parallel findings among adults which also demonstrated that exposure to Western influences was associated with more rivalrous behavior on this procedure.

After returning to New Zealand, we also collected a Pakeha comparison group: forty-eight boys and thirty-nine girls in grades K–2 from an inner city and a rural school in the greater Auckland area. A comparison between the behavior of five- to eight-year-olds in the Cook Islands with the similar aged non-Polynesian children in New Zealand is presented in figure 10.3. (These data were not yet available when we published the report on our fieldwork contained in Volume II, article 10.)

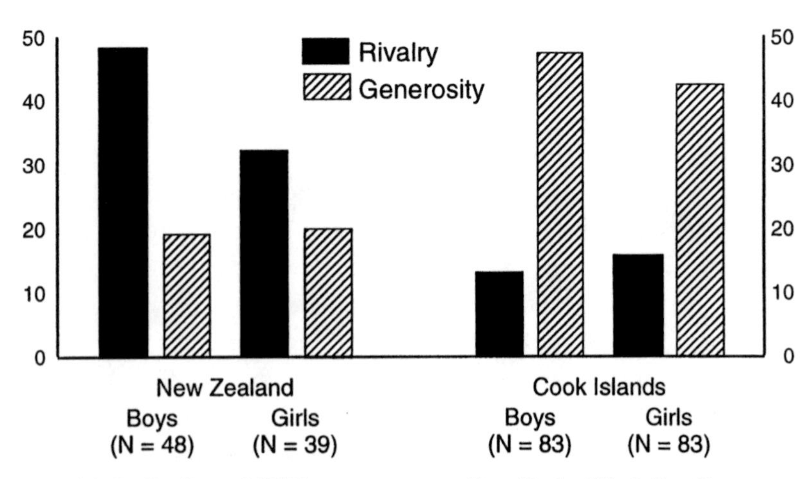

Figure 10.3. Cultural Differences on the Coin Distribution Task

Among New Zealand Pakeha children, 44% of the boys and 31% of the girls were already behaving in a rivalrous manner on this procedure even at the beginning of their school experience. (This sex difference in rivalry was not statistically significant, although it may reflect early sex-role differences in socialization to rivalry.) By contrast, only about 14% of the Cook Islands children behaved in a rivalrous manner, whereas 45% were generous. Only 18% of the Pakeha children were generous. These differences are highly significant statistically, of course, and are striking examples of the early impact of "culture." As Cook Islands children got older, however, they began behaving more and more like Pakeha New Zealand children. Our task was to discover under what circumstances this change in behavior would occur.

Interestingly, both ethnic groups were almost identical in their self-maximizing scores: The average child, whether Cook Islander or White New Zealander, chose the option which gave them the most money about three-quarters of the time it was offered. As a result, choosers in both groups averaged the same amount of money for themselves. The difference between the two groups, therefore, was not in how much they were willing to sacrifice their own interests, but *for what purpose* they would do so. Cook Islands children frequently gave up some of their possible earnings so that the other child would receive *more* money; New Zealand children sacrificed so that the other child would receive *less*.

Since the children in both societies were only beginning school, it seems reasonable to conclude that these dramatic contrasts in behavior are a result of the two distinct cultural contexts in which they had grown up, rather than differences in education or cognitive capacity. Furthermore, the behavior of neither group fits an egocentric stage model. If these young children were unable to consider the gains and losses of the observing child, they should simply have self-maximized whenever possible. In fact, only about a quarter of the children in both ethnic groups self-maximized all the time; the rest made calculated decisions at some time to take a personal loss in order to achieve some social purpose. For New Zealand children the situation was perceived as a chance to "win" more than someone else, and this was explicitly stated by many of them or displayed nonverbally by a triumphant grin as a rivalrous choice was made. By contrast, among the Cook Islands children, choices that involved taking more than the observing child often produced embarrassment, displayed by hesitation to choose, downcast eyes, or hands to face. (Systematic observations of the behavior of the experimental subjects were an important—and unusual—aspect of our procedure.)

The school system in Aitutaki, though predominantly staffed by native Aitutakians, was imported from New Zealand and reflected modern, Western value systems and norms of interaction. During their primary years, Cook Islands children must not only master academic skills, but they must also learn new interpersonal behavior. The classroom setting required the suppression of help-giving under most circumstances (in Western classrooms "helping" is typically considered "cheating"), rewards were individually distributed rather than shared by a group, and children had to vie for these rewards by "doing better" than their peers. (Standing out from others is very un-Polynesian behavior: As the saying goes, "The tallest palm is the first to be cut.") Furthermore, classroom authority was vested in a single adult, the teacher, rather than spread among peers, siblings, cousins, and a wide variety of adults. Thus the social context and behavioral expectations within the school were in sharp contrast to those found in traditional Polynesian homes. (See N. Graves and T. Graves 1979.) And with each passing year in school, these generous young Cook Islands children became increasingly more rivalrous, until by forms I and II most were acting very much like little White New Zealand children.

As our research progressed among these older children and among their parents, we wanted to document the ways in which Western influences ("acculturation") undermined traditional Polynesian patterns of cooperation and generosity, and led to the adoption of Western patterns of competition and self-centered individualism. Obviously, simply being in a Western-oriented school system was an important factor, but some children were more responsive to this influence than others. Who were the most susceptible to Western influence?

Because the adults we interviewed and tested on this same Coin Distribution Task were the parents and caretakers of our student and preschool sample, rather than a random sample of all adults on the island, we had ample family background data on all our subjects to draw on for this analysis. The results were exciting. (See Volume II, article 10.) Among adults, *exposure* to Western influences—years of education and having spent time in New Zealand, as well as living in the more Westernized (town) section of the island—and *adoption* of a Western-style nuclear family structure, all seemed critical in promoting rivalry. Among children, living in nuclear families and within the more Westernized villages were similarly influential.[11]

The strongest correlates with rivalry were still school variables, however, such as the condition of their school uniforms and their academic performance. Those who identified most strongly with the school system (well-kept uniforms) and received its rewards (high marks) were the most likely to display rivalrous behavior. This appears to be a systemic, feedback relationship, in which those children who exhibited the most competitive behavior in the classroom were the most likely to be noticed by their teachers and receive academic recognition. In the classroom, for example, we observed that teachers responded to the most competitive children in ways which rewarded and strengthened their competitive tendencies. As we noted in article 10, "many teachers concentrate their efforts on those perceived most likely to do well, while tending to ignore the slower children, allowing them to get what they can from school without being pushed." Consequently, year-end achievement scores, rather than falling into a normal curve, were clearly *bimodal*, and those in the upper half were *twice* as likely to be rivalrous on our Coin Distribution Task as those in the lower half. (For further details, see Volume II, article 10.)

Experiment Two: The Cooperation Board

In November, toward the end of the school year, we began testing form I children on the Madsen Cooperation Board. Briefly, this task requires subjects in groups of four to manipulate a pen over a piece of paper by pulling or slacking off on chords from the pen to each of them seated at the four corners of the experimental table. To succeed and obtain small rewards (in our case pennies with which they could purchase sweets) requires cooperation among them. If each pulls individualistically against the others, the pen remains near the center of the paper and no one receives rewards. This proved to be an ideal experimental procedure for studying cooperative behavior, and ultimately we tested 152 form I children, ranging in age from eleven to thirteen, in same-sex groups of four.

(A full description of the Madsen Board, our procedure and results is contained in Volume II, article 10.)

As we had anticipated, Cook Islands children proved to be far more successful than White New Zealand children at solving this cooperative task. Forty-five percent of our groups succeeded in cooperating, using the same criteria as Thomas; only 12% of the similar-aged Pakeha groups he had tested in New Zealand were successful. But these cultural differences, though supportive of ethnic stereotypes of Polynesian children (and adults) as more cooperative than Western children (and adults) were only a beginning. We wanted to understand *why* some Polynesian groups were successful and some were not.

A fruitful part of our data-gathering procedure was to include systematic observations of the participants while the children were engaged in the experimental task to discover what interpersonal behaviors led to success or failure. Almost 1,500 acts were recorded and scored. (See table 8 in article 10.) Briefly, an effective leader might help a group cooperate by directing and reproving the behavior of other participants. We observed twice as many acts of effective leadership in successful groups as in unsuccessful groups. But in general the quality and quantity of this leadership behavior seemed less important for success than the *membership* behavior. If this behavior was directed towards a group goal (listens to, looks at, watches, confers, and agrees with others) the group was far more likely to be successful; if this behavior was rivalistic and directed toward individual goals, the group was far less likely to be successful. Overall, furthermore, 59% of the children in unsuccessful groups had displayed a rivalrous behavioral predisposition on our Coin Distribution Task, compared to only 39% in unsuccessful groups.[12]

Equally interesting were our observations of how groups managed to overcome the rivalrous predispositions of some members. Since we had already learned that high academic achievement was strongly associated with more rivalrous behavior on the Coin Distribution Task, we anticipated that those students in the upper half of the bimodal distribution of marks would have more trouble cooperating on the Madsen Board than those students in the lower half. Contrary to our expectations, however, successful groups on the Cooperation Board contained 61% "high academics," whereas unsuccessful groups contained only 38% high academics." Solving this task probably requires certain cognitive skills. But we also observed many specific strategies used repeatedly by successful groups to overcome rivalrous tendencies among their members. The most common of these, particularly among girls (two-thirds of the successful girls groups used this strategy) was "buying off" a rivalrous member by allowing her to pull the pen to her circle first, after which she was more prepared to let the other children have a turn. But if a group of girls had more than one member who had tested rivalrous on the Coin Distribution Task, this strategy would not work and none of these groups were successful.

Another strategy used by successful problem solvers was to designate someone other than themselves to go first. Otherwise, their suggestion that they all take turns was likely to be ignored. Their willingness to be generous in this fashion often depended on their readiness to suppress rivalrous tendencies. Successful groups not only had fewer rivalrous members on the Coin Distribution Task to begin with, but only a third of these rivalrous persons behaved as rivalrous role models on the Cooperation Board. In unsuccessful groups, however, 70% of the rivalrous children competed fiercely. The most successful cooperative groups of all were careful to rotate first turns among all four members over the four trials.

These rich observations of participant behavior are unusual in experimental tasks of this kind, and were a major innovation in our procedure.

Systematic Observations in the Home

Nan's observational study of five-year-old preschool children on the island, conducted at the same time as the school study and adult survey and reported in a complementary publication (N. Graves and T. Graves 1983), was designed both to discover how traditional Polynesian patterns of prosocial behavior were learned in the home, and how Western influences were changing that learning environment for a growing number of Polynesian children. So her study had both a traditional "cultural learning" goal and an "acculturation" component.

Most of those who study "prosocial development" can be divided into two camps: Those who focus on processes *within* the child (the "cognitive development" approach, e.g., Piaget 1932; Kohlberg 1964 and 1969) and those who focus on influences *external* to the child (the "socialization" or "enculturation" approach of most sociologists and anthropologists). This is that old nature/nurture problem again. We attempted to synthesize both, in what we referred to as an "ecological" model. This resembles the social channeling of psychological predispositions, illustrated among Navajo migrants in chapter 8, but emphasizes the subtle ways in which prosocial behavior is an "emergent" from a contextual system that requires interdependence among persons in daily interaction.

Soon after we arrived in Aitutaki and settled into our village home, for example, it became apparent to us that our Polynesian neighbors expended little effort explicitly training children in prosocial behavior. As soon as they could toddle, most children seemed eager to be involved in the busy round of family and neighborhood activities, which they were allowed to join as they became physically capable.

We were particularly struck by the rarity of "object attachment" (Linus's blanket), "parallel play" (where children play in each other's presence but not *with* each other), "private speech" monologues, or other manifestations of "egocentrism" that characterize early developmental stages in the West. Instead, the children around us appeared to have a strong *group* orientation from infancy, which was being reinforced continuously in dozens of ways: They were being raised in large families by a variety of caretakers; they attended and participated in most family and community affairs; they were sent with food or goods to share with other people; they would take the family's contribution to the front of the church on Sunday; and they learned to work, drum, and dance on the perimeter of groups to which their older siblings, cousins, uncles, aunts, or parents and grandparents belonged.

This high degree of group participation and identification and the many manifestations of prosocial behavior that flow from it, we came to recognize, has its roots in the economic, social, and psychological interdependencies fostered by their subsistence economy. With Western influence, however, these interdependencies were breaking down, and with them are passing the need for and support of the high level of sociocentric behavior that has characterized island life.

Traditionally, for example, a fisherman who catches more than his family can eat that day will "store the surplus in his neighbor's belly." Then he and his family can count on a constant supply of fresh fish through gifts from others in return. Thus a network of mutual obligation, caring, and concern is formed throughout the village. With the advent of electricity, however (which only came to Aitutaki in 1964, but was being used by 90% of the households a decade later), refrigerators and freezers became popular. (A quarter of the adults in our survey owned them.) Now, a family's surplus could be stored at home, and the need for networks of food redistribution diminished. The same process was occurring with the introduction of sheet metal roofing, which eliminates the periodic need for communal thatching parties; commercial beer, which can be bought a few bottles at a time, replacing the large batches of home brew which would then be consumed communally; tractors rented from the agriculture department plowing individual fields which earlier would have been worked by labor exchange groups; outboard motors reducing the need for communal fishing by extending the range of individual boats, and so forth. People could now "afford" to quarrel with their neighbors, and the social skills that had developed to prevent, deflect, or resolve such quarrels would atrophy or never be learned.

Underlying all these changes was the dramatic growth in a cash economy on the island since World War II, which we were documenting. As more and more men were shifting from a subsistence economy to wage work, their neighbors would report "he's fishing in the shops these days." Furthermore, low wages and high prices make the "cost" of generosity greater, just as the desire for more material possessions, now within their grasp, was increasing. Some Islanders saw these economic changes as the growth of an un-Christian, selfish materialism, whereas others welcomed the opportunity to escape what they saw as physical drudgery and unreasonable obligations imposed on them by family and community.

Our understanding of the interconnections within this process of change grew during our six months of participant observation. Then, while Nan and I tested students in the schools and conducted interviews with the adults, she began the task of documenting changes in child rearing as well, with the help of five native Aitutakian female teachers whom she trained in systematic observational techniques. During the Christmas holidays (South Pacific summer, 1974–1975) they observed twenty-eight girls and twenty-one boys between the ages of five and six, who would be entering school the following year. These observations were conducted in the child's homes or surrounding environs during four 45-minute sessions, two during the mornings and two in the afternoons.[13] Upon entering the setting, usually unannounced, the observer recorded everyone present, the activities they were engaged in, and their kin or non-kin relationship to the target child. This placed all subsequent action within its social context, which was updated throughout the observation period as activities shifted and people came and went.

Using a structured, narrative procedure which Nan developed with their help, these observers recorded the target child's behavior in "action units." Each act included the verb or action, the initiator of the action, the responder (either the target child or another in the environment if the act was interpersonal), and modifiers of the action (including adjectives, adverbs, and expressions of affect). After translation, the "action units" in each protocol were coded into a variety of categories. In addition to our own categories concerning the social makeup of the environment and the "chore opportunities" within it, we also scored the protocols for categories used in the Six Cultures Study (Whiting and Whiting 1975) to make direct comparisons with the Whitings' work possible: "altruism" (offering or giving help, offering or giving support, and suggesting responsible behavior to others); "egoism" (asking for help or support, seeking attention, and seeking dominance or competing); and "mands" (commands, demands, or requests made to or by the target child). Protocols were scored by two coders with a reliability ranging from .84 to perfect, and any differences were then resolved through discussion and agreement.

Since we were interested in the effects of modern structural changes on prosocial behavior, we divided our sample of children by two cross-cutting dimensions: nuclear or extended family household structure and rural or town residence, both of which were strongly related to differences in "rivalry" in the Coin Distribution Task among parents. Each cell contained at least five boys and five girls. This four-cell division resulted in a "most traditional" category of rural children raised in extended families (N = 12) and a "most modern" category of town children raised in nuclear families (N = 10). The other two cells, rural-nuclear (N = 17) and town-extended (N = 10) were intermediate and mixed in degree of modernization.

A major determinant of children's behavior, we believed, would be the cast of characters found in that setting. Although we found no substantial differences between families with different degrees of modernization as to the *number* of persons present during these observations (all averaged between 4 and 5), they did differ sharply in the *type* of persons available to the child. The most traditional children (from extended families in a rural setting) had mostly kinsmen (89%) and few nonrelatives (11%) around, whereas the most modern children (nuclear/town families) had many more nonrelatives present (34%). Over half the time when observers visited rural-extended families, the mother was *absent* throughout the observation period (53%), and the child was mainly interacting with kin—brothers and sisters, cousins, aunts and uncles, and grandparents—who served as caretakers. Unrelated persons were present less than a quarter of the time. By contrast, in the town-nuclear households, the mother was present during 85% of the observations, and unrelated persons were present over three-quarters of the time.

The type of persons *present*, of course, will largely determine who a child interacts *with*. Almost half the time (47%), children in traditional households (extended families in a rural setting), engaged in social acts with extended kin, secondarily with nuclear kin (39%), and seldom with nonfamily persons (7%). Modern children showed the opposite pattern, interacting mostly with nuclear family members (55%) or unrelated persons (31%) and relatively rarely with extended kin (14%).

These differences in personnel and resulting interaction mean that traditional children are surrounded by and must learn to relate to a wide and varied circle of *relatives*, many of whom have authority over them (including older siblings and cousins). This group provides them with their sense of identity and belonging. Modern children, by contrast, are probably learning to *differentiate* themselves from others through their participation in a smaller, more exclusive family group and frequent contact with persons not belonging to this group at all. This could perhaps provide them with less sense of social *interdependence* than is experienced by traditional children. Furthermore, since nonrelatives are not directly responsible for these children's behavior, they may not as often actively promote the positive social behavior expected within the family.

Contrary to the Whitings' suggestion in their Six Cultures Study, we believe from these observations that the opposite of prosocial behavior is not egoism, but *individualistic* behavior. In our study this involved playing on one's own, often without others or ignoring their presence (as in parallel play), and often with one's attention on objects—things rather than people. Here the important ecological determinant in our study was town residence. Whereas children from extended or nuclear families did not differ in the amount of such nonsocial, solitary behavior, fully half of all the acts by town children were nonsocial, as compared to less than a third for the rural children. This probably reflects the dispersion of the family and the relative paucity of cooperative joint tasks in town, as well as an increase in interesting modern objects in the child's environment.

Sex Differences in the Learning of Cooperative Behavior

These children's learning experience is further shaped not only by *who* they interact with, among those available to them, but also by *what form* that interaction takes. Here significant sex differences emerged. First, in rural-extended families preschool girls were interacting with adults at a far higher rate than preschool boys: 34 acts per hour for girls compared with only 9 per hour for boys. Instead, boys were spending more of their time in play groups interacting with other boys.

Second, almost a quarter of these girls' interactions with adults involved *mands*: commands, demands, or requests directed toward the target child. By contrast, only 11% of adult interactions with boys in these traditional family settings involved such mands. Thus girls were having far more practice than boys in meeting the needs of adults, whereas the boys were often playing outside the arenas within which adults were working. In town settings, however, boys and girls did not differ in the number of mands they received from either adults or children.

Finally, we found that in the traditional (rural-extended) families girls were performing useful chores for the household at the rate of over eight per hour, whereas boys were doing only about one. So traditional girls were receiving a great deal of experience in contributing useful work to the family group, whereas boys were seldom called away from their play groups to perform chores. Again, in town boys and girls were not much different, although girls continued to do more chores than boys: 2.6 per hour compared to 1.8 for town boys.

These differences between boys and girls are related to three things: the *number* of chores available to be done in the country as compared to town that are at a level five-year-olds could be expected to handle; cultural values concerning the *appropriateness* of these tasks for boys or girls; and *how many other* eligible children are around to do them.

As Nan had found among Hispanic families in Colorado and Baganda families in East Africa, rural environments provide many more opportunities than town environments for children to help the family. On Aitutaki, men do more of the fishing, planting, and maintenance of food crops, and gathering, husking, and processing of coconuts, while women are expected to maintain the home, prepare food and clothing, and care for infants. Preschool boys are not considered old enough to participate in the men's work, whereas common and easy household tasks, such as collecting leaves and rubbish, keeping the fire going, running errands, washing dishes, sweeping, and a variety of child-care activities are usually performed by girls, if any are available. All of these except errands, fall under the sex-role division of labor. For example, although preschool boys *could* care for babies and seemed to enjoy them, we found only eight of the twenty-one boys ever did so during our observations, whereas twenty-four of the twenty-eight girls in our sample did so (chi square = 12.0, $p < .01$). These patterns parallel those found in other cross-cultural studies (Whiting and Edwards 1973; Ember 1973).

These circumstances create a situation in traditional families where cooperative behavior directed toward family goals is learned earlier for girls than boys, except in cases where few little girls are present. This "underwomaning," however, is more likely to occur in nuclear than in extended families. Consequently, the boys whom we observed in nuclear households actually performed *more* chores than those in extended households: 2.7 per hour compared with 1.3 per hour. *All* children, however, experience a radical reduction in the number of chores available to them when their families lived in town: The mean number of "chore opportunities" for children observed in nuclear-town settings was only 5.5 compared to 17.9 for children observed in rural-extended families.

The result of this is not only fewer family contributions and less responsibility for modern preschoolers, as Nan had observed in Denver and Kampala, but probably lower maternal expectations for them, and therefore, fewer adult-directed learning experiences (N. Graves 1971). In addition, in town there are more attractions outside the home—nearby friends and amusements—to tempt the child from family work. In Aitutaki, "wandering" was cited by town mothers as a major problem with children this age.

These sex differences in family work around the home have important implications for the development of prosocial behavior. It is clear from our observations that supportive and helpful behavior, as well as suggestions to others that they behave responsibly (the behaviors categorized as "altruism" in the Whitings' scoring system), often occurred in conjunction with family work around the home. Thus we found that *being given responsible tasks promotes altruistic acts.* Because much of this help is given in situations where others are involved in the work as well, chores also promote cooperative behavior involving coordination of effort. In extended families in rural settings girls displayed the most altruistic behavior—24% of all their acts—whereas this was true for only 8% of the boys' acts. In modern, nuclear families in town, however, *both* boys and girls are similarly low in altruistic behavior: between 5% and 8% of their acts.

Boys and girls also differed in the *type* of prosocial behavior they displayed. At this age boys acted altruistically mainly in relation to their *playmates*, for example, by sharing toys and food. Most of the girls' altruism took the form of responsible behavior in conjunction with family chores. Thus girls were learning to be cooperative within a hierarchical system of family responsibility, whereas boys were learning altruism in an egalitarian peer situation. In adolescence, however, boys will join older men in their fishing and other cooperative tasks, and it is then that they will mainly learn how to relate to older authority.

Conclusions

This research included our first systematic study of cooperative *teamwork*, which was to become the focus of the next phase of our professional career. It was from observing the contrast between traditional Polynesian learning experiences in cooperative groups and the individualistic and competitive strategies commonly used to motivate children in conventional Western classrooms that we became interested in *cooperative learn-*

ing, a movement within education which we recommended to Cook Islands politicians and educators as a way to avoid undermining traditional group-oriented values. (See chapter 13.)

In addition to this work on cooperation, generosity, and rivalry, we also looked at the way in which modernization, particularly among men, was affecting their physical and mental health. These findings were published in T. Graves and N. Graves (1979); reprinted as article 11 in Volume II. I will also discuss these findings along with a companion study of stress and health among Pakehas and Polynesian migrants in New Zealand in chapter 13.

In conclusion, this concatenation of systematic information, collected in different ways from a variety of sources and settings, shed new light on the origins of the cultural differences in "inclusive" and "exclusive" behavior which we had observed in New Zealand, as well as the process by which Polynesians are increasingly becoming like individualistic, rivalrous Westerners. This is a good example of a behavioral science approach to ethnographic analysis and interpretation, and contrasts sharply with more conventional ethnographic accounts.

Methodological Lessons for Behavioral Anthropology

The substantive lessons learned from this work were rich and rewarding, and a major report on our work (Volume II, article 10, first published in 1978) received the Stirling Award in Culture and Personality from the American Anthropological Association in 1975, the year we returned from the field. But the methodological lessons are equally important.

1. Systematic observations of small children's socialization experiences in or near their homes are extremely time-consuming and labor intensive. Using a team of knowledgeable local observers—schoolteachers on holiday eager to earn additional money—proved extremely helpful, not only because of the number of children who could be observed, but because of their knowledge of kin relationships and other local information which we would have overlooked. Involving these observers in the construction of the simple observational scheme served not only to improve its relevance, but also to help train and motivate the observers and create a true "insider-outsider" team. But close supervision by the behavioral scientist is necessary to maintain motivation and quality control.

2. Systematic observations of behavior enormously enrich data from other sources, such as interviews and experimental tasks, and in turn are enriched by them. A *convergence* of data from a variety of sources provides our fullest understanding of personality development and its contribution to behavior.

3. Systematic observations of subjects' behavior during a task such as the Madsen Cooperation Board can enormously enrich the empirical findings from these behavioral experiments.

4. The Cooperation Board also presented us with some unique theoretical and methodological issues. Although this task served as an excellent, objective, and replicable measure of cooperative behavior, prediction of that behavior from the personal characteristics of each group member was limited, because the outcome depended on the way the group functioned as a *team.* This forced us to look at cooperative behavior from a *contextual, ecological* perspective. This approach has now become leading edge within social psychology (Ross and Nisbett 1991), but at the time we were conducting our fieldwork was relatively rare. It came to serve as the guiding theoretical orientation in our subsequent analysis of prosocial development (N. Graves and T. Graves 1983).

5. Although we were able to observe and record impressive "cultural" differences in behavior using a variety of methods, variation in this behavior *within* a group contributed extremely valuable information on the sources of these differences, when related to variation in background experiences and psychological attributes of the actors. Increasingly we also came to recognize the importance of evaluating the *objective circumstances* under which such behavior takes place. This would become an important methodological strategy in our systematic observations of drinking behavior in New Zealand pubs, discussed in the next chapter.

Notes

1. Some well-publicized examples: Mead 1935 vs. Fortune 1939; Mead 1928 vs. Freeman 1983 and 1999; Redfield 1930 vs. Lewis 1951. See also, Schwartz and Schwartz 1955.

2. I did write a delightful ethnographic introduction to the tri-ethnic community (Graves 1966a), but Jessor did not want to include it in our more formal research report (Jessor, Graves, Hanson, and Jessor 1968).

3. Our anthropological colleagues, Tony Hooper and Judy Huntsman, who had invited us to New Zealand, were already studying another, small group of migrants from the Tokelau Islands. See Hooper and Huntsman 1972.

4. New Zealand life was also being affected by Islanders—"Polynesian Panthers" were active in Auckland when we arrived, the behavior of islanders was a popular topic in the press and casual conversation, and islander immigration became a divisive political issue in the next parliamentary election. But this impact was far smaller than that of the West on island life.

5. Fortunately, we had been able to maintain cooperative relationships with our former spouses, each of whom kept one of the girls during this year of fieldwork.

6. Aitutaki had two elementary schools on opposite sides of the island and its middle school (forms I and II) near the center. Children who wanted more education had to go either to the capital island of Rarotonga or to New Zealand.

7. Seventh-Day Adventists, who have become the second-largest denomination on the island, celebrate their sabbath on Saturday, the others on Sunday; the fish never get a rest. There are strong community sanctions against working or fishing on the Sabbath, supplemented among some by a lingering belief in possible divine punishment. This makes it difficult to schedule any community-wide cooperative activities over the weekend.

8. The decision *not* to interview a randomly selected sample of adults was deliberate. Our interest was more in exploring *relationships* among variables (including relationships between parent characteristics and the behavior of their children) than in making population estimates. For more on sampling decisions, see chapter 8.

9. In our original report we referred to this procedure as the "Coin Game." When administering it, however, we were careful not to use the term "game" to avoid introducing a competitive set.

10. Despite the fact that our results were striking and serve to document substantial cultural differences in the distribution of these personality traits and related behavior, to date I know of no other researchers who have tried using this task. I wish they would!

11. For purposes of the annual all-island rugby match, the administrative center and the two adjacent villages, including our village of Amuri, were designated as "town," while the other four villages combine forces to create a "country" team. This corresponds fairly well to the spatial distribution of intense Western influence on the island, and has psychological reality as well. For both men and women, those living in town were almost twice as likely to be "rivalrous" on our Coin Distribution Task as those living in the country. See article 10, table 6, p. 242 in Volume II.

12. These differences are "statistically significant" on a chi-square test at the .05 level. But since individual outcomes on the Cooperation Board are not independent events—all four children in a successful group will be classified as "successful"—it is not strictly legitimate to apply this test. We did so only to provide some standard for judging the magnitude of our results.

13. Nan dropped in on these observers on a random basis. They both recorded their observations, which were later compared as a check on reliability.

11

Interplay between Theory and Research

When we flew back to Auckland in 1975 at the end of our year of field-work on the tiny island of Aitutaki, I remember being overwhelmed by sensual stimuli: the lights, sounds, smells of the city. Walking into a supermarket I felt flooded by the multitude of choices: six varieties of toilet tissue, a dozen varieties of breakfast cereal, breads of all kinds, white, whole wheat, rye, raisin, French, sourdough. Option overload. I remember wondering what would this be like for Pacific Islanders arriving in New Zealand for the first time? Wouldn't they feel even more overwhelmed? How would they cope?

We had become immigrants ourselves in 1972 when we moved our family from California to New Zealand, so our personal lives and intellectual interest in migrant adaptation had converged. One of our first professional undertakings in our new home was writing a review article on urban migration for the *Annual Review of Anthropology* (N. Graves and T. Graves 1974). This proved to be an excellent exercise, forcing us into a thorough review of the literature and launching a fruitful new theoretical direction: examining the alternative adaptive strategies of urban migrants. And in the process of exploring the implications of this emerging theory we again found ourselves looking at drinking behavior, but in a new way.

This chapter returns to an important theme in behavioral anthropology—and in all science—the interplay between theory and research. It has been said that there is nothing so practical as a good theory. It guides and directs your empirical eye to observe and record from the infinite variety of possible "facts" those which are the most likely to make "sense" when brought together. But there is nothing more pregnant with theoretical possibility than well-chosen "facts" when they have been selected and examined in relationship to each other in this way. A second theme of this chapter involves strategies for conducting exploratory, theory-generating research, and then moving on to a more systematic theory-testing follow-up study. This, in turn, usually results in refinement of the theory. A third topic examines once more the strengths and limitations of systematic behavioral observations, this time, of drinking behavior in New Zealand pubs.

The Seeds of a Theory

When we first arrived in New Zealand, we had neither friends nor family already there to help us settle in. But we had been raised to be self-reliant, we had good educations and worldwide experience, money, and a job already waiting for us. So we drew on our own resources for coping with our new environment. But New Zealand is a small town, and we often found that without schoolmates or kin ties to call on we had difficulty adjusting or getting things done. How did other migrants cope?

The Navajo migrants we had studied in Denver had BIA sponsorship which paid their transportation, found them a job and a place to live, and helped them settle in. This was a quite unnatural migration situation, which perhaps made the move too simple. Young, single men were often encouraged to migrate who certainly would not have done so on their own, and who might have been better off never to have gone. Their social network, made up mainly of other young men, was not much help in their adaptation, in fact, their friends often contributed to their failure. (See chapter 7.) For the quarter who were married, only their wives provided an effective check on their drinking (McSwain 1965). Among the Hispanic and Baganda families Nan had studied, her focus had been on the impact of their new urban environment on their child-rearing behavior rather than on how they had gotten there. So a study of the migration process under natural conditions was a new topic of interest to us.

All over the world population pressures and Western influences have been leading more and more rural villagers to migrate to cities in search of jobs and excitement. Our own migration experience was hard enough; how would relatively unsophisticated people like Pacific Islanders, with limited education and few resources cope? And what might be the consequences of their strategy choices for other aspects of their behavior and on their health?

Among many topics, our 1974 review examined the ways immigrants managed to solve the practical problems of getting to the city, finding a job and a place to live, making friends, etc. The seeds of what would later become our theory of *preferred adaptive strategies* among urban migrants appeared in the distinction we drew in this early article between *individualistic* strategies such as we had used ourselves and *group-oriented* strategies such as were more typical of non-Western people:

> We can consider as *individualistic* those strategies where a migrant relies essentially on his own resources or his own initiative for a solution. If he uses institutional resources made available by the host community, he does so as an individual or a nuclear household head. By contrast, in *group-oriented* strategies the migrant turns for help to other people, usually kinsmen, fellow villagers, or migrants from his own ethnic group. Although such strategies tap a larger pool of resources than those possessed by the migrant himself, these are shared within a framework of reciprocity norms which require him to contribute his own resources to swell the adaptive potential of the group as a whole. Such strategies constitute the typical adaptive mode of many cooperative, kin-based societies described by anthropologists, and contrast with the individualistic strategies more common within Western society. Intragroup variations can usually be found, however, and ultimately we hope more attention will be given to specifying factors which lead to the choice between these alternatives. (N. Graves and T. Graves 1974:128–129)

An Exploratory Study of Worker Adaptation

This germ of a theory, with its attention to alternative strategies migrants may use for getting to the city, finding a job and a place to live, and generally coping with their new environment, would become the guide for what we looked at in our next research project. Meanwhile, however, we needed a job. In order to remain in New Zealand and take advantage of the research opportunity afforded by my Captain James Cook Fellowship (which paid for our research in Aitutaki) Nan had been forced to resign her position at UCLA, and I had resigned my own tenured professorship in solidarity. But our fellowship had now come to an end, and the anthropologists at Auckland University were happy not to have us stirring up student interest in contemporary race relations. So we took a position in the Department of Management Studies teaching social psychology, with a particular focus on Polynesian workers, both Pacific Islanders and indigenous Maoris.

Island people had been migrating to New Zealand in growing numbers since World War II, in search of jobs and educational opportunities. By 1975 there were more Cook Islanders living in New Zealand than in the Cooks, and the Samoan community was even larger. Smaller numbers had also come from Niue and the Tokelaus (both New Zealand protectorates) and the Kingdom of Tonga, among others. Although islanders made up only about two percent of the overall New Zealand population, their concentration in a few urban areas (particularly Auckland, the country's major industrial center) made them a significant and conspicuous minority group. Over half the indigenous Maori population (then roughly 8% of the total New Zealand population) were also now living in these same urban areas. As a result, almost half the floor-level workers in New Zealand's factories were Polynesian.

Responding to this challenge, the Vocational Training Council of New Zealand had recently established a Polynesian Advisory Committee, and when our friend and former anthropology graduate student, W. Frazer McDonald, completed his master's degree he took a position as its first director. He suggested that we might be interested in conducting a study to assist management (almost invariably Pakehas—New Zealanders of European cultural heritage) to better understand and motivate their multicultural workforce. It seemed to us that this project would fit in well with our overall research program on Polynesian urban migrant adaptation.

Since this project was to be conducted under the auspices of the Polynesian Advisory Committee, we decided to focus particular attention on ways to better understand Polynesian employees. Topics to be covered would include factors influencing job satisfaction, relations with supervisors and coworkers, and work-relevant attitudes. But we wanted to develop a theoretical model which would be just as useful for understanding European and Pakeha workers as Polynesians, and to link this research to our general interest in migrant adaptation. Would adaptive strategies for getting to New Zealand and adjusting to urban life have implications in the workplace? Would European migrants differ from Pacific Islanders in strategy choice, or from the everyday strategies of Pakeha and Maori New Zealanders who were not migrants?

We began our research by conducting exploratory interviews with management in over thirty major factories in the Auckland area concerning their experiences working with their Polynesian and non-Polynesian labor force. Rather than interview a few workers in each of a large number of factories, however, we then decided to conduct a more intensive, but still exploratory study of worker attitudes and behavior within two contrasting factories. This would enable us to control roughly for certain features of size, technology, and working conditions, while varying others. At the "theory generating" stage this method of "controlled comparison" is an extremely useful approach. (See Glasser and Strauss 1967.)

As our focus for intensive study we chose two large carpet mills which presented theoretically interesting similarities and differences. The factories were about equal in size—roughly 250 production-level workers onsite—and in both, Polynesians constituted a majority of the hourly workers. Both manufactured wool carpets, but Factory A employed a traditional weaving technique, whereas Factory B produced their carpets by a technologically simpler "tufting" process in which loops of wool are inserted into a thin, fibrous material which is later backed with latex and cloth to prevent the wool loops from pulling out. "Weaving" has traditionally been considered a skilled job taking several years of experience to master, and in Factory A workers passed slowly up through a hierarchy of machines from "narrow loom" to "broad loom," each of increasing complexity and speed. "Tufting" machines, although also variable in speed and complexity, can be mastered in a matter of months, and in Factory B machine operators were routinely rotated from one machine to another every two weeks. The management style in Factory A was hierarchical and strict and the union was strong and somewhat adversarial. In Factory B management was more relaxed, the union was weak, and (against union rules) supervisors often pitched in to help their workers. The reward structure in the two factories also differed: All workers in Factory A were paid on a production bonus basis; in Factory B most workers received higher hourly wages, but without production bonuses.

In line with our theory-generating design, we began with a period of informal observations and discussion with key personnel at all levels. We then conducted semi-structured interviews of from one to three hours in length with 157 production-level workers, both men and women, from the following ethnic groups:

20 Pakeha New Zealanders
38 Maori New Zealanders
10 European immigrants
42 Samoans
35 Cook Islanders
10 Niueans
2 Tongans

We used a quota-sampling procedure to obtain interviews with a preset proportion of eligible men and women representing different ethnic groups and levels of skill. This ensured that our sample would be representative of the labor force as a whole, while providing the flexibility necessary to minimize disrupting ongoing factory activities. I conducted all the interviews with men; Nan and Renée Haman, a mature sociology graduate student working on her master's thesis under our supervision, interviewed the women. The data reported below are drawn from our report on this research, prepared for the Polynesian Advisory Committee (N. Graves and T. Graves 1977a).

All interviews were conducted in English. Although a majority of our subjects were Polynesian, some of whom might have felt shy or uncomfortable talking with Pakeha interviewers, and some of whom had English language difficulties, we made a deliberate decision at this exploratory stage to conduct the interviews ourselves in order to learn as much as we could from talking with all types of workers directly. As researchers, we have found we remember what we see and hear ourselves better than what we read, and can use this material more readily in theory construction.

Characteristics of the interviewed sample are presented in table 11.1. Noteworthy is the similarity between men and women workers. Despite a slight advantage in age, education, and seniority, however, women were

Table 11.1. Characteristics of Interviewed Sample

	Men (N = 72)	Women (N = 85)
Average age	30	32
(range)	(17–64)	(18–64)
Percent married	64%	58%
Average household size	5.0	4.7
(range)	(1–11)	(1–11)
Average years of education	9.6	10.0
Median number of jobs in NZ	3	3
Percent on First Job	17%	24%
Average years on present job	3.4	3.6
(range)	(0–17)	(0–18)
Average weekly take-home pay (after taxes)	$88.51	$82.57

receiving on the average about $6 less per week in pay. (We found no evidence for *ethnic* discrimination in pay, however.)

Questions in this exploratory interview covered a broad range of topics, including our subjects' work history, relations with supervisors and coworkers, attitudes toward money and major financial needs, background experiences, particularly of the migrants, and finally, household composition, family life, and spare-time activities. Guiding our choice of questions was our general philosophy that a person's adjustment to work is part of a larger, total life adaptation and cannot be understood in isolation. Many questions were open-ended in format, allowing subjects to express their own attitudes and feelings, rather than having to choose among alternatives we provided as outsiders. For example, "What do you like *best* about working for [Company A or B]?" "Can you tell me something you *don't* like about working for ___?" Open-ended responses (as I have described in chapter 2 and Volume II, article 4) can later be subjected to systematic content analysis to yield quantitative scores. At the same time, such questions allowed us to probe more deeply whenever it seemed appropriate, and to follow many paths even though some of them might eventually prove deadends. This type of interviewing is more time-consuming and requires more skill than questionnaires with preset answers, but is an essential discovery technique during the exploratory phases of any study. Follow-up research, as I will discuss later in this chapter, can be designed in more structured ways and conducted in each subject's first language by trained interviewers from the same ethnic groups.

These exploratory interviews usually lasted between one and two hours. This can be exhausting for both interviewers and subjects, particularly those answering questions in their second language or who are not used to thinking about themselves and their situations analytically. To help overcome this problem we attempted to create an atmosphere of relaxed informality, allowing subjects to smoke if they wished and to think about their answers at leisure while we wrote down what they had said previously. We wanted verbatim answers to many questions, so that in our reports subjects could speak for themselves about their lives and work. This makes for more interesting reading and like case studies helps flesh out statistical analyses. But a tape recorder can inhibit a shy subject, and tapes are very time-consuming to transcribe and analyze.

For their data, behavioral scientists are heavily dependent on what their subjects are willing and able to tell them, and are then faced with the issue of how accurately what they are told reflects the true feelings of their subjects. To increase the honesty (validity) of these self-reports all interviews were conducted in private rooms provided by management, and subjects were guaranteed anonymity. We also took pains to define ourselves as "outsiders," emphasizing that we were not employed by management, but by the University of Auckland and the Vocational Training Council. No worker was forced to be interviewed, and no one lost any pay as a result of participation. By interviewing opinion leaders first, word quickly spread that the questions were fun and interesting and provided ample opportunity to offer observations and complaints about their work in a safe and relaxed atmosphere.

Subjects talked freely about how they obtained their job and why they changed jobs. Here are two contrasting examples with both theoretical and practical implications. It is from such raw data that our theory of adaptive strategies began to evolve:

> *I was a leading hand at ____. When my cousin first come to New Zealand from Samoa, he can't speak much English, so my boss wouldn't give him a job. So I come up here with my cousin, going around to other factories*

> *with him. So I talked with the Personnel Officer [at Factory B]. She said she got a job for me, but not for my cousin, because he can't speak English. I said I'd take the job here if she took my cousin. She said ok, if I worked here with my cousin.*

Consequently, he left his well-paying and responsible job at another firm.

> *I explained to my old factory why I finished: I feel sorry for my cousin who can't get a job if I don't work with him. They send me a letter, want me to come back. But I told them, it's too bad, too late, because they didn't get a job for my cousin. They wrote back that they have a job for my cousin. But I wrote back, "Sorry, it's too late because my cousin like this job, and me too."*

This is a good example of how kin ties aided a migrant's adaptation. A Cook Islander described the way in which informal friendship networks lead to jobs, a somewhat different strategy:

> *One of my mates (from the same island) had been working here for two years. I met him in the pub and he said he was going to Australia. "Is anyone taking your job at ___?" I asked. "No." So one day he brought me to the factory to have a look. He said, "Oh yes, it's quite a clean job. You get nice overalls." Well," I say, "it's good working here for my health." So he took me to the Personnel Officer and signed me up.*

We looked at sex and ethnic differences in responses to each of our topics. For example, with respect to job satisfaction, Polynesians were more influenced by their relations with coworkers than Europeans and Pakehas. Pacific Islands immigrants, who also reported heavy financial obligations to support relatives and their churches, were more concerned about pay and availability of overtime than Europeans and New Zealanders (including New Zealand–educated Maoris and Islanders), who were more concerned about convenient *hours* than Islanders. Men were far more motivated by opportunities for "self-growth" on the job (advancement, change, acquiring new skills) than women, but women were far more sensitive to the quality of their working conditions (cleanliness of work space, toilets, etc.) than men. Men feel little embarrassment being on the street, riding the bus, shopping, or going to the pub in their work clothes, for example, but women wanted showers available. Otherwise, "you just have to go home in your dirt," one commented ruefully.

We also looked for *situational* differences which seemed to influence worker attitudes and behavior regardless of sex or ethnicity. For example, if workers are given a bonus incentive for high production, they tend to be less open to various innovations in machines or production methods, less willing to take the time to train new workers, and less willing to cooperate with fellow workers to get a job done, since such deviations from routine may potentially cut into their bonus. This gives management less flexibility in adapting its operation to changing conditions.

A Theory of Preferred Adaptive Strategies

Out of this work emerged our theory of *preferred adaptive strategies* (N. Graves and T. Graves 1977b). We now came to differentiate three such strategies: *kin-reliance, peer-reliance,* and *self-reliance.* (See T. Graves and N. Graves 1980; reprinted in Volume II, article 12.) These represent relatively consistent *behavioral choices* in a variety of life areas. For example, when obtaining their first job most of our subjects from a European background (both immigrants and Pakeha New Zealanders) found it on their own, and this tendency increased for subsequent jobs. By contrast, the vast majority of Pacific Islands immigrants found their first job with the help of relatives, although this tendency decreased as they gained New Zealand experience.

Fifteen of the Pacific Islanders in our sample were either born in New Zealand or received at least part of their formal education there. As we later learned, this set them apart in many important ways from co-ethnics who had migrated as adults, and resulted in behavior more similar to indigenous Maoris than to other Islanders. For example, New Zealand–educated Islanders and Maoris depended increasingly on their friends for help in finding jobs. (Volume II, article 12, table 8.1.) Many Pacific Islands immigrants had relatives working in the same factory. This was far less common among Maoris and Islanders educated in New Zealand, and almost totally absent among Europeans. Island immigrants often lived with extended family members, particularly when they were new arrivals; unmarried Maoris and Islanders educated in New Zealand were apt to live with friends or relatives of their own generation, while the typical European/Pakeha pattern was to live in their own nuclear family. Kin made up a significant part of most Islanders' social network: they spent a lot of their spare time with relatives and regularly helped support relatives financially. This was rare for Europeans. Maoris and New Zealand–educated Islanders usually spent their spare time and money with friends. By giving a point for each objective indicator within six life areas—household composition, use of money, spare-time activities, social networks, how their present job was obtained, and workmates—we were able to classify each subject in our sample as predominantly *kin-reliant*, *peer-reliant*, or *self-reliant* in their behavioral choices. (See Volume II, article 12, table 8.2.) The distribution of these behavioral tendencies by sex and ethnic group is presented in table 11.2 (adapted from Volume II, article 12, table 8.3):

Table 11.2. Preferred Adaptive Strategies—Sex and Ethnic Differences

	Kin-Reliant	Peer-Reliant	Self-Reliant
Europeans/Pakehas			
Men (N=16)	0	38%	62%
Women (N=14)	14%	7%	79%
NZ-educated Maoris & Islanders			
Men (N=26)	35%	46%	19%
Women (N=28)	28%	36%	36%
Pacific Islands immigrants			
Men (N=27)	41%	22%	37%
Women (N=43)	56%	2%	42%

Several things are noteworthy about this table. First, there are clear ethnic differences in strategy choices, with Pacific Islands immigrants preferring *kin-reliance*, New Zealand–educated Polynesians preferring *peer-reliance*, and people with a European cultural heritage preferring *self-reliance*. Nevertheless, *within all three groups there is a range of variation, with substantial numbers preferring adaptive strategies more typical of other ethnic groups*.

Sex differences are also noteworthy, and not surprising. Within all three ethnic categories women are more dependent on their spouse and involved with nuclear family activities (*self-reliance*) than men. And within all three ethnic categories, turning to their buddies for help (*peer-reliance*) is a more common adaptation among men.

For many Pacific Islands immigrants *kin-reliance* is a rational and efficient strategy, and in most cases is simply an extension of a migrant's traditional rural lifestyle. In most non-Western communities kinship is the major determinant of appropriate social behavior, and reliance on a wide circle of extended kinsmen the major strategy for dealing with life's challenges. In a new urban environment this kin-based adaptation may become even stronger, at least at first, because of the migrant's dependence on kin sponsorship and help in moving to the city, providing initial shelter and finding a job. This can have psychological benefits as well, in providing a dependable and "stress-buffering" social support system, which our own family lacked when we first moved to New Zealand in 1972.

Within most kin-oriented traditional societies, however, there also exists a cross-cutting structure of age-graded "peer groups," which are nonhierarchical and egalitarian in form. These are particularly important for boys, as we saw in the last chapter, where participation in peer play groups begins at a very early age. Polynesian girls are more apt to work and play under the authority of older women—their mothers and later their mothers-in-law—contributing to the work around the home, while taking responsibility themselves for supervising and caring for younger children. Thus from a very early age girls are socialized to accept and work comfortably within a hierarchy of both male and female authority. This may help explain why, among the Polynesian workers we interviewed, problems with their supervisors were far more commonly reported by men than by women.

Within Western society age-graded peer groups are familiar as teenage cliques and gangs, which emerge most distinctly at that point in the life cycle when the yoke of adult authority weighs most heavily. But given our Western cultural commitment to independence, we normally remove this parental yoke in late adolescence and most middle-class parents then expect their offspring to abandon these childish ways and adopt a *self-reliant* adult lifestyle. Among non-Western, kin-based societies, however, the authority of the elders remains well into maturity. Consequently, so do the egalitarian peer groups.

It is not surprising, therefore, that indigenous New Zealand Maoris and Pacific Islanders raised and educated in New Zealand, particularly men, find *peer-reliance* an attractive adaptive strategy. Not dependent on their elder kinsmen for help in migrating to urban areas, these Polynesians often prefer to turn to their friends (and same-age relatives) for help in coping with the new challenges of urban life. Within these groups they share information, goods and services, and enjoy a position of equality. In fact, escaping the authority of elder kinsmen, we found, was frequently mentioned as an important motivation for a young Maori to leave the countryside and migrate to Auckland.

Peer-reliance is often an attractive choice among working-class members of Western society as well. Although working-class parents often abandon efforts to assert their authority by the time children reach adolescence, the wider society takes up the slack. Teachers, police officers, military officers, the "boss" at work, and powerful representatives of the middle class who serve as gatekeepers to the rewards and privileges of our society provide an alternative authority system. Consequently, we believe the peer friendship group continues to function as an important counterbalance to the authority system of the wider society. In addition to the egalitarian sanctuary which it provides, moreover, it also serves as a viable system for coping with economic marginality, through labor exchange and barter with friends, information about jobs, prices, and services.

When analyzing and presenting our data, in addition to sex and ethnic differences in work-relevant attitudes, values, and behavior, we also looked at these in relation to our subjects' preferred adaptive strategy. In general, *adaptive strategy choice was a better predictor of worker attitudes, values, and behavior than ethnicity*. This was particularly true with respect to how well they related to supervisory authority and to working in cooperative teams.

When we first began our fieldwork in Aitutaki I remember watching a group of men from our village build us a cookhouse. Wanting to understand what was going on, I asked who was the foreman? "We're all foremen here," they told me. But young men watched and copied older ones and turned to the most experienced whenever they had a question. In another construction project a returnee with many years of New Zealand experience tried to assume the role of a supervisor, but was pointedly ignored or put down. So we knew from casual ethnographic experience that Polynesian men were typically resentful of authoritarian supervision. But among the workers we studied in New Zealand, it was *peer-reliant* men, regardless of ethnicity, who were most likely to have problems with their boss.

It seems unlikely that employers and supervisors can be persuaded to abandon their use of ethnic categories, which are readily observable, when thinking about how to respond to their workers. Each ethnic group's *preferred adaptive strategy* then becomes simply another typical "culture trait." But if employers come to recognize that these three major strategies will usually be found within *all* ethnic groups, and that a worker's preference for one or another strategy has many implications in the workplace, then we may have helped break down some ethnic stereotypes and produced more sensitive and differentiated managerial responses (N. Graves and T. Graves 1977b).

Adaptive Strategies and Drinking Behavior

As our investigation progressed, we learned that each of these three adaptive strategies has a negative side. For example, a *self-reliant* adaptation tends to be more costly in dollars and cents. A kinsman may be able to get something for you wholesale, and a friend may do a job for you at "mate's rates." But a self-reliant person pays retail.

A major cost of *kin-reliance* is being enmeshed in a hierarchical authority system, and the kinship obligations and pressures which flow from these. As we will document more fully in chapter 13, for Samoan immigrants this can amount to as much as 20% of their income.

One of the most important costs of *peer-reliance* is that the *pub* is a major arena within which this adaptation plays itself out. Male peer groups may meet elsewhere, of course, the coffeehouse among Greek immigrants, for example. (See Baddeley 1977.) But a "home bar" provides a more typical clubhouse (Anderson 1978; Cavan 1966; Clinard 1962; Harrison et al. 1943; Macrory 1952; Sommer 1965). And even though the primary goal for going to the pub appears to be to have a good time with your friends, as we had learned from our research among Navajo migrants, when public bars serve as their most important recreational outlet, participants are at risk for alcohol abuse, violence, and arrest.

Among those carpet workers in our sample, regardless of ethnicity, who were classified as predominantly *peer-reliant*, 83% of the men and 65% of the women reported that they went to a pub *at least once a week*. This is about *three times* as high as the proportion of regular pub-drinkers among those who preferred a *kin-reliant* or *self-reliant* adaptive strategy. See table 11.3 (adapted from N. Graves and T. Graves 1977a, table 4.3). Without intending to do so, our research had again led us back to drinking behavior.

Table 11.3. Adaptive Strategies and Drinking Behavior

	Proportion who go to the pub at least once per week		
	Kin-Reliant (N = 54)	Peer-Reliant (N = 46)	Self-Reliant (N = 64)
Men (N = 69)	24%	83%	28%
Women (N = 85)	20%	67%	15%

Drinking and Violence in New Zealand's Pub Settings

While our research in these two carpet mills was still in progress, we were approached by a Samoan graduate student in psychology, Vineta Semu, who wanted to conduct systematic observations of drinking behavior for her master's thesis. My prior research on drinking behavior in the United States made me an obvious candidate to serve as a faculty advisor, and perhaps a source of additional funding as well. Furthermore, when we had first moved to New Zealand and taught a course on race relations at the University of Auckland, Nan and I had encouraged one group of students to observe cross-ethnic interactions in New Zealand's public bars. So the idea of extending this exploratory work through the use of more systematic observational procedures was appealing. Vineta recruited a fellow Samoan graduate student in psychology, Iulai Ah Sam, to help her. This research, and a complementary study of pub violence, proceeded over the following four years, and the results were reported in T. Graves, N. Graves, Semu, and Ah Sam 1981 and 1982. (See Volume II, articles 13 and 14.)

Although systematic observational studies of drinking behavior in public bars had become fairly common by the time we undertook these studies (our articles cited eight references from England, Scotland, Canada, and the United States), as far as we know this was the first systematic observational study in multiethnic settings such as New Zealand affords. Similar to stereotypes of American Indians and Australian Aborigines, there is a widespread belief among Pakeha New Zealanders that Polynesians (both indigenous Maoris and Pacific Islands immigrants) "can't hold their liquor." Besides a desire to bring systematic data to bear on these stereotypes, our research was designed to test a leading theory of public drinking behavior: the "Rounds Hypothesis." This states that the amount of alcohol consumed is closely related to the size of your drinking group, since drinking etiquette requires that each group member buy (and therefore consume) at least one "round" of drinks for their friends. I had observed this phenomenon ethnographically in the tri-ethnic community and in Denver, but this was our first attempt to study it systematically.

Our observations were conducted in twelve of the seventy bars in the Auckland metropolitan area, carefully selected to represent a wide range of typical settings which would differ in size and ethnic mix: four from the central city, five from the surrounding industrial/residential area, and three from outlying suburbs north, south, and west. Our two Samoan observers entered each pub at 5:00 P.M., selected a table which commanded a good view of the drinking area, bought drinks and took a quick census of the clientele. They then selected for systematic observation the next two (male) Maoris, two Islanders, and two Pakehas (white New Zealanders) to enter the bar, each taking responsibility for observing one member of each ethnic group.[1] They continued recording their observations of each subject at five-minute intervals until all six had left the bar. These observations were recorded unobtrusively on 3x5 cards held in their laps.

A recording system was developed which included the subject's estimated age, the size and ethnic composition of his drinking group (including the occasional woman), the length of time he remained in the pub, and the number of glasses of beer (or occasionally spirits) he consumed. Before the final data collection began, Nan and I helped Vineta and Iulai pretest and refine their observational system in three bars not included in the final study. This is an important step in any systematic research, and enabled us to ensure and demonstrate a high level of agreement (94% to 99%) between their observations and our own (reliability).

The systematic observations Vineta and Iulai went on to collect permitted extremely accurate and refined conclusions about ethnic similarities and differences in drinking behavior within New Zealand's pubs. For example, over 95% of the consumption by all three groups was beer. And rates of consumption within all three groups were also similar: about nine minutes per glass. But because the average Maori and Islander remained in the pubs significantly longer than the average Pakehas, as a group Polynesians drank about half again as much beer as their white New Zealand neighbors.

The social context of their drinking was also dramatically different: The vast majority of Polynesians drank in groups of three or more companions (84%), whereas a large proportion of Pakehas (over 40%) avoided such group settings and drank alone or with only one other companion (what we termed an "exclusive" drinking pattern, to tie this to the observational research on preschool behavior reported in chapter 9).

Unlike a conventional ethnographic analysis, however, which would typically focus on these "cultural" differences, this analysis depended on carefully documenting *variability* in drinking behavior within *each* ethnic group, so that correlations could be run among these variables. Then by statistically "controlling" for ethnic differences in only two traits—drinking group size and time spent in the pub—we were able to demonstrate that ethnic differences in consumption essentially disappeared. (See Volume II, article 13.) In other words, Polynesians who drank in smaller groups and didn't stay long in the pub, did not consume any more alcohol than their Pakeha neighbors. And those Pakehas who *did* participate in large drinking groups and *did* stay in the pub as long as their Maori and Islander mates, drank just as much. This research therefore took a major step toward "emptying out" a purely "cultural" explanation, by documenting substantial *within-group variation* in drinking behavior and identifying the two factors which accounted for most of this variation *within all three ethnic groups.* This form of analysis is a typical goal of my work as a behavioral anthropologist.

But the ethnographic question remains: Why do Polynesians typically drink in large groups? To answer this question we drew on the research by ourselves and others on Polynesian "culture," not as a set of uniform "traits," but as behavioral "tendencies" or "predispositions" which we had shown to vary among Maoris and Islanders, but which have their roots in their typical socialization experiences. As discussed in the last chapter, for example, Islanders are typically raised in large families and in addition to their parents are cared for by a variety of older siblings, cousins, uncles, aunts, and grandparents as well. Children raised in such "extended families" tend to become group-oriented, generous, and cooperative. But as we documented through the use of our Coin Distribution Task and Cooperation Board, those raised by their parents in small "nuclear" families, like typical Pakehas, often do not exhibit these characteristics. (See Volume II, article 10.)

In article 13 we brought together all our research evidence of this type to explain the tendency of Polynesians to drink in larger groups, including our observations of Polynesian tendency to exhibit "inclusive" behavior in school settings and to select "group-oriented adaptive strategies" in other areas of their lives. But because we had no information about the specific background experiences of the Polynesian subjects we had been observing in the pubs, we could only *infer* that those from a Maori or Islander background were more likely to have had socialization experiences of this kind than those from a European or Pakeha background. For behavioral anthropologists, this is a major limitation of an observational study of this kind. A complete analysis would require systematically collecting information from each of the subjects under observation. But this was not feasible under these circumstances.

Similarly, for the amount of time subjects chose to spend in the pub, some of the between-group differences we documented could be "explained" by these same ethnic differences in their tendency to drink in large groups. Those drinking with a number of their peers (usually Polynesians) tended to stay in the pub longer than those drinking alone or with only one other person (usually Pakehas). And the larger the drinking group, the longer they tended to stay. We documented this relationship within all three ethnic groups. But as we will see in the next chapter, the norm of "drinking in rounds" does *not* account for how long a drinker remains in the pub. Some men remain longer than strict adherence to this norm would predict, others decide to go home sooner than we would anticipate from the size of their drinking group. In fact, contrary to the classic "rounds hypothesis," our analysis demonstrated that how long a person remains in the pub is the *primary* determinant of the amount consumed, and the size of their drinking group is *secondary*.

Because we had no personal information about the individual drinkers we were observing—such as their home situation—in our article we could only offer speculations worthy of further research: for example, whether or not the drinker had a non-working wife who would be home with a hot dinner waiting for him. Since Polynesians more often than Pakehas have working spouses, and since even non-working Polynesian women typically eat with their children and feed their husbands whenever they return home, Polynesian drinkers often lack this incentive to return early. But this ethnographic explanation, though plausible, remains empirically untested.

Probably as important as such sociocultural factors, however, are differences in individual *motivation* to get drunk. Among Navajo migrants we were able to measure a variety of psychological pressures to drink and to demonstrate empirically that they were associated with more frequent bar drinking and getting arrested more often. (See chapters 6 and 7.) Again, unfortunately, information about individual differences of this type in psychological motivation was missing from our New Zealand pub-drinking population, and in this study we could only offer plausible speculations as a stimulus to further research. This is typical in behavioral science: Each empirical study raises additional questions to be investigated.

In our published report (Volume II, article 13) we didn't discuss these explanatory limitations. What we *did* discover and demonstrate statistically was compelling enough, and nicely complemented our previous research among Cook Islanders. Together they provided an interesting concatenated explanation of ethnic differences in pub behavior. But these observational data lacked the subtle attention to determinants of within-group variation in drinking behavior *outside of the immediate situation we were observing* which we were able to document so well among Navajo migrants. Again, this is an almost inevitable limitation of systematic observations in public places.

Addressing Another Stereotype: Polynesian Pub Violence

"Running a city pub can be a bloody business" an Auckland newspaper headline blared (*Auckland Star*, 16 August 1976). The Polynesian reputation for pub violence was another issue we hoped to address in our observational studies. Our intent was to collect a large pool of "critical incidents" (Flanagan 1954) of pub violence in order to examine factors associated with their frequency and seriousness. But in over 100 hours spent in twelve different pubs Vineta and Iulai rarely saw any incidents of this kind. With seventy public bars in the Auckland region, even one serious fight a year in each would provide the press with plenty of journalistic fodder. To obtain a good sample of incidents for research purposes, however (including ones which might have led to a fight but did not), we had to change our research strategy, by hiring and training others to conduct observations for us over an extended period of time. The "security officers" hired by pub owners who experienced the most social problems, we felt, would make ideal surrogate observers.

With the help of Vineta's husband, who worked for a private security firm, we enlisted the participation of nineteen such security officers to record all "incidents" that came to their attention while on duty over a three-week period. (Because it was their job, they had a keen eye for events which might lead to a fight, even when they did not.) In this manner we collected 119 incidents of varying degrees of seriousness which could be systematically scored for a number of potentially important factors responsible for how serious they became. (For details of our procedure and results, see Volume II, article 14.)

Contrary to popular belief and ethnic stereotypes, the most important determinant of incident seriousness was *not* the ethnicity of the initiator or how drunk he was, but *the size of his drinking group*. And again, the *pattern* of correlations was repeated among Maoris, Islanders, and Pakeha New Zealanders alike. (See Volume II, article 14, figure 3.) Clearly, we were not dealing with a uniquely Polynesian problem here, as some white New Zealanders believed, but with one common to all those, regardless of ethnic background, who adopt a "peer-reliant" lifestyle, with a "home bar" as their "clubhouse." Within these settings, the larger your drinking group, the more likely you will inadvertently be drawn into a fight. When one of your friends gets into trouble, you will be expected to come to his rescue. On the battlefield this is heroism; in a bar it is a cause for arrest.

There are important Polynesian-Pakeha differences, however. As we have already discussed with respect to amount consumed, Polynesians are more likely than Pakehas to be drinking in large groups. Because of their strong kinship ties as well as the likelihood that their drinking buddies include a number of co-ethnics, Polynesians are more likely than Pakehas to join in to help a friend or relative when he gets into a fight. They are also quicker to move a conflict from the verbal to the physical level. Europeans have a relatively high tolerance for verbal aggression ("Sticks and stones can break your bones . . . "). A typical Samoan aphorism suggests that they are more apt to view such verbal assaults as damaging to their family's reputation: "A good name is better than a good face. . . ." Perhaps as a consequence, Samoans (but not Cook Islanders) are far more likely than Europeans to get into pub fights.

At this point the two prongs of our research were coming together: We knew that drinking with a relatively large groups of friends was strongly associated with a more general *peer-reliant* adaptive strategy for coping with life, and that this strategy was quite commonly chosen among working-class men from all three ethnic groups in New Zealand: Maoris, Islanders, and Pakehas. We were therefore eager to explore determinants of strategy choice other than ethnicity, and the wider implications of such choice for other aspects of their behavior. Our next major research project, a complementary survey study among working-class New Zealanders—both Polynesian and Pakeha—was designed in part to address these issues.

Polynesian Migrant Adaptation Survey

During 1977–1978 we spent a year at the Center for Advanced Study in the Behavioral Sciences in Palo Alto and the following fall semester at the Center for South Pacific Studies, University of California, Santa Cruz, writing up our research on Aitutaki. When we returned to New Zealand, with our hearts (and most of our family) still in California, it was clear that we would be returning "home" to the United States as soon as we finished up our research projects. Following completion of the pub observational studies, however, we still felt we needed a complementary survey study of Polynesian migrant adaptation to answer the many questions our research had been raising. For example, we wanted to test the hypothesis that "persons who have adopted a predominantly *peer-reliant* strategy in other areas of their life will go to the pub more often, will spend more time there when they do go, and will drink in larger groups than those who have adopted predominantly *kin-reliant* or *self-reliant* strategies." *Peer-reliance* was strongly associated with pub drinking among carpet-mill workers whom we had interviewed. But these interviews had served to help us formulate this theory (an *inductive* process—moving from data to theory.) To test and refine this theory we needed to undertake a *deductive* study in which we moved in the *opposite* direction—from theory to data. This is the way scientific knowledge accumulates and builds, moving back and forth between data-based theory and theory-based data collection. We also wanted to know a lot more about the *private* drinking behavior of New Zealanders, both Polynesian and Pakeha, and how this fit in to their overall adjustment to life. Finally, we wanted to know more about the *pressures* of everyday life, both objective (situational) and subjective (psychological) which might motivate some subjects, regardless of ethnicity, to drink more than others as a form of escape.

Undertaking a survey study of Polynesian urban adaptation had been our initial goal when we first migrated to New Zealand in 1971. We also wanted this to be a comparative study, including samples of both

Samoans and Cook Islanders plus indigenous Maoris and Pakehas who were living in the same working-class neighborhoods and working together in Auckland's factories. So building on the exploratory study we had conducted in the two carpet factories, Iulai, Vineta, Nan, and I set to work designing a survey instrument for use during the southern hemisphere's summer months at the end of 1979 and early 1980. This was an exciting "insider–outsider" task, in which our goal was to design a data-collecting instrument so simple in language and format and concrete in content that it would permit an approximation to the ideal of "decentered" translations into English, Samoan, and Cook Islands Maori (Werner and Campbell 1970).

The issue of translating questionnaire items from English into some often exotic non-Western language is an important one for any behavioral scientist working cross-culturally. It is particularly important for psychological measurement, because the subtlety of psychological concepts may make them particularly difficult to translate. (In the next chapter I'll give an example of a problem of this kind that we faced when developing a measure of "Type A" personality.) Following the principles for a decentered translation, instead of simply writing our questions in English and then translating them, we would work back and forth between Samoan and English, so that basic concepts would be equivalent in both languages and neither version of the survey interview would simply be a "translation" of the other. (Polynesian languages are sufficiently similar that once a "decentered" version had been constructed in Samoan and English, a translation into Cook Islands Maori was relatively straightforward. And for most indigenous Maoris, English had become their "first language".) Interviews could then be conducted in the subjects' primary language by same-sex native speakers.

The interview, which generally took between one and two hours, was theory-based in its design, with the explicit intent of making possible an empirical examination of the role of adaptive strategies for coping with urban life. Because Hooper and Huntsman's work had included a major focus on Tokelauans' *health* both before and after migration, we had included a health component in our research on Aitutaki, and wanted to do so again in New Zealand. But rather than simply document changes in health status associated with migration as they had done, we wanted to undertake a more ambitious, hypothesis-testing design in which we examined the relationship between the stress of modernization, urban adaptation, and the subjects' health status. In the next chapter I will present this "stress and health" model and results from both Aitutaki and Auckland; here I will only discuss migrants' economic adjustment and leisure activities, with a focus on their drinking behavior.

We selected our subjects by a mixture of area and quota sampling from three working-class neighborhoods of Auckland where all four ethnic groups live side-by-side. Our aim was not to obtain a "random sample" of Pacific Islands immigrants, Maoris, and Pakehas, but a representative sample of those occupying a similar economic stratum. (Otherwise, we could anticipate, the substantial economic differences among "average" members of these groups would probably account for most of the other ethnic differences we might find. Not a theoretically interesting outcome.) Interviewers would go to a randomly selected block in an integrated, working-class neighborhood, begin at a randomly selected spot, and knock on doors consecutively until they found an eligible subject. In total, 664 usable interviews were completed from Pakehas and the two Pacific Islands groups, but only from 64 Maori women and no Maori men. The New Zealand government had a summer work-study program which provided the funding for our interviewers. Unfortunately, however, we were unable to recruit and keep Maori interviewers; that summer young Maori university students all seemed to be involved in political activism. "What use will this survey be to Maoris?" we were asked. A legitimate question for behavioral anthropologists from the subjects of their research, and one not easily answerable to their satisfaction. See chapter 13 on "Research and Application." Time ran out and we reluctantly had to abandon our plans for obtaining a good Maori comparison group.

Characteristics of the sample we did obtain are presented in table 11.4. Note that the groups are relatively homogeneous in age, marital status, and rate of pay. This suggests that our sampling technique was successful in obtaining subjects from each ethnic group of roughly similar age and economic standing. There were several important background and demographic differences among the groups, however. The native-born New Zealanders of European cultural background (Pakehas) had significantly more formal education, and were far more likely to have passed

Table 11.4. Survey Sample Characteristics

	Samoans (N = 230)	Cook Islanders (N = 217)	Pakehas (N = 233)
Age			
Mean	31.0	31.5	30.0
(s.d.)	(7.8)	(9.4)	(9.4)
Years of education			
Mean	6.8	7.2	8.3
(s.d.)	(2.1)	(1.4)	(1.1)
School certificate pass	14%	4%	43%
Married	75%	64%	64%
Household size (median)	6	5	4
Children under 16 (mean)	1.8	2.4	1.1
Urban-raised	9%	10%	77%
Hourly wages (median)			
Men	$3.97	$3.75	$3.96
Women	$3.35	$3.45	$3.30

the School Certificate examination, a prerequisite for higher education or most trade apprenticeships. They were also far more likely to have been raised in urban environments (77%); only about 10% of the Pacific Islanders were raised in New Zealand, although about a quarter of the Samoans and over 40% of the Cook Islanders in our sample were raised in or near the capital towns in their home islands. Most of the immigrant Polynesians were clearly disadvantaged in language, training, and experience for coping with urban-industrial life. In addition, their households were significantly larger than those of their Pakeha neighbors, mainly because they had more dependent children. (These Pakeha-Polynesian differences in household size would be even larger if it were not for a number of unmarried Pakeha subjects who were "flatting" with several of their friends to cut down on rent.) This means that the working adults in Polynesian households had an extra burden of nonproductive members to support.

The distribution of preferred adaptive strategies by ethnic group is presented in table 11.5. In general, these data support the findings from our exploratory carpet factory research, and because of the larger and more representative sample size, give us added confidence in the validity of

Table 11.5. Preferred Adaptive Strategies—Sex and Ethnic Differences

	Kin-Reliant	Peer-Reliant	Self-Reliant
Samoans			
Men (N = 106)	67%	11%	22%
Women (N = 124)	58%	10%	32%
Cook Islanders			
Men (N = 100)	51%	10%	39%
Women (N = 28)	42%	4%	54%
Pakeha New Zealanders			
Men (N = 112)	6%	39%	55%
Women (N = 121)	13%	26%	61%

our theoretical conclusions. Pakeha New Zealanders with a Western cultural background overwhelmingly chose *self-reliance* as their dominant adaptive strategy, whereas the majority of Pacific Islands immigrants chose *kin-reliance*. Note, however, that the Cook Islanders were less *kin-reliant* than Samoans, and more *self-reliant* like their Pakeha neighbors. This was even true of a small *majority* of Cook Islands women. Cook Islanders appear to be more Westernized than Samoans, and as we will see below, this is true of their drinking behavior as well.

Our failure to obtain a Maori sample was a major setback for our goal of looking at the relationship between *peer-reliance* and drinking behavior. Our factory research had led us to anticipate that this strategy would be found most commonly among Maoris, particularly men. Only twenty-three Pacific Islands men chose a predominant *peer-reliant* adaptive strategy in this survey study. When we returned to the United States, therefore, an analysis of drinking behavior by adaptive strategy assumed relatively low priority, and when time, funds, and enthusiasm ran out it was never completed. Ethnic group differences in drinking behavior, however, are presented in table 11.6.

Table 11.6. Ethnic Differences in Drinking Behavior

	Samoans	Cook Islanders	Pakehas
Percent who are drinkers			
Men	41%	73%	90%
Women	4%	44%	86%
Percent who drink at home at least monthly			
Men	8%	49%	69%
Women	2%	30%	50%
Percent who drink in pubs at least monthly			
Men	24%	36%	51%
Women	1%	22%	25%
Percent who drink in other settings at least monthly			
Men	7%	33%	64%
Women	0%	24%	38%
Percent of pub drinkers who prefer the lounge bar			
Men	25%	4%	70%
Women	50%	55%	88%
Percent who usually drink with relatives in the pub			
Men only	28%	10%	2%
Percent who reported being involved in one or more fights last year			
Men	56%	22%	47%
Women	-0-	-0-	-0-
Percent of men who drink in pubs weekly, but reported no fights	15%	80%	57%

These data complemented our systematic observations and critical incidents by providing additional information on who is going to public bars regularly and who is not. Polynesian drinking patterns are distinct in several ways. First, almost 60% of Samoan men and 96% of Samoan women said that they did not drink at all. (Iulai and Vineta considered this a valid finding, with abstinence supported among Samoans by their very high involvement in the church.) More than a quarter of Cook Islands men and more than half of Cook Islands women also reported being abstainers. (Note that in their drinking behavior Cook Islanders are intermediate between Samoans and Pakehas.) By contrast, the vast majority of both Pakeha men and women are drinkers. For those Islanders who *do* drink, it is more a male activity than among Pakehas, and less likely to be tempered by the presence of women.

Second, the *settings* in which Polynesians and Pakehas do most of their drinking tend to be different. Although half of the Pakeha men in our sample have a drink in the pub at least monthly, they are more likely to drink at home, at their friends' homes, or in other settings such as sporting events or private clubs. This is less true for Cook Islands men, and for Samoan men the pub is the *major* setting in which their drinking takes place. Furthermore, when they *do* drink in pubs, Pakehas prefer to drink in the lounge bars, whereas Polynesian men overwhelmingly prefer the public bars, where the decor is simpler and there is no dress code, and where the arrangements of tables and stools permit drinking in larger groups. Consequently, Islanders more frequently place themselves in an arena where they are likely to become embroiled in fights. Finally, Islanders (and particularly Samoans) are far more likely to be drinking with relatives, so that family reputation and family loyalty may draw them into a conflict started by somebody else.

Not surprisingly, we found a positive correlation within all three ethnic groups between the number of fights a man reported in the last year and the frequency he drank in the pub. And among Samoans this relationship achieved a high level of statistical significance ($r = .41$). Among Samoan men, 85% of those who drank in pubs at least weekly also reported at least one fight in the last year. By contrast, this was true of only 43% of the weekly Pakeha pub drinkers and only 20% of the weekly Cook Islands pub drinkers.

It is the Cook Islanders who stand out most sharply in this analysis. This conforms with the data we had collected independently from the security guards. Of all the pub "incidents" they reported, Cook Islanders were involved in only a handful of cases, and rarely as initiators. The majority of Islanders who got into fights were Samoans. (No likelihood of ethnic bias here; the majority of the security guards were *also* Samoans.)

The way Cook Islanders avoid interpersonal conflicts and their techniques of conflict resolution would make a fascinating study in itself, but one we must leave for others to undertake.

In sum, we now know that pub drinking is strongly associated with a more general *peer-reliant* adaptive strategy for coping with life, but we still need to explore determinants of strategy choice other than ethnicity (since not all members of an ethnic group made the same choices), and the wider implications of strategy choice for other aspects of life. If we had remained in New Zealand, answering questions such as these would have become our next focus of inquiry. For traditional cultural anthropologists the group results reported above could comfortably serve as the conclusion of their research; for behavioral anthropology they are just a beginning.

Methodological Lessons for Behavioral Anthropology

1. In this chapter I have described the way we designed and executed an exploratory study of worker adaptation, which helped us to develop and refine a theory of adaptive strategies, examine some implications of this theory for public drinking behavior, and then design a more systematic survey study to test hypotheses derived from this exploratory work. This is the way behavioral science builds on itself. We move back and forth from inductive to deductive research, from theory generating to theory testing, and then back to theory refinement.

2. I also described our two observational studies of drinking behavior and violence in public bars. Systematic observations of this type lend themselves particularly well to the study of *group* and *situational* differences in behavior, since relatively large numbers of persons can be observed unobtrusively in public places. This can be a very useful tool for cultural anthropologists. But as behavioral anthropologists we typically want to go beyond such observations to examine differences in the background experiences and present circumstances of our subjects, and differences in their psychological characteristics, which could help account for their within-group and within-situation *variability* in behavior. Such information is normally not available for the subjects you observe in public places. And what about their drinking behavior in private places?

3. Systematic observations such as those reported in this chapter typically require complementary survey research. Among both Polynesians and Pakehas, for example, some will be more "group oriented" than others. Do background differences in family composition and size lead to these different propensities to participate in large groups and to choose group-oriented adaptive strategies? Do they then choose group settings more often for activities such as drinking? Are some people more motivated to *seek out* drinking groups than others by the psychological or social needs which these groups fill, such as we had found and documented among Navajo migrants? And once choosing to participate, do some members conform more than others to group norms? Finally, may motivational factors actually *give rise to* "cultural" forms, such as the typical American Indian weekend "binge drinking" group and the Polynesian recreational drinking groups? As we have already seen in chapter 7, such questions go to the heart of the "meaning" of "culture" for individuals raised and living within different ethnic groups, and should go a long way toward "emptying out" that meaning in ways relevant to all human beings.

Note

1. In this study we made a deliberate decision to focus on *male* drinking behavior. The presence of women was noted because this impacted the behavior of the male group, but their own drinking behavior was not studied.

12

Multivariate Analysis and Causal Inferences

One of the most pleasurable parts of being a behavioral anthropologist is playing with the data. Systematically collecting behavioral observations, abstracting dusty records, or conducting dozens of interviews can be numbing work. But once the coding is completed and the numbers are in, the fun begins.

I love the challenge of devising novel ways of measuring personality variables, of using formal records, of constructing meaningful indices from the sloppy material at hand. I love theory-building, making hypothetical sense of the world. But above all, I love finding out what the world has to teach me through feedback from empirical data. Of course I love having my hypotheses supported. But I also love surprises.

Given the complexity of human behavior and the multitude of factors which influence it, multivariate analysis is a necessary part of behavioral anthropology, but one which is often difficult for researchers to master and readers to understand. In this chapter I want to present and compare three forms of multivariate analysis which I have had fun using in my work: *pattern analysis, multiple regression,* and *path analysis*. Like different strategies for measuring psychological variables or behavior, each has its advantages and disadvantages, its strengths and limitations. And each may be more appropriate under some conditions, with some types of data, or for some purposes. Behavioral anthropologists need simple ways to handle a variety of determinants of behavior simultaneously. These three approaches have served me well.

Pattern Analysis

When Nan and I spent our year in East Africa (1967–1968) I brought a deck of IBM cards with me containing all the data from the Navajo Urban Relocation Research Project. They had no computer at the Makerere Institute of Social Research in Kampala where I had my office. So while our children were in school and Nan was interviewing Baganda mothers and observing their child-rearing practices in Kampala and a Baganda village far to the south, I was spending long and happy hours at the Institute's counter-sorter. Many of the complex analyses I reported over the next few years (articles 5, 6, and 7 in Volume II) had their origin in this work.

As already described in chapter 4, pattern analysis starts with the simplest form of two-by-two contingency tables, which can graphically show the relationship between some outcome behavior—such as quickly returning home to the reservation—and some potential determinants—such as negative economic experiences in the city. This process can be repeated, adding one variable after another, to demonstrate the impact of several determinants simultaneously. An example from the Navajo project will illustrate this process. Our outcome ("dependent") variable here is whether or not a migrant remained in the city at least eighteen months. Table 12.1 shows the effect of three *initial* economic variables on this outcome.

Table 12.1. Initial Economic Experiences versus Returnee Rates

	Proportion of all migrants	Percent remaining at least 18 months
Initial % unemployed		
Less than 15%	(50%)	43%
15% or more	(50%)	18%
Initial job level		
Skilled or semiskilled	(46%)	41%
Unskilled	(54%)	24%
Starting wage		
More than $1.25 per hour	(37%)	41%
$1.25 per hour or less	(63%)	24%

What this table is showing is that each of these three initial economic experiences appears to have a roughly similar effect on the outcome: If a new migrant experiences many days without work during the first half of his stay (or his first six months in Denver if he remained more than a year) the likelihood of his soon returning home more than *doubles*. Similarly, if his first job in the city is only as an unskilled laborer, or if it pays him a minimum wage of only $1.25 per hour or less, in each case his chances of returning home in less than eighteen months also almost doubles.

But then we want to put these predictors together to show their *joint* effect on the behavior in question, which is usually greater than the effect of any one predictor alone. Pattern analysis accomplishes this simply by crosscutting each of the four cells in your first two-by-two table by whether the subjects within each cell have high or low scores on some *second* potential determinant. This results in eight cells, and the proportion of subjects displaying our outcome behavior can be calculated for each cell. In this way I am "controlling" for the effect of one variable *mechanically* (because all the subjects in the cell have roughly similar scores on the first variable) while varying a second (because we divide them into those who are "high" or "low" on the second variable). In the above example, we would look at subjects who had relatively little initial unemployment and relatively *good* (skilled or semiskilled) jobs, versus those with little initial unemployment but relatively *poor* (unskilled) jobs. Then we would look at those with relatively high initial unemployment who still got relatively good jobs, versus those who got only poor, laboring jobs. What we found was that it didn't seem to matter *which* of these two unfavorable initial experiences a migrant had, in either case about three-quarters of them returned home relatively quickly.

If you have enough subjects this process can be repeated for yet a *third* determinant (resulting in sixteen cells) or even a *fourth* (resulting in thirty-two cells) as we were able to do in the Tri-Ethnic study. (See for example Jessor, Graves, Hanson, and Jessor 1968:349 and the tables reprinted in chapter 4.) In the Navajo project I normally stopped with three variables. Again, we are engaged in a form of *mechanical* control: For example, we looked at subjects who had an unfavorable initial economic experience through both high rates of initial unemployment *and* a poor job, and then examined what happened if they *also* received a low wage. What we found was that when they experienced *all three* of these strikes against them, 86% were out of there and back home within eighteen months. (Most, of course, returned to the reservation much sooner.)

Contrasting this cumulative *negative* effect is a cumulative *positive* effect of initial economic experiences. For example, it didn't much matter if migrants had relatively little initial unemployment or relatively good initial jobs, in either case roughly 40% remained in the city at least eighteen months. But when we crosscut these by yet a *third* initial economic experience, how high their starting wages were, we again improved our prediction. Among those with all three favorable initial economic experiences—little initial unemployment and a good job at a decent wage—almost 80% remained in the city at least eighteen months. This is what it takes to insure migrants of a reasonably good chance of "making it" in the city; anything less and the majority will soon return home. Unhappily, less than 10% of the young Navajo men who tried migrating to Denver for work had the type of initial experiences in the Denver job market which would predict long-term success. The other 91% had a less than 40% chance of making a successful adjustment and remaining in the city. This is a strong empirical indictment of the government's relocation program, at least for Navajos.

Table 12.2. Initial Economic Experiences vs. Returnee Rates

Pattern variables:

1. Initial % unemployed
   (Less than 15% vs. 15% or more)
2. Initial job level
   (Skilled/semiskilled vs. unskilled)
3. Starting wage
   (Over $1.25 per hour vs. $1.25 or less)

Pattern Analysis:	Proportion of all migrants	Percent remaining at least 18 months
Favorable on all three predictors	(09%)	79%
Favorable on two out of three	(30%)	39%
Favorable on only one of three	(39%)	23%
Unfavorable on all three	(22%)	14%

Table 12.2 summarizes these results in a typical pattern analysis. Note: this is a truly "predictive" model, since all three of the "pattern variables" *preceded* in time a migrant's decision to return home. And using only these three predictors we have managed to account for about 65% of the variability in returnee rates (from 14% to 79%). These are pretty impressive results within behavioral science.

More on Interaction Effects

One of the additional virtues of pattern analysis, already noted in chapter 4, is its ability to uncover "interaction effects." These occur when some relationship between one predictor and an outcome takes place only under certain circumstances but not under others. These interaction effects are difficult to spot in a computer-generated correlation matrix (the correlations are simply too low to attract attention), but when I was working with two-by-two contingency tables, they would pop out at me. Article 1 in Volume II, which I discussed in chapter 4, was my first published example of these interaction effects. Article 5, discussed in chapter 7, presents some others. Article 11 (to be discussed in the next chapter) presents a plethora of these interaction effects with very different subjects (Pacific Islanders) in a very different setting (Polynesia) and a very different research problem: the stress of modernization and its effects on health.

Pattern analysis is a good example of controlling for the effect of one variable *mechanically* while examining the joint effect of a second variable. This is a powerful analytic approach that has the virtue of working with groups of real people, and is therefore easily understandable to readers. But when working with several predictor variables simultaneously it becomes awkward and requires a large number of subjects. Both multiple regression and path analysis enable you to do essentially the same thing, but to do so *statistically* rather than mechanically. Although I knew about these techniques while working on the Tri-Ethnic and Navajo projects, and our data were in a form which would have lent themselves to this type of statistical manipulation, I was still skeptical about their use. But I was intrigued, and when I moved to UCLA in 1969 I seized the opportunity to learn more about them and give them a try.

Multiple Regression

A. Kimball Romney, a professor at Harvard, was a pioneer in the use of quantitative methods in anthropology and had engaged in many interesting manipulations of his data which I wanted to learn about. (In his self-deprecating manner he referred to his studies as "tight little turds.") But before I could take up a Special NIMH Fellowship to spend a year working with him[1] he moved to the new University of California campus at Irvine to help found a very quantitatively oriented anthropology department there. He invited me to join him, but the full professorship at UCLA and the research training program that came with it seemed to offer more professional opportunities. Nevertheless, I arranged to take up this fellowship at UC Irvine on a part-time basis during 1970–1971, while still taking responsibility for leading the new Research Training Program in Behavioral Anthropology at UCLA.

It was a fruitful year. Nan and I drove down to UCI for two days each week, renting a motel room overlooking the ocean on a regular basis every Thursday night, attending classes, participating in seminars, and working with faculty members on their projects and our own. It was like a two-day intellectual holiday each week.

The interdisciplinary environment at Irvine was familiar and stimulating. Nan and I became close friends with Charlie and Jean Lave, a young Harvard-trained academic couple. Charlie's specialty was the economics of public transportation, and Jean was an anthropologist who had conducted systematic research in Liberia on everyday mathematics (Lave 1988).

Charlie gave me a crash course in multiple regression. He emphasized it as a *discovery technique*, using flexible and sophisticated ways to manipulate and play with your data. So I brought all the Navajo data to Irvine to see what we could do with them.[2] It was out of this collaboration that our joint paper on "Determinants of Urban Migrant Indian Wages" emerged (Graves and Lave 1972; reprinted in Volume II, article 8).

In a regression analysis you start by looking at a correlation matrix in which all your potential "predictors" can be seen in relationship to some outcome variable. (See article 8, table 1.) We chose to explore the determinants of a migrant's *starting wage*, because we knew it was a key "mediating" factor in his subsequent economic, social, and psychological adjustment to the city. It also displayed a wide range of variability. A binary outcome—such as voting Democratic, or in our case, remaining in the city at least eighteen months—is exactly what you want for a pattern analysis. But for a correlational analysis such as multiple regression, a dependent variable with a lot of variation in scores among your subjects to explain is better. (The starting wages of Navajo migrants in our sample ranged from $.63 per hour to $2.70.)[3] Charlie also liked the fact that a migrant's starting wage occurred at a uniform point in his urban experience, regardless of when we had interviewed him.

I had been suspicious of regression analysis. At this early stage it looks a bit like the *post hoc* analysis of the Tri-Ethnic data Jessor and I had performed when we first ran our correlation matrix, and suffers from similar dangers. (See chapter 4) And it magnifies any artificially high correlations may be the result of chance factors, since the computer program orders predictor variables by the magnitude of their correlation with the outcome. But warned of these dangers and guided as much as possible by explicit theory, it is a valuable tool.

In its simplest form multiple regression examines how much each "predictor" variable contributes to some outcome when the *co-variation* among the predictors is eliminated. For example, in their hypothetical height and weight research described in chapter 4, our Martian investigators might have obtained even better prediction of a football player's weight if they also measured the weight of his *parents*, to get at the genetic component. But clearly his genes *also* contributes to a player's height, and therefore contributes some of the *same* predictive power as height alone. Multiple regression serves to eliminate this overlap in prediction and calculates the *independent* contribution of each predictor to some outcome *at the present time*. (This is an important point to remember. Later in this chapter I will discuss causal path analysis, which examines the contribution of various predictors *through* time.)

In our initial matrix (Volume II, article 8, table 1) we looked at all the factors Bob Weppner had considered when testing his Economic Adjustment Model, plus attributes of the Denver economy at the time of a migrant's arrival, which he had not. Although these were strongly related to a migrant's amount of *initial unemployment* (another important mediating factor in his subsequent adjustment), they were only weakly related to his initial *wages*. (Contrary to popular belief, Charlie knew as an economist that high unemployment rates have more effect on the *standards* employers apply when screening applicants than on the *wages* they offer.) But they demonstrate how to create potentially important *new* variables out of old ones, by mathematical manipulations, such as adding, squaring, or multiplying them together.

Multiplying a father's occupation by how successful he was as a provider ("Family Wealth") is another example. If a migrant's father had wage-labor jobs most of the year, his son apparently learned something about the cash economy, which translated into a higher starting wage in Denver. We wondered, however, if perhaps a wage-laboring father might prove to be a more influential role model if he were also a *successful* provider. So we multiplied having a wage laborer for a father (scored yes or no, 1 or 0) by whether the migrant reported his family as richer—scored 1—rather than poorer—scored 0—than his neighbors. (Only wage-laboring fathers whose families were richer would then end up with a score of 1; all others would be scored 0.) This is how you can explore the possibility of *interaction effects* with multiple regression. If the resulting correlation with starting wage had been substantially *higher* than that with Father's Occupation or Family Wealth *alone,* we would explore this effect further. But it was not.

Squaring years of education to see if it had a nonlinear relationship with starting wage *did* have an empirical payoff, however. (See the text of article 8 and table 1.) This led us to create a series of new variables: Years of Formal Education beyond Six, beyond Seven, etc. until we achieved a maximum correlation with starting wage of .37 at Years of Education beyond Ten. This, then, replaced our original Years of Education variable in subsequent analyses. With respect to his starting wage in the city, *only education beyond the tenth grade* made any difference at all. Less than that and a migrant might just as well have no education. All he could command was unskilled work. This empirical finding has important policy implications as well.

In this manner we also discovered that anything less than *skilled vocational training* was also useless. As employers had told Bob Weppner in his interviews, much of the vocational training being given Navajo kids in school was simply unrelated to the urban job market. Another finding with important policy implications.

Months of premigration work experience and premigration urban experience were also unrelated to his starting wages; only the *size* of his premigration wage made any difference.

Two personality attributes which employers seemed to consider important deficits among their Navajo employees ("Is the worker ambitious?" and "Is he able to plan ahead?"; see Weppner 1968; 1971; and 1972) also proved to be unrelated to the wages they were being offered. This further supports our empirical challenge to "culture of poverty" theorists. (See chapter 6 and Volume II, article 6.)

Finally, it was interesting to us that employers seemed to recognize that married migrants were a better bet than single migrants, and therefore offered them on the average 17 cents per hour higher starting wages. Given the positive role most wives played in controlling their husbands' drinking behavior, and therefore less likelihood of absenteeism due to drunkenness and arrest, this seems a highly rational act on the part of employers. I therefore expected marital status to play a particularly strong role in the wages being offered migrants for *skilled and semiskilled* jobs, where employers often made a significant investment in training their new employees, and therefore had a strong interest in keeping them on the job. I was wrong. Employers made the greatest allowance for a migrant's marital status in the *poorest* day labor jobs, where wages were the lowest and undependable employees could easily be replaced. We decided that this was more a matter of *charity* on the part of employers than a concern for promoting *stability,* as I had guessed. Employers appeared to recognize that a migrant with a wife and particularly with children to support simply needed to earn more to be able to remain in the city. And this fact was even more true among those in laboring jobs than in more highly paying jobs requiring special skills.

Article 8 was written as much to convey the power of multiple regression as a research tool as to examine the substantive issues concerning the determinants of a Navajo's starting wage in Denver. Although it sometimes requires a degree of mathematical sophistication to follow, I hope an average reader can at the very least come away with some sense of this technique's potential. For example, even sophisticated statisticians may not recognize that multiple regression is capable of handling nonlinear interaction effects, or finding nonlinear relationships within a linear variable, as we did for years of education.

Although multiple regression is a far more refined statistical technique than the differences between Stayers and Leavers which Bob Weppner looked at variable by variable in his dissertation, *both* approaches begin by looking at associations between some outcome and its presumed determinants *after the fact.* The use of multiple regression to produce a "prediction formula" is seductive and somewhat deceptive to the uninitiated. If we were to replicate our analysis among another sample of migrants from another Native American tribe, or even another sample of Navajo migrants to Denver or to some other city, for example, we might come out with somewhat different results. We would hope that the same group of variables would prove predictive of starting wages, at least to some degree. But in general we can expect that in different settings with different subjects the *magnitude* of the relationships among predictors and outcome variables will probably differ.

Some determinants, however, may prove to have a similar effect in a quite different research setting. For example, the nonlinear contribution of years of education to starting wage was replicated among African migrants to Monrovia in Liberia. (See Lave, Mueller, and Graves 1978.) The Monrovia data *also* showed that less than eleven years of education had relatively little economic value for a migrant: He was better off dropping out of school and getting informal training experience while earning money. This is a good example of "sloppy replication": finding a similar relationship among *theoretical* variables even when the measures, the setting, and the subjects are quite different. This type of replication provides a good deal of confidence in the *generality* of a theoretical relationship, since idiosyncratic aspects of the subject population or measures could not be responsible for similar outcomes in both research settings.

Multiple regression is typically used to give you and your readers a sense of how much of the variation in outcome your explanatory factors can account for. For example, in the case of Navajo migrant starting wages, our "multiple correlation coefficient" (R) was .54. In our case, though respectable, this is relatively low and accounts for only a little more than a quarter of the variation in migrant starting wages (R squared = .29). It is humbling to remind ourselves that this leaves 71% of that variation for other researchers to account for in other ways.

From an applied standpoint, multiple regression can also serve to help give you some sense of where may be the most strategic points to intervene. In the case of migrant wages, for example, being sure that potential migrants complete high school before migration is clearly primary. Offering only *skilled* vocational training in American Indian schools is probably the second, so that the migrant has something really worthwhile to offer his employer.

Finally, a standard use of multiple regression only concerns itself with *direct effects* of the predictor variables at one point in time, and usually ignores *indirect effects* of more remote variables in a causal chain. This can seriously distort our understanding of *process*, a key goal of any behavioral research enterprise. Charlie and I addressed this issue briefly in our article, particularly with respect to the indirect effects of a Navajo father's nontraditional occupation on preparing his son for successful migration. But a modified form of multiple regression known as *path analysis* does a far better job of this.

Path Analysis and Causal Inferences

As just noted, multiple regression examines the contribution of each explanatory variable to some outcome *at one point in time*. The model, using our analysis of the determinants of a migrant's starting wage as an example, looks as follows:

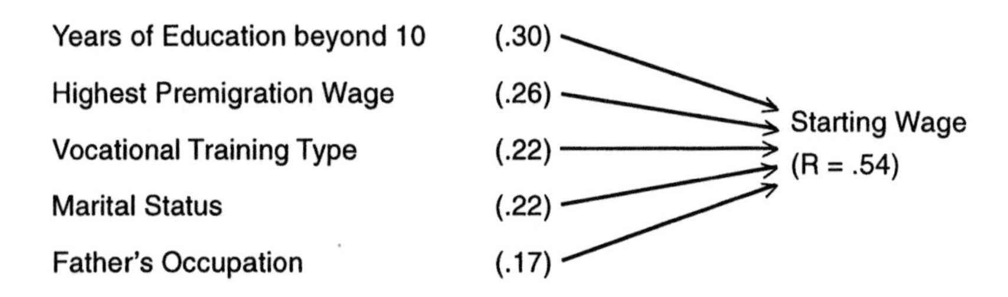

Figure 12.1. Determinants of a Navajo Migrant's Starting Wage—A Multiple Regression Model

"Partial correlations" are in parentheses after each variable. These represent the "direct" effect of each variable on the "outcome" (starting wage) when all the other variables in the equation are "controlled."[4] But in the real world the effects of other variables are *not* controlled. This is particularly true of variables whose effect may be mediated by other variables in some "causal chain." A path analysis looks at this causal chain. The model is quite different from multiple regression, and is probably a more realistic picture of what is actually going on. For example, with respect to a Navajo's starting wage, the model might look like this:

Father's Occupation → Years of Education beyond 10 → Vocational Training Type → Highest Premigration Wage → Starting Wage

Figure 12.2. Determinants of a Navajo Migrant's Starting Wage—A Causal Path Analysis

Clearly a father's occupation precedes his son's educational experience, and if instead of being a traditional herder the father has been participating in the cash economy, he may well help influence his son to remain in school beyond the tenth grade. Those years of education will probably effect what type of vocational training the son receives, although this is an issue to be tested empirically. Both years of education and vocational training type will probably influence both the highest wage a potential migrant receives before migration and his starting wage in Denver. Where marital status fits into this causal chain is unclear *a priori*, but should be examined empirically.

A model of this type can often be constructed logically, and then each step examined empirically to discover both a variable's "direct" effects and its "artifactual" or "indirect" effects: those mediated wholly or in part by more proximal variables in the causal chain. The empirical relationships among the variables in your model can then be tested mathematically to see how well they "fit" mathematical expectations. This is the essence of path analysis. (For sociological examples, see Duncan 1966. For psychological examples, see Werts and Linn 1970. And for anthropological examples, see Hadden and DeWalt 1974.)[5]

"Causal inferences" from correlational data arranged in this manner are a natural corollary of path analysis. Braxton Alfred had introduced me to the work of Hubert Blalock on *Causal Inferences in Nonexperimental Research* (1961) at an early point in our Navajo migrant research. I was skeptical about the validity of such analyses, however, and never applied Blalock's technique to our data. (Recall, for example, the possible *reversal* in causal direction which I demonstrated in my analysis of "psychological acculturation" in the tri-ethnic community: Volume II, article 2, discussed in chapter 4.) Nevertheless, I was intrigued by the logic of the mathematics involved. And when I moved to UCLA an opportunity to put Blalock's approach to a test presented itself.

One of the rewards of going to all the trouble to collect systematic data is that you can use them over and over again, as fresh ideas and insights come to mind. I am a great believer in "secondary analyses" of both my own and other people's data. If the data are good, it doesn't really matter who collected them or why, they may still prove useful for other purposes.

Dick Jessor, with his commitment to "construct validity" (strictly designing your measures for some theoretical purpose), was somewhat skeptical about the value of secondary analyses. But I am not so much of a purist. In fact, if the data are sound to begin with, I love the challenge of figuring out creative new ways to use them. The first two articles reprinted in Volume II (and already discussed in chapter 4) were both secondary analyses of Tri-Ethnic data, with which I had intimate familiarity. I found them fascinating, and full of surprises. Earlier in this chapter I discussed a secondary analysis of our Navajo Migrant data which Charlie Lave and I conducted, using the powerful tool of multiple regression. It, too, yielded surprises, and deepened our understanding of our data. Here is a third example, using path analysis.

When we moved to UCLA I had the good fortune to work with Clyde Woods in a secondary analysis of the systematic data he had collected on the adoption of Western medical practices in San Lucas Tolimán, a mixed Mayan Indian and Ladino community on Lake Atitlán in Guatemala. Nan and I visited the area over Christmas in 1970, and intended to do fieldwork in San Lucas during the following summer,[6] but unhappily I developed paratyphoid that spring and my doctor advised against going. Nevertheless, this brief visit gave me a "feel" for the community and the area Clyde was writing about. What a beautiful spot! Stanford researchers were smart to make this lake area in the southwestern highlands, surrounded by thirteen communities for comparative purposes, a center for their interdisciplinary research program on modernization and health. After completing his dissertation under my direction at Colorado, Pete Snyder participated in this project before joining us at UCLA.

Clyde's data were collected in 1965–1966 while he was a graduate student at Stanford University, but I could immediately see that they would lend themselves well to constructing and testing a causal path analysis, a sophisticated form of multivariate analysis that I was eager to try. The results were published as a monograph (Woods and Graves 1973), a large section of which is reprinted as article 9 in Volume II of this series. It is an excellent example of a fruitful combination of traditional ethnography and quantitative methodology, and demonstrates how this can help answer questions, resolve theoretical disputes, and discover subtle relationships which would probably not be apparent to a more casual ethnographic observer.

There are over 3,000 inhabitants in San Lucas Tolimán, and more than 80% of these consider themselves "Indios." The rest are "Ladinos" who pride themselves on their part-Spanish heritage. This distinction is probably more related to socioeconomic status than biological ancestry, however: Ladinos are the "modern" segment of the population, speaking Spanish, better educated, and more likely to be engaged in the cash economy. The Indians tend to retain their native dialect, distinctive dress, traditional subsistence agricultural activities, and traditional worldview. And it is they who maintain the traditional religious life of their communities through the *cofradía* system: Religious fraternities each of which has responsibility for the care and adoration of a particular saint, and whose members take turns serving a costly one-year period of community and ceremonial service (*cargo*).

But all this is changing. Western influences and temptations abound, and Ladinos offer a local model of a more modern way of life. Table 12.3 compares the proportion of Indian men (or their households) and Ladinos who had adopted various "modern" traits at the time of Clyde's fieldwork:

Table 12.3. Adoption of Modern Practices in San Lucas Tolimán

	Indians	Ladinos
Can speak Spanish	89%	100%
No longer uses sweat bath	84%	100%
Wears modern dress	84%	100%
Wears factory-made shoes	13%	91%
Had a Western education	15%	92%
(Children now in school)	22%	97%
Single household plot	63%	94%
Civil or religious marriage	21%	77%
Nonagricultural occupation	14%	73%
Outhouse	17%	86%
Radio	9%	57%
Raised cooking hearth	4%	96%
Running water	3%	58%
Electricity	2%	44%

In addition to this transition from traditional to modern in material culture, economic activity, education, and lifestyle were changes in medical beliefs and practices. These were the focus of Clyde's dissertation research (Woods 1968). Although some thirty-six shamans had been in practice twenty-five years earlier, by 1966 only thirteen were active, none on a full-time basis. A number of traditional midwives and lay curers (mainly women herbalists) were available, but these were in increasing competition from Ladino pharmacists, practical nurses, and trained doctors. Faced with an illness, most Indians used a combination of traditional, folk, and modern services, but in varying proportions.

The basic problem we were addressing in this monograph was to discover what accounts for differences among Indians in their medical beliefs and practices. Note that as usual in behavioral anthropology research, our dependent variable (the thing we wanted to explain) included within-group variation in *behavior*—the degree to which they were using traditional or Western medical services—as well as the degree to which they had retained a belief system about the nature of the world and man's place in it which underlies and supports their traditional curing practices.

Clyde's dissertation described traditional beliefs and practices ethnographically and the changes in these which were currently underway. But he had also collected systematic data from a sample of forty Indian household heads using a forty-eight-item scale of traditional beliefs, and had observed and recorded their medical practices over a six-month period. In addition, he had collected a large quantity of systematic data on their exposure to Western influences through education, the media, military service, and travel, a test of their political awareness, information about their economic activities and wealth, and an inventory of a Western lifestyle. It was the availability of these systematic data which attracted my attention. By constructing and manipulating indices of key concepts, such as exposure, innovativeness, and economic status, we could put to an empirical test alternative theories about the process of modernization, such as which changes first, behavior or the cultural beliefs which are thought by most anthropologists to underly and determine this behavior.

The inferential steps we followed are carefully spelled out in the monograph. First we calculated a matrix of correlation coefficients among these indices and our outcome variables and placed them in a causal sequence based on the strength of these correlations. Blalock's rule, which makes intuitive sense, is that because of the intervening effects of chance circumstances and other causal factors, correlations should be highest among adjacent links in a causal chain and diminish as you proceed outwards in both directions. Four variables—exposure, innovativeness, medical practices, and beliefs—ordered themselves nicely in this manner. See table 7 in Volume II, article 9. As this table clearly demonstrates, traditional beliefs, though changing, are lagging behind changes in medical practices (as I and many social psychologists have argued): The correlation between beliefs and behavior is higher than between beliefs and innovativeness, and that between beliefs and exposure is lower still. Once modern beliefs about disease etiology begin to take hold, however, and replace more traditional beliefs, they will probably give rise to an increase in the use of modern medical facilities. A feedback system of "co-evolution" is initiated which will increase the correlation between these two variables. But this will not change their relative position in this "causal chain."

The role of *wealth* in this process, which had been a source of both theoretical and empirical controversy in the literature, confronted us with an empirical paradox: The wealthiest Indians in San Lucas also held the most traditional beliefs. Yet wealth seemed to set the whole process in motion.

Unanticipated empirical findings of this type are an exciting and challenging dividend of systematic research, compelling a search for an explanation which often enriches your theoretical formulations and ethnographic understanding. In our case it led first to a reconceptualization of wealth into two relatively independent streams: traditional (control over land) and modern (control over cash). The first is more common among older men, the second more common among younger. A Land Index showed no consistent pattern of relationships with the variables in our modernization model; a Cash Index fit quite neatly at the beginning of our causal chain: Involvement in the cash economy, whether by older or younger men, increasingly exposes them to the outside world. But control over cash was still associated with the maintenance of traditional beliefs.

An exploration of the alternative ways a man comes to acquire and spend relatively large amounts of cash helped resolve this paradox. A key intervening variable was participation in the *cofradía* system (ceremonial service) which requires large sums of money and family support, but also reinforces traditional beliefs. Relatively affluent Indians are thereby subjected to competing and often incompatible influences. Through participation in the cash economy they are exposed to modern beliefs, but by participation in the *cofradía* system their traditional beliefs are reinforced. "Controlling" for the influence of *cofradía* and related variables statistically produced a set of correlation coefficients which both fit mathematical expectations and made ethnographic sense. (Blalock provides clear mathematical tests of a causal model. This helped us recognize that our initial model was incomplete as well as reassuring us that our final model was probably valid.)

Clyde and I concluded our monograph by noting:

> Woods, who knew the community well, learned things about the process of modernization in San Lucas which he had not suspected or understood at the point when the data were collected. At the same time, however, it was his intimate familiarity with the research community which enabled him to help Graves construct meaningful additional indices of key concepts to be investigated, to interpret and make sense of the relationships which emerged, and to direct us to the solution of an apparent empirical paradox. The point seems obvious and would not be worth laboring if it

were not for the fact that both anthropologists and their more quantitatively oriented colleagues in other social sciences are apt to ignore the substantial contribution which each can make to the other. (Woods and Graves 1973:56)

Causal Inferences from Correlational Data: Testing the "Rounds Hypothesis"

After we moved to New Zealand, I used Blalock's approach once again in order to test the "Rounds Hypothesis" concerning the determinants of alcohol intake and barroom drinking patterns. While this was a much simpler and more straightforward use of path analysis, the results were both surprising and unexpected. (See Volume II, article 13.) Most observers, including myself, assumed that the social norm of "buying rounds" for everyone in your group would cause those who drank in larger groups to drink more than those in smaller groups. The size of a drinking group, therefore, would determine how many "rounds" participants consumed (and how drunk they got) and therefore how long they stayed in the pub. But the pattern of correlations we obtained through systematic observations in New Zealand pubs did not fit this model. Instead, group size consistently correlated more highly with the amount of time a person stayed in the pub than with the amount he consumed. In fact, the correlation between group size and glasses consumed ("rounds") consistently dropped to zero when the mediating influence of time spent was controlled. (See article 13, figure 1.)

The fact that an identical pattern of correlations was found within all three ethnic groups—Pakehas, Maoris, and Pacific Islanders—and was also replicated three times by researchers working independently (without our knowledge or theirs) in Canadian pubs (see article 13, figure 2), has given me a good deal of confidence in these results. But inferences about the direction of causality among these three variables required the construction of another variable and further statistical manipulation.

The logic of this analysis is carefully spelled out in article 13. After eliminating possible alternatives, the causal chain which emerged was as follows: The size of a drinking group influences how long its members stay in the pub, and this in turn largely determines how much they drink.

Clearly the norm of drinking in rounds is important, and results in the very high correlations between time spent and amount consumed. And clearly drinking in rounds influences how long a person remains in the pub, since those who drank in large groups (primarily Polynesians) remained in the pub longer. (And this was our major explanation of why Polynesians drank more than Pakehas.) So what difference does it make? Was this simply an exercise in statistical sophistry?

I'm now tempted to admit that to a large degree it was. At the time I was delighted with the mathematics involved and with the consistency of our results and those of another independent researcher. But this causal sequence *does* make a difference; I simply failed to spell it out in the article. *The subcultural norm of drinking in rounds patterns behavior only to the extent a drinker chooses to participate in it.* He can go home sooner or stay later than would be expected by rigid adherence to this norm. Other factors also determine that choice. In this research we could not specify what those other factors might be; in our Navajo migrant research we could. (See chapter 7 on the psychological motivation and social channeling of their drinking behavior.)

A cultural anthropologist would typically focus on their drinking group norms; a behavioral anthropologist would consider group norms to be only one factor among many to take into consideration when accounting for within- and between-group variation in behavior.

This finding is important for recognizing limitations in the role of "culture" for understanding human behavior, a topic to which I will return in the final chapter.

Methodological Lessons for Behavioral Anthropology

By way of summary, let me briefly outline the conditions under which the various types of data analysis presented in this chapter and earlier in chapter 3 are appropriate.

1. For presenting relationships between each "predictor" (a,b,c . . . n) and some outcome(s) (x, y, and z), simple two-by-two tables will be more easily understood by most readers than correlation coefficients, though matrices of these coefficients are useful to some readers as supplements. For example :

	Low on X	High on X
High on A	# or % of subjects	# or % of subjects
Low on A	# or % of subjects	# or % of subjects

This presentation is made even easier for readers to comprehend by converting your raw frequencies of subjects in each quadrant into percentages. Often I simply list the percentage high on the outcome (X) for those high on A and low on A, although this is really just a simplified two-by-two table. (In the Navajo project, I calculated the arrest rates for those high on A versus those low on A, which enabled me to control for differences among subjects in the amount of time they had remained in the city.)

2. For "interaction effects," where variable A has an effect on some outcome X only when variable B is either high or low (for example, among Navajo migrants marital controls on their drinking behavior are important only when economic status is poor—see chapter 7) the percentage of subjects high (or low) on some outcome can be calculated and presented in each of the four cells. One will clearly stand out. (For another clear example, see Volume II, article 1.)

3. For a multivariate analysis of two predictor variables where no such interaction effects occur, a pattern analysis provides the simplest and most readily understandable mode of presentation:

High on both predictors A and B	% high on outcome X
High on only one predictor, A or B	% high on outcome X
Low on both predictors A and B	% high on outcome X

This approach can be extended to three predictors, or even more, if you have enough subjects that the numbers in the two extreme groups (all favorable or all unfavorable) don't get so small that the presence of one or two "deviant cases" throws off your nice linear sequence of percentages.

4. Pattern analysis can serve as a basis for selecting and presenting illustrative "case" material. Readers can then develop a "feel" for the group of real people represented by each "pattern." This approach can also serve as a neat way to *summarize* "case" material. At the end of article 5, for

example, I did this for the case study of "Harrison Joe," the Navajo migrant who introduced that article. Of fifteen variables which might have been used to predict his success or failure in the city he had a favorable score on only three. Not a good prognosis.

5. By cutting each predictor into high or low, present or absent, you may be losing a lot of information and predictive power, however. When your measures have been carefully constructed and validated and your audience is sophisticated you may prefer to use more fine-grained analytic procedures, such as multiple regression and path analysis.

6. If you have a large number of potential determinants of some outcome and want to see how much of the variation in this outcome you can account for, a multiple regression analysis will quickly give you the answer. But don't be seduced (or seduce your reader) into thinking that your results can be generalized to other subjects, times, and places. Multiple regression is a *post hoc* procedure which takes maximum advantage of "chance" outcomes which may not necessarily occur again. What is called for is *replication* of your findings by an independent investigator. And the more varied the context, subjects, and measures the better ("sloppy replication"), as happened in Monrovia, for example (Lave, Mueller, and Graves 1978).

7. I love path analysis because it results in models of "process": How some outcome came about as the result of a historical sequence of prior events. Often the hypothetical sequence of determinants is clear from the nature of the variables, and you can then test your model mathematically for "goodness of fit," using Blalock's mathematical criteria. And sometimes this analysis will help uncover subtle relationships which would escape ethnographic observation. But this, too, is a *post hoc* enterprise which can be seductive, and lead you and your reader to believe that you know more than you actually do. The best defense is *replication*, as we did among the various ethnic groups under investigation in articles 13, 14, and 15.

Whenever using the sophisticated statistical techniques discussed in this chapter, and when interpreting the results for myself and my readers, I like to evoke the skeptic's dictum: "Chew well, but don't swallow it all."

Notes

1. As noted in chapter 2, I had avoided going to Harvard as an undergraduate, and again skipped my chance to do so for my Ph.D. The ball was pitched, but I struck out on this third opportunity as well. Too bad. My father was a Harvard graduate.

2. This also provided Irvine students with hard data to work on in their statistics courses. Over the years they have conducted a number of interesting secondary analyses of these data, something which normally cannot be done with more qualitative anthropological material.

3. We could have used how many months a migrant remained in Denver, which would have served as an interesting methodological contrast to our pattern analysis presented above. But Charlie was an economist, and determinants of a migrant's wages seemed more interesting to him.

4. By squaring these partial correlations—to indicate how much of the "variance" in the outcome each determinant independently accounts for—and adding them up you get the square of the multiple correlation (R), or how much of the variation in starting wages these determinants account for in total (just under 30%).

5. These papers are difficult for nonmathematicians to follow, however, and perhaps were written as much to impress as to inform. The underlying models need not be so complex.

6. This would have been an unusual opportunity to test the validity of causal inferences from correlational data through a longitudinal restudy of Clyde's subjects to see if they had changed in the ways our model had predicted. As far as I know, that type of validation of a causal model has yet to be performed.

13

Research and Application

My first job after graduating from college in 1954 was as an elementary school teacher in an off-reservation hospital for tubercular Navajo Indians. (See chapter 2.) In my spare time I took graduate classes in the behavioral sciences at the University of Colorado. "Applied anthropology" particularly appealed to me, because it seemed to offer the perfect opportunities to express my social concerns while learning the way of life of peoples very different from my own.

But I was also a "scientist," with a background in the physical and social sciences, and was convinced that providing "hard data" to decision makers would give them powerful arguments for enlightened social policy. Over the years I have learned just how naive that idea was. Nevertheless, I also learned that practical, "applied" topics of study are just as interesting and theoretically rich as "basic" ethnographic research, and might possibly prove to be more useful. Finally, there is the pragmatic fact that it is a lot easier to obtain grant funds to study barroom brawling in New Zealand than cockfighting in Bali.

The Tri-Ethnic Community Research Project was undertaken specifically to address the practical problems associated with excessive drunkenness among Southern Ute Indians living side by side with Hispanics and Anglo Americans on their checkerboarded reservation community in southwestern Colorado. It was this that motivated Omer Stewart to seek research funds, with the hope that our data would be useful to tribal leaders in addressing these problems. We did good research, and perhaps we helped motivate tribal leaders and members to look at their alcohol problems more seriously, though these were obvious enough to any casual observer. After we concluded our project the tribe sponsored an "Alcoholism" conference where we reported our findings. But thirty-five years later their problems are as obvious—and intractable—as ever.

The data we collected and the hypotheses we tested didn't lend themselves easily to applied intervention. What might have been the most useful to investigate we largely ignored. For example, most observers believed that the monthly "per capita" allotment payments each tribal member received from the government as part of their reservation land settlement contributed to their drinking problems. Although some of this money was spent for home improvements, education, and other useful things, purchases at the local liquor stores and bars increased each month following these payments. Many (mainly WASP) critics also felt these payments, however "deserved," contributed to Indian "dependency" and undermined their motivation to work. We don't know, because this was not an issue we addressed in our research. In fact, this topic is not even mentioned in our book (Jessor, Graves, Hanson, and Jessor 1968).

Another unaddressed topic, which I think probably accounts for much Indian problem-drinking throughout the country, was their self-fulfilling negative expectations. I remember a promising Ute high school senior, who after our research was completed came up to Boulder on his own to visit us. The first we heard of this was from the county jail, which was holding him on a public drunkenness charge. We visited him there, and somewhat defensively he explained, "My father is a drunken Indian; my mother is a drunken Indian. So are my two older brothers and most of my uncles and aunts. Of course I am going to be a drunken Indian." "Exposure to deviant role models" *was* one of the variables we examined and it *was* associated with deviant drinking behavior. And such exposure *was* significantly higher for the Indians than the two other ethnic groups. But despite within-group variation in such role models within the immediate family, *all* Indians suffer from the generalized negative ethnic self-image held by the wider community.

Jessor, however, wanted to avoid consideration of variables *unique to one ethnic group*, such as "culture" or "contact history," so that we could develop and test a theory which would be equally applicable for understanding within-group variation in drinking behavior *regardless of the subject's ethnicity*. Our resulting theory did just that, and "worked" quite well (although least well for the Indians, as I discussed in chapter 4). But perhaps we left out exactly the variables which best accounted for the substantial *between-group differences* in behavior which set the Native American population apart so conspicuously. It had nothing to do with their traditional Ute "culture," but with their particular reservation circumstances as a tribe, and their general circumstances as a defeated indigenous minority forced to give up their traditional hunting and warrior way of life to live as peaceful farmers on small plots of land like Anglo Americans.

The Navajo Urban Relocation Research also avoided addressing historical or cultural factors which would potentially impact *all* our Indian subjects, since our focus was on accounting for *within-group variation* in urban adaptation. Our explanatory models were carefully grounded in the specific circumstances our subjects were confronting, and were therefore better able to account for this variation. Following this research I went to Washington and reported on our findings to the Bureau of Indian Affairs, and in Denver to the staff of the BIA Office of Employment Assistance. They were interested in our findings, which had many practical implications for their relocation program. But as far as I know, our research had no impact whatsoever on the way the program continued to be implemented.

Almost all the research I have undertaken during my career has had an "applied" focus of this kind: Besides social problem behavior like excessive drunkenness and its consequences, migrant adaptation, acculturation, and assimilation, which I have covered in the bulk of this book, I have looked at interethnic attitudes and race relations, stress and health, and educational strategies, which I will address in this chapter.

Measuring Ethnic Attitudes

When Nan and I first arrived in New Zealand in January of 1972 and were given the task of teaching a course on ethnic relations at the University of Auckland, we wanted to learn what New Zealanders themselves thought of various ethnic groups, including Americans, but particularly various Polynesian groups. Since we hoped to be studying the urban adjustment of Island immigrants, we felt knowing how they might be viewed by their host community would be a useful first step. We also thought investigating these interethnic attitudes might serve as a useful and educational exercise for our students.

New Zealanders pride themselves in their egalitarianism and lack of the intense prejudices they ascribe to white Americans, particularly our attitudes toward Blacks. "We love our Maoris," they would say. In addition to obvious paternalism, we suspected that there might be far more negative attitudes here than they acknowledged or perhaps were even aware of. We wanted to bring these to the attention of our students by having them help us learn about the prejudices of their countrymen. But how to go about doing this?

We had been struck on arrival by how freely New Zealanders of European cultural heritage ("Pakehas") exchanged "ethnic" jokes, barbs, and stereotypic comments at the expense of other group around them. These had not yet become "politically incorrect." We asked students to share some of them:

> *"My family is better off than your family," a Maori child taunts his Pakeha neighbor. "'T isn't." "'T is. At least we don't live next door to a bunch of Maoris!"*

Or closer to home:

> *"Did you hear about the bus-load of American tourists that drove over a cliff and killed everyone aboard?" "No! What a shame!" "Yes. There were three empty seats!"*

As our first strategy, therefore, we asked our students to keep a "Stereotype Notebook" in which they recorded any remarks overheard in casual conversation with or between other persons, whether positive or negative in content, which referred to some presumed attribute or attributes of any ethnic group. These notebooks were kept for at least a month to help sensitize students to the prevalence of such remarks among New Zealanders. They also provided us with our first taste of the content of these stereotypes and their emotional tone. But we also wanted to measure these intergroup attitudes more systematically.

Measuring attitudes which may run counter to socially acceptable standards, for example, prejudicial ethnic stereotypes, is a particularly difficult problem within any research setting. In a course on Research

Methods which I had taken as a graduate student at the University of Colorado, my professor Ken Hammond was immensely concerned with how to overcome a subject's natural tendency to try and hide attitudes which are not socially acceptable or culturally valued. How to get subjects to cooperate and not fake it, or keep them unaware that they are revealing politically incorrect attitudes?

"Error-choice" techniques are one useful strategy under such circumstances, since subjects think they are only being asked "facts" and are unaware that their answers are being used as an indirect measure of their underlying attitudes (Hammond 1948). Hammond's method involves presenting subjects with a multiple choice "test" of their "knowledge" about one or more ethnic group(s) about which they may harbor negative feelings. For example, "What percentage of black males between the ages of 18 and 30 are currently in prison or on parole?" For each item they are given four alternative "answers" none of which is factually correct. Instead, these range in degree of accuracy from way too low, low, high, to way too high. Respondents reveal their underlying attitudes by the direction of the "errors" they make when choosing from a series of such items. If their errors are close to the correct answer, and vary from a bit too low to a bit too high, their underlying attitude toward that group is assumed to be relatively neutral; consistent errors in one direction or the other reveal negative or positive attitudes. These errors can be scored, their sum ranged along a continuum, and this measure of their attitudes related to their behavior, such as a willingness to rent or sell their home to a minority family.

Error choice was the neatest strategy Ken Hammond taught us for measuring potentially negative attitudes, and I had wanted to put it to use for some time. But the development and validation of an error-choice test is a long and arduous process. Furthermore, Nan and I didn't know enough about the various Polynesian and immigrant European groups we wanted to ask about to construct and validate a traditional error-choice test. But we came up with a much simpler alternative, which students could use without much training and which is flexible enough to use under many circumstances encountered by behavioral scientists. This procedure also has the virtue that it begins with an open-ended "discovery technique" which can be carefully refined as experience accumulates.

We simply gave students a list of fifteen ethnic groups prominent within New Zealand society and asked them each to interview several of their Pakeha friends and neighbors, asking them to describe, in their own words, what each group was like, including their own. The list included five Polynesian groups (Maoris, Samoans, Cook Islanders, Niueans, and Tokelau Islanders), five English-based groups (Americans, Australians, Canadians, Englishmen, and New Zealand Pakehas), and five other groups (Dutch, Yugoslavs, Greeks, Chinese, and Indians) which had a significant number living in New Zealand. (To avoid simple repetition and response set, these groups were randomly mixed on their interview sheets.) Students were instructed to tell their subjects that "You may have a friend or associate from some of these groups who is different from the average. But please put these out of your mind and describe for us as best you can a *typical* member of each group." Students then recorded each adjective used.

To avoid as much as possible having interviewers influence these responses, we didn't tell our students that we were attempting to measure their subjects' *attitudes* toward these ethnic groups; we simply explained that as Americans we were curious to know how these groups (including our own) were *perceived* by average New Zealanders. We promised to pool their data and report to them the results. Since we had over 100 students in this class and each collected several protocols, we soon had lots of data to analyze: over six thousand scorable adjectives from the community at large and almost four thousand from fellow students.[1]

The resulting data were fascinating on two levels: descriptive and evaluative.

First, through a systematic *content analysis* of these questionnaires, we were able to formulate a composite picture of each ethnic group through the eyes of an "average" white New Zealander. Each adjective was written on a separate piece of paper. Then working with a small group of graduate students in our research methods course, through discussion and consensus we grouped these adjectives into twenty-six natural categories. Each category was formed around one or more high-frequency adjective(s), which provided its core meaning. The questionnaires were then rescored using these twenty-six categories and analyzed statistically to see which categories tended to go together (*factor analysis*).

From this work three "clusters" of adjectives emerged, each with high internal consistency and clearly differentiated from the other two. Table 13.1 presents the proportion of descriptive adjectives falling into each of these three clusters for each ethnic group:

Table 13.1. Proportion of Adjectives Used as a Description of Each Ethnic Group, by Cluster

	Cluster 1 ("arrogant," etc.)	Cluster 2 ("easy-going," etc.)	Cluster 3 ("hard-working," etc.)
Americans	62%	25%	6%
Australians	53%	28%	5%
English	52%	27%	13%
Canadians	36%	42%	16%
Pakeha	34%	40%	7%
Maoris	7%	81%	5%
Niueans	6%	78%	10%
Samoans	11%	75%	8%
Cook Islanders	8%	75%	11%
Tokelau Islanders	11%	72%	11%
Chinese	23%	30%	45%
Dutch	43%	19%	35%
Yugoslavs	18%	42%	31%
Indians	19%	47%	29%
Greeks	17%	48%	23%

In general, the five English-based groups were defined by the first cluster (although Canadians and New Zealand Pakehas were frequently described by adjectives within *both* Clusters 1 and 2), the five Polynesian groups by the second cluster, and the five other foreign groups by the third (although these groups were often described by adjectives from other clusters as well.) The English-based groups were seen (in order of frequency used) as arrogant, loud-brash, materialistic, intelligent, serious, self-reliant, ambitious, and progressive. By contrast, the Polynesian groups were primarily seen as easy-going, happy, quick-tempered, friendly, uneducated, quiet, clannish, generous, musical, and dirty. The other foreign groups were typically seen as hard-working (over half the responses), shrewd, polite, honest, and clean.

Note that Americans, with the highest percentage, emerge as the "type case" for Cluster 1, Maoris for Cluster 2, and Chinese for Cluster 3. Judging from these percentages, the most clearly stereotyped ethnic group, by these Pakeha New Zealand subjects, are the Maoris.

Nevertheless, important differences among these groups are also identified. Pakehas see themselves as the most self-reliant, Americans as the most materialistic, English as the most arrogant and serious, Canadians as the most friendly and intelligent, and both Americans and Australians as far and away the most loud and brash. Similarly, among Polynesian groups, the Maoris are seen as most easy-going and friendly, whereas Samoans, Niueans, and Tokelau Islanders are seen as the most quick-tempered. And among the other foreign groups, Dutch, Yugoslavs, and Chinese are seen as the most hard-working, while Greeks, Chinese, and Indians stand out as the most shrewd.

But more than this. Few adjectives in the English language are truly "neutral." Most carry a valance, either positive or negative. And since the words we use represent a choice among possible alternatives, their valance probably reflects our underlying attitudes. If so, the open-ended descriptions students initially obtained could serve the same function as the "errors" in a conventional error-choice test. All we needed was a way of rating them reliably for their positive or negative connotation. (Of course, speakers may be careful in their choice of words, as all of us are when trying to be polite. But in this instance we hoped the subjects would view their task as providing an "accurate description" rather than conveying their attitudes toward each group, in a manner analogous to the "factual" task in a conventional error-choice test.)

Enlisting the help of three graduate students in our Research Methodology course who differed in age, sex, and social class, we had them independently rate each adjective collected along a simple five-point scale from very positive to very negative. These ratings were quite consistent, and by pooling them and discussing those which contained any substantial degree of disagreement, we were able to construct a dictionary of adjectives for English-speaking New Zealand Pakeha in which each entry could be given a score of positive, neutral, or negative. All the adjectives in the original protocols could then be scored and mean scores calculated for each ethnic group.

To our chagrin, and to the delight of our students, "Americans" turned out to have the *most* negative ratings of any ethnic group described: We were seen as arrogant, materialistic, loud, brash, and generally obnoxious. Australians received very similar ratings, with the English following close behind. Even "Pakeha New Zealanders" were described by themselves using almost as many unfavorable adjectives as favorable ones. Among English-speaking groups only Canadians came off looking good: They received almost four times as many positive descriptors as negative ones.

Contrary to our initial expectations, the attitudes of white New Zealanders toward native Maoris, as suggested by these descriptive adjectives, were overwhelmingly positive: two and a half to one. Pacific Islanders, however, received about as many negative descriptors as positive ones.

To speed up data collection and analysis in subsequent research, the initial open-ended procedure was simplified by using twenty key words (ten positive, ten negative) from our content analysis. Then additional subjects were simply asked to chose five adjectives from this list which they considered most accurately described each ethnic group. Using this same list of adjectives, we later asked subjects to describe a variety of idealized roles, such as "employer," "doctor," "lawyer," "friend," and "son-in-law." We could then match the role profiles we obtained with the descriptions of various ethnic groups. Again we discovered something we had not anticipated: The best ethnic match with "ideal son-in-law" was with the description of a typical New Zealand Maori! (As one validation of this finding, as early as 1960 over 40% of all Maori marriages in the Auckland area have been with New Zealand Pakehas.) We published this study in New Zealand under the title, "Would you want your daughter to marry one?" with the answer being a resounding "yes!" (T. Graves 1977).

This research was both fun and interesting, but it was not strictly "behavioral anthropology" by my definition because we had no measures of *behavior* to which these attitudes could be related. Attitudes *can* be important determinants of behavior (and many theorists believe behavior can be an important determinant of attitudes) and the overall rate of intermarriage between Maoris and Pakehas may reflect (and help determine) the positive attitudes toward Maoris which we found. In our survey study, introduced in the last chapter, we found that about half the working-class Pakehas we interviewed reported having a Polynesian relative. Would this have been associated with more positive attitudes toward Polynesians? Unfortunately, we didn't ask.

From an "applied" perspective, this research was mainly valuable in the way it (and the direct observations of interethnic encounters students also undertook, reported in chapter 9) opened the eyes of our students to the society they lived in. In many respects this was the most rewarding class I ever taught.

Stress and Health

Tony Hooper and Judy Huntsman, who originally invited us to come to New Zealand, were conducting their own research among Tokelau Islanders in cooperation with the Epidemiology Unit of the Wellington Hospital, with changes in the health status of these Polynesian immigrants constituting a major focus. (See Salmond et al. 1985; and Wessen 1993 for results of this effort relevant to the theme of migration, stress, and health.) In an early lecture to this group we included stress and health in our model of migrant adaptation (N. Graves and T. Graves 1972), drawing in part on the model Braxton Alfred had developed for the Navajo project. (See chapter 5.) And when we planned our own field research in Aitutaki, we decided to include measures of the health status of these Islanders as a baseline for a subsequent analysis of stress and health among Cook Islands immigrants in New Zealand.

But we also anticipated that Westernization would have health implications *within* the islands themselves. Our initial model for this process is presented in T. Graves and N. Graves (1979; reprinted in Volume II, article 11). Westernization, we hypothesized, would lead to a more rivalrous and individualistic personality orientation, which would result in more social conflicts and in turn to more symptoms of poor health.

As we demonstrated in N. Graves and T. Graves 1978 (reprinted in Volume II, article 10 and discussed in chapter 10), the first link in this inferential chain was strongly supported by our data. But the following steps received weak or mixed support or empirical disconfirmation. It is always exciting when the data do not conform to your expectations, and often this leads to new theoretical and empirical insights. Article 11 provided ample opportunity for us to trace not only our emerging understanding, but also the way we went about arriving there.

In brief, what we found was that a significant number of Aitutaki men were modernizing *without* Westernizing: They were successfully taking advantage of modern opportunities without taking on Western personality characteristics or abandoning their cooperative group orientation. Instead of one, we found *two* streams of modernizing individuals: those who were becoming more individualistic and opting out of the traditional communal system, and those who were not. Regardless of whether we used high Western Exposure or high Economic Status as our measure of modernization, those who *retained* their group orientation reported fewer social conflicts and fewer health problems than the rest of their community.

These findings fit what we know from other research about the *stress buffering* effect of being well integrated socially. They also provide an excellent example of how I have gone about searching for *interaction effects*: when variables such as Western exposure and economic status lead to one outcome under one set of conditions but a very different outcome under another.

This analysis was completed during the year Nan and I were residents at the Center for Advanced Study in the Behavioral Sciences in Palo Alto (1977–1978). When we returned to New Zealand what we had learned became part of our thinking and entered the design of our survey study of Polynesian adaptation in Auckland. (See T. Graves and N. Graves 1985; reprinted in Volume II, article 15.) One of our hypotheses was that adaptive strategies such as kin-reliance and peer-reliance, which were based on the maintenance or even intensification of a group-orientation, should be stress-buffering, and therefore related to fewer symptoms of poor health. But from a review of the literature two other hypotheses were added.

Prior social science research on stress and health can be neatly divided into two traditions: the sociological, which looks at the relationship between the *amount of change* in a person's objective circumstances as a source of stress leading to poor health (a research tradition initiated by Rahe et al. in 1964 and Holmes and Rahe 1967), and psychological, which looks at typical ("Type A" or "Type B") personality traits which may predispose someone to stress and therefore to poor health (initiated by Friedman and Rosenmann in 1959). As I read this literature I was struck by the fact that *there was almost no mutual citation*: Sociologists and psychologists were essentially ignoring what members of the other discipline were doing in this topic of investigation.

My interdisciplinary antennae went up, and I thought to myself, what an ideal opportunity to demonstrate the *complementarity* of these two approaches. And what better groups for doing so than among Polynesian and Pakeha New Zealanders. Pacific Islands immigrants would be experiencing major "life changes" to differing degrees, but they would also be likely to display relaxed "Type B" personality traits. One of their classic ways of coping with life is to downplay the significance of their struggles and setbacks. (My friend Alan Howard at the University of Hawaii had written a whole book about this, 1974, aptly titled *Ain't No Big Thing*.) By contrast, native New Zealand Pakehas, with their European cultural background, should on the whole have less objective changes in their lives to cope with but be more likely to approach these from a hard-driving "Type A" personality perspective. Testing these expectations and the interactions among these complementary types of variables became a second focus of our survey research study.

As I discussed in chapter 11, working with Iulai and Vineta to design this survey was both rewarding and fun, and occupied much of our time during our last year in New Zealand. From our research in Aitutaki we already had a good measure of Health Status, a modified version of the Cornell Medical Index, but we changed the format somewhat to ask "How often have you had each of these problems in the past year?" We also added "colds or flu" and "little accidents, like cutting yourself, taking a bad spill, and so on, either at home or at work?" and a couple of additional psychosomatic items: "having difficulty concentrating," and "not caring about things anymore." (These two scales are reprinted in Volume II, articles 11 and 15.)

Methodologically, it is worth noting that we never felt compelled to continue using a measure in the exact form we had used it before, both because of our recognition that behavioral science is still in its infancy and its measurement instruments in constant need of improvement, and because of my dedication to "sloppy replication": studying the same set of theoretical relationships using different measures and very different subjects. My goal has been to replicate the *pattern* of relationships among theoretical variables, not their exact magnitude.

We also needed new measures of both situational stressors and Type A/B personality traits which would be appropriate for use among Polynesians and Pakehas in New Zealand. Situational stressors could be couched as objective events which we could ask about relatively easily, but we needed to be sure our list sampled fully the types of situations residents of the city might typically encounter. This required all four of us to draw on our experience as immigrants, as well as our knowledge of Polynesian urban adaptation. We also wanted to add a number of "daily hassles" to our list, which other researchers were suggesting might be at least as predictive of health symptoms as more serious "life changes" (Kanner et al. 1981). Methodologically, again, this was an interesting scale, because unlike most psychometric measures, these items represented *alternative* sources of situational stress. Consequently, experiencing one stressor could not be expected to imply experiencing others, and we could not appropriately test the "reliability" of our scale by calculating item-total score biserial correlations. (See table 3 in Volume II, article 15.)

Measuring Type A/B personality traits presented a greater challenge. The typical "Type A" personality scale asked about certain types of behavior which is more appropriate for executives than laborers, and Europeans than Polynesians. Instead, we chose to focus directly on psychological characteristics underlying these behaviors. We couched these in the form of contrasting adjectives, such as "relaxed—tense" and "patient—impatient" which could be rendered equally well in Polynesian languages as in English. ("Striving," however, is not an easy concept for Polynesians to describe in their own language, itself an interesting ethnographic observation.) We then used each pair to define the ends of a ruler, and asked subjects to place themselves along each scale. (This was our own adaptation of Osgood's classic "semantic differential" for measuring meaning applied to the measurement of one's own personality. See Osgood, Suci, and Tannenbaum 1957.) Six of our eight pairs survived careful statistical analysis, and correlated highly with each other, forming a single dimension. (See Volume II, article 15, table 4.)

As anticipated, overall the Pakehas in our sample described themselves as much farther toward the "Type A" end of these semantic scales than did the Polynesians. But contrary to our expectations, the Polynesians overall did not report having to cope with more situational stressors than their Pakeha neighbors, though the *types* of stressors they typically faced tended to differ: Polynesians reported more stress in money matters and kinship relations; Pakehas reported more problems dealing with authority—more troubles at work, more brushes with the law—and more job changes. Finally, Polynesians reported somewhat fewer health symptoms.

A typical ethnographic description might stop here. But as behavioral anthropologists our focus was not simply on *between-group* differences, but on determinants of *within-group* differences as well. Here our results were equally striking. Within both sex groups and all three ethnic groups, Type A personality traits were positively associated with more reported symptoms of poor health at highly significant levels, just as we had anticipated. And so were more situational stressors, at even higher levels. (See Volume II, article 15, table 5.) Yet these two sources of stress—personality and situational—had only a weak positive correlation with each other (.18 overall). In other words, within all three ethnic groups, personality traits and the objective situation served as *alternative* routes to poor health.

As further validation of this thesis we constructed a two-by-two contingency table to define two contrasting groups of subjects: those who were high in situational stressors but low in Type A personality traits, and those low in situational stressors but high in Type A personality traits. *These two groups were essentially identical in health status*: There were no statistically significant differences between them on *any* of the thirty items in our health survey.

Because of the low correlation between our measure of Type A personality traits and situational stressors (an indicator of *discriminant validity*, by the way), by combining them the overall multiple correlation coefficient rose to .5, a very respectable empirical result that accounts for about a quarter of the variation in reported health symptoms. (See Volume II, article 15, figure 1 for a simple *causal model*.) This illustrates once again how a "field theoretical" approach to explanation, which combines psychological and sociological variables, increases our understanding of the determinants of some outcome (Lewin 1951, Yinger 1965). Sociologists, psychologists (and anthropologists) need not see themselves as "rivals" in their quest for an understanding of the human condition, but as complementary allies. And because in most cases a large portion of "variance" remains unaccounted for even after our best interdiscipinary efforts (in our case, 75%), there is plenty of room for other disciplines to contribute as well.

One brief caveat. Some critics have suggested that when measures of situational stressors, personality attributes, and health symptoms are all based on self-reports, as is true of ours and most research of this type, there is the possibility that these measures are somewhat confounded, and that this may account for the empirical findings. May not subjects who are sensitive to the impact of situational stressors (perhaps a somewhat "neurotic" personality trait) also be more likely to experience and report physical and psychosomatic symptoms on the Health Symptoms Survey? Richard Lazarus and his colleagues at Berkeley, who first developed a "daily hassles" scale, have addressed this general issue (Lazarus, et al. 1985) and conclude that it doesn't really matter, that all "explanations" in behavioral science are somewhat circular. What is important in measuring "stress," for example, is not how many objective, environmental stressors actually occur, but how persons *appraise* these situations with respect to their own well-being. It is the person–environment *relationship* that is stressful.

I would only add, as I learned early in my career (see chapter 3), that when your dependent variable (the thing you want to explain—in our case, variations in reported health symptoms) and your independent variables (in our case situational stressors and Type A/B personality traits) are all measured by self-reports, then it is important that you design these measures to be *maximally different in content and format*, as we did in this case, to avoid the problem of confounded measurement as much as possible. The low correlation between our situational stressors and Type A/B personality scales suggests that indeed we seem to have been quite successful in doing this. Our large samples size and the replication of our findings within three distinct ethnic groups and both sex groups provides even further confidence in the empirical and theoretical validity of our findings.

Our primary motivation for conducting this survey was to examine the effect of different "adaptive strategies" on the adjustment of Pacific Islanders to life in New Zealand. With respect to health we anticipated that *group-oriented* strategies—kin-reliance and peer-reliance—would be *stress-buffering* and therefore associated with better health. In this we were disappointed. Among both Pakehas and Cook Islanders, a variety of measures of social support yielded weak and inconsistent results. And among Samoans the empirical evidence was clearly in the *opposite* direction anticipated: The more they were mapped into a network of kin and co-ethnics the *more* stress and health symptoms they reported. (See Volume II, article 15, table 6.)

Our *post hoc* ethnographic explanation of these findings (supported at least by other data from our survey) was that for many Samoans, kin ties may be more stressful than stress-buffering, because of the high *cost* of maintaining their social obligations. The average Samoan in our sample reported spending about $1,500 during the last year for kinship and community obligations. (Cook Islanders reported only spending a third as much, and Pakeha only a sixth as much.) For floor-level production laborers making an average of under $4 per hour (under $8,000 per year), this is close to 20% of their income! But even more stressful for Samoans, according to our survey results, were the demands of "mutual aid" within their ethnic community: food, services, and hospitality. Among Samoans this variable was strongly associated with more reported health symptoms ($r = .4$), whereas among Cook Islanders and Pakehas these correlations were negligible. Our empirical findings and interpretation are supported by a more recent study of stress and health within an urban Samoan community (Janes 1990). Janes found that among these Samoan immigrants in California social support from adult siblings was associated with *lower* blood pressure, but other kinds of extended kin obligations were associated with *higher* blood pressure.

Doubtless there are many fascinating interaction effects of this kind still lying hidden within this body of data. But by this time in our lives Nan and I were back home in the States, grant funds had run out, and we were devoting our energies full-time to promoting cooperative learning.

Cooperative Learning

"These Cook Islanders simply aren't motivated," lamented a teacher to us during our fieldwork in Aitutaki. She was a Cook Islander herself, but trained as a teacher in Western methods of instruction. I demurred. Almost every evening while lying in bed we would hear the drums beating from the village community hall. There Island youths composing the village dance team would be diligently practicing their routines for hours in preparation for the annual Constitution Day dances, honing them to a high level of perfection. Not motivated? Just not motivated in school.

We talked about this problem with our language and culture tutor, Tangaroa Elia. He was a retired schoolteacher and understood the problem. "Cook Islanders like to work in groups," he explained. "They don't like to compete with each other as individuals, or to stand out as better than somebody else. There's an old Island proverb: 'The tallest coconut palm is the first to be cut.' But when they are part of a *team* they will work hard for the success of their team. So, when I was a teacher I put my students into teams, rather than having them compete against each other as individuals."

As our research progressed we increasingly came to recognize, and deplore, the way the schools were promoting an individualistic, competitive ethic among the most promising students, thereby undermining traditional community-centered values. (See Volume II, article 10.) In our final report to the Cook Islands government summarizing the results of our research (September 1975) we concluded:

> [S]ince most Cook Islands teachers, like their European counterparts, reward competition and rivalry among children as a way to motivate them in school, it seems evident that the child who learns his academic subjects quickly is also learning these personality traits most thoroughly. This creates a moral dilemma for the Cook Islands Government, its teachers and its people: Those children who are being trained most vigorously and most successfully for future leadership roles are also the ones who will be the least likely to want to use their talents for the welfare of Cook Islands society as a whole.

Then in our recommendations we noted:

> Faced with this dilemma, Cook Islands leaders may decide to continue their present educational policy, even though it may be undermining traditional values, out of a belief that this is the best way to equip their children to deal effectively with modern life.

> The undesirable psychological and social side-effects are then accepted as the necessary price to be paid for the benefits of Western technology. We believe it is not necessary to pay this price. Recent educational research has shown that it is possible to motivate children to learn just as well through the use of cooperation amongst pupils as through competition between them.

We then went on to outline advantages of such an approach for Cook Islands society, what it would require to implement, and how it fitted in with national goals.

Even before we completed our field work we had begun formulating alternative teaching methods based on group cooperation rather than individual competition. We were preadapted for this: I had been trained as part of a research team and had always encouraged my graduate students to work in teams. Nan prepared for her Ph.D. orals in a team of fellow graduate students. Then we team-taught at UCLA and the University of Auckland and encouraged our students to discuss their observations and to prepare for their exams in small groups.

We had gotten into a controversy with the anthropological faculty at the University of Auckland for our unconventional teaching and grading methods. Within the British system students are normally marked on a strict curve, with as many failures being given out as As and as many Ds as Bs. This creates a competitive and individualistic reward structure, in which the success of one student reduces the chances of success for another. Consequently, students are discouraged from helping each other. But helping each other is just what we wanted them to do. So we changed the reward structure. We told our students that everyone in our classes could receive an A if they performed well during the year and on their final exam. Then a week before the end of term we gave students some twenty or more integrative essay questions to study in groups, and promised that the four or five questions on their final exam would be drawn from this list. The results were astoundingly good essays, many As and Bs and only the occasional failure. Students learned the material, which is what we wanted them to do. The exams served to demonstrate what they *did* know rather than what they did *not* know, as was more commonly the case among our colleagues. Since I was acting chair of the department we got away with this, but our colleagues were not happy.

After we returned to New Zealand from Aitutaki, our friend David Thomas, who had encouraged us to study cooperation and competition in the islands, put us in touch with a social psychologist at the University of California at Santa Cruz, Elliot Aronson, who had recently designed a system of cooperative instruction for use in the Austin, Texas, schools which were currently being integrated (Aronson 1975). His "jigsaw method" was designed to help improve race relations among students at the same time they were learning cooperatively, and had many of the characteristics we were attempting to develop: Students were placed in interdependent groups where the success of each depended on the cooperation and mutual support of all.

In the fall of 1975 we flew back to the States to receive the Stirling Award in Culture and Personality for our research in Aitutaki (Volume II, article 10) and while there we visited Aronson at Santa Cruz. He in turn put us in touch with a whole movement within education which we knew nothing about: "Cooperative Learning." Suddenly we discovered that a lot of people, including some excellent psychologists like Spencer Kagan, whose research had served as the stimulus for our Coin Distribution Task, were involved in this movement and were thinking along the same lines as we were.

At about this point I was invited to spend a year at the Center for Advanced Study in the Behavioral Sciences in Palo Alto. We arranged to go for the 1977–1978 session when Aronson would also be at the Center completing a book on his "jigsaw" method (Aronson, et al. 1978). Although we spent much of that year writing up our research, we took the occasion to meet many leaders in the field of Cooperative Learning at conferences, including one we sponsored ourselves at the Center. And we began developing our own "ecological approach" to restructuring classrooms to promote cooperative behavior among students (N. Graves and T. Graves 1983 and 1985).

On returning to New Zealand we hoped—and expected—that Cook Islands educators and government leaders would be enthusiastic about the possibility of training their teachers in the use of cooperative instructional methods which would be a much better "fit" with their traditional culture. We even dreamed, somewhat tongue in cheek, that "Cook Islanders could then perhaps someday serve as educational consultants for culturally disadvantaged European children with the 'Nyaa-nyaa' syndrome, training their teachers to help them learn cooperatively without developing destructive rivalistic tendencies" (quoted from the final paragraph in Volume II, article 10). But we were wrong. The New Zealand educational model was the standard to which Cook Islanders aspired, and their leaders feared that any use of cooperative methods would undermine the ability of their students to compete successfully with New Zealanders and leave them in an intellectual and cultural backwash.

So Nan applied for and received a research grant for an applied study of cooperative learning in New Zealand schools. Our thinking was that if we could demonstrate the efficacy of these methods to New Zealand educators, then Cook Islands educators and government decision makers would also become more receptive. But this never happened. A change in government in the Cook Islands brought in a progressive administration, led by our friend Dr. Terepai Maoate from Aitutaki, who had treated us and our children while we were doing our fieldwork. Ironically, he and his colleagues were even more dedicated to competitive educational approaches than the former conservative government.

Despite this setback, however, we were hooked. And on our return to the United States in 1981 we became increasingly involved with the Cooperative Learning movement. Nan continued her applied research project in integrated classrooms in California, anticipating that she could demonstrate that these methods were particularly effective among Hispanic children, who also came from a "cooperative" and group-oriented cultural tradition. Instead she found that *most* children, *regardless of cultural background*, seemed to respond well to these methods. The changes which we observed in classrooms where Cooperative Learning was effectively introduced were magical. From a competitive situation where teachers and students seemed to be in a constant power struggle with each other, happy and friendly "learning communities" emerged.

By 1983 we had abandoned all our academic research activities and were devoting full-time to training teachers in these methods. Offering a workshop on cooperative learning to a "classroom" of about thirty-two teachers, which we structured and ran as we hoped they might structure and run their own classrooms of roughly thirty students each, we were able indirectly to touch the lives of about a thousand students through each workshop. During the 1980s we conducted hundreds of workshops of this type, published a manual for training teachers in these methods (N. Graves and T. Graves 1990) and co-edited *Cooperative Learning* magazine, a quarterly publication of the International Association for the Study of Co-operation in Education. Although this applied work was a major departure from our former research careers, in many respects, this proved to be the most rewarding period of our lives.

The Application of Social Research

It's hard to say if *any* social research actually influence the direction of social policy. More often it seems to be used by politicians and reformers to justify programs which are launched for other reasons. "The Culture of Poverty," a notion derived primarily from anthropological research by Oscar Lewis (1966a and 1966b) is a good example. To many anthropologists and other critics, this was bad theory and bad research. (See the various papers in Leacock 1971. For my own empirical challenge, see Volume II, article 6, discussed in chapter 6.) But it was in line with the prevailing popular wisdom and political will of the time, and became justification for some bad programs during the "war on poverty."

Postcolonial, feminist, and Marxist critics of anthropology argued during the 1970s and 1980s that the objectivity of (Western male) anthropologists was undermined by their priviledged position, while their research frequently served to reinforce or extend colonial political and economic power and exploitation. Anthropological descriptions of "primitive" societies served as one basis for the Marxian critique of the modern capitalist state (Diamond 1975), but anthropological research by Western scholars has also served as a handmaiden of Western political influence. Closer to home, some anthropological fieldwork in sensitive areas of the world has been financed by the CIA and the information gathered used for counterinsurgency programs. (For insight into the dark side of anthropology, see Langner 1967 and Berreman 1969.)

I experienced this firsthand. Beginning as soon as I held a faculty position at the University of Colorado, I was visited each year by representatives of the CIA with offers of funding for graduate students to conduct field research in sensitive parts of the world. The funds would be channeled through "respectable" agencies, of course, and their true source kept confidential. Although I always ushered these visitors to the door with an admonition about what this could do to the principle of open scholarship and relations with the academics and other citizens of a host community, they persisted in returning with such offers each year. I presume my colleagues were similarly approached, though we never talked about it. Nan and I ran into "respectable funding" of this kind during our year in East Africa (1967–1968), and one of the tenured faculty at UCLA apparently recruited students for research in politically sensitive areas of the world for many years, with secret financial support from our government. This was the focal issue which set some of my junior colleagues at UCLA against some of their senior colleagues during the student strikes of 1970.

The social, political, and economic biases of Western scholars will best be countered, in my opinion, by training women and minority researchers—one of the explicit goals of the Research Training Program in Behavioral Anthropology at UCLA—and joining them as colleagues in our research endeavors. I learned most about a feminist perspective from working closely with Nan, and the perspective of colonial subjects from working with Iulai Ah Sam and Vineta Semu.

The application of our research findings was disappointingly limited, however. I had made a point of sharing the findings from our Navajo migrant research with key personnel in the Denver Office of Employment Assistance and the Bureau of Indian Affairs in Washington. But I probably could only have had any real impact on policy by joining their operational staff. And then I probably would not have been able to continue conducting research. Similarly in New Zealand. With respect to cooperative learning, it soon became apparent to us that we did not have the energy both to conduct further research on its effectiveness and to promote its use. We made a choice.

Methodological Lessons for Behavioral Anthropology

"The methodological requirements of applied work are not always the same as in academic anthropology" (Pelto and Pelto 1978:xi).[2]

People involved in practical problems which provide services to members of a non-Western ethnic group typically want and need at least two things:

1. Help in making their approach relevant and appropriate to the group they are serving ("Focused ethnographic studies"—see Pelto and Pelto 1997—"Formative Assessment"—see Gittelsohn, et al. 1998a) and "Rapid Assessment Procedures" (Gittelsohn, et al. 1998b).
2. Evaluation of the effectiveness of their interventions. (See, for example, Marchione 1980.)

Both of these needs require rapid feedback from the anthropologists on their staff. But behavioral anthropology, as should be apparent to those who have read this far or have done such work themselves, is slow and tedious work. And the outcomes tend to be complex, not easy for others to grasp or apply in their work. One result is that dedicated applied anthropologists are frequently forced to employ traditional ethnographic methods—participant observation and key informant interviewing—to provide rapid but stereotypic descriptions of the "typical" ways of thinking, feeling, and doing in a community rather than the more complex and differentiated description of the range of within-group *variability* within the community and correlates of this variability, which a behavioral anthropologist would want to undertake.[3]

I don't have an answer to this problem, which has become a particular methodological focus for Pertti Pelto in recent years. Perhaps we must simply view behavioral anthropology as more appropriate for *basic* research than *applied* research and each of us choose how to invest our time and energy. For Nan and me, our research activities and our applied interests within education proved incompatible, and it became a matter of choice between them.

Notes

1. Adjectives describing physical-racial characteristics ("dark-skinned"), typical occupations ("vintner"), ethnic nicknames ("coconuts"), or simply positive or negative evaluations ("wonderful," "total loss") were eliminated from this analysis. We were also interested to see if students and the community at large held similar ethnic stereotypes. They did. But as one might expect, the tendency for

Pakeha respondents to stereotype Polynesians, and to describe themselves and other English-based groups as quite distinct was somewhat stronger within the wider community than among students.

2. Chapter 10 of their book *Anthropological Research* provides an excellent discussion, and the Peltos continue their concern with these issues to this day.

3. For a wide-ranging discussion of these issues within medical anthropology, see Vol. 11, No. 2 of *Medical Anthropology Quarterly*, 1997. Also, see Handwerker (2001) and Bernard (2002:331-333) for a more positive view of rapid assessment procedures than my own.

14

Anthropology in the Twenty-first Century

Throughout my career I have been a marginal member of my profession. There is no single non-Western group with whom I am deeply identified. Nor single subject specialty. But whether I call myself a psychological anthropologist, urban anthropologist, medical anthropologist, applied anthropologist—or behavioral anthropologist—I am always an anthropologist. Anthropology is at the core of my personal identity. More than any other of the human sciences ours embodies my basic values: an interest in, appreciation of, and respect for individual and group differences. Throughout our history, anthropologists have taken as our primary responsibility to describe as accurately and empathetically as possible these differences in the ways people think of, talk about, and engage in their daily lives so that others, too, might understand, appreciate, and learn from them. I revel in this human variability.

In the twenty-first century, the cultural homogenization taking place through the pervasive power of the mass media and economic globalization—"McWorld"—is fostering an equally disturbing "tribal" reaction in which many ethnic groups are reasserting their claim to a unique human identity. Tribalism is as old as the earliest human band. Each group has tended to see itself as "the people" and others as somehow lesser beings. The conflict and misery which this ethnic chauvinism has caused throughout human history can no longer be sustained if we are to survive as a species. As the most holistic of the human sciences, anthropology has a key role to play in promoting mutual respect and tolerance, helping others both to understand and appreciate these group differences *and* the common humanity which underlies them (Spiro 1978).

But the research strategies and insights of our sister disciplines also have important lessons for us as anthropologists. It is my hope that this book may help to make these lessons clear, and thereby contribute to the evolution and enrichment of my own chosen profession.

The Evolution of Anthropology as a Behavioral Science

As I come to the end of this personal and professional saga, I would like to look back on both my own research career and the field as a whole from a twenty-first-century perspective. How has anthropology changed during the last few decades? In many respects, what my students and I were trying to do in the 1960s and 1970s was ahead of the times. We were anticipating and responding to trends within anthropology and pressures from the wider society which are finally working themselves out. The kind of research we were doing forty years ago now seems more in tune with the field today than it was back then.

The essence of science, Spiro (1986) has cogently argued, is working with *variability*, its causes, correlates, and consequences. In the early days of our profession this variability was demonstrated at the *societal* level by ethnographic accounts of the typical "way of life" of exotic societies that contrasted with our own. When enough of these ethnographies had been collected to make systematic comparisons possible on a worldwide basis, some anthropologists began to use this variability to formulate and test propositions about possible determinants of these group differences in culture traits. Over the years "holographic studies" using the Human Relations Area Files have become increasingly sophisticated (Levinson 1977; Levinson and Malone 1980; Ember and Ember 2001) and have served to help move our profession from purely idiographic description to nomothetic explanation, as Marvin Harris (2001) and others had been urging.

But questions arose about the reliability and validity of these ethnographic reports. Contrasting patterns of culture and temperament often seemed too pat. When dependent solely on the intuitive skill and insight of a single observer, no matter how perceptive, ethnographies of this type are only the *beginning* of science. They serve as *hypotheses* about a society and its typical patterns of thinking, feeling and behaving which have yet to be tested through the systematic collection of empirical data. In taking this next step key elements are that the hypotheses be potentially refutable, that the process be public and potentially repeatable, and that the data be based on objective procedures of known (or potentially knowable) reliability and validity — all basic cannons of the scientific method.

This is exactly what Mike Watson and I did when testing Edward Hall's hypotheses concerning Arab and American differences in proxemic behavior (Watson and Graves 1966, discussed in chapter 9). And it is what Florence Kluckhohn and her colleagues had done a bit earlier in their classic study of *Variations in Value Orientations* (1961) among five culture groups in the American Southwest. And what the Whitings and their colleagues then did on a more ambitious scale among *Six Cultures* carefully selected on a worldwide basis (B. Whiting 1963; Whiting and Whiting 1975). These studies usually served to provide empirical support for more casual ethnographic observations, but in a far more convincing and differentiated manner. And Kluckhohn's clearly stated hypotheses also enabled someone like me to offer an empirical challenge to her formulation of a *past, present, and future time perspective* among Native Americans, Hispanics, and Anglo Americans (presented in chapter 2 of this book).

When anthropologists began collecting systematic data of this kind to demonstrate modal differences *between* groups, furthermore, we were also inevitably struck by the range of variation in beliefs and behavior to be found *within* these same groups, no matter how homogeneous they seemed. A logical next step was to use this variability as a research tool as well. Then *within-group variability* could serve to test the cross-cultural *generality* of hypotheses about human behavior. In complementary fashion, these within-group analyses also help explain factors responsible for *between-group* differences as well (Jessor, Graves, Hanson, and Jessor 1968 and many of the articles reprinted in Volume II of this series).[1] Thus was born Behavioral Anthropology.

What ever happened to Behavioral Anthropology at UCLA? The Research Training Program in Culture Change at the University of Colorado, which I initiated in 1962 was a great success, and a lot of fun for those who participated in it. We had a supportive, interdisciplinary home within the Institute of Behavioral Sciences, plenty of grant funds and other resources, and a flexible research laboratory among migrants in Denver and on the Navajo reservation. The Research Training Program in Behavioral Anthropology at UCLA, however, which we launched in 1969 with great enthusiasm, was hardly conceived before it was aborted.

There were a number of reasons for this. The student strikes following Nixon's Cambodia incursions in the spring of 1970, in which several of my (untenured) junior colleagues were actively involved, created a rift between them and the more traditional, more politically conservative (and tenured) senior faculty. As the department's youngest full professor I found myself caught in the middle. Things fell apart. Pete Rodgers, who coined the term "behavioral anthropology" and lured me to UCLA, built a boat and sailed off to the Bahamas, never to be heard from again within the profession. By the fall of 1971 I was fed up with national and departmental politics, with UCLA, with Los Angeles, its freeways and its smog, with the United States and "the arrogance of power." It seemed like a good time to do more fieldwork. Once Nan and I left UCLA, however, only one of my junior colleagues was given tenure (Dwight Read), and behavioral anthropology there suffered an unceremonious demise.

But these idiosyncratic circumstances probably mattered very little. As anthropologists know well, innovations need a receptive climate to flourish; our program in behavioral anthropology was launched in an inappropriate time and place. Although archaeologists and physical anthropologists have been using increasingly sophisticated measurement procedures and statistics, within cultural anthropology there was a growing antipathy toward "positivism," disparagingly dismissed as "scientism." In the 1970s this burst forth into open warfare, led by neo-Marxists, feminists, postcolonial and postmodern theorists and the challenge of "interpretive anthropology." We didn't stand a chance.

I am sympathetic to all of these challenges, and believe each has contributed something of value to our field. But not when they claim absolute truth, and dismiss other paths to understanding as wrong-headed and a waste of time.

It has been thirty years since Nan and I packed up our family and sailed off to New Zealand, thereby effectively ending our promising academic careers. We did good work in New Zealand. But we didn't have a prestigeful podium from which to speak, or the faculty support and financial resources to promote a substantial body of behavioral research. We were outsiders, juggling two careers and raising six children.[2] I'm impressed by the quantity and quality of what we *did* produce, but sad about what was left undone. And sad that our baby, behavioral anthropology, never had a chance to grow and prosper.

Looking back over these last thirty years from my present perspective, I am encouraged to see several promising trends which bode well for the future role of anthropology within the behavioral sciences, and for the kind of research strategies my students and I pursued.

Exorcising the Demon of Reflexivity

For more than a quarter century this post-modern perspective has cursed social science in general and anthropology in particular. Many anthropologists have questioned whether scientific "objectivity" is even *possible* within our field, or whether we might be better off recognizing that in human affairs, particularly when working cross-culturally, an interpretive or hermeneutic stance may be more appropriate. The field even spent a year recently (1995–1996) debating in our *Newsletter* whether or not anthropology is a "science." If not science, Roy D'Andrade asked impatiently, "What *do* you think you're doing?" (D'Andrade 1995b.)

This postmodern critique has been useful in reminding us of the influence of the researcher on our subject matter, on what we see and report, and the validity of our interpretations. But denying the possibility of valid reference to an independent reality is needlessly paralyzing. All science struggles with these threats to objectivity; scientific methods continue to evolve for gathering reliable (replicable) and public knowledge, and for formulating and testing explanatory theories. These are the best set of practices available for overcoming subjective bias.

Part of the problem is a misunderstanding of what "science" is all about; part is a prejudice by number-phobic colleagues against statistics of any kind. Even "counting" something can be seen as dehumanizing and bad. But this prejudice seems to be abating, and an effort is now well underway to proceed toward a "post-postmodern" orientation in which it is again acknowledged that we may hope to achieve some reasonable and objective description of another way of life (Spiro 1986; Allan 1998), and that many of the distinctions that have been made between "qualitative" and "quantitative" approaches to doing so are spurious (Hamersley 1992).[3]

Bringing the "Culture Wars" to an End

Within anthropology an inordinate amount of time and talent has been engaged in arguing about what "culture" really is. These "culture wars" began in earnest with the publication of Kroeber's classic paper on "the superorganic" in 1917. In this essay he argued that organic heredity and social tradition are distinct phenomena, and that the latter involved "a leap to another plane" which must be studied on its own terms. His "autonomy of the social" was immediately challenged by Edward Sapir (1917) with his classic reposte: "And yet it is always the individual that really thinks and acts and dreams and revolts." To which Kroeber is reported to have responded, "I don't give a red cent whether cultural phenomena have a reality of their own, as long as we treat them as if they had" (Darnell, Irvine, and Handler 1999:32).

Kroeber's intent was to stake out a distinct subject area within academia as a source of professional identity and focus of research for our field: the nonbiological evolution of that uniquely human phenomenon called "culture." Although "cultural evolution" may not have become the central focus of anthropological attention as Kroeber had hoped, the concept of "culture" surely did. It rests at the core of our professional identity, and for the rest of the twentieth century most anthropologists worth their salt felt a need to offer their own perspective on the concept. Within the "culture" of anthropology, this concept rapidly became a "low consensus" trait. By 1952 Kroeber and Kluckhohn had collected and classified 171 distinct definitions, each designed to emphasize some aspect of culture seen as neglected by others: social heritage, normative rules, psychological traits, structural patterning, ideas, or symbols. And this process continues to this day: See, for example, White 1959 and 1975; Geertz 1965 and 1973; Kaplan 1972; Goodenough 1973 and 1989; Wagner 1975; Rohner 1984; Shweder and LeVine 1984; Romney, Weller, and Batchelder 1986; D'Andrade and Strauss 1992; Shweder 1996; Romney and Moore 1998.

In the 1970s and 1980s this lack of agreement about what it is we are supposed to be studying threatened to tear our field apart, with the utility of the concept itself being challenged in books and papers with provocative titles like "On the demise of the concept of culture" (Yengoyan 1986); "The predicament of culture" (Clifford 1988); "Culture and truth" (Rosaldo 1989); "Writing against culture" (Abu-Lughod 1991); "Forget culture" (Brightman 1995); and "The fate of 'culture'" (Ortner 1999). In 1986 a new journal, *Cultural Anthropology*, was launched by George Marcus, himself a key player in this game, with the explicit aim, according to his opening editorial, of providing a forum for these debates:

> [T]he treatment of the key concept of culture, we believe, is an index and expression of the debates occasioned by [various] challenges. Many embrace culture as *the* symbolic capital of anthropology and as the most fertile ground for the exercise of theoretical imagination; others acknowledge culture in a mundane way, as one factor among many in research; while for others, culture is distinctive by its absence, a concept that has lost its utility and has dissolved into other frameworks. By constituting a forum for all contemporary and emerging perspectives on culture, this journal intends to expose the broader intellectual currents affecting anthropology and other related disciplines at an uncertain but exciting time. (Marcus 1986:4)

These debates are a form of professional masturbation: We may find them stimulating, but I doubt if anyone outside of anthropology will receive much satisfaction. (See Marshall Segall's 1984 commentary, "More than we need to know about culture, but are afraid not to ask.") With the publication of an entire supplemental issue of *Current Anthropology* devoted to "Culture—A Second Chance?" edited by Richard Fox (February 1999) perhaps this debate can finally be put to rest, if for no other reason than physical exhaustion.

Christoph Brumann's lead essay, "Writing for Culture. Why a successful concept should not be discarded," is sensible and thorough. Using the term "culture" to refer to the typical way of life which characterizes a particular group of people is a useful shorthand, and collecting systematic data on a group's cognitive, affective, and behavioral domains to demonstrate the degree of within-group commonality and between-group differences is a worthy research goal. This more sophisticated form of ethnography is alive and well, and there are many good books now available to teach the novice how to do it. See, for example, Wolcott (1995 and 1999) and the excellent new series of seven texts comprising *The Ethnographer's Toolkit* (LeCompte and Schensul 1999).

It is also time to recognize, as Brumann points out, that anthropologists no longer "own" the concept of culture, which is now firmly established within the mainstream. Not as anthropologists originally conceived it, however—as a group's nonbiological inheritance from the past—but as a shorthand reference to a group's distinctive "way of life" *in the present.* Journalists and other laypeople speak and write freely about "contemporary American culture" (*not* referring simply to High Culture—music, art, and literature), the "culture" of a business group like Hewlett-Packard, and even the distinctive "culture" of a particular classroom, interest group, or family. These are references to what characterize various groups *at the moment*; their origin is not part of the conceptualization, and in my opinion should be a matter for research, not embedded in the concept of culture itself.

In the past I have railed against "the poverty of culture" as an explanatory concept, and have suggested that our fixation on it as a focus of anthropological theory and research has been a barrier to more creative thought and practice (Graves 1972a). Brumann's review touches on most of the criticism I and others have voiced: overgeneralization, homogenization, boundedness, stability. Perhaps most problematic has been a tendency to turn this scientific abstraction into a "thing" capable of causing the behavior from which it is abstracted. All the social sciences have hypothetical constructs of this type: "roles," "personality," "the invisible hand of the marketplace." (An errant CEO pleads in court, "It was the invisible hand of the marketplace that made me do it, Judge.") Saying that the Bula-Bula behave as they do "because of their culture" explains nothing. And in today's world justifies nothing.

In chapter 6 I discussed personality and its component traits as "constructs" which have no reality except in the minds of those who use them. At the group level "culture" and its component traits occupy a similar philosophic status, as Homer Barnett (1954) pointed out almost a half century ago. But habits of thought and action, whether shared or idiosyncratic, are "sticky": It may take years of psychotherapy to change them. It is this *stickiness* which gives them their semblance of causality. To the extent they unconsciously "mold" future behavior it is not unreasonable to treat them as having some degree of causal power. It is only when they are *unconscious, unquestioned,* however, that they have this power. When raised to consciousness and examined their power is diminished, following them becomes a *choice,* and determinants of that choice become a necessary part of any behavioral explanation.

The Diminishing Influence of Cultural Tradition on Human Behavior

Theories of the evolution of culture have generally seen it as playing a complementary role to biological evolution, ultimately replacing most genetically determined "instinctive" behavior by "culturally" determined noninstinctive behavior, which had been passed down from one generation to the next by imitation and social learning. (This was made both possible and necessary by the long period of human infant dependency.) The adaptive advantage of this increased behavioral flexibility is obvious. But such flexibility occurs only if groups can *change* their behavior more rapidly in response to changing environmental conditions than would be possible through mechanisms of natural selection. So, from the start, "cultural" ways of doing things had to be subject to change under changing circumstances. That's what makes us more adaptable than creatures whose behavior is genetically programmed.

Culture itself, furthermore, became an integral part of this evolutionary process, by changing the "environment" to which human groups were adapting. Each new "invention" (a change in the body of "tradition" being passed down to the next generation) made other adaptive changes possible or necessary (Burke and Ornstein 1995). "Invention is the mother of necessity." For thousands of years this accumulating process of change was so slow that for all intents and purposes humans could continue behaving pretty much as did their ancestors for many generations, unless they migrated into new physical environments. Cultural tradition as a guide to how individuals and groups should live their lives was highly adaptive, and "worked" for most people most of the time.

The "agrarian revolution" radically changed the physical and social environment of human groups in many parts of the world. The necessary social adaptations were made over several thousands of years. The "industrial revolution" initiated another series of radical culture changes. Again, the necessary social adaptations were made, this time over several hundred years. Our current "information revolution" is initiating even more radical changes in the way we think, feel, and do things, and this time adaptations are being made within a single generation. In fact, Western culture in general and contemporary American culture in particular is changing so rapidly that much of its content and style was unknown to past generations, and children are now teaching significant aspects of it to their parents and grandparents, a *reversal* of the typical path of cultural transmission.

Conquering armies, traders, missionaries, even anthropologists, have all participated in this process of culture change, by introducing isolated groups of people to alternative ways of thinking, feeling, and doing (Sharp 1952). This has undermined the authority of parents, elders, and of "tradition" in general, and has resulted in more and more people choosing to behave in ways quite different from those of a previous generation. One of the attractions of anthropology as a field of study for me was that I viewed it as a "subversive" science, which would help students to recognize how "tradition" might be unconsciously molding their ways of thinking, feeling, and doing, thereby freeing them to make more conscious behavioral choices.

Contemporary social movements, most particularly "feminism," have explicitly been aimed at undermining the authority of the male-dominated culture of previous generations, challenging the legitimacy of "traditional" roles for women and "traditional" treatment of women by men—for example, clitorectomy, blocking access to education and jobs, contraception, abortion rights, etc. The guardians of "traditional values," conspicuously in Islamic countries, but also in the United States and elsewhere in the West, are struggling hard to maintain their authority and hold back this tide of "secular humanism," but ultimately it will be a losing battle.

A recent letter to the editors of the San Francisco *Chronicle* (April 9, 2000) illustrates the degree to which "the yoke of tradition" is being challenged, especially by women:

> Poor Africa! Famine, poverty, violence, a rampaging AIDS epidemic, and now apocalyptic Christian visions. It is easy to look for outside forces to blame: colonialism, the CIA, the evil eye—but the hard part is looking within for the real source of the problem: tradition.
>
> It is tradition that encourages absolute obedience to some "elder" or "priest." It is tradition that deprives women of rights, of education, of contraception. It is tradition that discounts Western medicine and seeks the cure for AIDS in sleeping with young virgins.
>
> The solution to Africa's political, ecological and epidemic problems does not lie in revived tribalism; it lies in seeking the world's best ideas available to help reduce population voluntarily, to help raise the productivity of agriculture and to disarm the generals and their teenage armies who are otherwise reducing the population involuntarily.
>
> —Laina Farhat-Holzman

"Western" education, radio, TV, and now the Internet are all playing a role in this process of culture change, by exposing more and more people to alternatives. The role of cultural tradition in determining human behavior is steadily decreasing, its "moral authority" diminishing. More and more people are making conscious choices about how they want to think, be, and behave. They may choose to revive and "relearn" a traditional language, like Hebrew in Israel, or Maori in New Zealand, but this is a matter of conscious choice for purposes of ethnic identity, not an automatic following of a traditional "cultural norm." Contemporary cultures are being constructed by their carriers from a multitude of sources. This process is itself a worthy subject of research. But the resulting "way of life" each cultural and subcultural group creates for itself is both an end-product and through feedback a determinant of that process as well. Although "tradition" may continue to play a role in some areas of contemporary life, most of the typical ways of thinking, feeling, and doing displayed by most groups throughout the world will increasingly be determined by *other* factors, particularly personal identity and contact with Western alternatives.

Anthropologists Are Changing Our Own Culture

In response to this changing world we live in, anthropologists have been changing some of our own most cherished beliefs and behavior as well. As Eric Wolf noted, "the strength of anthropology has always been in its eclecticism, or—what may be the same thing—its respect for reality" (Wolf 1980:9). We are a flexible, adaptive, and evolving profession.

1. Studies of "Contemporary Culture"

Perhaps the most dramatic shift has been in our typical focus of inquiry. With anthropological investigations in the New Guinea highlands and the Amazon valley, all "untouched" non-Western societies have probably now been "discovered" and thoroughly "corrupted" by Western influences, leaving little but an account of their acculturative stress and adaptive changes for modern anthropologists to document. All "peasant" societies are now closely linked to and influenced by the "global economy," through television and urban migration (Abu-Lughod 1999). Those of us who go back and revisit our field sites after many years are often dismayed by the changes taking place and the loss of that more isolated and integrated culture we once idealized and loved. (See, for example, Rosaldo 1989.)

More and more ethnographers now choose to document the dominant features of contemporary cultures that are living and growing, and actively being constructed by those who display them. As she had done so often, Margaret Mead anticipated this shift in focus with *Culture and Commitment: A Study of the Generation Gap* (1970). In this book she contrasts "postfigurative" cultures in which the young look to their elders as sources of values, wisdom, and authority and our modern, international "prefigurative" culture in which the young set the goals and pace for their elders to follow. This may be ethnographic stereotyping at its most blatant, but she also identified at an early point the diminishing role of "tradition" in contemporary society.

Aspects of contemporary society and its many subcultures are now a popular focus of research. See, for example, the variety of studies collected by Richard Fox in *Recapturing Anthropology: Working in the Present* (1991), Hugh Gusterson's study of nuclear weapons scientists (1996), Paul Rabinow's book on the "culture" of the research institute within which the polymerase method to synthesize DNA was discovered (1996), the collection edited by George Marcus in *Critical Anthropology Now* (1999) such as Sherry Ortner's study of her own "Generation X" (Ortner 2003), and Barbara Joans' study of Harley bike culture, especially the role of women riders (2001).

2. Documenting Within-Group Variability in Culture and Behavior

Before Edward Sapir published his influential article (1938) pointing out that a respected Omaha elder could disagree with other informants ("Two Crows denies this"), the idea that there might be variability within a culture group in ways of thinking, feeling, and doing was quite novel. Cultural beliefs, values, and behavior were assumed to be relatively homogeneous, at least within the "primitive" societies anthropologists typically studied and described, and any normal member of the group might therefore serve equally well as a "key informant." But evidence for within-group variability slowly accumulated, and in 1975 Bert and Gretel Pelto published an excellent, widely cited essay on "Intra-cultural diversity: some theoretical issues" as the lead article for a special issue of the *American Ethnologist* on "Intra-Cultural Variation" (Volume 2, No. 1). This was followed in 1985 by a symposium on intracultural variation at the annual meeting of the American Anthropological Association, which served as the basis for an entire issue of the *American Behavioral Scientist* devoted to this topic (Boster 1987). Recognition and acceptance of cognitive, affective, and behavioral variability within all culture groups now seems widely accepted within our field.

Several prominent anthropologists, however, have managed to retain a model of a shared, uniform "culture" while acknowledging within-group diversity in what informants may tell us, by ascribing this diversity to differences in the "cultural competence" or "knowledge" of the *informants* rather than to variability within the "culture" itself. For example, D'Andrade (1987:200) argues that "the fact that one can be an expert in a cultural system implies that there is a definite reality to such cultural systems."

With their "culture as consensus" model Kim Romney and his colleagues have gone a step further, developing a mathematical procedure for objectively identifying both the degree of an informant's "cultural competence" *and* "the *correct* answers to cultural questions" (italics added to Romney, Weller, and Batchelder 1986:313; see also Romney and Moore 1998, and Romney 1999). The focal task of anthropology can then remain an ethnographic description of the "true culture" underlying this diversity in informant expertise.

The model has been validated using Weller's data from twenty-four urban Guatemalan women on their "knowledge" about twenty-seven diseases. When there is "high consensus" among informants in their responses to questions about their culture—whether or not these diseases were contagious, for example—this model works quite well, but is then unnecessary. Since almost everyone agrees, the cultural "truth" is self-evident. When there is "low consensus," however—whether or not these same diseases were "hot" or "cold," a truly "cultural" issue, in my judgment, since arbitrary and not grounded in scientific fact—then the model doesn't seem to work at all. So what's the point?[4]

Romney's approach has the great virtue of promoting a more systematic, empirical basis for describing shared cognition. But given the growing variety of influences now bearing on people's beliefs and behavior, it would seem both wise and practical to abandon the search for any underlying "true" culture, and devote our attention instead to describing and explaining the observable diversity, as critics of "cultural consensus" theory urge (Aunger 1999). In Weller and Romney's case, for example, it would have been far simpler and more straightforward to calculate the women's knowledge of contagion by comparing their answers to a doctor's. Then the extent of their expertise could again be correlated with other factors, resulting in the interesting and not totally self-evident conclusion reported by Romney that it is *the number of children* they have, not their age, which has resulted in women acquiring the greatest accumulation of accurate medical knowledge about contagion. What may account for their differences in opinion about whether or not a disease is "hot" or "cold," however—an equally interesting issue with the practical implication that it may influence their decisions about appropriate treatment—appears yet to be explored.

3. A Shifting Emphasis toward the Study of Behavior

Perhaps because of our dedication to the concept of culture as our primary research focus, anthropologists have tended in the past to devote more attention to such topics as the norms of appropriate behavior (the "grammar" of a culture) than to what the people they were studying actually do. Sherry Ortner, in her influential paper on "Theory in anthropology since the sixties" (Ortner 1984), however, argues that a shift in this direction is now taking place, that since the 1980s there has been a growing focus within anthropology on the study of "practice." She uses a number of synonyms—praxis, action, interaction, activity, performance—and defines "practice" briefly as "anything people do" (149), which makes it sound suspiciously like the "behavior" that behavioral scientists have been studying for some time. But her interest, doubtless influenced by the Marxist, feminist, and postcolonial theorists of the late 1960s and 1970s, is in a very limited segment of that behavior: "modern practice theory," she writes (148), "seeks to explain the relationship(s) that obtain between human action, on the one hand, and some global entity which we may call 'the system,' on the other." And within these relationships, she emphasizes "the specific realities of asymmetry, inequality, and domination."

Studies of the impact of the system on practice and the impact of practice on the system are obviously important. Much of the effort by women, minorities, and members of third world societies to overcome the power of "tradition" and of colonial and postcolonial exploitation falls within this purview. But the anthropology of everyday life goes well beyond this limited power struggle. That's not to say that "the system" doesn't have an influence on almost *all* behavior. Navajo drinking and drunkenness, for example, is heavily influenced by their economic marginality within a system which exploits minorities, then strongly promotes striving for material goods which they cannot afford. Navajo drinking is also influenced by norms of appropriate behavior within their recreational drinking groups which may have developed in part to flaunt "the system." But Navajos vary tremendously in the frequency with which they participate in these groups and follow these norms. It is this within-group *variation* in their behavior which I have sought to understand and explain, and a full explanation goes well beyond any "cultural" or "systemic" analysis. (See chapter 7.)

4. Limiting the Role of Culture as an Explanation of Behavior

In response to our more sophisticated understanding of the culture concept, it is now widely recognized within our field that "shared cultural constructs do not automatically impart motivational force" (D'Andrade and Strauss 1992:13). The relationship is *problematic* rather than automatic, and thereby becomes an appropriate object of empirical research. Through a number of case studies the contributors to this interesting book explore how this linkage may or may not come about. I missed any empirical tests of the various theories these case studies have produced, however, and I suspect that "the directive force of cultural models" which D'Andrade touts (1984) may be overstated. Situation pressures and constraints, I predict, may account for more of the variance in behavior than cultural models.[5]

My own definition of culture is basically statistical: a description of "the typical ways of thinking, feeling, and doing which characterize some ethnic group." And in my experience it is more "a thing of shreds and patches" than an integrated whole. I have very few examples from my own research, furthermore, where "culture" has proved to be useful as an *explanatory* concept. I have no other explanation for the striking differences Mike Watson and I found between Arab and American students in "proxemic behavior," however, than that Arabs and Americans differ culturally in this regard (Watson and Graves 1966, discussed in chapter 9). But this statement simply acknowledges our ignorance as to *how* and *why* children raised within these contrasting culture groups typically learn such different ways of behaving. Similarly, Nan and I invoked cultural differences between Polynesians and Pakehas in "group orientation" to help "explain" their differences in drinking behavior, although in this case we had collected substantial empirical data showing how typical Polynesian social learning experiences promoted this group orientation, and how this was changing under the impact of Westernization (chapter 10).

When our research goal is to explain within-group *variation* in behavior or *changing* patterns of behavior, the concept of culture has not proven useful, since even when variation is acknowledged, the concept of culture refers to the "typical" ways of thinking, feeling, and doing of a particular group, not to the deviations which over the long run are precursors to change.

Another way some behavioral anthropologists have used the concept of "culture" in our research is as a basis for measuring the degree to which our subjects ascribe to the "traditional" beliefs of their ethnic group, or have achieved their shared goals. In the Navajo migrant research, for example, we employed a measure of Navajo "traditionalism"—the varying degree to which our subjects clung to a "traditional" Navajo "way of life" or identified more with a contrasting "Western" way of life—as one "predictor" of their success and satisfaction living in a Western urban environment (chapter 6). And in the Guatemalan health study Clyde Woods and I used a measure of the degree to which subjects still held "traditional" beliefs about health and illness a "dependent" variable: one of the things we wanted to explain (Woods and Graves 1973, discussed in chapter 12).

Potentially, measures of variation in the degree to which subjects ascribe to the beliefs and values held by typical members of their ethnic group could be used as interesting variables in behavioral research. A description of the "cultural" model would then serve as the "standard" against which subjects' own beliefs and values were compared. For example, using the technique developed by Romney and associates (1986), Dressler and his associates defined a "cultural consensus" in Brazil as to what material items might constitute a "successful lifestyle," what they describe as "middle-class domestic comfort." They then used this as a standard against which to evaluate how successful their subjects were in actually attaining this lifestyle. Increasing "cultural consonance in lifestyle" was associated with *lower* blood pressure (Dressler et al. 1998). Dressler (1999) also refers to "lifestyle incongruity," the degree to which subjects may be attempting to maintain a material lifestyle that is beyond their economic means, as a source of "stress," which he has found associated with *elevated* blood pressures. These complementary measures sound suspiciously like what Merton (1957) referred to as a "means/goals disjunction," and which we have repeatedly found to be associated with greater alcohol consumption and other forms of social deviance (T. Graves and N. Graves 1978).

Finally, there is no question but that "norms of appropriate behavior" exist to varying degrees either consciously or unconsciously in people's minds, and serve as templates guiding their behavior. But how frequently they *choose to participate* in situations where these norms obtain, and the degree to which they embrace these norms when they do, is a matter of psychological *motivation* determined by other causal factors, as we saw among Navajo drinkers in chapter 7 and Polynesian drinkers in chapter 12.

5. Increasing Methodological Eclecticism

The typical research methods employed by cultural anthropologists have been and continue to be participant observation and key informant interviewing. Nevertheless, quantification has a respectable history within our field. (See the review in Johnson 1978.) And there have long been a few "deviants" like myself who have employed more systematic research design and data collection in our research. Bert Pelto's 1970 text on *Anthropological Research* was the first to bring this work to the attention of the anthropological mainstream, and this coverage was expanded in the revised edition co-authored with Gretel Pelto (1978). In 1987 Bert Pelto and Russ Bernard founded the summer Institute on Research Methods at the University of Florida ("Methods Camp") which over succeeding years exposed many colleagues and students to these nontraditional approaches. An even larger audience has read Bernard's 1988 text on *Research Methods in Cultural Anthropology* and his edited *Handbook of Methods in Cultural Anthropology* (1998) which covers a wide range of quantitative and qualitative approaches. The third edition of Bernard's text (2002) is advertised as "the standard textbook for methods classes in anthropology programs." So there is a growing market within our field for information about systematic research methods appropriate for cross-cultural use.

Meanwhile, one of the promising trends outside our field during the last couple of decades is an increasing appreciation and acceptance of "qualitative" ethnographic methods within our sister disciplines. (See particularly the chapters by the sociologist Howard Becker and psychologist Donald Campbell in Jessor, Colby, and Shweder 1996.) When even my old mentor Dick Jessor can endorse "an ecumenical orientation to social inquiry" which includes qualitative methods (9), I know a major epistemological shift has taken place within the behavioral sciences.

Perhaps the respect now being given to conventional ethnographic methods outside our field may help us in turn to be more open to the use of systematic quantitative methods in the type of "qualitative-quantitative mix" I have long advocated. Bernard, for example, subtitled the 1994 and 2002 editions of his methods text for anthropologists "*Qualitative and Quantitative Approaches*," and published a separate edition (2000) specifically aimed at a broader nonanthropological audience. The evolution of anthropology as a behavioral science seems well underway, and the emergence of an integrated science of human behavior in which we can play an important role is now emerging.

Three Steps along This Evolutionary Path

As in most evolutionary processes, earlier stages persist into the present in modified form. Here are three examples from our own field.

1. Cockfighting in Bali

Clifford Geertz can serve as a contemporary spokesperson for the earliest, ethnographic stage of our profession's development. As a leading exponent of an "interpretive" anthropology, Geertz argues forcefully that human social life is a matter of *meaningful* activity which can only be studied superficially through the "objective" methods of science. I take issue with this. Inferences about the "meanings" underlying social acts are not "superficial" when they are based on systematic data collected from a random sample of 100-plus subjects rather than a handful of nonrandom "informants" such as Geertz normally depends on. In a very real sense we are *all* "Geertzians," since we are all engaged in making inferences and interpretations from our data. The difference may simply be that *my* "thick descriptions" are woven from a web of statistical relationships by which I am attempting to "validate" my interpretations and make the process by which I arrived at them as public as possible, rather than simply depending on the intuitive skill and insight of the ethnographic observer.

Geertz himself seems to recognize that at least rough quantification may be useful at times to bolster the credibility of his interpretations. In one of his most widely read, delightful, and well-written articles, for example, "Deep play: Notes on the Balinese cockfight," (reprinted as chapter 15 in Geertz 1973), he uses cockfighting as a way into his analysis of (male) Balinese character. "As much of America surfaces in a ball park, on a golf links, at a race track, or around a poker table, much of Bali surfaces in a cock ring. For it is only apparently cocks that are fighting there. Actually, it is men" (417).

This article is a good example of what his admirer Sherry Ortner cogently refers to as "ethnographic journalism" (Ortner 1999). Geertz makes a lot of stereotypic statements about "the Balinese," which can make a behavioral scientist wince. But these are artistic shorthand to make a rhetorical point (of which he is a master), and must constantly be reframed as "this appears to be statistically *typical* Balinese ways of thinking, feeling or doing." "To anyone who has been in Bali any length of time," he asserts for example, "the deep psychological identification of Balinese men with their cocks is unmistakable" (417.) (The double entendre is intended.)

"The Balinese never do anything in a simple way that they can contrive to do in a complicated one, and to this generalization cockfighting is no exception." To demonstrate this point Geertz then goes on to analyze in a way which clearly illustrates widespread within-group variability in social and economic position, determinants of the magnitude of two types of bets: the (usually large) "center bet" between the two cock owners (though typically involving money raised from family members and other allies), and smaller "side bets" between pairs of observers in the audience. The "cultural rules" which create a framework within which these bets are formed are clearly shared as "high consensus" traits. But the actual behavior (how much money is bet and at what odds) is extremely variable, and depends on many factors, including the economic and social status of the bettors and the size of the center bet. The larger the center bet, for example, the closer the odds are to even money. Geertz collected fairly precise data on fifty-seven matches, and if he had been inclined to do so, he could probably have constructed a mathematical model for "predicting" the size of these bets. Such an exercise in "behavioral anthropology" would have clarified the relative importance of these various determinants and added to the specificity of his analysis. It might even have revealed relationships which his ethnographic observations had missed.

There is a place for intuition and inference in a science of human behavior as a source of hypotheses to be tested. There is also a place—and a market—for the type of untested ethnographic descriptions Geertz and his followers provide. Geertz is a storyteller, journalist, humanist, philosopher, textual interpreter, and writer of nonfiction. But he is not a scientist. He does not follow the rules of the game. He and I came to anthropology from opposite directions—Geertz from the humanities, I from the physical sciences—so we tend to emphasize different things. His major goal is to articulate and celebrate human *diversity*, mine our *unity*, by testing hypotheses and formulating laws of human behavior which apply across these varying cultural groups.[6] These are *complementary*, not antagonistic goals. And anthropology is a large enough tribe that there is room within it for all of us.

2. Sleeping Arrangements in India

Richard Shweder can serve as a spokesperson for an intermediate stage in our professional development, where ethnographic hypotheses are put to empirical test. Shweder is a firm believer in the value of "culture" as an explanation of social behavior. In somewhat convoluted fashion he defines culture as "a reality lit up by a morally enforceable conceptual scheme composed of values (desirable goals) and causal beliefs (including ideas about means-ends connections) that is exemplified or instantiated in practice" (Shweder 1996:20).

Shweder's research on sleeping arrangements in Orissa, India, and Hyde Park, a suburb of Chicago, serves as a major source of his faith in the importance of a group's "morally enforceable conceptual scheme(s)" in determining their behavior. Not all of a group's typical ways of thinking, feeling, and doing have the "moral" component Shweder emphasizes in his definition, of course. I drive on the right-hand side of the road and stop at red lights because it is convenient and safer to follow these cultural conventions, as is true of much else that I choose to do in conformity to middle-class Anglo-American norms. But when it comes to sleeping arrangements, his work seems both interesting and useful. A careful analysis of this research, however, also provides support for the importance of alternative, noncultural influences.

Shweder and his colleagues believe that "sleeping arrangements are a joint product of cultural preferences (for example, the particular moral goods promoted by a people) and local resource constraints (for example the amount of space available)" (1995:30). In the community they were studying in Orissa, India, they collected reports on the sleeping arrangements during the previous night from a member of each of 160 Hindu households. These sleeping arrangements were so variable, however, that they found it impossible to infer the underlying "moral principles" guiding them. To provide a more standardized data set, they devised a "Sleeping Arrangements Task" with a hypothetical family of seven: father, mother, sons fifteen, eleven, and eight, and daughters fourteen and three. Then under varying resource constraints—from one room to seven—informants were asked to sort these family members into acceptable sleeping arrangements. Nineteen Hindu adults from Orissa and nineteen American adults from Hyde Park, Illinois, completed this task.[7]

From these data the researchers extracted what they believed to be the "moral preferences" guiding their informants' choices. (Exactly how they went about doing this is unspecified.) For the Hindu subjects, these were "incest avoidance, protection of the vulnerable, female chastity anxiety, and respect for hierarchy." For middle-class Americans, by contrast, they hypothesized that the moral preferences were "incest avoidance, the sacred couple, and autonomy." The above ordering of these moral preferences was determined by a second, "Preference Conflict Task," in which a smaller number of informants (four from Orissa, sixteen from Hyde Park) were presented with a series of hypothetical sleeping arrangements "selected to exemplify breaches of the moral preferences" and were asked to rank them from "most offensive" to "least offensive."[8] They then validated their analysis of Indian moral preferences by seeing how well these predicted the sleeping arrangements reported by family members in their 160 Orissa households. In 87% of the households, actual sleeping arrangements were consistent with all four hypothesized Indian preferences. The principle of "incest avoidance" was violated only eight times (5%), "protection of the vulnerable" (co-sleeping with a small child) was never violated, "female chastity anxiety" (young unmarried girls are not left to sleep alone) was violated only twice, and "respect for hierarchy" (sexually mature boys should not sleep with their fathers) was violated twelve times (7.5%). When it comes to sleeping arrangements, this seems to me a convincing demonstration of the power of a small number of hypothetical "cultural norms" to predict actual behavior under a variety of circumstances. And I suspect the same would be true for data gathered on sleeping arrangements among middle-class American families.

In my own family, for example, when our youngest son was born Nan took him to work during the day strapped to an Apache cradle board and breast fed him at her desk. But despite our familiarity with typical non-Western co-sleeping arrangements for infants, at night we put him to bed alone in his own room adjacent to ours. I don't think he liked this very much, and it seemed as if every time we started to make love, he would begin to cry for attention. But the "sacred couple" principle prevailed. And although my youngest daughter and her husband frequently "co-slept" with their baby daughter for convenience in nursing (as appears to be a growing trend in contemporary American society), if she were to have a second child, she hoped it would also be a girl, because otherwise she felt she would have to give up her private office and craft room for a second children's bedroom, in conformity with the principle of brother–sister "incest avoidance."

I applaud Shweder's creative construction and use of a standardized task to collect data for extracting underlying cultural norms, as well as the collection of a large body of actual sleeping arrangements by his team (their "behavioral criterion measure") for validating this analysis. An excellent test of an ethnographic hypotheses.

These data make it possible, furthermore, to develop and test additional hypotheses. For example, although the authors state that "there is no sacred couple principle in force in Orissa," in thirty-five cases (22% of the 160 household) exclusive father–mother sleeping arrangements were reported. Furthermore, when Indian informants selected their hypothetical solutions to sorting seven family members into varying numbers of bedrooms, under the three-room constraint a *majority* of their solutions (53%) also conformed to the "sacred couple" principle. (There are clear cultural differences, however: Under the same conditions, 88% of the American informants' solutions conformed to this principle.) This suggests to me the strong possibility that the "sacred couple" principle, being widely promulgated by Hollywood, may now be emerging as a new "cultural norm" in India. What would be needed to move this analysis from the systematic validation of an ethnographic hypothesis to a true example of behavioral anthropology would be to relate the within-group *variation* in preference for exclusive father–mother sleeping arrangements among his informants to variation in their degree of exposure to Western influences. This type of analysis is central to the next example.

3. Child Rearing in Kenya

Ever since their ambitious *Six Cultures* studies (B. Whiting 1963) Beatrice and John Whiting have set the highest standards for systematic data collection to test clearly formulated hypotheses both between and within culture groups. In a recent publication (1996) Beatrice Whiting reports the results of a study of culture change in Kenya.

What could be more "cultural" than conceptions of "the good child"? This is the set of character traits mothers attempt to instill and reward in the next generation. Thirty years ago she and her local university research apprentices were attempting to document these beliefs among the Kikuyu. Drawing on classic ethnographies of Jomo Kenyatta and Louis Leakey, key informants, and the cultural expertise of her student interns, Whiting and her team selected four character traits which they believed would traditionally be considered "praiseworthy": respectful, obedient, good-hearted, and generous. (These are the best English translations bilingual students could come up with; their research was conducted, of course, in Kikuyu.) Note that these are all positive *social* (group-oriented) traits, which promote harmonious family and community interaction.

Through interviews with four key informants, the researchers then identified four contrasting personality traits which they thought would help make a child successful in school: clever, brave ("bold"), confident, and inquisitive. Note that these are all *individualistic* traits, what the Whitings refer to as "self-traits."

In order to explore the possible effects of exposure to Western-style schools on the hierarchy of maternal values, each of these four "modern" traits was paired with each of the four "traditional" traits in a sixteen-item questionnaire, and administered to twenty-four mothers who varied in their degree of exposure to formal schooling. Each mother was asked, "Which is better, that your child be generous or clever? Bold or generous? Generous or inquisitive? Generous or confident? Clever or respectful? Respectful or bold?" and so on. (To avoid response set, the items were paired and administered in random order.) Each trait was then scored from 0 to 4, *depending on how often it was chosen as the more important*. These scores were then correlated with the mother's years of schooling. These correlations varied from +.41 to –.46, with all the "modern" traits receiving positive correlations, and all the "traditional" traits receiving negative correlations. Clearly, the "valued child" was changing under the impact of changing conditions, and traditional Kikuyu "culture" was no longer determining what kind of a child these mothers would seek to promote.

To explore this phenomenon in other ways, key informants from the community were asked to identify families they considered "most modern." Then the researchers analyzed the demographic indices associated with these judgments, such as the father's years of education and occupation, house type, monogamous or polygynous marriage, membership in one of the new Protestant or Catholic churches, etc. Nine of these were found to be closely associated with each other statistically, and through factor analysis were then combined into a single "modernization scale." This scale correlated with the mother's choices of an "ideal child" even higher than had her years of education alone. The highest correlations of all, however, (+.55 to -.57), were reported for *the presence of a radio* in the home. What is clear from this analysis is that traditional Kikuyu "culture" is rapidly receding as the major source of these mothers' value choices; exposure to Western ideas and the adoption of a more Western way of life is taking its place. For a behavioral anthropologist, the next step would then be to demonstrate an empirical association between these differences in parental values and differences in observations of their child-rearing *behavior*.

Toward an Integrated Science of Human Behavior

Anthropology, Eric Wolf has observed, is "the most scientific of the humanities" and "the most humanist of the sciences." (Quoted by Yengoyan in his forward to Wolf 2001.) As a field we have an important contribution to make to our sister disciplines, both in providing this bridge between these different ways of knowing, and more particularly in humanizing behavioral science. "The Other" is no longer a distant tribe, but out neighbor, and behavioral science in the twenty-first century must needs help us all learn ways to live with, benefit from, and enjoy these cultural differences. All behavioral science, perforce, must therefore to some degree become "anthropological." And accurate description of the typical ways of thinking, feeling, and doing which characterize all these groups with which we are now in such intimate contact (cultural anthropology) are more needed than ever, *including the range of variation within each of these groups*—to avoid cultural stereotypes.

From my reading of the contemporary anthropological literature, particularly that being published outside the mainstream anthropological journals, more of us within anthropology are joining members of our sister disciplines in taking one further step: using this range of both within- and between-group variation to formulate and test hypotheses concerning the *causes, correlates, and consequences* of this variation (behavioral anthropology). Both activities—description and explanation—are worthy and important, and in many ways complementary. But it is in undertaking the latter, I believe, that we anthropologists have an opportunity to make our greatest contribution to an integrated and cumulative science of human behavior.

Notes

1. Rohner's tests of Parent Acceptance–Rejection Theory—*They Love Me, They Love Me Not* (1975), his follow-up reports (1984 and 1986), and his community study with Chaki-Sircar (1988) provide the best example I know of a cumulative body of cross-cultural, psychological, and community research designed explicitly to take advantage of these complementary approaches. I wish there were many more.

2. Two of our children found New Zealand partners and live there still. So now we have three nuclear-free New Zealand grandchildren.

3. There will be some who question whether we have truly been successful at driving a stake through the heart of this demon, which keeps rearing up to haunt us.

4. It's the rare anthropologist, furthermore, with the mathematical skills to apply their technique. But see the creative use by Dressler et al. (1998).

5. Within social psychology the same has been true for the concept of "personality," which occupies for them a theoretical position similar to "culture" for anthropologists. And here, too, situational factors have often proved to have more explanatory power. See Ross and Nisbett (1991).

6. What Rohner (1986:165) refers to as "anthroponomy."

7. The researchers were struck by the fact that less than 15 of the 877 logically possible solutions were chosen with any frequency within either culture, and about 95% of the possible solutions were never chosen at all. They interpret this as evidence for the strong influence of "culture," and believe the unchosen solutions were ruled out as "immoral, unacceptable, or otherwise 'ungrammatical' by informants in both cultures" (Shweder et al. 1995:31) .

8. The authors acknowledged "that the particular set of offending arrangements presented to American informants" was "not ideal for determining the full ordering of American moral preferences," and "[m]ore work needs to be done to establish the precedence ordering of American values." I suspect that if middle-class American informants were given the following three hypothetical two-bedroom, four-person sleeping arrangements to order from "most offensive" to "least offensive," that in the majority of cases the "sacred couple" principle would emerge as more important than "incest avoidance" (as it does in my ordering below). But this in an empirical task I will leave to someone else.

References

Abu-Lughod, Lila

1991 Writing against culture. *In* Richard G. Fox (ed.) *Recapturing Anthropology: Working in the Present.* Santa Fe: School of American Research Press, pp. 137-162.

1999 The interpretation of culture(s) after television. *In* Sherry Ortner (ed.) *The Fate of "Culture." Geertz and Beyond.* Berkeley: University of California Press, pp. 110-135.

Alfred, Braxton

1965 *Acculturative Stress among Navaho Migrants to Denver, Colorado.* Ph.D. dissertation, Department of Anthropology, University of Colorado, Boulder.

1970 Blood pressure changes among male Navaho migrants to an urban environment. *Canadian Review of Sociology and Anthropology* 7:189-200.

Allan, Kenneth

1998 *The Meaning of Culture: Moving the Postmodern Critique Forward.* Westport, CT: Praeger.

Anderson, Elijah

1978 *A Place on the Corner.* Chicago: University of Chicago Press.

Aronson, Elliot

1975 Busing and racial tension: The jigssaw route to learning and liking. *Psychology Today* Vol. 8, No. 9, pp. 43-50.

Aronson, Elliot, Nancy Blaney, Cookie Stephen, Jeff Sikes, and Matthew Snapp

1978 *The Jigsaw Classroom.* Beverly Hills, CA: Sage Publications.

Aunger, Robert

1999 Against idealism/contra concensus. *Current Anthropology* 40 (Supplement): S93-S101.

Baddeley, Josephine

1977 The church and the coffeehouse: Alternative strategies of urban adaptation among Greek migrants to Auckland. *Urban Anthropology* 6:217-236.

Barker, Roger G. and Herbert F. Wright

1954 *Midwest and Its Children. The Psychological Ecology of an American Town.* Evanston, IL: Row, Peterson.

Barnett, Homer G.

1954 Comment appended to Broom, et al. *American Anthropologist* 56:1000-1002.

1960 Review of *Leadership and Culture Change in Palau* by Roland W. Force. *American Anthropologist* 1962:1099-1101.

Barnouw, Victor
1963 *Culture and Personality.* Homewood, IL: Dorsey Press. (Revised edition 1973.)
Bassett, I. J., and K. W. Thomson
1968 Land use and agrarian change on Aitutaki, Cook Islands. *South Pacific Bulletin* 18:25-30.
Becker, Howard
1996 The epistemoloy of qualitative research. *In* R. Jessor, A. Colby, and R. A. Shweder (eds.) *Ethnography and Human Development.* Chicago: University of Chicago Press, pp. 53-71.
Benedict, Ruth
1934 *Patterns of Culture.* New York: Houghton Mifflin.
Bennett, John W.
1946 The interpretation of Pueblo culture: A question of values. *Southwestern Journal of Anthropology* 2:361-374.
1954 Interdisciplinary research and the concept of culture. *American Anthropologist* 56:169-179.
Bennett, John W., and Gustav Thaiss
1967 Sociocultural anthropology and survey research. *In* Charles Y. Glock (ed.) *Survey Research in the Social Sciences.* New York: Russell Sage Foundation, pp. 269-314.
Bernard, H. Russell
1988 *Research Methods in Cultural Anthropology.* Beverly Hills, CA: Sage Publications.
1994 *Research Methods in Anthropology: Qualitative and Quantitative Approaches.* (Second Edition.) Thousand Oaks, CA: Sage Publications.
2000 *Social Research Methods: Qualitative and Quantitative Approaches.* Thousand Oaks, CA: Sage Publications.
2002 *Research Methods in Anthropology: Qualitative and Quantitative Approaches.* (Third Edition.) Walnut Creek, CA: AltaMira Press.
Bernard, H. Russell (ed.)
1998 *Handbook of Methods in Cultural Anthropology.* Walnut Creek, CA: AltaMira Press.
Berreman, Gerald
1969 Not so innocent abroad. *The Nation,* November 10, pages 505-509.
Blackmore, Susan
1999 *The Meme Machine.* New York: Oxford University Press.
Blalock, Hubert M., Jr.
1961 *Causal Inferences in Nonexperimental Research.* Chapel Hill: University of North Carolina Press.
Boggs, Stephen T.
1956 An interactional study of Ojibwa socialization. *American Sociological Review* 21:191-198.
1958 Culture change and the personality of Ojibwa children. *American Anthropologist* 66:47-58.

Boggs, Stephen T. *(continued)*
1973 The meaning of questions and narratives to Hawaiian children. *In* C. Cazden, D. Hymes, and V. John (eds.) *The Function of Language in the Classroom.* New York: Columbia Teachers College Press.
Boster, James S.
1987 Why study variation? *American Behavioral Scientist* 31:150-162.
Brightman, Robert
1995 Forget culture: replacement, transcendence, relexification. *Cultural Anthropology* 10:509-546.
Brumann, Christoph
1999 Writing for culture. Why a successful concept should not be discarded. *Current Anthropology* 40 (Supplement):S1-S27.
Bruner, Edward, and Julian B. Rotter
1953 A level-of-aspiration study among the Ramah Navaho. *Journal of Personality* 21:375-385.
Burke, James, and Robert Ornstein
1995 *The Axemaker's Gift. A Double-Edged History of Human Culture.* New York: G.P. Putnam's Sons.
Campbell, Donald T.
1996 Can we overcome worldview incommensurability/relativity in trying to understand the other? *In* R. Jessor, A. Colby, and R. A. Shweder (eds.) *Ethnography and Human Development.* Chicago: University of Chicago Press, pp. 153-172.
Campbell, Donald T., and Julian C. Stanley
1966 *Experimental and Quasi-Experimental Designs for Research.* Chicago: Rand McNally & Co. (First published in 1963.)
Cavan, Sherri
1966 *Liquor License. An Ethnography of Bar Behavior.* Chicago: Aldine.
Chamberlin, Thomas C.
1890 The method of multiple working hypotheses. *Science* (Old Series) 15:92-96.
Chance, Norman
1965 Acculturation, self-identification, and personality adjustment. *American Anthropologist* 67:372-393.
Clifford, James
1988 *The Predicament of Culture.* Cambridge, MA: Harvard University Press.
Clinard, Marshall B.
1962 The public drinking house and society, *In* D. J. Pittman and C. R. Snyder (eds.) *Society, Culture and Drinking Patterns.* New York: John Wiley, pp. 270-292.
Cloward, Richard A., and Lloyd E. Ohlin
1960 *Delinquency and Opportunity. A Theory of Delinquent Gangs.* Glencoe, IL: The Free Press.
Conger, John J.
1956 Reinforcement theory and the dynamics of alcoholism. *Quarterly Journal of Studies on Alcohol* 17:296-305.

Cronbach, Lee J., and Paul E. Meehl
1955 Construct validity in psychological tests. *Psychological Bulletin* 52:281-302.
Curley, Richard T.
1967 Drinking patterns of the Mescalero Apache. *Quarterly Journal of Studies on Alcohol* 28:116-131.
D'Andrade, Roy G.
1981 The cultural part of cognition. *Cognitive Science* 5:179-195.
1984 Cultural meaning systems. *In* Richard A. Shweder and Robert A. LeVine (eds.) *Culture Theory: Essays on Mind, Self, and Emotion.* New York: Cambridge University Press, pages 88-119.
1987 Modal responses and cultual expertise. *American Behavioral Scientist* 31:194-202.
1995a *The Development of Cognitive Anthropology.* Cambridge: Cambridge University Press.
1995b What *do* you think you're doing? *Anthropological Newsletter,* Vol. 36, No. 7, pp. 1, 4.
D'Andrade, Roy, and Claudia Strauss (eds.)
1992 *Human Motives and Cultural Models.* New York: Cambridge University Press.
Darnell, Regina, Judith T. Irvine, and Richard Handler
1999 *The Collected Works of Edward Sapir III: Culture.* New York: Mouton de Gruyter.
Denée, Edite
1973 Mother–child interaction at an ethnically mixed Auckland play centre—an exploratory study. Master's thesis, Department of Anthropology, University of Auckland.
Devereux, George
1948 The function of alcohol in Mohave society. *Quarterly Journal of Studies on Alcohol* 9:207-251.
Diamond, Stanley
1975 The Marxist tradition as a dialectical anthropology. *Dialectical Anthropology* 1:1-5.
Dozier, Edward P.
1966 Problem drinking among American Indians: The role of sociocultural deprivation. *Quarterly Journal of Studies on Alcohol* 27:72-87.
Dressler, William W.
1999 Modernization, stress, and blood pressure: New directions in research. *Human Biology* Vol. 71, No. 4, pp. 583-603.
Dressler, William W., Mauro Campos Balieiro, and Jose Ernestos Dos Santos
1998 Culture, socioeconomic status, and physical and mental health in Brazil. *Medical Anthropology Quarterly* 12:424-446.
Duncan, Otis Dudley
1966 Path analysis. Sociological examples. *The American Journal of Sociology* Vol. 72, No. 1, pp. 1-16.
DuToit, Bryan M.
1964 Substitution: A process in culture change. *Human Organization* 23:16-23.

References

Eiseley, Loren
1957 *The Immense Journey.* New York: Random House.

Ember, Carol R.
1973 Feminine task assignment and social behavior of boys. *Ethos* 1:424-439.

Ember, Carol R., and Melvin Ember
2001 *Cross-Cultural Research Methods.* Walnut Creek, CA: AltaMira Press.

Ferguson, Frances N.
1968 Navajo drinking: Some tentative hypotheses. *Human Organization* 27:159-167.

Firth, Raymond
1936 *We the Tikopia.* New York: American Book Co.

Fjellman, Stephen M.
1976 Natural and unnatural decision-making: A critique of decision theory. *Ethos* 4:73-94.

Flanagan, John C.
1954 The critical incident technique. *Psychological Bulletin* 51:327-358.

Fortune, Reo F.
1939 Arapesh warfare. *American Anthropologist* 41:22-41.

Fox, Richard G. (ed.)
1991 *Recapturing Anthropology: Working in the Present.* Santa Fe: School of American Research Press.
1999 Culture—A Second Chance? *Current Anthropology* 40 (Supplement).

Freeman, Derek
1983 *Margaret Mead and Samoa: The Making and Unmaking of an Anthropological Myth.* Cambridge, MA: Harvard University Press.
1999 *The Fateful Hoaxing of Margaret Mead: A Historical Analysis of Her Samoan Research.* Boulder, CO: Westview Press.

Freilich, Morris (ed.)
1970 *Marginal Natives. Anthropologists at Work.* New York: Harper & Row.

Friedman, M., and R. H. Rosenmann
1959 Association of a specific overt behavior pattern with blood pressure and cardiovascular findings. *Journal of the American Medical Association* 169:1286-1296.

Gallimore, Ronald, W. S. MacDonald, and Stephen T. Boggs
1969 Education. *In* Ronald Galimore and Alan Howard (eds.) *Studies in a Hawaiian Community: Na Makamaka o Nanakuli.* Honolulu: Bernice P. Bishop Museum.

Garfinkel, Harold
1967 *Studies in Ethnomethodology.* Englewood Cliffs, NJ: Prentice-Hall.

Geertz, Clifford
1965 The impact of the concept of culture on the concept of man. *In* J. R. Platt (ed.) *New Views on the Nature of Man.* Chicago: University of Chicago Press.
1973 *The Interpretation of Cultures.* New York: Basic Books.

Geertz, Clifford *(continued)*

2000 *Available Light: Anthropological Reflections on Philosophical Topics.* Princeton, NJ: Princeton University Press.

Gittelsohn, Joel, Marguerite Evans, Deborah Heltzer, Jean Anliker, Mary Story, Lauve Metcalfe, Sally Davis, and Patty Iron Cloud

1998a Formative research in a school-based obesity prevention program for Native American school children (Pathways). *Health Education Research* 13:251-265.

Gittelsohn, Joel, Pertti J. Pelto, Marguret E. Bently, Karabi Ghattachayya, and Joan Jensen

1998b *Rapid Assessment Procedures (RAP): Ethnographic Methods to Investigate Women's Health.* Boston: International Nutrition Foundation.

Gladwin, Christina

1983 Contributions of decision-tree methodology to a farming systems program. *Human Organization* 42:146-157.

1989 *Ethnographic Decision Tree Modeling.* Newbury Park, CA: Sage Publications.

Glasser, Barney, and Anselm L. Strauss

1967 *The Discovery of Grounded Theory: Strategies for Qualitative Research.* Hawthorne, NY: Aldine De Gruyter.

Goffman, Erving

1971 *Relations in Public: Microstudies of the Public Order.* New York: Basic Books.

Goldschmidt, Walter, and Robert B. Edgerton

1961 A picture technique for the study of values. *American Anthropologist* 63:26-47.

Goode, William J., and Paul K. Hatt

1952 *Methods in Social Research.* New York: McGraw-Hill.

Goodenough, Ward H.

1973 *Culture, Language, and Society.* Menlo Park, CA: The Benjamin/Cummings Publishing Co. (Second Edition 1981.)

1989 Culture: concept and phenomenon. *In* Morris Freilich (ed.) *The Relevance of Culture.* New York: Bergin & Garvey, pages 93-97.

Graves, Nancy B.

1971 *City, Country, and Child Rearing: A Tri-Cultural Study of Mother–Child Relationships.* Ph.D. Dissertation, Department of Anthropology, University of Colorado, Boulder.

1974 Inclusive versus exclusive interation styles in Polynesian and European classrooms: In search of an alternative to the cultural deficit model of learning. *South Pacific Research Institute Research Report No. 5.*

1976 Egocentrism and cultural deprivation: Empirical evidence for the ethnocentric bias of Piagetian theory. *South Pacific Research Institute Research Report No. 12.*

Graves, Nancy B., and Theodore D. Graves

1972 Social-psychological factors in urban migrant adaptation. *In* J. M. Stanhope and J. S. Dodge (eds.) *Migration and Related Social and Health Problems in New Zealand and the Pacific.* Wellington, New Zealand: Wellington Postgraduate Medical Society, pp. 73-89.

Graves, Nancy B., and Theodore D. Graves *(continued)*

1974 Adaptive strategies in urban migration. In *Annual Review of Anthropology* Volume 3, pp. 117-151.

1977a *Understanding New Zealand's Multicultural Workforce.* Report to the Polynesian Advisory Committee of the Vocational Training Council of New Zealand.

1977b Preferred adaptive strategies: An approach to understanding New Zealand's multicultural workforce. *The New Zealand Journal of Industrial Relations* 2:81-90.

1978 The impact of modernization on the personality of a Polynesian people. Or, how to make an up-tight, rivalrous Westerner out of an easy-going generous Pacific Islander. *Human Organization* 37:115-135. (Reprinted in *Studies in Behavioral Anthropology* Volume II, article 10.)

1979 Children in a multi-cultural society: Building on cultural assets in the school. *In* Arch Jelley (ed.) *Children in New Zealand: The Raw Materials of Our Society.* Auckland, New Zealand: Auckland Primary Principals Association, pp. 19-35.

1983 The cultural context of prosocial development: An ecological model. *In* Diane Bridgeman (ed.) *The Nature of Prosocial Development: Interdisciplinary Theories and Strategies.* New York: Academic Press, pp. 243-264.

1985 Creating a cooperative learning environment. An ecological approach. *In* Robert Slavin et al. (eds.) *Learning to Cooperate, Cooperating to Learn.* New York: Plenum Press, pp. 403-436.

1990 *A Part to Play. Tips, Techniques and Tools for Learning Co-operatively.* Victoria, Australia: Latitude Publications.

Graves, Theodore D.

1961 *Time Perspective and the Deferred Gratification Pattern in a Tri-Ethnic Community.* Ph.D. Dissertation, Department of Anthropology, University of Pennsylvania.

1964 Review of *Culture and Personality* by Victor Barnouw, and *Personality and Social Systems* by Neil J. Smelser and William T. Smelser (eds.). *American Anthropologist* 66:483-484.

1966a Introduction to the Tri-Ethnic Community. Unpublished manuscript.

1966b A guide to survey interviewing on the Navajo reservation. University of Colorado, Institute of Behavioral Science, Navajo Urban Relocation Research Report No. 18.

1966c Alternative models for the study of urban migration. *Human Organization* 15:295-307. (An expanded version appears in *Studies in Behavioral Anthropology*, Volume II, article 3.)

1967a Acculturation, access, and alcohol in a tri-ethnic community. *American Anthropologist* 69:306-321. (Reprinted in *Studies in Behavioral Anthropology*, Volume II, article 1.)

1967b Psychological acculturation in a tri-ethnic community. *Southwestern Journal of Anthropology* 23:337-350. (Reprinted in *Studies in Behavioral Anthropology*, Volume II, article 2.)

Graves, Theodore D. *(continued)*

1970 The personal adjustment of Navajo Indian migrants to Denver, Colorado. *American Anthropologist,* Vol. 72, No.1, pp. 35-54. (Reprinted in *Studies in Behavioral Anthropology,* Volume II, article 5.)

1971 Drinking and drunkenness among urban Indians. *In* J. O. Waddell and O. M. Watson (eds.) *The American Indian in Urban Society.* Boston: Little-Brown, pp. 275-311.

1972a Behavioral Anthropology and the Poverty of "Culture." (Unpublished manuscript.)

1972b *There But for Fortune. The Role of Alcohol in Navajo Urban Adaptation.* (Unpublished book manuscript.)

1973 The Navajo urban migrant and his psychological situation. *Ethos* 1:321-342. (Reprinted in *Studies in Behavioral Anthropology,* Volume II, article 7.)

1974 Urban Indian personality and the "culture of poverty." *American Ethnologist* 1: 65-86. (Reprinted in *Studies in Behavioral Anthropology,* Volume II, article 6.)

1977 Would you want your daughter to marry one? *Multi-Cultural School* 6:28-31.

Graves, Theodore D., and Nancy B. Graves

1976 Demographic changes in the Cook Islands: Perception and reality. Or, Where have all the *mapu* gone? *Journal of the Polynesian Society* Vol. 85, No. 4, pp. 447-461.

1978 Evolving strategies in the study of culture change. *In* G. D. Spindler (ed.) *The Making of Psychological Anthropology.* Berkeley: University of California Press, pp. 518-555.

1979 Stress and health: Modernization in a traditional Polynesian society. *Medical Anthropology* 3:23-59. (Reprinted in *Studies in Behavioral Anthropology,* Vol. II, Article 11.)

1980 Kinship ties and the preferred adaptive strategies of urban migrants. *In* Linda S. Cordell and Stephen Beckerman (eds.) *The Versatility of Kinship.* New York: Academic Press, pages 195-217. (Reprinted in *Studies in Behavioral Anthropology,* Volume II, article 12.)

1985 Stress and health among Polynesian migrants to New Zealand. *Journal of Behavioral Medicine* 8:1-19. (Reprinted in *Studies in Behavioral Anthropology,* Volume II, article 15.)

Graves, Theodore D., Nancy B. Graves, and Michael J. Kobrin

1969 Historical inferences from Guttman scales: The return or age-area magic? *Current Anthropology* 10:317-338.

Graves, Theodore D., Nancy B. Graves, Vineta N. Semu, and Iulai Ah Sam

1981 The social context of drinking and violence in New Zealand's multi-ethnic pub settings. *In* T. C. Harford and L. S. Gains (eds.) *Social Drinking Contexts.* Rockville, MD: National Institute on Alcohol Abuse and Alcoholism, Research Monograph No. 7, pp. 103-120.

1982 Patterns of public drinking in a multiethnic society. A systematic observational study. *Journal of Studies on Alcohol* 43:990-1009. (Reprinted in *Studies in Behavioral Anthropology,* Volume II, article 13.)

Graves, Theodore D., and Charles A. Lave
1972 Determinants of urban migrant Indian wages. *Human Organization* 31:47-61. (Reprinted in *Studies in Behavioral Anthropology*, Volume II, article 8.)
Graves, Theodore D., and Minor VanArsdale
1966 Values, expectations and relocation: The Navaho migrant to Denver. *Human Organization*, Vol. 25, No. 4, pp. 295-307. (Reprinted in *Studies in Behavioral Anthropology*, Volume II, article 4.)
Gusterson, Hugh
1996 *Nuclear Rites: An Athropologist among Weapons Scientists*. Berkeley: University of California Press.
Hadden, Kenneth, and Billie DeWalt
1974 Path analysis: Some anthropological examples. *Ethnology* 13:105-128.
Hall, Edward T.
1959 *The Silent Language*. Greenwich, CT: Fawcett.
1963 A system of notation of proxemic behavior. *American Anthropologist* 68:1003-1026.
Hallowell, A. Irving
1955 *Culture and Experience*. Philadelphia: University of Pennsylvania Press.
Hammersley, Martin
1992 *What's Wrong with Ethnography?* London: Routledge.
Hammond, Kenneth
1948 Measuring attitudes by error-choice: An indirect method. *Journal of Abnormal and Social Psychology* 43:38-48.
Handwerker, W. Penn
2001 *Quick Ethnography*. Walnut Creek, CA: Alta Mira Press.
Hansen, Morries H., William N. Hurowitz, and William G. Madow
1953 *Sample Survey Methods and Theory. Vol. I.* New York: John Wiley.
Harris, Marvin
2001 *The Rise of Anthropological Theory*. (Updated edition. First published in 1968.) Walnut Creek, CA: AltaMira Press.
Harrison, Tom et al. ("Mass Observations")
1943 *The Pub and the People. A Worktown Study*. London: Victor Gollancz Ltd.
Hart, C. W. M.
1954 The sons of Turimpu. *American Anthropologist* 56:242-261.
Heath, Dwight B.
1964 Prohibition and post-repeal drinking patterns among the Navajo. *Quarterly Journal of Studies on Alcohol* 25:119-135.
1987 Anthropology and alcohol studies: Current issues. *Annual Review of Anthropology* 16:99-120.
Henry, William E.
1947 The Thematic Apperception Technique in the study of culture-personality relations. *Genetic Psychology Monographs* 35:3-135.
Hinkle, Lawrence E., Jr., and Harold G. Wolff
1958 Ecological investigation of the relationship between illness, life experience and the social environment. *Annals of Internal Medicine* 49:1373-1388.

Hocart, A. M.
1929 *Lau Islands, Fiji.* Honolulu: Bernice P. Bishop Museum Bulletin 62.
Holmes, Thomas H., and Richard H. Rahe
1967 The social readjustment rating scale. *Journal of Psychosomatic Research* 4:189–194.
Honigmann, John J., and Irma Honigmann
1945 Drinking in an Indian–White community. *Quarterly Journal of Studies on Alcohol* 5:575-619.
1955 Sampling reliability in ethnological fieldwork. *Southwestern Journal of Anthropology* 11:282-287.
Hooper, Antony, and Judith Huntsman
1972 The Tokelau Island Migration Study. *In* J. M. Stanhope and J. S. Dodge (eds.) *Migration and Related Social and Health Problems in New Zealand and the Pacific.* Wellington, N.Z.: Wellington Postgraduate Medical Society, pp. 97-102.
Howard, Alan
1970 *Learning to be a Rotuman; Enculturation in the South Pacific.* New York: Teachers College Press.
1974 *Ain't No Big Thing. Coping Strategies in a Hawaiian-American Community.* Honolulu: The University Press of Hawaii.
Hurt, Wesley R. and Richard M. Brown
1965 Social drinking patterns of the Yankton Sioux. *Human Organization* 24:222-230.
Janes, Craig R.
1990 *Migration, Social Change, and Health: A Samoan Community in Urban California.* Stanford, CA: Stanford University Press.
Jessor, Richard, Anne Colby, and Richard Shweder (eds.)
1996 *Ethnography and Human Development. Context and Meaning in Social Inquiry.* Chicago: University of Chicago Press.
Jessor, Richard, Theodore D. Graves, Robert C. Hanson, and Shirley L. Jessor
1968 *Society, Personality, and Deviant Behavior. A Study of a Tri-Ethnic Community.* New York: Holt, Rinehart & Winston.
Jessor, Richard and Kenneth R. Hammond
1957 Construct validity and the Taylor Anxiety Scale. *Psychological Bulletin* 54:161-170.
Joans, Barbara
2001 *Bike Lust. Harleys, Women, and American Society.* Madison: University of Wisconsin Press.
Johnson, Allen W.
1978 *Quantification in Cultural Anthropology. An Introduction to Research Design.* Stanford, CA: Stanford University Press.
Johnston, Kenneth M.
1967 *Village Agriculture in Aitutaki, Cook Islands.* Wellington, New Zealand: Victoria University Department of Geography, Pacific Viewpoint Monograph No. 1.

Kagan, Spencer, and Millard C. Madsen
1971 Cooperation and competition of Mexican, Mexican-American, and Anglo-American children of two ages under four instructional sets. *Developmental Psychology* 5:32-39.
1972 Rivalry in Anglo-American and Mexican children of two ages. *Journal of Personality and Social Psychology* 24:214-220.
Kanner, A. D., J. Coyne, C. Schaefer, and R. S. Lazarus
1981 Comparison of two modes of stress measurement: Daily hassles and uplifts versus major life events. *Journal of Behavioral Medicine* 4:1-39.
Kaplan, Abraham
1964 *The Conduct of Inquiry. Methodology for Behavioral Science.* San Francisco: Chandler Publishing Co.
Kaplan, David, and Robert Manners
1972 *Cultural Theory.* Englewood Cliffs, NJ: Prentice Hall.
Kilpatrick, F. P., and Hadley Cantril
1960 *Self-Anchoring Scaling. A Measure of Individuals' Unique Reality Worlds.* Washington, DC: The Brookings Institute.
Klopfer, Bruno, Mary D. Ainsworth, Walter G. Klopfer, and Robert R. Holt
1954 *Developments in the Rorschach Technique. Volume I: Technique and Theory.* Yonkers-on-the-Hudson, NY: World Book Co.
Kluckhohn, Florence
1953 Dominant and variant value orientations. *In* Clyde Kluckhohn, Henry A. Murray, and David M. Schneider (eds.) *Personality in Nature, Society, and Culture.* New York: Alfred Knopf, pp. 342-357.
Kluckhohn, Florence, and Fred L. Strodtbeck, et al.
1961 *Variations in Value Orientations.* Evanston, IL: Row, Peterson & Co.
Knupfer, Genevieve, R. Fink, W. B. Clark, and Angelica S. Goffman
1963 Factors related to amount of drinking in an urban community. The California Drinking Practices Study. Report No. 6.
Kohlberg, Lawrence
1964 Development of moral character and moral ideology. *In* M. L. Hoffman and L. W. Hoffman (eds.) *Child Development Research.* New York: Russell Sage Foundation, pages 383-432.
1969 Stages and sequences: The cognitive-developmental approach to socialization. *In* D. Goslin (ed.) *Handbook of Socialization Theory and Research.* New York: Rand McNally.
Kroeber, Alfred L.
1917 The superorganic. *American Anthropologist* 19:163-213.
Kroeber, Alfred L., and Clyde Kluckhohn
1952 *Culture: A Critical Review of Concepts and Definitions.* Cambridge, MA: Paper of the Peabody Museum of Archaeology and Ethnology, Vol. 47, No. 1.
Kunitz, Stephen J., and Jerrold E. Levy
1994 *Drinking Careers. A Twenty-five Year Study of Three Navajo Populations.* New Haven, CT: Yale University Press.
2000 *Drinking, Conduct Disorder, and Social Change: Navajo Experiences.* New York: Oxford University Press.

Langner, Elinor
1967 Foreign research: CIA plus Camelot equals troubles for U.S. scholars. *Science* 156:1583-1584.

Langner, Thomas S.
1965 Psychophysiological symptoms and the status of women in two Mexican communities. (Unpublished manuscript.)

Lave, Charles A., James V. Mueller, and Theodore D. Graves
1978 The economic payoff of different kinds of education: A study of urban migrants in two societies. *Human Organization* Vol. 37, No. 2, pp. 157-162.

Lave, Jean
1988 *Cognition in Practice.* Cambridge: Cambridge University Press.

Lazarus, Richard S., Anita DeLongis, Susan Folkman, and Rand Gruen
1985 Stress and adaptive outcomes. The problem of confounded measures. *American Psychologist* Vol. 40, No. 7, pp. 770-779.

Leacock, Eleanor B. (ed.)
1971 *The Culture of Poverty; A Critique.* New York: Simon & Schuster.

LeCompte, Margaret D., and Jean J. Schensul
1999 *The Ethnographer's Toolkit. Book 1. Designing and Conducting Ethnographic Research.* Walnut Creek, CA: AltaMira Press.

Leighton, Alexander H., T. Adeoye Lambo, Charles C. Hughes, Dorothea Leighton, Jane M. Murphy, and David B. Macklin
1963 *Psychiatric Disorder among the Yoruba.* Ithaca, NY: Cornell University Press.

Lemert, Edward M.
1958 The use of alcohol in the Salish Indian tribes. *Quarterly Journal of Studies on Alcohol* 19:90-107.

LeShan, Lawrence L.
1952 Time orientation and social class. *Journal of Abnormal and Social Psychology* 47:589-592.

Levinson, David
1977 What have we learned from cross-cultural surveys? *American Behavioral Scientist* 20:757-792.

Levinson, David, and Martin J. Malone
1980 *Toward Explaining Human Culture: A Critical Review of the Findings of World-Wide Cross-Cultural Research.* New Haven, CT: HRAF Press.

Levy, Robert I.
1969 Child management structures in Tahitian families. *Journal of the Polynesian Society* 78:35-43.

Lewin, Kurt
1951 *Field Theory in Social Science. Selected Theoretical Papers.* (Edited by Dorwin Cartwright.) New York: Harper & Brothers.

Lewis, Oscar
1951 *Life in a Mexican Village: Tepoztlan Restudied.* Urbana: University of Illinois Press.

1966a *La Vida. A Puerto Rican Family in the Culture of Poverty—San Juan and New York.* New York: Random House.

1966b The Culture of Poverty. *Scientific American* Vol. 215, No. 4, pp. 19-25.

Lindesmith, A. R. and A. L Strauss

1950 A critique of culture-personality writings. *American Sociological Review* 15:587-600.

Lindzey, Gardner

1961 *Projective Techniques and Cross-Cultural Research.* New York: Appleton-Century-Crofts.

Macrory, Boyd E.

1952 The tavern and the community. *Quarterly Journal of Studies on Alcohol* 13:609-637.

Madsen, Millard C.

1967 Cooperation and competition motivation of children in three Mexican subcultures. *Psychological Reports* 20:1307-1320.

Madsen, Millard C., and Ariella Shapira

1970 Cooperative and competitive behavior of urban Afro-Americans, Anglo-American, and Mexican village children. *Developmental Psychology* 3:16–20.

Maher, Robert F.

1960 Social structure and culture change in Papua. *American Anthropologist* 62:593-602

Mangin, William

1960 Mental health and migration to cities: A Peruvian case. *New York Academy of Sciences* 84:911-917.

Marchione, Thomas

1980 Factors associated with malnutrition in the children of Western Jamaica. *In* Norge W. Jerome, R. F. Kandel, and Gretel Pelto (eds.) *Nutritional Anthropology: Contemporary Approaches to Diet and Culture.* New York: Redgrave, pp 223-273.

Marcus, George E.

1986 "A beginning." (editorial) *Cultural Anthropology* 1: 1-4.

1999 *Critical Anthropology Now. Unexpected Contexts, Shifting Constituencies, Changing Agendas.* Santa Fe, NM: School of American Research Press.

Maxwell, M. A.

1952 Drinking behavior in the state of Washington. *Quarterly Journal of Studies on Alcohol* 13:219-239.

Mazur, Allan

1977 Interpersonal spacing on public benches in "contact" vs. "noncontact" cultures. *The Journal of Social Psychology* 101:53-58.

McClelland, David C.

1953 *The Achievement Motive.* New York: Appleton-Century-Crofts.

McCleland, David C., John W. Atkinson, Russell A. Clark, and Edgar A. Lowell

1958 A scoring manual for the achievement motive. *In* J. W. Atkinson, (ed.) *Motives in Fantasy, Action, and Society*. Princeton, NJ: D. Van Nostrand Co., Inc. pp. 179-204.

McClelland, David C., and David G. Winter

1969 *Motivating Economic Achievement.* New York: Free Press.

McClelland, David C. et al.

1969 *Achievement and Economic Development.* Princeton, NJ: Van Nostrand.

McCracken, Robert D.
1968 *Urban Migration and the Changing Structure of Navajo Social Relations.* Ph.D. dissertation, University of Colorado, Boulder.
1999 *Directors' Choice. The Greatest Film Scenes of All Time and Why.* Las Vegas, NV: Marion Street Publishing Co.

McSwain, Romola M.
1965 *The Role of Wives in the Urban Adjustment of Navajo Migrant Families to Denver, Colorado.* MA thesis, Department of Anthropology, University of Hawaii.

Mead, Margaret
1928 *Coming of Age in Samoa: A Psychological Study of Primitive Youth for Western Civilization.* New York: Morrow.
1935 *Sex and Temperament.* New York: William Morrow.
1970 *Culture and Committment: A Study of the Generation Gap.* New York: Doubleday.
1972 *Blackberry Winter.* New York: Simon & Schuster.

Merton, Robert K.
1957 *Social Theory and Social Structure.* (Revised 1949 edition). New York: Free Press.

Metzger, Duane G., and Gerald E. Williams
1966 Some procedures and results in the study of native categories: Tzeltal "firewood." *American Anthropologist* 68:389-407.

Michener, Bryan P.
1965 The Development and Scoring of a Test of Need-Achievement for Navajo Indians. Navajo Urban Relocation Research Report No. 6.
1971 *The Development, Validation and Application of a Test for Need-Achievement Motivation among American Indian High School Students.* Ph.D. Dissertation, University of Colorado, Boulder.

Mischel, Walter
1958 Preference for delayed reinforcement: An experimental study of a cultural observation. *Journal of Abnormal and Social Psychology* 56:57-61.
1961a Delay of gratification, need for achievement, and acquiescence in another culture. *Journal of Abnormal and Social Psychology* 62:543-552.
1961b Father-absence and delay of gratification. *Journal of Abnormal and Social Psychology* 63:116-124.

Morrison, Denton, and Roman Henkel
1970 *The Significance Test Controversy.* Chicago: Aldine Publishing Co.

Mulford, Harold A., and Donald E. Miller
1959 Drinking behavior related to definition of alcohol: A report of research in progress. *American Sociological Review* 24:385-389.
1960a Drinking in Iowa: II. The extent of drinking and selected sociocultural categories. *Quarterly Journal of Studies on Alcohol* 21:26-39.
1960b Drinking in Iowa: III. A scale of definitions of alcohol related to drinking behavior. *Quarterly Journal of Studies on Alcohol* 21:267-278.
1960c Drinking in Iowa: IV. Preoccupation with alcohol and definitions of alcohol, heavy drinking and trouble due to drinking. *Quarterly Journal of Studies on Alcohol* 21:279-291.

Mulford, Harold A., and Donald E. Miller *(continued)*
1963 Preoccupation with alcohol and definitions of alcohol: A replication study of two cumulative scales. *Quarterly Journal of Studies on Alcohol* 24:682-696.
Ortner, Sherry
1984 Theory in anthropology since the sixties. *Comparative Studies in Society and History* 26:126-166.
1999 *The Fate of "Culture." Geertz and Beyond.* Berkeley: University of California Press.
2003 *New Jersey Dreaming—Capital, Culture, and the Class of '58.* Durham, NC: Duke University Press.
Osgood, Charles E., George J. Suci, and Percy H. Tannenbaum
1957 *The Measurement of Meaning.* Urbana: University of Illinois Press.
Parker, Seymour
1964 Ethnic identity and acculturation in two Eskimo villages. *American Anthropologist* 66:325-340.
Parker, Seymour, and Robert J. Kleiner
1970 The culture of poverty: An adjustive dimension. *American Anthropologist* 72:516-527.
Pelto, Pertti J.
1970 *Anthropological Research. The Structure of Inquiry.* New York: Harper and Row.
Pelto, Pertti J., and Gretel H. Pelto
1975 Intra-cultural diversity: some theoretical issues. *American Ethnologist* 2:1-18.
1978 *Anthropological Research. The Structure of Inquiry.* (Second Edition.) New York: Cambridge University Press.
1997 Studying knowledge, culture, and behavior in applied medical anthropology. *Medical Anthropology Quarterly* 11:147-163.
Piaget, Jean
1932 *The Moral Judgment of the Child.* London: Kegan Paul.
Pitt, David C., and Cluny Macpherson
1974 *Emerging Pluralism: Samoan Migrants in New Zealand.* Auckland: Longman Paul.
Quinn, Naomi
1978 Do Mfantse fish sellers estimate probabilities in their heads? *American Ethnologist* 5:206-226.
Rabinow, Paul
1996 *Making PCR: A Story of Biotechnology.* Chicago: University of Chicago Press.
Rahe, Richard H., M. Meyer, M. Smith, G. Kjaer, and Thomas H. Holmes
1964 Social stress and illness onset. *Journal of Psychosomatic Research* 8:35.
Redfield, Robert
1930 *Tepoztlán: A Mexican Village.* Chicago: University of Chicago Press.
Remland, Martin S., Patricia S. Jones, and Heidi Brinkman
1991 Proxemic and haptic behavior in three European countries. *Journal of Nonverbal Behavior* 15:215-232.

Remland, Martin S., Patricia S. Jones, and Heidi Brinkman *(continued)*
1995 Interpersonal distance, body orientation, and touch—effects of culture, gender, and age. *Journal of Social Psychology* 135:281-297.

Riesman, David
1950 *The Lonely Crowd. A Study of the Changing American Character.* New Haven, CT: Yale University Press.

Ritchie, James E.
1957 *Childhood in Rakau—The First Five Years.* Wellington, New Zealand: Victoria University College Publications in Psychology No. 10.
1972 New families: New communities. *In* G. Vaughan (ed.) *Racial Issues in New Zealand.* Auckland: Akarana Press.

Rogers, Everett M.
1962 *Diffusion of Innovations.* Glencoe, IL: The Free Press.

Rogers, Everett M., and A. E. Havens
1962 Predicting innovativeness. *Sociological Inquiry* 32:34-42.

Rohner, Ronald P.
1975 *They Love Me, They Love Me Not: A Worldwide Study of the Effects of Parental Acceptance and Rejection.* New Haven, CT: HRAF Press.
1984 Toward a conception of culture for cross-cultural psychology. *Journal of Cross-Cultural Psychology* 15:111-138.
1986 *The Warmth Dimension. Foundations of Parental Acceptance-Rejection Theory.* Beverly Hills, CA: Sage Publications.

Rohner, Ronald P., and Manjusri Chaki-Sircar
1988 *Women and Children in a Bengali Village.* Hanover, VT: University Press of New England.

Romney, A. Kimball
1999 Culture concensus as a statistical model. *Current Anthropology* 40: Supplement 103-115.

Romney, A. Kimball, and Carmella C. Moore
1998 Towards a theory of culture as shared cognitive structures. *Ethos* 26:314-337.

Romney, A. Kimball, Susan C. Weller, and William H. Batchelder
1986 Culture as consensus: A theory of culture and informant accuracy. *American Anthropologist* 88:313-338.

Rosaldo, Renato
1989 *Culture and Truth. The Remaking of Social Analysis.* Boston: Beacon Press. (Second edition 1993.)

Ross, Lee, and Richard E. Nisbett
1991 *The Person and the Situation. Perspectives of Social Psychology.* Philadelphia: Temple University Press.

Rotondo, H.
1960 Psychological and mental health problems of urbanization based on case studies in Peru. *In* Philip M. Hauser (ed.) *Urbanization in Latin America.* New York: Columbia University Press, pp. 249-257.

Rotter, Julian B.
1954 *Social Learning and Clinical Psychology.* Englewood Cliffs, NJ: Prentice-Hall, Inc.

Rotter, Julian B. *(continued)*
1966 Generalized expectancies for internal versus external control of reinforcement. *Psychological Monographs* 80 (1).
1971 External control and internal control. *Psychology Today* Vol. 5, No. 1, pp. 37-42, 58-59.

Salmond, Anne
1975 *Hui: A Study of Maori Ceremonial Gatherings.* Wellington, New Zealand: A.H. and A.W. Reed.

Salmond, C. E., J. G. Joseph, I. A. Prior, D. G. Stanley, an A. F. Wessen
1985 Longitudinal analysis of the relationship between blood pressure and migration: The Tokelan Island Migration Study. *American Journal of Epidemiology* 122:291-301.

Sapir, Edward
1917 Do we need a "superorganic"? *American Anthropologist* 19:441-447.
1938 Why cultural anthropology needs the psychiatrist. *Psychiatry* 1:7-12.

Schneider, Louis, and Sverre Lysgaard
1953 The deferred gratification pattern: a preliminary study. *American Sociological Review* 18:142-149.

Schwartz, Morris S., and Charlotte G. Schwartz
1955 Problems in participant observation. *American Journal of Sociology* 60:343-353.

Seeman, Melvin
1959 On the meaning of alienation. *American Sociological Review* 24:783-791.

Segall, Marshall H.
1984 More than we need to know about culture, but are afraid not to ask. *Journal of Cross-Cultural Psychology* 15:153-162.

Sharp, Lauriston
1952 Steel axes for stone age Australians. *In* E. H. Spicer (ed.) *Human Problems in Technological Change.* New York: Russell Sage Foundation, pp. 69-90.

Shweder, Richard A.
1996 True ethnography: The lore, the law, and the lure. *In* Richard Jessor, Anne Colby, and Richard Shweder (eds.) *Ethnography and Human Development.* Chicago: University of Chicago Press, pp. 15-52.

Shweder, Richard A., Lene Arnett Jensen, and William M. Goldstein
1995 Who sleeps by whom revisited: A method for extracting the moral goods implicit in practice. *In* Jacqueline J. Goodnow, P. J. Miller, and F. Kessel (eds.) *Cultural Practices as Contexts for Development.* Number 67, pp. 21-39. San Francisco: Jossey-Bass Publishers.

Shweder, Richard A., and Robert A. LeVine (eds.)
1984 *Culture Theory: Essays on Mind, Self and Emotion.* New York: Cambridge University Press.

Snyder, Peter Z.
1968 *Social Assimilation and Adjustment of Navajo Indian Migrants to Denver, Colorado.* Ph.D. dissertation, Department of Anthropology, University of Colorado.

Snyder, Peter Z. *(continued)*
1971 The social environment of the urban Indian. *In* J. O. Waddell and O. M. Watson (eds.) *The American Indian in Urban Society.* Boston: Little, Brown & Co., pp. 207-243.
1973 Social interaction patterns and relative urban success: The Denver Navajo. *Urban Anthropology* 2:1-24.

Sommer, Robert
1965 The isolated drinker in the Edmonton beer parlour. *Quarterly Journal of Studies on Alcohol* 26:95-110.

Spiro, Melford E.
1978 Culture and human nature. *In* G. D. Spindler (ed.) *The Making of Psychological Anthropology.* Berkeley: University of California Press, pp. 331-360.
1986 Cultural relativism and the future of anthropology. *Cultural Anthropology* 1:259-286.

Spiro, Melford E., and Roy G. D'Andrade
1958 A cross-cultural study of some supernatural beliefs. *American Anthropologist* 60:456-466.

Steiner, Stan
1968 *The New Indians.* New York: Harper & Row.

Stewart, Omer C.
1964 Questions regarding American Indian criminality. *Human Organization* 23:61-66.

Strieb, Gordon F.
1952 The use of survey methods among the Navaho. *American Anthropologist* 54:30-41.

Stycos, J. Mayone
1966 Sample surveys for social science in underdeveloped areas. *In* R. N. Adams and J. J. Press (eds.) *Human Organization Research.* Homewood, IL: The Dorsey Press, pp. 375-388.

Thomas, David R.
1975a Cooperation and competition among Polynesian and European children. *Child Development* 46:948-53.
1975b Effects of social class on cooperationand competition among children. *New Zealand Journal of Educational Studies* 10:135-39.

Thompson, Laura
1948 Attitudes and acculturation. *American Anthropologist* 50:200-215.

Valentine, Charles A.
1968 *Culture and Poverty.* Chicago: University of Chicago Press.

Von Neuman, John, and Oskar Morganstern
1944 *Theory of Games and Economic Behavior.* Princeton, NJ: Princeton University Press.

Wagner, Roy
1975 *The Invention of Culture.* Chicago: University of Chicago Press. (Revised and expanded 1981.)

Wallace, Anthony F. C.
1952 The modal personality structure of the Tuscarora Indians. *Smithsonian Institution, Bureau of American Ethnology Bulletin* 150.

Wallace, Melvin
1956 Future time perspective in schizophrenia. *Journal of Abnormal and Social Psychology* 52:240-245.
Watson, O. Michael
1970 *Proxemic Behavior. A Cross-Cultural Study.* The Hague & Paris: Mouton.
Watson, O. Michael, and Theodore D. Graves
1966 Quantitative research in proxemic behavior. *American Anthropologist* 68:971-985.
Webb, Eugene J., Donald T. Campbell, Richard D. Schwartz, and Lee Sechrist
1966 *Unobtrusive Measures. Nonreactive Research in the Social Sciences.* Chicago: Rand McNally & Co.
Weller, Susan C.
1983 New data on intracultural variability: The hot/cold concept of medicine and illness. *Human Organization* 42:249-257.
1984a Cross-cultural concept of illness: Variation and validation. *American Anthropologist* 86:341-351.
1984b Consistency and concensus among informants: Disease concepts in a rural Mexican town. *American Anthropologist* 86:966-975.
Weppner, Robert S.
1968 *The Economic Absorption of Navajo Indian Migrants to Denver, Colorado.* Ph.D. Dissertation. University of Colorado, Boulder.
1971 Urban economic opportunities: The example of Denver. *In* J. O. Waddell and O. M. Watson (eds.) *The American Indian in Urban Society.* Boston: Little, Brown & Co., pp. 245-273.
1972 Socio-economic indicators of assimilation of Navajo migrant workers in Denver, Colorado. *Human Organization* 31:303-314.
Werner, Ozzie, and Donald T. Campbell
1970 Translating, working through interpreters, and the problem of decentering. *In* R. Naroll and R. Cohen (eds.) *A Handbook of Method in Cultural Anthropology.* New York: Natural History Press, pp. 398-420.
Werts, Charles E., and Robert L. Linn
1970 Path analysis: Psychological examples. *Psychological Bulletin* 74:193-212.
Wessen, Albert F. (ed.)
1993 *Migration and Health in a Small Society: The Case of Tokelau.* Oxford, UK: Oxford University Press.
White, Leslie A.
1959 The concept of culture. *American Anthropologist* 61: 227-251.
1975 *The Concept of Cultural Systems. A Key to Understanding Tribes and Nations.* New York: Columbia University Press.
Whiting, Beatrice B. (ed.)
1963 *Six Cultures; Studies of Child Rearing.* New York: John Wiley & Sons.
1996 The effects of social change on concepts of the good child and good mothering: A study of families in Kenya. *Ethos* 24: 3-35.
Whiting, Beatirice B., and C. P. Edwards
1973 A cross-cultural analysis of sex differences in the behavior of children aged three through eleven. *The Journal of Social Psychology* 91:171-188.

Whiting, Beatrice, and John Whiting
1975 *Children of Six Cultures: A Psycho-Cultural Analysis.* Cambridge, MA: Harvard University Press.
Whiting, John W., Irvin L. Child, William W. Lambert, Ann M. Fischer, John L. Fisher, Corinne Nydegger, William Nydegger, Hatsumi Maretzki, Thomas Maretzki, Leigh Minturn, A. Kimball Romney, and Romaine Romney
1966 *Six Cultures Series: 1. Field Guide for a Study of Socialization.* New York: Wiley.
Williams, Roger J.
1956 *Biochemical Individuality. The Basis for the Genetotrophic Concept.* New York: Wiley.
Wolcott, Harry F.
1995 *The Art of Fieldwork.* Walnut Creek, CA: AltaMira Press.
1999 *Ethnography. A Way of Seeing.* Walnut Creek, CA: AltaMira Press.
Wolf, Eric R.
1980 They divide and subdivide, and call it anthropology. *New York Times,* Sunday, November 30, Section E, page 9.
2001 *Pathways of Power. Building an Anthropology of the Modern World.* Berkeley, CA: University of California Press.
Woods, Clyde M.
1968 *Medicine and Culture Change in San Lucas Tolemán: A Highland Guatemalan Community.* Ph.D. dissertation, Stanford University.
Woods, Clyde M., and Theodore D. Graves
1973 *The Process of Medical Change in a Highland Guatemalan Town.* Latin American Center, UCLA. (Reprinted in part in *Studies in Behavioral Anthropology,* Volume II, article 9.)
Yengoyan, Aram
1986 Theory in anthropology: On the demise of the concept of culture. *Comparative Studies in Society and History* 24:368-374.
Yinger, J. Milton
1965 *Toward a Field Theory of Behavior. Personality and Social Structure.* New York: McGraw-Hill Book Co.
Young, Frank W., and Ruth C. Young
1961 Key informant reliability in rural Mexican villages. *Human Organization* 20:141-148.
Young, James C.
1980 A model of illness treatment decisions in a Tarascan town. *American Ethnologist* 7:106-131.
Ziegler, Suzanne, and Theodore D. Graves
1972 An Urban Dilemma: The Case of Tyler Begay. In *There But For Fortune. The Role of Alcohol in Navajo Urban Adaptation.* (Unpublished book manuscript.) See appendix B.
Zipf, George K.
1949 *Human Behavior and the Principle of Least Effort.* Boston: Addison-Wesley.

Appendix A

Navajo Urban Relocation Research Survey Questionnaire

1. NAME
2. ADDRESS (or nearest trading post)
3. TYPE OF INTERVIEW
   ___ Denver migrant
   ___ returnee
   ___ comparison
4. When were you born?
5. Are you married? YES NO
   (IF YES) Is your wife living here with you? YES NO
6. (BACKGROUND) While you were growing up, what did your father (or head of household) do for a living?
   (PROBE FOR AMOUNT OF TIME PER YEAR DOING NON-HERDING FARMING)
7. Compared to other Navajo families you know on the reservation would you say your own family was richer or poorer? RICHER POORER
8. Tell me about your schooling.
   What was the first school you ever went to?
   (NAME AND LOCATION)
   When did you start there?
   How long did you go there?
   Did you go to school there with white children?
   (FOR HS OR SNP) Did you receive a degree there?
   (GET DATE)
   (REPEAT FOR EACH SCHOOL ATTENDED)

Note: Alternative versions for admininstration of this questionnaire to migrants in Denver, on the reservation, and the reservation comparison group have here been compressed into a single form. Spaces for responses, coding, etc., have been eliminated.

9. Did you have any vocational training or job training while you were in school? YES NO
   (IF YES)
   Where?
   What kind?
   How many years? (GET DATES IF POSSIBLE)
10. Did you have any vocational training after you finished school? YES NO
   (IF YES)
   Where?
   What kind?
   How many years? (GET DATES IF POSSIBLE)
11. Were you ever in the armed services? YES NO
   (IF YES)
   How many years? (GET DATES IF POSSIBLE)
   Did you have any special training while you were in the service? YES NO
   (IF YES) What kind?
   How long?
12. (JOB HISTORY) What was the <u>first</u> job you ever had working for somebody else?
   Where was that?
   What were you doing on this job?
   How much were you being paid? ($/hr.)
      How long did you work there? (GET ESTIMATED START AND END DATES)
   (MIGRANTS AND RETURNEES: REPEAT THIS SERIES FOR EACH JOB <u>UP TO MOVE TO DENVER</u>)
   (COMPARISONS: REPEAT THIS SERIES FOR EACH JOB <u>UP TO THE PRESENT</u>)
13. (MIGRANTS AND RETURNEES ONLY—COMPARISON GROUP SKIP TO QUESTION 26)
   Before you came/went to Denver, were there any other places you lived that you haven't mentioned yet? YES NO
   (IF YES) Where did you go?
   How long were you there?
   What were you doing there?
   (REPEAT FOR ALL EXPERIENCES UP TO MOVE TO DENVER)
14. When was the first time you came/went to Denver?
   (GET AS EXACT DATE AS POSSIBLE, MONTH, DAY, AND YEAR)
15. What were the reasons you decided to come/go to Denver to live?
   (Any other reasons?)

16. What was the *first* job you had after you got to Denver?
    Who was your employer? (NAME OF FIRM AND ADDRESS IF KNOWN)
    How long were you there (out of work) before you got this job?
    How did you get that job? (i.e., BIA, Colorado Employment, friend, etc.)
    What were you doing on this job? (GET SPECIFIC DESCRIPTION)
    How much were you being paid?
    How long did you work there? (GET START AND END DATES IF POSSIBLE)
    (REPEAT THIS SERIES FOR EACH JOB UP TO PRESENT OR RETURN TO RESERVATION)
17. When you came/went to Denver did any friends or relatives go with you? YES NO
    (IF YES) Can you give me their names?
    What was _______________'s relationship to you?
    Is _________________ still living in Denver?
    (REPEAT FOR EACH NAME)
18. When you came/went to Denver were any of your friends or relatives already living here/there?YES NO
    (IF YES) Can you give me their names?
    What was _______________'s relationship to you?
    Is _________________ still living in Denver?
    (REPEAT FOR EACH NAME)
19. Who is/was your <u>best</u> friend (here) in Denver?
    Who else was/is a close friend of yours (here) in Denver?
    Is/was there anyone else you consider to be a good friend in Denver?
    Are these all Navajos? YES NO
    (IF NO, SPECIFY ABOVE WHETHER INDIAN OR OTHER)
20. (RETURNEES ONLY—DENVER MIGRANTS SKIP TO QUESTION 32.)
    What was your first job after you <u>left</u> Denver?
    Who was your employer?
    How long were you out of work before you got a job?
    How did you get that job?
    What were you doing on this job?
    (GET SPECIFIC DESCRIPTION)
    How much were you being paid?
    How long did you work there?
    (GET START AND END DATES IF POSSIBLE)
    (ASK THIS SERIES FOR EACH JOB UP TO PRESENT)
21. Why did you come back down to the reservation?

22. Were you working at the time you left Denver? YES NO
    (IF NO) How long were you out of work before you left Denver?
    (IF YES) Were you having any trouble with your boss at the time you left? YES NO
23. Did you buy a car or truck while you were in Denver? YES NO
    (IF YES) How much were you in debt?
24. Did your relatives on the reservation ask you to come back? YES NO
25. Did you come home to have a sing? YES NO
26. (COMPARISON GROUP ONLY—MIGRANTS SKIP TO QUESTION 32.)
    Have you ever gone on relocation? YES NO
    a. (IF YES)
       Where did you go?
       How long were you there? (GET DATES IF POSSIBLE)
       Have we gotten all your jobs while you were there?
       (IF NOT FILL IN ON QUESTION 12)
       Why did you leave?
       (REPEAT THIS SERIES FOR EACH RELOCATION EXPERIENCE)
    b. (IF NO)
       Why haven't you ever gone on relocation?
       Did you ever apply for relocation? YES NO
27. Were there any (other) places you lived away from the reservation that you haven't mentioned yet? YES NO
    (IF YES, REPEAT QUESTION 26a.)
28. Do you have any friends or relatives living in Denver? YES NO
    (IF YES)
    Who are they? (NAME AND RELATIONSHIP)
29. Do you have any friends or relatives on relocation in any other cities? YES NO
30. (IF YES) Have you had a chance to talk with anyone about life in the city? YES NO
31. (IF YES) Who?
    What kinds of things did they tell you?
    What did they say was good about city life?
    What did they say was bad about city life?
    Did they say they were having a hard time? YES NO
    (IF YES, GIVE DETAILS)

(ALL SUBJECTS)

32. Now let's talk a little more about your present (last) job.
    What do (did) you like best about this job?
    (What else? Anything else?)

33. What do (did) you not like about this (last) job?
    (What else? Anything else?)
    (IF PRESENTLY UNEMPLOYED, SKIP to question 36.)
34. Let's see. You are making ________________ at your job.
    How much money do you think you <u>should</u> be paid?
    (IF HIGHER THAN PRESENT WAGE)
    How long from now do you think it will be before you are paid this much?
35. Do you ever worry about getting laid off from your job? YES NO
    Why do you feel this way?
36. (UNEMPLOYED RETURNEES AND COMPARISONS ONLY)
    Do you feel you need a job here on the reservation? YES NO
    (IF YES) What have you been doing to try to get a job?
37. (DEBT) Everybody from time to time finds that he can't pay all his bills and has to borrow money. How often have you found it necessary to borrow money in the last year?
    (FOR EACH INCIDENT) Can you tell me about it?
    Whom did you borrow money from (what company)?
38. How much money did you borrow?
    How much are you now in debt?
39. (EXPECTATIONS) We're interested now in a little different <u>kind</u> of information from you. Everybody wants certain things in life. When you think about what really matters to <u>you</u>, how would you describe the <u>best</u> life you can imagine?
    (If you could have everything just as you want it...)
40. Now think of the kind of life you would <u>not</u> want. How would you describe the <u>worst</u> life you can imagine?
41. (SHOW THE LADDER CARD.) Here is a picture of a ladder. Let's say that at the top (POINTING) is the <u>best</u> kind of life that you have just described. At the bottom is the <u>worst</u> kind of life. Where on the ladder (MOVING FINGER RAPIDLY UP AND DOWN LADDER) do you feel that you personally stand at the <u>present time</u>?
42. (DENVER MIGRANTS ONLY—RETURNEES AND COMPARISONS SKIP TO QUESTION 44.)
    Where do you think you will be on the ladder <u>5 years from now if you stay in Denver</u>?
43. Where do you think you will be on the ladder <u>5 years from now if you returned to the reservation</u>?
44. (RETURNEES AND COMPARISONS—DENVER MIGRANTS SKIP TO QUESTION 46.)
    Where do you think you will be on the ladder <u>5 years from now if you stay on the reservation</u>?

45a. (RETURNEES) Where on the ladder do you think you would be 5 years from now if you had stayed in Denver?
b. (COMPARISONS) Where on the ladder do you think you would be 5 years from now if you went to Denver?
46. Where on the ladder would you say the average Navajo on the reservation stands?
47. Where would you place the average Navajo living in Denver?
48. How about other Indians living in Denver?
49. (DENVER MIGRANTS ONLY) Where do you think the average white man in Denver stands?
50. (RETURNEES AND COMPARISONS) Where would you stand on the ladder right now if you were living in Denver?
51. (VALUES) Let's talk some more about your life (here) in Denver. What are the things that you like (liked/would like) best about living in Denver?
(What other things? Anything else?)
52. What do/did/would you not like about living in Denver?
53. What do/did you like best about living on the reservation?
(What other things? Anything else?)
54. What do/did you not like about living on the reservation?
55. Do you ever plan to go (back) to the reservation/a city to live? YES NO
(IF YES)
When do you think you'll go?

(COMPARISON GROUP—SKIP TO QUESTION 65.)

56. (URBAN SOCIAL RELATIONS) (While you were living in Denver) about how often do/did you get together with other Navajos?
(RATE PER MONTH)
57. Do/did you have any Indian friends in Denver who were not Navajo? YES NO
(IF YES)
How often do/did you get together with them?
(RATE PER MONTH)
58. Do/did you have any friends in Denver who were not Indians? YES NO
(IF YES)
How often do/did you get together with them?
(RATE PER MONTH)

59. Do/did you belong to any clubs or athletic teams in Denver? YES NO
    (IF YES) About how often do/did you meet (practice, play, etc.)?
    (PROBE FOR AVERAGE NUMBER OF TIMES PER MONTH)
    Is/was it an all-Indian club (team, etc.)? YES NO
    (IF YES) Were/are they all Navajo? YES NO
60. (While you were in Denver) Do/did you ever attend activities of the White Buffalo Council? YES NO
    (IF YES) How many times do/did you attend (while you were there)?
61. (DENVER MIGRANTS ONLY—RETURNEES SKIP TO QUESTION 65.)
    Here is a list of other Navajos living in Denver.
    I wonder how many of these people you know.
    How about ____
    (IF YES) Have you seen him in the last month?
    (IF YES) Did you see him last week?
    Is he still living in Denver?
    (LIST OF 111 NAVAJOS KNOWN TO BE LIVING IN DENVER AT THE TIME FOLLOWED)
    Do you know any other Navajos working here in Denver?
    (IF YES, GET NAME, ADDRESS, AND FREQUENCY OF CONTACT)
62. When was the last time you sent a letter to anyone on the reservation?
    When was the time before that?
    Is this about average for you? YES NO
    (IF NO) Well, about how often do you <u>usually</u> send letters to the reservation?
63. When was the last time you went home to the reservation for a visit?
    How long were you there?
    (REPEAT FOR THE TIME BEFORE THAT, ETC., THROUGH THE LAST YEAR)
64. Suppose you took a trip back home to the reservation.
    How many people back home would you want to visit while you were there?
65. (ACHIEVEMENT MOTIVATION—USE TAPE RECORDER)
    Here are some pictures that a Navajo artist drew.
    I'd like you to make up a story about each one.
    1. Here is the first one. (MAN TALKING WITH SUPERVISOR)
       What is happening?
       What happened before this picture?
       What is the young man thinking or wanting?
       What will happen next?
       How will the story end?

2. Here is the second one. (STUDENT IN CLASSROOM)
   What is happening?
   What happened before this picture?
   What is the young man thinking or wanting?
   What will happen next?
   How will the story end?
3. Here is the third one. (MAN WATCHING JEWELRY RECEIVE PRIZE)
   What is happening?
   What happened before this picture?
   What is the young man thinking or wanting?
   What will happen next?
   How will the story end?
4. Here is the fourth one. (FAMILY GETTING ONTO BUS)
   What is happening?
   What happened before this picture?
   What is the young man thinking or wanting?
   What will happen next?
   How will the story end?
5. Here is the fifth one. (MAN SPEAKING TO GROUP)
   What is happening?
   What happened before this picture?
   What is the young man thinking or wanting?
   What will happen next?
   How will the story end?
6. Here is the last one. (MAN COUNTING PAPER MONEY)
   What is happening?
   What happened before this picture?
   What is the young man thinking or wanting?
   What will happen next?
   How will the story end?

66. (HEALTH STATUS) Let's talk a few minutes about your health.
    (DENVER MIGRANT) How have you been feeling since you came to Denver?
    (RETURNEE) How have you been feeling since you came back from Denver?
    (COMPARISON) How have you been feeling this last year?
67. (DENVER MIGRANT) When was the last time you had to stay home from work because of sickness?
    How many days work did you miss?
    (RETURNEES AND COMPARISONS) When was the last time you were sick?
    How many days were you sick?
    (ALL) When was the time before that, etc.
    (FOR THE LAST YEAR)

Appendix A

68. (CORNELL MEDICAL INDEX)

1. Do you often have bad pains in the arms or legs?
2. Do you worry a lot?
3. Do you ever find it hard to breathe just sitting still?
4. Do you often feel sick all over?
5. Does your heart ever beat hard enough for you to hear it?
6. Do you often have small accidents or hurts?
7. Do you get upset or mad easily?
8. Do you often have bad headaches?
9. Do you ever feel like you are going to pass out?
10. Do you often break out in a cold sweat?
11. Do you often have bad pains in the stomach?
12. Do you worry very much about your health?
13. Are you often dizzy?
14. Does it upset you when someone says you did something wrong?
15. Do you ever have pains in the heart or chest?
16. Do you often worry about having TB?
17. Do you often feel like not eating?
18. Do you often have twitches in your face, head or shoulders?
19. Do you get confused when you have to work fast?
20. Do you often have a hard time falling asleep?
21. Do you often feel tired when you get up in the morning?
22. Do you get nervous or shaky when your boss asks you questions about your work?
23. Do you often wish you could start your life all over again?
24. Do you get tired after even a little work?
25. Do little things make you nervous?
26. Is it often hard for you to make up your mind and decide things?
27. Do you think a lot about bad things that have happened in your past?
28. Do pains in your head often keep you from doing your work?
29. Are you often jumpy?
30. Do you often get completely tired out for no reason?
31. Do you usually take at least one alcoholic drink a day?
32. Are you often sick and unhappy?
33. Do you get mad even at little things?

34. Do you often think life looks hopeless?
35. Do noises or movements at night make you nervous?
36. Are you shy or bashful even with your friends?
37. Do you always seem to feel a little bit sick?
38. Do you often have bad dreams or nightmares?
39. Are your muscles or joints often hard to move?
40. Do you often feel very discouraged?
41. Do pains in your back make it hard for you to work?
42. Do you have to scratch yourself very much?
43. Do you feel alone and sad even when you are with friends?
44. Do sudden noises make you jump?
45. Does it make you mad to have people tell you what to do?
46. Do you ever find it hard to breathe when you are working?
47. Are you often too tired to eat?
48. Do you often have to clear your throat?
49. Do you often have trouble breathing?
50. Do you often feel lonesome?

69. Let me take your blood pressure.
    (GET TWO READINGS, SUBJECT SEATED)
70. (NAVAJO TRADITIONALISM)
    Here are some pictures that another Navajo artist drew of life on the reservation.
    1. Take a look at the first one. (HAND TREMBLER)
       What is happening in this picture?
       (RECORD VERBATIM RESPONSE. USE NONDIRECTIVE PROBES, THEN:)
       a. What do you think this lady is doing?
       b. Do you think she will find out what's wrong with him?
       c. Do you think he will get well?
       d. If you were sick, what would you do?
       e. What are the main reasons why you would do this?
    2. Here is the second picture. (DOCTOR AND SINGER)
       What is happening in this one?
       (RECORD VERBATIM RESPONSE. USE NONDIRECTIVE PROBES, THEN:)
       a. Do you think that man (FIRST PATIENT) will get well?
       b. Do you think that man (SECOND PATIENT) will get well?
       c. If you were sick, which would you go to first, a doctor or a singer?

d. What are the main reasons why you would do this?

3. Here is the last picture. (FAMILY IN TRUCK) (RECORD VERBATIM RESPONSE. USE NONDIRECTIVE PROBES, THEN:)
   a. (POINT TO DANCE) What's going on over there?
   b. (POINT TO CHURCH) What's going on over there?
   c. Which way do you think that truck (IN FOREGROUND) will go?
   d. If you were driving the truck, which way would you rather go?
   e. What are the main reasons you would want to go there?

71. (INTERNAL-EXTERNAL CONTROL)

I'm going to read some questions now, each of which has two parts. I'd like you to tell me for each question which part you believe is more true. In some cases you may believe both parts are true. But for every question, I'd like you to choose the statement which <u>you</u> believe from your <u>own</u> experience is <u>more</u> true. Okay? (CIRCLE 1 OR 2 CLEARLY)

1. 1) If you've got ability, you can always get a good job, or
   2) Getting a good job depends partly on being in the right place at the right time.
2. 1) It's really easy to have friends; a person just needs to try to be friendly, or
   2) Making friends depends on being lucky enough to meet the right people.
3. Suppose a Navajo gets picked up by the police.
   1) Does this often happen when he hasn't done anything wrong, or
   2) Has he probably done something to deserve it?
4. 1) When I make plans, I am almost certain that I can make them work, or
   2) I have usually found that what is going to happen will happen regardless of my plans.
5. 1) Working hard and steady is the way to get ahead in a job, or
   2) Getting ahead in a job depends on what kind of boss you happen to have.
6. Suppose someone starts a fight with you.
   Is this probably
   1) because you did something to make him mad, or
   2) because he was born mean?

7. If a person fails in life, is it
   1) because he couldn't help it, or
   2) the result of his own doing?
8. 1) In the long run we ourselves are responsible for bad government, or
   2) There's not much the average person can do about how the government runs.
9. Suppose a man gets sick and can no longer work.
   1) Is this usually a misfortune which cannot be helped, or
   2) Did this probably happen because he didn't take proper care of himself?
10. 1) Getting into trouble depends completely on the kind of life you lead, or
    2) If the breaks are against you, you can get into trouble anyway.
11. People get rich
    1) because they work hard, or
    2) because they have good luck.
12. Suppose a man loses a lot of his livestock during the winter.
    Would this probably happen
    1) because he didn't take proper care of them, or
    2) because of bad luck?
13. If a man's child turns out badly, would this be
    1) The result of the way the man and his family brought up the child, or
    2) because the child was born bad?
14. When a man finds a job, is it usually
    1) because of good luck, or
    2) because he spent a lot of time looking for one?
15. 1) No matter how much a person tries, it's hard to change the way things are going to turn out, or
    2) A person can make whatever he wants out of his life.
16. When a farmer has a good crop, is it mainly
    1) because he was lucky and got good rain that year, or
    2) because the farmer has worked hard on his fields?
17. Suppose a man doesn't get along with his wife.
    Would this probably be:
    1) because he had been drinking too much, or
    2) because he was unlucky and married a mean woman?

18. 1) Most people who get into trouble start out looking for it, or
    2) Often trouble starts because a person happens to be in the wrong place at the wrong time.
19. When a child does well in school is it usually
    1) because he was born with intelligence, or
    2) because he studied hard?
20. What happens to a man in his life
    1) depends on what he decides to do, or
    2) is something he cannot change, no matter how hard he tries?

72. (FUTURE TIME PERSPECTIVE) Now we'd like to know the kinds of things Navajos <u>expect</u> to do during their lives. Look ahead for a minute and then tell me five things that you <u>think</u> you'll do or <u>think</u> will happen to you. These don't have to be important things, just the first things that come to your mind. (PAUSE)
Anything at all that you think you'll do or think will happen to you.
(AFTER EACH RESPONSE SAY:)
("Alright, tell me something else that you think you'll do or think will happen to you.")
(IF S GIVES A <u>PROCESS</u> ITEM, LIKE "live in Denver", SAY, "Now that's something you'll be doing over a period of time. We're interested in more specific things you think you'll do at some particular time. OK?")
Now I want to know how long it is from now that you expect each of these future things to happen.
How long from now do you expect...(event 1)?
(REPEAT FOR EACH EVENT LISTED)

73. (DRINKING BEHAVIOR) Let's go on to something else now. What kind of alcoholic drink do you like best, beer, wine, or liquor?
Beer____ Wine____ Liquor____ (Never drink)____
(IF NEVER) Most people drink at least once in a while. What are the reasons why you never drink?
(IF STILL NEVER—SKIP TO QUESTION 81)

74. About how often do you have a drink? Would you say...
____Three or more times a day
____Two times a day
____About once a day
____Three or four times a week
____Once or twice a week
____Two or three times a month
____About once a month
____Less than once a month

75. Where do you do most of your drinking?
76. With whom do you usually do most of your drinking?
77. What do you <u>usually</u> drink?
    Beer____ Wine____ Hard liquor____
    Combination (specify)______________________________
78. About how many drinks do you yourself usually have at a sitting?
79. How many times were you drunk last month?
    (IF NONE) How about in the last year?
    Is this about average for you? YES NO
    (IF NO) Well, what would you say is about average for you? _________ times per ______________
80. Let's talk about the kinds of problems drinking may have caused you.
    (PAUSE, OBTAIN DETAILS IF VOLUNTEERED)
    1. Does your wife or anybody argue with you because they don't like your drinking? YES NO
    2. When some guys get drunk they get happy. Some get sad, some get sleepy. Some want to fight. How is it for you?
    3. Have you ever driven a car when you've had a good bit to drink? YES NO
       (IF YES) How often did this happen last year?
    4. Have you ever busted up the place while you were drinking? YES NO
       (IF YES) How often did this happen last year?
    5. Have you ever gotten into a fight or been beaten up while you were drinking? YES NO
       (IF YES) How often did this happen last year?
    6. Have you ever had trouble with your boss or lost your job because of your drinking? YES NO
       (IF YES) How often did this happen last year?
    7. Has your landlord or landlady ever asked you to move because of your drinking? YES NO
       (IF YES) How often did this happen last year?
    8. Have you ever been hurt or had an accident while you were drinking? YES NO
       (IF YES) How often did this happen last year?
    9. Have you ever lost a friend because of your drinking? YES NO
       (IF YES) How often did this happen last year?
    10. Have you ever been picked up by the police for drinking or for driving while drinking? YES NO
       (IF YES) How often did this happen last year?
       (FOR EACH INCIDENT) Can you tell me about it?
       How did (EACH INCIDENT) turn out?

81. (ENGLISH LANGUAGE COMPREHENSION) Here's something a little bit different. I'm going to hand you some pictures. Each picture has three parts, A, B, and C. Then I'll read a sentence, and I want you to tell me which part, A, B, or C, you think is right. Let's try an example.

    (GIVE S THE EXAMPLE PICTURES)

    Example 1:

    There is a circle, a triangle and a square. Which is the triangle? (PAUSE)

    The correct answer is "C".

    Example 2:

    The man is playing the violin. (PAUSE)

    The correct answer is "B".

    Get the idea?

    (IF S DOES UNDERSTAND, START THE SCALE. IF NOT, GO THROUGH EXAMPLES 3 AND 4.)

    Example 3:

    The man is sitting on the chair.

    The correct answer is "B".

    Example 4:

    He shut his suitcase by sitting on it.

    The correct answer is "C".

    Ready?

    (HAND S THE FIRST TEST PICTURES)

    1. He is drinking a glass of water.
    2. They are studying now.
    3. She is giving him a flower.
    4. It's a beautiful day, and he is going fishing.
    5. It's his hat that fell in the water, not he.
    6. Which is the tablespoon?

    (HAND S THE NEXT CARD)

    7. The man is seated at the table.
    8. John said, "Did you find the ball?"
       Charles said, "I'm still looking for it."
    9. Did you turn off the light? Not yet, but I'm going to.
    10. The man is running after the dog.
    11. The man isn't smoking.
    12. The dog is on the table.

    (HAND S NEXT CARD)

    13. She is sitting at the right of the man who is wearing a hat.
    14. I just saw it. It's behind the door.
    15. The dog is farther from the ball than the cat.

16. The noise I heard was made by a baby chick with a milk bottle.
17. What time did you say it was? I said 10 of 5.
18. He can't open the bottle.

(HAND S NEXT CARD)

19. He wasn't able to maintain his balance.
20. He is giving her his hat and coat.
21. The fat man with the cigar is having his house painted.
22. He was so tired that he couldn't stand up any longer.
23. "What happened?" "He fell off the table."
24. She is sinking.

(HAND S NEXT CARD)

25. The man's horse is crossing the river.
26. He opened the door of his room.
27. Mrs. Smith is watching the baby.
28. He put on his coat and hat.
29. He ran out of paper early in the afternoon.
30. The boys had the bird tied with a string.
31. The boy is as tall as the girl.

(ASK IF THE SUBJECT HAS ANY QUESTIONS HE WOULD LIKE TO ASK)
(THANK AND PAY SUBJECT FOR HIS TIME)

Appendix B

A Test of Need-Achievement for Young Male Navajo Indians, Scoring Manual

The Stimulus Pictures

From an initial pool of some twenty achievement situations pertaining to employment, education, relocation, competition, leadership roles, creative endeavors, monetary utilities, and urban living, six were selected by two judges (Michener and Graves) who had direct field experience with reservation Navajos as well as Navajo urban relocatees. An attempt was made to sample typical Navajo achievement situations within both traditional and nontraditional contexts. A Navajo artist was then commissioned to illustrate the selected situations in realistic and natural settings. In order to maximize identification by the respondents, the artist included in each picture Navajo males of comparable age range to the relocatees, and dressed in a style common to both traditional and acculturated groups. The six pictures are presented next in their order of presentation.

Based on Michener (1965). This research report also includes a review of the literature, theoretical rationale, suggestions for scorers to increase reliability, a scorer training test, and scored sample protocols.

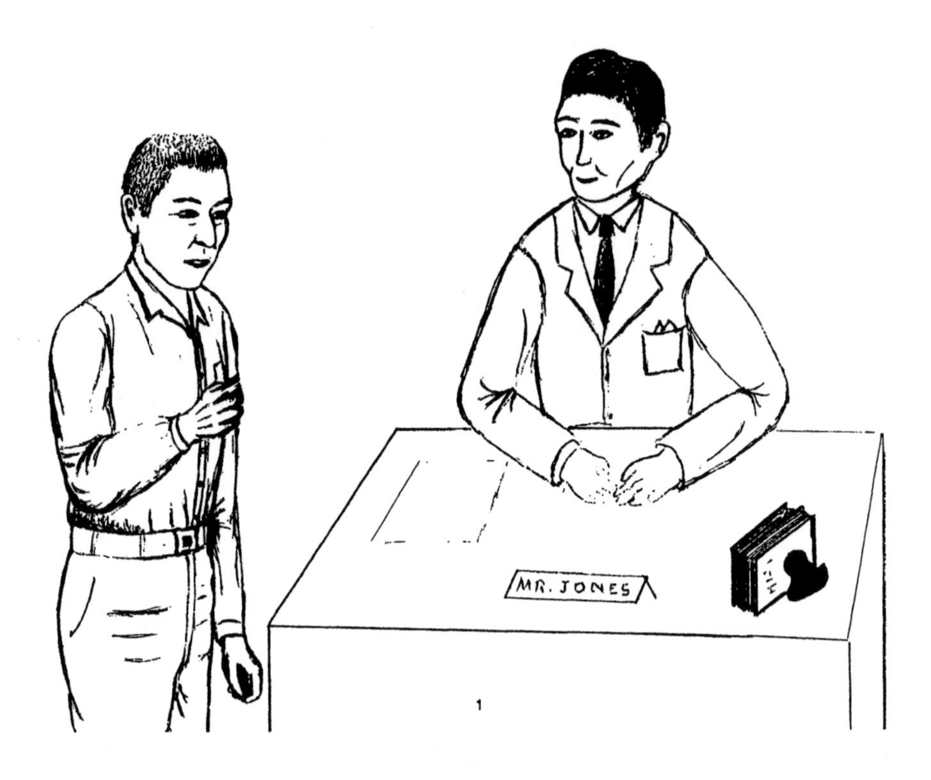

Picture #1 — Man Talking with Supervisor

A young Navajo adult is standing before a man who is seated behind a desk. Typical responses are: The man is seeking employment, asking for a raise, discussing a work problem, or telling his boss he's returning to the reservation.

Picture #2 — A Student Thinking

A young Navajo adult is seated at a school desk in a typical classroom situation, an open book is before him. Two other students are in the background. Typical responses are: He's listening to the teacher; he's studying hard to get educated; he's wishing school was out so he could just fool around.

Picture #3 — Man Watching Jewelry Receive a Prize

Two Navajo judges in traditional dress are awarding first prize to some fine silverwork while a young Navajo adult is looking on. Typical responses are: He made that fine silverwork; he's proud he won first prize; he's wishing that he knew how to do that silverwork so he could win, too; he just wants to buy some silverwork; or this man just pawned some silverwork to those men.

Picture #4 — A Family Getting onto a Bus

Shows a family getting onto a bus. Suitcases are present and the bus driver is assisting them. Typical responses are: This family is sending their boy away to get an education; these people are going on relocation; that family is going on vacation or going to Gallup to visit relatives.

Picture #5 — Man Speaking to a Group

A tribal chairman, accompanied by a younger man, is addressing a Navajo audience. The speaker's attitude, topic, and speech content are frequently quite informative, often referring to employment, education, economic development, and relocation.

Picture #6 — A Man Counting Money

This picture elicits a story about how the money was acquired—wages, gambling, found it—and how it will be spent—give to wife, buy a house, groceries, durable goods, savings, or liquor.

Administration

The test pictures are administered in a relatively informal manner, in the familiar environment of the subject's residence, as part of a larger survey questionnaire, following approximately thirty to forty minutes of questions concerning age, education, employment history, health, etc., which conveniently standardizes the immediate pretesting situation. (See Appendix A.) Each subject is assured complete confidentiality in all matters and is paid for his time. The picture responses are tape-recorded to insure accurate protocols for content analysis while obviating interviewer interruptions. The following procedure is used: "Here are some pictures that a Navajo artist drew. I'd like you to make up a story about each one. Here is the first one." Interviewer hands subject the drawing of a man talking with his supervisor. Then the following probes are asked:

a. "What is happening?"
b. "What happened before this picture?"
c. "What is the young man thinking or wanting?"

d. "What will happen next?"
e. "How will the story end?"

These probes are repeated for each picture shown.

Scoring

The following scoring method is derived from McClelland, Atkinson, Clark, and Lowell (1958) Scoring System C. All examples have been drawn from responses to the above set of Navajo pictures, and the explanations have been simplified and rendered more pertinent where possible.

All stories are first scored for the clear presence or absence of Achievement Imagery (AI) — whether or not the story meets one or more of the following prerequisites: (1) *competition with a standard of excellence;* (2) *unique accomplishment;* or (3) *long-term involvement with implied achievement goal.*

1. *Competition with a standard of excellence* is indicated when one of the characters within the story is engaged in competitive activity (excluding pure aggression) where winning or doing well or better than someone else is the primary concern. Alternatively, a standard of excellence may be evident by a concern with how well a task is done, e.g., specific mastery or true craftsmanship. Any use of adjectives of degree (good, better, best) will qualify as long as they evaluate the performance. If the goal is implicit, then the quality and intensity of the instrumental act must be clear, e.g., "The boy is working hard to finish his homework" may only indicate that he wants to go outside and play. In this case the context is crucial. However, the statement, "He is working slowly with great thoroughness" implies a concern with accuracy—a standard of excellence.

2. *Unique accomplishment* may be assumed when one of the characters is involved in doing something above the run-of-the-mill task or standard which will mark him as a personal success. Inventions, artistic creations, exceptional craftsmanship, or some other extraordinary accomplishment would fulfill this criterion. No explicit concern regarding the outcome is necessary where it is apparent that such an achievement would generally be acknowledged as an individual contribution. An example would be, "This silversmith can make anything out of silver and he has just made a new style."

3). *Long-term achievement involvement.* This kind of story depicts a character in the process of approaching a long-term goal. Any professional career such as becoming a medicine man, tribal chairman, or skilled worker are examples permitting the inference of competition with a standard of excellence *unless it is stated that another goal is primary* e.g., food for the children, personal security, etc.

Doubtful or Tentative Imagery (TI) and Unrelated Imagery (UI).

Stories which fulfill one or more of the above imagery criteria are given a score of +1 and are then scored further for the presence or absence of one or more of ten additional subcategories. (See below.) If some achievement reference is made but the story doesn't meet the criteria, it is labeled TI and given a score of 0. Stories without reference to an achievement goal are given a score of -1. Stories judged TI or UI are not scored further. These three categories—UI, TI, and AI—comprise a continuum of increasing certainty that the story contains imagery related to achievement motivation. While undoubtedly some achievement stories are lost, in the long run, only rigid adherence to the stated criteria can assure a high level of interscorer reliability. Examples:

AI (Picture #1) "Well, I guess they're talking, looking for a job I guess."
AI (Picture #1) "Well, I guess he's talking to his boss, want a raise in pay check."
[Often the first sentence is sufficient to establish an achievement-oriented goal.]

TI (Picture #2) "There's three guys in school. I think, the first guy who sits in front, he's thinking about what kind of lesson he's gonna study you know. The second one, he's just thinking. And the last one, he's the same, just thinking about, but the first one he tried to, he just opened a book, I guess want to read."
[Thinking about a lesson and reading are too nonspecific to be scored AI.]

UI (Picture #5)
a. "First, some people are going to town, I guess, to go shopping."
b. "He's taking a little boy on the bus."

c. "Oh, I think he's thinking about what in the world to buy for their family."
d. "How to get home."
e. "When they come home."

Subcategory Scoring

After a response has been scored AI, the story is further scored for the degree and intensity of the need-achievement displayed. One point only is given for the presence of each of the following, no matter how frequently they may appear in the story.

Need Imagery (N)

Someone in the story must state a desire to reach an achievement-defined goal. The accomplishment may be specific, such as "He *wants* to be tribal chairman," or general, "He hopes to succeed." Need may not be inferred from secondary or unrelated activity. For example, "The judge *wants* his assistant to hand him the blue ribbon for presentation" is not scored N. Examples:

N (Picture #1) "He wants the raise in pay check, he wants a little money."
N (Picture #2) "He wants to study."
[If the statement was, "The teacher wants the Navajo students to study hard," it obviously would not be scored N.]

Instrumental Activity (I)

This refers to a description of means or activity within the story directed towards the attainment of some stated goal, regardless of its success or lack of success, and independent of both the original statement of the situation and the final outcome of the story (in other words, exclusive of the responses to standard probes [a] and [e] generally.) Examples:

I (Picture #4)
a. "Looks like they going to Denver, on relocation."
b. "They going to work or school."
c. "I don't know." (?) "The whole family going."
d. "They going to relocation office to find a job for them."
e. "I don't know."

[Here the goal of going to school or getting a job is offered, and while the outcome is declined commentary, certainly getting on the bus and then going to the relocation office are instrumental activities, regardless of the outcome.]

I (Picture #5)

a. "They have a meeting, president, vice-president, talking over about their problems. . . . They want to have done it right away."
b. "Probably get together and talk about it, and what they really want to bring up at the meeting."
c. "What they all got together for, and how to talk it over before they go on doing something about it."
d. "So they don't have to worry about it."
e. "The job done, everything's fine, no problem."

[In this example the goal is only defined indirectly as an immediate problem to be solved through collective action. The affective concern manifested over the issue as well as the instrumental action of talking it out before final action and the outcome, all indicate some degree of instrumental problem-solving activity.]

Anticipatory Goal States (Ga+ and Ga–)

Someone in the story anticipates goal attainment (Ga+) or frustration (Ga–). The anticipatory states, however, must be related to the achievement goal of the story. Both (Ga+) and (Ga–) may be scored in the same story, but neither more than once. Examples:

Ga– (Picture #1)

a. "Maybe applying for a job or something like that."
b. "He might apply for a job or something."
c. "Could be hopeless." (Ga–)
d. "He might have or get himself a job."
e. "If he's pretty good, he might be successful." [clear doubt]

Ga+ (Picture #2)

a. "Looks like he's reading a book."
b. "Oh, I don't know." (?) "I don't think there's anything happened except probably he went in the classroom, set down and started reading a book."

c. "He probably studied hard and wants to be a really good student."
d. "I think that he's make out real good, be on his own, probably get a job on his own and work." (Ga+)
e. "Well, if he makes it good, probably all right. He might come out all right."

[Line d clearly indicates positive goal anticipation although in the final outcome he admits some doubt.]

Obstacles or Blocks (Bp and Bw)

Obstacles are scored when the character's progress toward a goal is hindered in some way. The obstacles may be located in the world at large ("He can't get a job because there aren't any jobs right now"—Bw) or within the person ("He isn't good enough to get this job"—Bp). Indications of past failure are scored Bp regardless of whether they interfere with the goal attainment. Both Bp and Bw may occur in the same story, and both can be scored once. Example:

Bp (Picture #1)
a. "Guess this guy is talking to the teacher or something."
b. "He's probably telling the teacher about his problem."
c. " I think he never did learn to talk English." (Bp)

Nurturant Press (Nup)

Some person within the story aids, assists, sympathizes, or encourages the character engaged in some achievement-related activity. The support must be in the direction of achieving his goal, and from the point of view of the character who is striving. Examples:

(Nup) (Picture #1)
a. "This man wants a promotion, and his boss say he'll help him to read blueprints so that he can get promoted." (Nup)

(Nup) (Picture #4)
a. "Think this guy's parents putting him on the bus to school."
b. "He probably just herd sheep or something."
c. "He been wishing he could go to school."

d. "His father will be proud to hear that he got education." (Nup)
e. "He probably be happy."

Affective States (Ga+ and Ga–)

This score normally requires an emotional statement by the character in response to goal attainment or nonattainment, and most commonly this category is found in the subject's response to the last probe (e): "How did the story end?" Positive affect (Ga+) is associated with active mastery, definite accomplishment: "He enjoyed winning first prize"; "He was proud of being elected tribal chairman." Alternatively, G+ may be scored based on a statement which implies definite objective benefit as a result of successful achievement and permits the inference of positive affect: "He became famous"; "The tribe was proud of him." (G–) is scored when a character in the story manifests negative affect over the outcome of his actions: "He was very unhappy because he didn't get such a good job," or "He was disgusted because he hadn't won." Alternatively, the outcome reveals objective concomitants of failure and deprivation: "He became a drunken bum." Occasionally both positive and negative outcomes may be scored for the same story: "He was happy that he won first prize, but his necklace was stolen."

Achievement Thema (Th)

Thema is scored when achievement behavior is the main plot of the story. If there is a major counterplot other than the achievement theme, or if there is any doubt about the achievement imagery being central to the story itself, Thema is not scored. Example:

(Th) (Picture #2)
a. "He's studying hard, math" (AI)
b. "How he flunked the last test." (Bp)
c. "Teacher is explaining the test."
d. "He'll try to study harder and do much better on next test." (I)
e. "He'll be able to understand the problems and do ok." (G+, Th)

Total Need-Achievement Scores

Each picture should be scored separately, without reference to the others in the same protocol. The best procedure is for scorers to score all subjects (in random order) for Picture 1, then all subjects for Picture 2, etc. Each subject's total Need-Achievement score is the sum of his scores on each of the six stories. For further information on test construction, reliability, and validity, see Graves (1974), reprinted in Volume II, article 6.

Index

Index

Index

Index

Index

About the Author

Dr. Theodore D. Graves is a retired professor of anthropology and social psychology who has taught at the University of Colorado at Boulder, the University of California at Los Angeles, and the University of Aukland in New Zealand. He has conducted field research in the American Southwest, Latin America, East Africa, and the South Pacific. Dr. Graves's distinctive behavioral science approach to cross-cultural research, Behavioral Anthropology, seeks to explain *within-group variation* in attitudes, beliefs, and behavior, and differences among group members in their health status. This involves the formulation of testable hypotheses about the causes, correlates, and consequences of this variation, which are then examined systematically by means of carefully constructed measures of relevant behavioral, psychological, social, economic, and cultural variables.